GOVERNING THE TERRAIN CALLED BEAUTY

Revolutionary Cuba does not recognize the liberal rights on which lgbtq advocates in the United States rely. How then has legal progress occurred for lgbtq people in Cuba? This book traces the history of lgbtq identity and law in Cuba and the US from the turn of the twentieth century through the legalization of same-sex marriage. It investigates material and discursive conditions during and after the Cold War and the under-recognized importance of legal consciousness. Applying comparative legal analysis, genealogy, critical social theories, and interviewing, the book produces an encounter between Cuba and the US that directs attention to the millions of constitutive run-ins that occur daily between the global and the local. Rich and insightful, it reveals how law and identity evolve under imperialism, anxious nationalisms, racial stratification, and economic hardship.

Libby Adler is Professor of Law and Women's, Gender, & Sexuality Studies at Northeastern University in Boston. She is the author of *Gay Priori: A Queer Critical Legal Studies Approach to Law Reform* (2018) as well as numerous articles on lgbtq legal issues. She serves as a commissioner on the Massachusetts Commission on LGBTQ Youth.

Governing the Terrain Called Beauty

THE QUEERNESS OF POLITICAL ECONOMY IN CUBA AND THE UNITED STATES

LIBBY ADLER
Northeastern University, Boston

CAMBRIDGE
UNIVERSITY PRESS

CAMBRIDGE
UNIVERSITY PRESS

Shaftesbury Road, Cambridge CB2 8EA, United Kingdom

One Liberty Plaza, 20th Floor, New York, NY 10006, USA

477 Williamstown Road, Port Melbourne, VIC 3207, Australia

314–321, 3rd Floor, Plot 3, Splendor Forum, Jasola District Centre, New Delhi – 110025, India

Cambridge University Press is part of Cambridge University Press & Assessment, a department of the University of Cambridge.

We share the University's mission to contribute to society through the pursuit of education, learning and research at the highest international levels of excellence.

www.cambridge.org
Information on this title: www.cambridge.org/9781009872324
DOI: 10.1017/9781009872317

When citing this work, please include a reference to the DOI 10.1017/9781009872317

First published 2026

Cover image: *AZUL / BLUE* by Enrique Rottenberg from Sleeping With series, 2010
Archival Grade Print on MOAB Metallic Paper 150 x 100cm / 59 x 39 in (Edition 3)
75 x 50 cm / 29 x 19 in (Edition 15) (Printed on Aluminium and Wood)

A catalogue record for this publication is available from the British Library

A Cataloging-in-Publication data record for this book is available from the Library of Congress

ISBN 978-1-009-87232-4 Hardback
ISBN 978-1-009-87233-1 Paperback

Didn't you want a close-up of the nocturnal habits of Havana gays?

I don't know … I wanted to get a sense of the scene…

*Well … what you want to see and know isn't that pleasant, I warn you. It's sordid, alarming, stark and almost always tragic, because it's the result of loneliness, eternal repression, mocking, hostility, contempt, even of monoculture and under-development. Do you understand?**

* This dialogue occurs between two fictional characters, an effeminate gay man and a police detective investigating the murder of another gay man whose body was discovered in drag. The excerpt comes from the popular Cuban mystery writer, Leonardo Padura, *Havana Red,* trans. Peter Bush (Bitter Lemon Press, 2005) 134, originally published in Spanish as *Máscaras* (Tusquets Editores, S.A., 1997).

Contents

Figures and Table

FIGURES

TABLE

Preface

While dying of AIDS in a sixth-floor walk-up in Hell's Kitchen,[1] and before taking his own life, the gay Cuban ex-pat writer, Reinaldo Arenas (1943–90) wrote a memoir.[2] In 2000, it was made into a motion picture starring Javier Bardem and featuring, among others, Sean Penn and Johnny Depp.[3]

In his memoir, Arenas recounted working in the Cuban National Library during the 1960s, at the height of Cuba's anti-homosexual persecution, while aspiring to a career as a writer. He encountered at the library other gay and lesbian intellectuals, including some of the giants of the Cuban literary scene.

The young Arenas entered a literary contest and came in second, earning Honorable Mention. The influential poet and writer, José Lezama Lima, thought Arenas was robbed; his entry should have won first prize. Lezama Lima, married to a woman but known to be homosexual, had been following Arenas's work. In the film adaptation, he invited Arenas to his home after the award ceremony. When Arenas arrived, he marveled at Lezama Lima's personal library, pulled a book from a shelf, and inspected it. The older man, assuming the posture of a mentor, advised Arenas,

> People that make art are dangerous to any dictatorship.
> They create beauty, and beauty is the enemy.
> Artists are escapists.
> Artists are counter-revolutionary.
> And so *you* are a counter-revolutionary, Reinaldo Arenas.
> Do you know why?
> Because there's a man that cannot govern the terrain called beauty.
> So he wants to eliminate it.[4]

Lezama Lima appears to be talking here solely about the beauty of art, but the broader context of the film tightly links art with sexuality. For example, narrating a scene from Arenas's time in prison, the actor Javier Bardem (who portrays Arenas) introduces the character of Bon Bon, a fellow inmate played spectacularly by Johnny Depp. Bon Bon appears in drag, or perhaps would be understood as transgender in contemporary US lexicon. She is important to the story in part because her rectum is said to be sufficiently capacious to smuggle contraband in and out of the prison, including pages from the novel Arenas was writing. But the film also invites us to appreciate Bon Bon for the infusion of "glamour" she provides to an otherwise dismal and colorless environment. As the camera introduces Bon Bon, striding coquettishly across the sun-brightened prison yard and donning a boa and other feminine accoutrement, Bardem (in voiceover) observes "Leonardo Da Vinci was homosexual, so was Michelangelo, Socrates, Shakespeare and almost every other figure that has formed what we have come to understand as beauty."

The scene seems to substantiate Lezama Lima's thesis: Bon Bon is ungovernable, not only because she can sneak goods past the guards in her commodious anatomy but also because even prison cannot suppress her beauty – understood at once as both her art ("glamour") and her sex. Joined together in both narration and image, they are too entwined to distinguish.

The film adaptation had to convert an autobiographical voice into dialogue, which is presumably why this idea about governance is expressed by Lezama Lima. In the memoir, however, it is Arenas who observes,

> A sense of beauty is always dangerous and antagonistic to any dictatorship because it implies a realm extending beyond the limits that a dictatorship can impose on human beings. Beauty is a territory that escapes the control of the political police. Being independent and outside of their domain, beauty is so irritating to dictators that they attempt to destroy it whichever way they can. Under a dictatorship, beauty is always a dissident force, because a dictatorship is itself unaesthetic, grotesque; to a dictator and his agents, the attempt to create beauty is an escapist or reactionary act.[5]

The term "governance" is introduced by the screenplay; the memoir speaks of "control." It appears that the scriptwriters derived their choice of terms by presuming Arenas to have been contemplating the prohibitory rule of the state. To *govern*, as the script interprets Arenas, is to rule, or to impose the law – presumptively brutal and ugly – by force of the police. It is a structural conception.

Law, though, is a mode of governance that can be analyzed not just structurally but also at a microlevel. This means not only that careful legal thinkers read the annotations and footnotes (though there is that) but also that they appreciate the effects of law as a discourse, influenced by related discourses, including those of legitimacy, systemic determinacy, and national mythology.

Michel Foucault used the term *governmentality* to designate an "analytical grid," encompassing all "the conduct of men," through which he proposed to view "relations of power," whether occurring on a large or intimate scale.[6] The "governmentality grid" envisioned by Foucault is granular in perspective; it is concerned with what he dubbed "micro-powers"[7] – exerted in quotidian encounters – as much as in structural power held because of position. As Janet Halley has explained and elaborated on the concept, *governance* is not limited to exercises of state power; it extends to all "ideas exert[ing] a governing will within human affairs," as well as to "human-inflected processes like knowledge formation."[8]

This book accepts Arenas's understanding of *beauty* but contests the film's conception of *governance*. In the film, beauty is ungovernable in the sense that it exists beyond law's reach. Borrowing from Foucault and Halley, however, the book takes a more expansive view of law according to which no element of human activity exceeds its domain – under dictatorship or otherwise. To begin with, where one might perceive law's absence, it can be understood merely as permission or nonenforcement[9] – a point that any course in legal theory would cover.

But deeper still, law is more than a list of prohibitions. It does more than regulate conduct and assign consequences for violation. Law, not unlike art, is a producer and product of knowledge[10] – those unspoken, circulating assumptions buried in lay as well as professional discourses. It shapes identities and is in turn shaped by them. Law is not merely external to individuals and enforced by the police; it is also interior to individuals; we self-govern according to shared cultural conceptions. Law subtly influences our perceptions of the world we inhabit, the people in it, and our relationships to nature, institutions, places, and things. This study engages comparative and genealogical inquiry to shed light on how, indeed, "the terrain called beauty" is "governed."

To see law, one can look at books (or webpages) containing statutes, regulations, and cases, but if law shapes us and we shape law, then it behooves us also to gaze periodically into a mirror – not only in search of beauty but also in search of governance. Examining the history of Cuba's position in global political economy, the evolution of its ideas about nonnormative sexuality and gender, and the assumptions circulating among legal professionals, sheds light on Cuba, but not only on Cuba. It also has the potential to reflect something to legal thinkers situated in a contrasting legal and political–economic environment – mainly, in this case, the US. Gazing into the mirror, I hope the reader will find that systemic thinking at the expense of dissecting ethnography, discourse, and legal transfer obfuscates, rather than discloses, the complexity of law's evolution. Such discovery has the capacity to reveal, as well, emancipatory prospects that have been left on the shelf due to the veneer of illegitimacy or impossibility that comes into being as a result of limits that we impose on ourselves.

Acknowledgments

This book took several years to write, and its completion depended upon the generosity and help of many friends, colleagues, and students along the way. Janet Halley and David Kennedy both dedicated hours to reading deeply and providing detailed feedback that radically improved the quality of the manuscript. Rashmi Dyal-Chand can always be counted on to read, listen, and strategize on my behalf, and this time around was no exception. Karl Klare taught me through deep exchange over ideas as he has been doing for many years. Aziza Ahmed is invariably the first person to whom I show everything I write, when I'm still feeling uncertain, and often the last person who sees it before I have the confidence to send it out the door. These friends and the characteristic engagement I enjoy with them are practically lifeblood.

I am fortunate to have the company of an international crew of brilliant, good-humored, and critical legal scholars that calls itself *Gender & Political Economy* (GPE). Its participants are my sisters and global compatriots. They put up with multiple phases of this project over the course of numerous meetings and panels and kept my head buzzing with critical insight.

Judge Isaac Borenstein (ret.) of the Massachusetts Superior Court, Cuban-born and maintaining ties to the Revolution, facilitated my initial contacts in Havana, including with Yamila González Ferrer, Vice-Chair of the National Union of Cuban Jurists, to whom I am grateful for having extended an invitation to the *Ninth International Conference on Women, Gender, and Law* in Varadero. Jorge Esquirol kindly invited me to a conference of the Association for the Study of the Cuban Economy (ASCE) held at Florida International University in 2022. There, he introduced me to, among others, Daimar Cánovas of the University of Havana Faculty of Law & Jurisprudence, who in turn helped me along with further contacts and direction when I arrived in Havana. Jorge also provided me with careful feedback at multiple junctures in the process of working out my arguments.

Additional colleagues from Northeastern and beyond provided comments, advice, and encouragement, including Helena Alviar, Amílcar Barreto, Amy Cohen, Lori Lefkovitz, Daniel Medwed, Fernanda Nicola, Russell Robinson, Sonia Rolland, Rachel Rosenbloom, Kara Swanson, and Suzanna Walters. Jessica Silbey and Ari

Waldman got me started on how to approach interviewing for the modest qualitative study discussed in Chapter 5. Luis Brens, who had previously taken a group of Northeastern students to Havana to study urban photography, kindly met with me to help me budget and otherwise prepare for my trip.

Quite a few research assistants advanced this study, helping with research in the early stages or (at the other end of the process) with citation. These Northeastern students, both undergraduate and law, are now mostly graduated and include Theo Babbitt, Adam Bubanich, Catalina Carbonell, Mike Charla, A.J. Jarrett, Emerson Johnston, Maria Kennedy, Kyanna Patterson, Natalie Peña, Cecilia Reichert, and Ana Paula Velarde.

Two additional research assistants warrant special mention. Thaís De Marco devoted hours (for no pay or credit) to the endnotes and bibliography, in some cases merely formatting and in others chasing down obscure Cuban sources. Annery Miranda, now an immigration attorney whom I count as a friend, worked closely with me for a couple of years, traveled to Cuba to help me with interviews of Cuban lawyers and law students, translated transcripts, and was otherwise indispensable to the production of Chapter 5. In addition, she put me in touch with David Guerra and Rodela Khan, each of whom provided helpful advice as we prepared for the interviews.

The Center for Law, Equity, and Race (CLEAR) at Northeastern University School of Law, where I was an inaugural fellow, funded my trip to Cuba in 2022, without which I could not have completed this work. I also had the support of the Northeastern Humanities Center, where I was a fellow during the conceptualizing phase of this project. This fellowship had the added value of putting me in dialogue with fascinating colleagues from around the university who were working on a range of interdisciplinary projects.

I benefited from numerous opportunities to present parts of this study at workshops, conferences, classes, and colloquia at the American University Washington College of Law, Washington University School of Law in St. Louis, University of Stellenbosch Faculty of Law (as host to the Global Scholars Academy of the Institute for Global Law & Policy at Harvard Law School), Stanford University Program on Feminist, Gender, & Sexuality Studies, Cornell Law School, University of Chicago Law School, University of Georgia School of Law, University of Toronto Faculty of Law, Rutgers School of Law, Sciences Po Law School, Law & Society meetings (in San Francisco [2025], San Juan [2023], and Lisbon [2022]), Florida International University College of Law (as host of ASCE), University of Colorado Law School, and of course my home base, Northeastern University, in both the School of Law and the Humanities Center.

Portions of this study in their initial iterations can be found in "From Contamination to Congratulation: The Discursive and Legal Careers of the Homosexual in the U.S. and Cuba," in *Enticements: Queer Legal Studies*, edited by Joe Fischel and Brenda Cossman (New York University Press, 2024); "Marriage as a Hustle: The Evolution of Property Law and the Arrival of Same-Sex Marriage in Cuba." *Family Court Review* 62, no. 4 (2024): 863–76 (which benefitted from comments by Albertina Antognini, Sally Goldfarb, and Aníbal Rosario Lebrón); and "On the Why of Same-Sex Marriage in Cuba." *Florida International University Law Review* 17 (2023): 485–505. I am grateful to the editors of each of these collections.

I was helped along by a few additional people, Cubans and Cuban ex-pats, who prefer not to be named. The absence of their names should not be read to indicate my lack of appreciation.

Finally, and as always, I am grateful to David Adler and Wendy Zazik for indulging frequent progress reports, reading occasional installments, and supplying moral support.

Author's Note and Dedication

As this book goes to press, the Trump administration has imposed a painful energy blockade on Cuba and threatens the possibility of "regime change." My thoughts turn to the people I met in Cuba and to the millions of ordinary Cubans who have been made to suffer as the geopolitics of the powerful deprive them of food, medicine, light, internet, and oil. With cognizance of how meager is the gesture, I nevertheless dedicate this book to them and will try my best never to forget their struggle merely to live.

Boston, Massachusetts
June, 2026

About the Cover

The cover image is a photograph taken by Enrique Rottenberg. It is one in a series entitled "Sleeping With," which can be viewed at www.enriquerottenberg.com/sleeping-with. As the artist describes the series, "Throughout the entire island of Cuba, hundreds of very diverse bedrooms were photographed, always encountering the unique characteristic of the Cuban idiosyncrasy that made it all possible: their hospitality. Trespassing the boundaries of public space in order to introduce ourselves into a home's most private place, where people spend a third of their lives, where they dream, lay sleepless, undress, procreate … The absence of its inhabitants gives life to the settings, objects, decorations, floors and walls, telling us the individual and collective history."

Introduction

On June 6, 2024, *KirrinFinch* (KF), a Brooklyn-based, lesbian-owned, company that "creat[es] menswear-inspired apparel designed to fit a range of female and non-binary bodies,"[1] sent an email blast to its customers. In honor of Pride Month, KF lent its "spotlight" to a Havana-based clothing and gift shop. The shop is called *Clandestina*, and it describes itself as "an independent collective of female-forward artists and designers that bring the Cuban spirit of 'resolver' [problem solving] and sustainable design to the world."[2] Its mission is to "revolutioniz[e] Havana fashion through the Cuban design lens of producing from what exists while championing representation for LGBTQ+ Cubans!"[3] KF provided a link that would take its customers to the Clandestina website to make purchases.

Clandestina is in a unique position under US law. One of its two co-owners holds Spanish citizenship,[4] rendering it possible for an otherwise Cuban brand to sell its fashion designs in the US.

But it took far more than the fortuitous circumstances of one business partner[5] to produce this potentially profitable partnership between a little lgbtq shop in Old Havana and another in Brooklyn. The shared identity, entrepreneurship, and capital mobility upon which the KF-Clandestina collaboration depends unfolded slowly, unevenly, and idiosyncratically, amid dynamic national and global conditions.[6] Events precipitating the chance to purchase a Clandestina T-shirt in the US reach at least as far back as the end of Spanish colonialism and the start of American imperialism in Cuba; they proceed through Prohibition, the Great Depression, the New Deal, sex tourism, gambling, the Mambo, the Castro-led Revolution, the rise and fall of sugar yields, the Cold War, the break-up of the Soviet Union, the ascent of neoliberalism, the COVID-19 pandemic, and more.

Governing the Terrain Called Beauty: The Queerness of Political Economy in Cuba and the United States follows the strands that brought us this moment. It narrates a story about travels and transformations in sexual and gender identity and the legal treatment of sexual and gender minorities under changing material and discursive conditions. *Governing the Terrain Called Beauty*, at first blush, is a study of lgbtq legal advances in Cuba, including legalization of same-sex marriage. In producing a genealogical and comparative encounter between Cuba and the US, however, it offers something deeper: a vision for the conduct of a richly contextualized political–economic analysis of sexual identity and the law by which it is governed.

Such an analysis reveals much that would be missed by confining one's attention to the cloud-cover of generalizations about socialism, capitalism, or other big systems. National jurisdictions, of whatever political–economic identities, host millions of constitutive run-ins every day between the global and the local. Getting underneath the clouds and beginning to account for these myriad occurrences enables not only thicker description but also a less obstructed line of sight to law reform possibilities. What follows, then, is a reconstituted history of Cuba and the US as it bears on the evolution of sexual and gender identities and their regulation, as well as an argument about what the comparative and genealogical method of study offers in contrast to one that draws its inferences from generalizations about socialism or capitalism.

WHY CUBA?

Once notorious for sending homosexual men to labor camps and quarantining HIV-positive persons, the Cuba of today has decriminalized same-sex sex, outlawed discrimination on the basis of sexual orientation, provided free gender-affirming health care (including gender confirmation surgery), permitted gender marker changes on national IDs, proliferated gay- and trans-positive sex education for every age-level and as part of medical training, and sponsored an annual conga line commemorating the depathologization of homosexuality by the World Health Organization. In 2022, Cuba became the thirty-second country in the world to legalize same-sex marriage while also extending access to adoption and assisted reproduction to same-sex couples.

Yet, Revolutionary Cuba recognizes none of the liberal rights on which lgbtq advocates in the US and other liberal democracies[7] have relied. It protects no rights to privacy, expression, association, or assembly and has historically frowned upon identity-based political movements as inconsistent with the unifying ideology of the Revolution. Cuba sustains few NGOs that could mount a campaign of impact litigation and lacks the kind of vigorous commercial sector wherein corporate competitors might independently take initiatives toward equality to attract personnel or appeal to consumers. While some grassroots organizing occurs in Cuba, it is typically squelched, exiled, or absorbed into the machinery of state.

How then, has Cuban progress for its lgbtq citizens occurred? How does the reformist path in a legal culture that is unfriendly to liberal rights differ from one that relies on them almost entirely? What might a country that routinely turns to command-and-control economic measures to distribute and redistribute resources across its population do differently from one (such as the US) that is notoriously resistant to downward redistribution and – even while clocking in triumph after triumph for those positioned to benefit from liberal rights gains – neglects the most economically disadvantaged members of the lgbtq community?

In contrast to the US, Cuba's path toward gay emancipation, as one might expect, has been largely state planned. Initially, its principal drivers were public health initiatives and sex education curricula, with decriminalization and anti-discrimination coverage following. In recent decades, a single figure, Mariela Castro, has propelled much of the progress. Mariela is the niece of Fidel Castro and the daughter of Fidel's brother Raúl and Raúl's wife, Vilma Espín. Mariela's revolutionary pedigree places her beyond reproach in the Cuban political arena. She sits as a member of Cuba's National Assembly, is a psychologist with a doctorate from the University of Havana, and has served as the longtime director of the Cuban National Center for Sex Education (CENESEX).

The rule changes Mariela has championed have been delivered in a top-down fashion rather than as a response to grassroots organizing or litigation, but that is not to say they sprang fully formed from her head as if she were Zeus. To understand the context in which Mariela and her allies have advanced the lgbtq cause requires one to appreciate the country's global position over the course of many years and specifically its relationship with the US before and since the 1959 Revolution that brought her family to power.

META-SYSTEMS

In the US, left-progressive legal thinkers often maintain one of two predominant orientations. The first is a *liberal rights* orientation according to which a group's identity is more or less fixed outside the law's purview, and it is the job of the civil rights lawyer to vindicate equality, privacy, or expressive interests on behalf of the group. The second is a *big system* orientation that locates injustice in the general condition of capitalism (or, in recent decades, neoliberalism), is wary – if not disdainful – of legal reforms that effectively reenforce the structural foundations of "the system," and underestimates the significance of factors that might be characterized as aesthetic, discursive, or affective, rather than structural and material. Both camps have yielded important insights. Still, when it comes to the former, my prior work has focused on critique,[8] arguing that liberal rights discourses can hide analytical holes through which regressive politics might sneak, causing the best laid legal reform plans to backfire or impose under-recognized costs on vulnerable constituencies. This book takes up the premises of the latter orientation, that of systemic determinacy, identifying its limits in a multi-determined world.

That is not, however, how the project started. My research into Cuba was initially premised on a hope that at its end I would return to the work of my own national jurisdiction to continue pressing the movement for lgbtq advancement in a direction that would benefit the most economically marginalized with fresh ideas for a more redistributive agenda. A socialist country that had made real progress for lgbtq people, I imagined, would have an arsenal of legal strategies that would be more attuned to the hazard of economic stratification. I would study Cuba to uncover them.

In some respects, this hypothesis was vindicated. Cuba did indeed make some of its advances in the socialized domains of public health and sex education, benefiting its lgbtq population without regard to other aspects of social position – such as race or geography – that often correlate with economic marginalization.

Yet, while the Cuban system is in many respects socialist – an identity to which its leadership fervently adheres – a close look at Cuban legal developments over the years reveals a far more conflictual, and constantly changing, picture. Cuba's continual struggle for survival and dignity in the international domain has affected all manner of internal developments, including regulation of the economy, but also in the domain of sexual identity. The codification of same-sex marriage in Cuba, for instance, seven years after the US Supreme Court found a constitutional right to same-sex marriage in *Obergefell v. Hodges*,[9] cannot be fully understood without also comprehending Cuba's global position over the course of decades, including the economic abyss in which it found itself after the Soviet downfall, the seemingly interminable US embargo, and the move from sugar to tourism as its prime industry.

Indeed, the ten-thousand-foot view of Cuba as socialist ends up contributing little to understanding Cuba's political economy or its effects on Cuba's sexual and gender minorities. "[L]aw," as international legal scholar David Kennedy has written, is located in "the middle space between big systems and ethnographic study."[10] In the Cuban context, formal and informal markets pervade at the ethnographic level, while legal codes, at moments big and small, adjust and "consolidate."[11] Once you break any system down into its numerous rules, rule gaps, standards, zones of discretion, and degrees of enforcement, you can see its intricacies, inconsistencies, exceptions, and accommodations to change. Systemic characterization thereby comes to seem more and more contingent, and even a bit in the way of a clear view of the ground.

The exploration of Cuban law in this book, therefore, does little in the end to illuminate specific legal reforms that might be transplanted from a socialist system into the US. Instead, my revised hope for this study is that it will serve as a mirror, reflecting back especially to left legal thinkers situated in the US (and other self-consciously liberal legal jurisdictions) the haplessness of investing too much confidence in meta-systems to explain legal developments.

COMPARISON, GENEALOGY, AND DISCOURSE

The initial intentions of this project were what comparative legal scholars refer to as "functionalist;" that is, a quest "to find (better) solutions to problems."[12] In this case, the problem was that of how to advance the cause of lgbtq people while bringing along economically marginalized subpopulations. The turn to a comparison with Cuba was born of curiosity regarding how a country with a command economy and an aspiration to economic destratification might "do" lgbtq legal advancement differently, and what US-based advocates might learn from observing an altogether different trajectory of lgbtq legal progress. The method, however, evolved as the study progressed.

Contra many mainstream legal comparative efforts, this one ultimately left behind the search for the "best" (i.e., most efficient or most advanced) answers to legal questions.[13] Nor is the objective of this project, as it is with some comparative investigations, to identify universals (i.e., to drill down through superficial legal variations to demonstrate that law reaches more or less the same solutions across borders).[14]

In addition to avoiding dependence on general characterizations of Cuba as socialist or the US as capitalist, the study also eschews over-reliance on *legal* systemic binaries (e.g., status/contract, civil code/common law, or primitive/modern)[15] to characterize contrasts between the two systems. Dichotomies such as these can be misleading. Legal systems are not monolithic; they contain exceptions, contradictions, gaps, and ambiguities.[16] They change constantly to accommodate new conditions and address new problems. As David Kennedy has written, "All countries have political characteristics once routinely thought anomalous and there is no one 'normal' or mature form for political life. Stable and significant political regimes come in many varieties – more or less authoritarian, more or less religious, more or less decentralized, more and less technocratic, with different blends of public and private economic power."[17]

A critical comparative analysis highlights this richness rather than suppressing it. Intentional "splitting,"[18] to use international law scholar Nathaniel Berman's term, results in a more comprehensive picture while also yielding insight into what "critical resources" each system makes available to emancipatory projects.[19]

Following comparative legal scholars Fernanda Nicola and Günter Frankenberg, the comparative method employed in this book extends itself instead to examining law as a *discourse*[20] – that is, as a largely unseen and fluctuating network of concepts that have real distributive effects in the world, not merely through regulation, but by shaping perceptions of what is legitimate and even what is possible. To that end, I have taken care to check any tendency toward logocentrism[21] (i.e., excessive focus on the two dimensions of constitutions, cases, statutes, or treatises as if legal texts provided a three-dimensional representation of the subject they purport to govern). Moreover, the study is *genealogical*: that is, it examines historical factors that helped to shape beliefs about law and sexuality and, in turn, traces the regulatory and distributive effects of those beliefs. *Governing the Terrain Called Beauty*, therefore, derives its insights by producing an encounter between Cuba and the US and directing attention to how law – understood as a formal regime of rules *as well as* a complex of discourses – evolved under imperialism, anxious nationalisms, racial stratification, economic hardship, and other material and discursive conditions. It is about how ideas travel and the under-recognized pertinence of legal consciousness to the limits of social change.

While Cuba occupies the principal focus of the book's narrative, events in the timeline of the US appear regularly. Inclusion of these events serves two purposes.

First, the US stands as a point of contrast. Despite all manner of front-page gains, such as prohibitions against employment discrimination and the right to marriage equality, lgbtq people in the US remain over-represented among the poor, the food insecure, and the homeless. US-based lgbtq advocacy has prioritized reform objectives designed to make sense within a discourse of equal rights. The resulting reforms have provided the greatest benefit to those least in need, leaving the most economically disadvantaged lgbtq people (typically distinguished by race, age, and/or region of the US) behind.[22]

Second, the US, as a once imperialist and still antagonistic neighbor, performs a powerful role within Cuba's own story. US policy toward Cuba, the Cold War between the US and the Soviet Union, the end of the Cold War, and geopolitics since, have helped to shape the status of sexual and gender minorities in Cuba before and since the 1959 Revolution. Even as Cuba witnessed the capitulation of formerly communist Eastern European nations to the norms of the global marketplace, this determined outpost of some ten million people has strived over the decades to withstand external influence and chart its own political–economic course. That said, among the most interesting aspects of this story is how geopolitics and global economic pressures have shaped identities, ideas about law, and the treatment of sexual and gender minorities inside Cuba.

A central objective of comparison in *Governing the Terrain Called Beauty*, typical of critical comparative undertakings, is to denaturalize assumptions underlying US law. Every effort, therefore, has been made to guard against ethnocentrism.[23] Indeed, the following pages are meant to reflect mindfulness of US legal scholastic conventions. To hold this aim steady requires – to the extent of my abilities – cognizance of the biases ingrained by my training as a US lawyer, an effort to treat Cuba as different on its own terms and not as an "exotic other,"[24] while also "defamiliarizing the familiar"[25] by maintaining critical distance from US law and a willingness to "discover [my own] pre-understandings."[26]

The book also tracks law as it travels across national boundaries. "[L]aws neither fall from heaven, as lawmakers' ingenious insights, nor do they grow organically from the soil of local culture."[27] Instead, they are often best "understood as products of the confluence of information – some local, some that have travelled from elsewhere.… [I]t is important to understand legal transfer as part of world-making," and to be cognizant that "in the process of transfer new layers of meaning are added."[28] Law is a producer and product of culture as well as a producer and product of encounters between the global and the local.

I began, therefore, with a few impressionistic ideas about what differentiates US and Cuban legal systems but held them lightly and with an openness to being disabused: US legal culture favors making change for an identity-based constituency by relying on a familiar set of higher order rights, including rights to privacy, assembly, expression, association, and identity-based formal equality – but *not* distributive equality (i.e., *not* an equalized distribution of resources such as wealth, housing, nutrition, etc.). The Cuban system, by contrast, is resistant to liberal rights and identity-based claims but is at ease with top-down redistributive pronouncements. These suppositions were merely a point of entry, which I anticipated would fracture, or at least become complicated, as the study progressed.

IDENTITY LEXICON

Governing the Terrain Called Beauty follows the gay subject as he travels through the twentieth century and into the twenty-first, illuminating the conditions within which he is continually being forged. Lesbians make an occasional appearance in this story, but it is the male homosexual that emerges as central. Moreover, sexual identity categories are shifting and unstable across time and place. This is reflected in the book's vocabulary, sometimes using *lgbtq*, other times *gay*, *lesbian*, or *trans*, sometimes *homosexual*, and finally at times *sexual and gender minorities*. This inconsistency is a feature, not a bug, in a comparative and genealogical exercise. Contemporary US vocabulary breaks down identity in a particular way that has not historically been controlling in Cuba, though the terminology has evolved in recent years. *Sexual and gender minorities* is the most neutral term I could find to speak across borders and eras. Another option was *queer*, but while I acquiesce to the *q* in *lgbtq*, I use *queer* to refer to a set of analytic tendencies, not an identity, in deference to *queer's* theoretic lineage. I use *trans* or *transgender* in both national contexts, though the meaning in Cuba is a bit narrower than it has become in the US – closer to the old term *transsexual* – and in Spanish is closer on a literal translation to *transvestite*, which has an altogether different English usage. When discussing Cuban history, the text makes frequent use of the term *homosexual* because it is closer to the practice predominating in Cuba until relatively recently, notwithstanding my cognizance that the term chafes against the sensibilities of some US-based and other Anglophone readers, sounding clinical and antiquated. *Homosexual* is not always synonymous with *gay*, which for decades in the US (and more recently in Cuba) has signified a preference for same-sex romantic and sexual attachment, usually referring to men, but sometimes encompassing lesbians, as well. Whether a man is butch or femme, whether he tops, bottoms, or is versatile, *gay* is equally applicable in contemporary US vocabulary. As in other parts of Latin America and the Caribbean, however, the conception of the male homosexual in Cuba has historically emphasized effeminacy and availability for penetration by a top, who is masculine and not coded homosexual. (Chapter 1 will review the applicable Cuban Spanish slang.) The term *homosexual* was also in more common usage in the US in the 1950s, and therefore will appear in discussions of that history, as well.[29] All of these terms are in constant flux and by the time this book goes to press, a revised lexicon could be emerging.

To affirm the semiotic point, none of these terms is an exact match for an underlying referent. Indeed, the homosexual and gay figures in the book are more often discursive figments than real human beings. This is especially the case as both the US and Cuba deploy their homosexuals and gays for nationalist purposes during and after the Cold War. During the second Red Scare in the US, for example, the homosexual was closely associated with the fear of communist infiltration. Meanwhile, Cuba – like other socialist societies – regarded homosexuals as redolent of capitalist imperialism and bourgeois decadence. (The homosexual archetype has rather obviously been inflected by misogyny, as well, positing the penetrated as feminine and humiliated and the penetrator as masculine and victorious.[30]) Both countries eventually reversed course, touting their progress toward gay emancipation as evidence of the redemptive capacities of their systems.

The volatility of sexual and gender identity categories joins with the contingency of political–economic systems to produce an unstable matrix that made my original, functionalist undertaking seem naïve. A key conclusion of this study, therefore, circles back to method. To apprehend the how and why of lgbtq advancement in a particular national jurisdiction one is best advised to hold the reins loosely. Over-dichotomization of either gay/straight or socialist/capitalist obscures rather than enlightens.

TONE

I approached Cuba as a novice, with no special expertise in Latin American or Caribbean Studies, but rather as a US-based legal scholar who maintains an interest in the range of avenues available to advance the welfare of those lgbtq persons whose oppression is most intransigent. Immersing myself in learning about Cuba for the past few years, it has been striking how ardently held are polar positions by those for whom Cuban politics remain extremely emotionally salient. From the perspective of a person who, at a much younger age, lived in Jerusalem and participated in Palestinian–Israeli peace activism, the raw nerve endings are strikingly familiar. My objective in engaging with Cuban studies is to maintain – as steadily as I can – the posture of a student: here to learn, open-minded, and with an aspiration to maintain my academic remove. I intend neither to valorize nor to demonize Revolutionary Cuba or its leadership. (I am much more comfortable making judgments about the US without fear of getting ahead of my learning.) In the course of reading, I have at turns been appalled (e.g., by the abuse of male and female homosexuals in Cuban prisons) and moved (e.g., by the solidarity displayed by the young literacy volunteers of the early revolutionary period). My tone, however, is meant to reflect neither zealotry nor reductionism, neither apology nor determined detraction. I am certain that this posture will disappoint some readers, but in my academic judgment, it is the soundest approach for achieving the purposes of this project.

ORGANIZATION

The book is in three parts. Each part consists of two chapters.

Part I selectively reconstitutes Cuban history, weaving it together with relevant, contemporaneous events in the US. The two chapters that compose Part I (which owe a debt to a collection of historical and ethnographic secondary sources) are genealogical in the sense that they illustrate the role of international and national politics, especially the relationship between the US and Cuba as well as between each of those two nations and the Soviet Union, in shaping sexual identities and legal advances. By reexamining pertinent events with sexual identity at the center, this Part illustrates the interplay between the global and the local, as well as between material conditions and discourses of identity.

Chapter 1 opens in 1898, when Cuba finally rid itself of Spanish colonial power only to find itself subordinated to US control. Over the course of the next six decades, US presence inflicted deep indignities on the Cuban people. The homosexual – conceived as a weak and effete provider of illicit pleasures to US businessmen, tourists, and military personnel – became discursively entangled with exploitation by the hated capitalists and mob bosses from the north, much of which occurred with the cooperation of corrupt Cuban leaders. When the new revolutionary era dawned, expunging the vice and national humiliation that the homosexual represented emerged as a regime priority. The 1960s and early 70s are remembered as the darkest years for Cuban homosexuals, marked by legal and social exclusion, surveillance, police round ups, and forced labor. Cuban nationalist sentiment manifested as a compulsion to win back Cuban honor by advancing the iconography of the socialist "New Man," while simultaneously stamping out his shameful counterpart, that painful reminder of imperialist subjugation. The US, meanwhile, had waded into the murk of its own Cold War fears, its conservatives depicting homosexuals as communist infiltrators hiding in government and among producers of arts and culture. These fantasized traitors would, many believed, destroy the family, men's industrial spirit, and the nation itself if they were not expelled from positions of trust and subjected to relentless policing. Taken together, Cuba's symbol of capitalist exploitation and the US's specter of communist infiltration introduce the homosexual not only as a depository for nationalist anxieties but also as a diacritical "other" crucial to the consolidation of each nation's systemic identity.

Anti-homosexual vitriol began to subside in Cuba in the mid 1970s, which is where Chapter 2 picks up the story. By this point, the US had entered its sexual revolution and gay liberation (gay equality's rebellious predecessor) had launched. Cuba also began to turn the tide. It launched a progressive sex education program aimed at every sector of society, promoting tolerance of homosexuality as a normal human variant and pushing modest law reforms. In the 1980s, a combination of the AIDS crisis and the Reagan era's new "family values" led gay rights advocates in the US to construct an activist and advocacy infrastructure and establish a reform agenda centered on partnership recognition. At the end of that decade, the US left the Cold War behind, enabling a wave of legal progress for gays and lesbians. For Cuba, though, the downfall of the Soviet Union spelled economic calamity. Even as it fervently maintained its socialist identity, the new revolutionary regime was forced to open itself to international tourism and foreign capital investment, resulting in an uptick in transactional sex that revived anxieties regarding national exploitation and prompted a rearrangement of sexual identities. For some homosexuals, old stereotypes became new again. The final decades of the twentieth century saw an uneasy conjunction of legal progress with social censure.

How then, Part II asks, did the next century bring gay marriage to Cuba? On September 25, 2022, Cubans voted in a national referendum by a margin of almost 2-to-1 to adopt a new Family Code that legalized marriage between two partners of the same sex. In a country that has a low marriage rate accompanied by a high divorce rate, is markedly less religious than its neighbors, rarely awards alimony, does not impose any legal consequences on children born of nonmarital parentage, has historically allocated little property using marriage or divorce, distributes most public resources (e.g., health care) such that they do not depend on marital ties, and accords marriage little social significance, why did same-sex marriage emerge as a law reform objective?

Chapter 3 begins with a brief explanation of Cuba's legal structure followed by an account of the process by which same-sex marriage, just one piece of a larger overhaul of Cuba's Family Code, became law. It then examines Cuba's old Family Code of 1975 and introduces its 2022 successor, along with coterminous regulatory changes in housing, foreign investment, entrepreneurship, and self-employment – all of which came as Cuba tried to navigate stormy economic waters. Legal changes converged to produce a strange contradiction: Family law over time rendered marriage *less important* while the beginnings of a real estate market and vastly increased opportunities for entrepreneurship made marriage seem *more important*. The chapter concludes by reviewing a misguided effort to achieve good order by incentivizing marriage among reluctant Cubans, ultimately damaging marriage's prestige and revealing how material benefits can affect marriage's social meaning.

Despite the low regard in which marriage had been held for many years in Cuba, Cubans suddenly lost sight of its devalued status when the question of gay equality came into the foreground. Chapter 4 supplies an ingredient to partially explain the sudden overvaluation of marriage when it came to gays and lesbians. Same-sex marriage as an egalitarian ideal for the benefit of those who hold a gay or lesbian identity acquired so much symbolic power globally that even a country that ostentatiously eschewed liberal rights and identity-based reform fell under its captivating spell. This chapter engages postcolonial and queer theory to explore the spread of gay identity into Cuba, along with same-sex marriage as the zenith of gay identity recognition. Gay identity slipped into Cuba with the tourists, ex-pat family visits, and foreign investment that Cuba was forced to admit by the dire economic conditions it has faced since the downfall of the Soviet Union. The chapter concludes by focusing on one specific figure, the *pinguero*, a type of male sex worker who arose to accommodate the demands of the sex tourism market. The pinguero's encounters exemplify a site at which the global meets the local, generating changes in the discourse of sexual identity. The chapter is designed to illustrate how political–economic changes can usher in discursive ones, and how these changes in turn facilitated the arrival of same-sex marriage.

Lawyers, by virtue of their training and participation in a culture of legal practice, engage in a profession-specific discourse that is embedded within a larger discourse of nationalist premises. Part III takes up this "legal consciousness" as a point of comparative analysis. Under-recognized aspects of one's own legal culture can appear more vividly in the reflection of another, illuminating capacities and limits that might otherwise go unnoticed. This part uses comparison to denaturalize the assumptions of US legal culture and shed light on how legal and nonlegal "discourses co-produce legal realities."[31]

Chapter 5 reviews the results of an investigation I undertook on a visit to Cuba in November of 2022. Along with a research assistant, I attended a conference of family lawyers, many of whom had participated in the drafting of and public advocacy for Cuba's recently adopted Family Code, including the new provision for same-sex marriage. We also conducted interviews with individual Cuban lawyers and met with a group of Cuban law students. Using an interview technique designed to open a window into legal consciousness, we facilitated a number of revelatory conversations regarding how these legal thinkers conceptualize problems and what tools they believe to be at their disposal to address them. Our conversations generated the remarkably consistent suggestion that our interviewees do not hold as their chief aspiration the performance of objective, linear deduction from rule to case outcome (a performance for which US lawyers continue to be rigorously trained). Instead, the lawyers and law students we interviewed idealized legal decision-making that is driven by a commitment to humanism, conceptualized in spiritual (though not deistic) terms. This belief fused with a more general Cuban discourse of socialism as a facet of national identity, entailing continuing suspicion and resentment toward the capitalist behemoth to the north, perceived (not without justification) as a perpetual antagonist, ideologically and pragmatically. All the Cuban lawyers and law students with whom we spoke were quite cognizant of the regulatory transitions Cuba has undergone in recent years and the resulting growth in the aboveground private sector. They nevertheless did not view same-sex marriage or other changes for lgbtq people as affected by economic pressures from, or ideological concessions to, external forces.

Chapter 6 treats the Cuba study as a mirror in which to view the liberal legal imagination, especially in the US. What stood out in Chapter 5's interviews with Cuban lawyers and law students (i.e., lack of interest in neutral deduction in favor of a humanistic spirit and defiant attachment to socialist identity amid hostile, capitalist, and imperialist forces) makes visible a propensity among some left-legal thinkers in a contrasting legal system to over-attribute distributive outcomes to capitalist predetermination and to underestimate the pertinence of discursive power to law. This chapter brings together the thesis that distributions are produced by multifaceted encounters between global and local, as well as material and discursive, factors. Those factors can be excavated genealogically, viewed in the light of comparison, and used to assist in understanding how one's own legal consciousness might unwittingly legitimate unjust distributions or artificially set bounds on possibilities for change.

The book concludes by considering one last example of a specific mode of governance that engages both formal regulation and internalized norms: space. Queer theorists have observed the norm-setting capacities of spatial boundaries that purport to separate public from private, producing discourses of family, sexuality, race, and so on. These writers also propose the queerness of disturbing these norms, of disorienting the sense of order they provide, and of serving them up for critical examination. This final example encapsulates the queerness that *Governing the Terrain Called Beauty* endeavors to bring to political–economic analysis, making room for contradiction and surprise and illuminating discourses of law and identity that might otherwise seem natural.

PART I

A Queer, Comparative Genealogy

1

Expulsion of the Homosexual Figment

1898–1970s

The "homosexual" introduced in this chapter is not a person; he is a figment. This is not an assertion that there are no homosexuals, or that in some vulgar postmodern sense the term has no content – though to be sure its content varies, including by national context, as this chapter describes. Nor is the assertion made without recognition that real human bodies, marked as homosexual, have endured disdain, terror, arrest, imprisonment, torture, murder, and all other manner of abuse. The homosexual subject of this chapter is a figment because he – not invariably but typically, *he* – functions as a potent constitutive element in (at least) two rival nationalist discourses.

The instability of the category is immaterial to the homosexual's performance of this role, as long as the term manages to signify moral weakness and compromised masculinity. In Cuba, the homosexual stood for these defects and then some during the period spanning from the end of Cuba's status as a Spanish colony well into the Cold War period. The term's adverse connotations did not then mercifully drop off the ledge of history, but around the mid 1970s the homosexual idea did begin to undergo some salutary interventions, initially medical in nature, which are discussed in Chapter 2. This chapter, however, trudges through the bleakest expanse, where the Cuban homosexual amassed and then bore his most despised characteristics.

In the US, particularly during the Cold War, some parallel features afflicted the American homosexual. What follows is a selective reconstitution of Cuban history from the end of its Spanish colonial period until the mid-1970s, interspersed with relevant developments in the US. The history is selective in that it is designed to highlight the emergent place of the homosexual in Cuban nationalist discourse and the part that the US played in that evolution. The histories of the two nations entwined, as did their homosexual notions, as relations of imperialism and Cold War antagonism between them unfolded. The part of the story told here begins with the formal entry of the US into Cuban governance.

Like other Caribbean nations, Cuba endured centuries of colonialism, slavery, and economic plunder. In 1898,[1] with the Treaty of Paris concluding the

Spanish-American War,[2] Cuba gained its nationhood from what had been, but was no longer, the Spanish Empire. Genuine independence for Cuba was not, however, imminent. The US had intervened on Cuba's behalf in its liberation struggle against Spain after the USS Maine mysteriously exploded in Havana Harbor killing 260 American sailors.[3] The result of Spain's defeat included US acquisition of Puerto Rico, Guam, and (temporarily) the Philippines. While Cuba was not similarly "acquired," the US would impose four years of military rule[4] and thereafter exert a powerful influence over Cuba's governance and economy for decades.

Documenting and cementing this influence was the Platt Amendment. Named for its author, Senator Orville Hitchcock Platt (R-CT) and signed by President William McKinley in 1901, the Platt Amendment ostensibly committed the US to cede control of the island to its people, but conditionally.[5] The conditions, seven of them, were stringent. The Platt Amendment limited Cuba's freedom to enter into treaties with foreign powers and to borrow money; it granted the US an indefinite "right to intervene" in Cuba to preserve the latter's independence and to protect "life, property, and individual liberty;" and it entitled the US to purchase or lease land for use as naval bases.[6] Withdrawal of US troops remaining in Cuba in the aftermath of the Spanish-American War was contingent upon Cuba's adopting the terms of the Platt Amendment into its new constitution. In 1902, the first Cuban Republic officially constituted itself, the US withdrew, and a further treaty was signed in 1903 by which the US acquired Guantánamo Bay.

The next few decades saw periodic instability, including uprisings and the hatching of a variety of political groups organized around dissatisfaction with economic and labor conditions, racial inequality, and governmental corruption. University students and professors as well as workers saw their small revolts put down by some combination of Cuban military might and US intervention.

Cuba abolished slavery late – 1886 – but abolition was not followed by a US-style Jim Crow period of legally sanctioned racial exclusion. The war in which Cuba won its independence from Spain was fought on the heels of slavery's end. Its revolutionary premise, according to historian Alejandro de la Fuente, included a vision of racial equality that drew Afro-Cubans into battle,[7] many of whom distinguished themselves as leaders and war heroes. José Martí, a poet and writer and perhaps Cuba's most revered historic figure, who gave his life for the cause of ending Spanish rule, left a corpus of written work that instilled the ideal of a nation "with all, for all."[8] The precise meaning of this racially inclusive dream, however, which continues to inflect the Cuban national imaginary, has been a matter of some disagreement.

A key debate within Cuba,[9] for example, during the period known as the *first republic* (1902–33), regarded whether race-conscious political organizing was consistent with the spirit of a Cuban nation that was truly "for all." In 1908, in response to Black electoral losses, a Black political party arose, the *Partido Independiente de Color* (PIC), to address economic concerns as well as to ensure Black representation and participation in governance. Its platform included nondiscrimination in public sector employment and access to education and land.[10] The party was banned in 1910 as an affront to Cuba's "nationalist ideology of racial fraternity."[11] Martí wrote, "'There can be no racial animosity, because there are no races.'"[12] Deference to this racial "denial"[13] constrained the array of strategies available to redress racism. Race-based organizing was widely perceived to be "un-Cuban" and even "racist." Party activists continued to rally until they were finally put down in 1912 in the form of a massacre resulting in approximately 3,000 Afro-Cuban deaths.[14] The US (without being asked) provided assistance in this brutal act of suppression[15] out of fear that a country with a dominant Black population would be unsuited to self-rule.[16] Apprehensions about the possibility of "another Haiti" ran through the discourse, with some opponents claiming that PIC's leaders were themselves Haitian.[17] The Cuban government also repressed Santería and other African-based religions to avoid conveying an impression of Cuba as primitive,[18] but it is not clear that such measures had any impact on official US thinking.

In these early decades of the century, sugar was king. It was Cuba's chief export, relentlessly harvested and produced to satisfy US demand. Workers migrated from around the Caribbean and beyond to toil under slave-like conditions in the cane fields. US corporations, monumentally the United Fruit Company, invested massive amounts of capital in sugar production in Cuba, as well as bananas and other crops around the Caribbean. Buyers from the US and other countries bought up Cuban agricultural land, so that, according to historian Ada Ferrer, "less than a decade after independence, perhaps three-quarters of Cuban territory belonged to foreigners."[19] The US absorbed Cuban sugar, creating a lucrative export market, but the profits predominantly went right back to US companies.[20] Meanwhile, coffee and other agricultural products went neglected, resulting in a risky strategy of near-monoculture.[21] When, as a result of World War I, the European beet sugar trade crumbled, companies in Cuba moved in on the European market, further intensifying the Cuban economy's reliance on this single export. The strategy disclosed its shortcomings when the Great War ended and sugar production across the globe returned, sinking prices. Cane cutters in Cuba, including many former slaves, lost their meager salaries while US corporations – diversified throughout the region – took a hit but continued to prosper.[22]

Prohibition in the US began in 1920 and lasted until 1933. Cuba, conveniently situated just ninety miles from the Florida Keys, enjoyed year-round sun and served legally produced rum using the molasses derived from the sugarcane crop. Unsurprisingly, Cuba began to emerge as a popular tourist spot for Americans, many of whom were flush thanks to the post–World War I economy. Rum, once regarded as a déclassé, third-rate spirit, rose in reputation and appeal. This occurred thanks in part to Bacardi, the family-owned rum maker founded decades earlier in Santiago de Cuba.[23] Famously, Ernest Hemingway, who lived for three decades on the island, sipped daiquiris with a double shot of Bacardi rum at the renown Floridita Bar in Old Havana.[24]

Over the course of the 1920s, Cuba's tourist appeal flourished – and it was not the rum alone that drew visitors. "Vibrant nightlife, plentiful alcohol, drugs, gambling, pornography, live sex shows, and ubiquitous brothels drew ever-increasing hordes of visitors each year."[25] US investment dollars rushed into Havana, some of them going to bribe local officials, smoothing the way to building permits and past other bureaucratic hurdles to erecting nightclubs and cabarets.

Meanwhile, in the countryside, US corporations established sugar plantations and processing plants that employed Black Caribbean and other migratory workers at a meager wage. The US was deep in its Jim Crow era. American companies either sent American managers down to Cuba or entrusted Spanish (i.e., white) local men to serve as on-site managers. (Angel Castro, whose sons Fidel and Raúl would lead the Cuban Revolution, was one such Spaniard entrusted by the Americans, and he became wealthy as a result.) The island was awash in money, but only some Cubans were in a position to benefit; most were left impoverished, ill-housed, and illiterate.

With so many people working in the sugar industry, its ebb and flow was a major determinant of Cuba's economy, and therefore also a major determinant of political sentiment toward both the national government and its continuing subservience to US interests. Conditions slowly improved in the early 1920s but then worsened again with the 1929 stock market crash.

In the US, the crash brought the Roaring '20s to an end and hurled the country into the Great Depression. In 1932, with unemployment at a record high and the inability of President Herbert Hoover and the Republicans to salvage the economy painfully evident, Americans voted to install President Franklin Delano Roosevelt, whose New Deal meant a profusion of new economic regulations – including labor laws, price controls, and social insurance programs – and the evolution of an enormous federal bureaucracy.

Though popular with the electorate, the New Deal was despised by conservatives. A swirl of interrelated anxieties attached to its proto-socialistic features. Conservatives staunchly opposed government interference in the "free market" and reviled the new social insurance programs, which they deemed at odds with American "self-reliance."[26] They charged that the New Deal robbed Americans of their virility and independence, producing dependency in its stead.[27] As historian David K. Johnson, leading chronicler of the anti-homosexual witch hunts of the era, observed, "To many critics, bureaucracy was guilty of smothering the individual will of American citizens .... accomplishing on a societal level what … mothers … were feared to be doing on a familial level."[28]

As literary critic Lee Edelman explains, it was a short distance to an invigorated homophobia:

> [G]ay men were assumed … to be overly fond of and close to their mothers, even as they were assumed … to hate women .... It was … the too loving mother that heterosexual culture loved to hate, the smothering mother who destroyed her son through overprotection and overindulgence .... [T]he mother stands accused …

of effeminizing her son, of preventing his "natural" development into heterosexual manhood.[29]

Federal aid functioned, conservatives worried, like an overbearing mother – the cause, many believed, of male homosexuality.[30] This was by no means the origin of the imagined homosexual in the US, but it did represent an important moment of his rhetorical integration into left-right conflict over economic policy.

The massive expansion of government meant a concomitant accretion of federal job openings. New opportunities prompted thousands to move to Washington, DC.[31] Critics suspected that men who worked in government, rather than laboring in manly jobs or striking it out on their own as entrepreneurs, evidenced a lack of masculine independence.[32] Worst among them were the intellectuals, whose expertise in social science or statistics was viewed as professorial, effete,[33] and Jewish.[34]

While racial discrimination remained intransigent, white job applicants could often rely on their merits and exam performance.[35] Some jobs were reserved for men, but there was nonetheless a fresh set of work opportunities for white single women.[36] Growth in population alone meant more homosexuality in the District[37] as increasing urbanization, the Great Migration of Black southerners to northern cities, and European immigration all contributed to the emergence of gay and lesbian social and political community.

US racism came to Cuba in the form of corporate employment practices, thereby feeding anti-American sentiment among Cuban workers and contributing an obdurate layer of inequality. Cubans generally supported racial egalitarianism – at least in the abstract – a testament to the widespread influence of the most salutary rendition of Martí's vision. The struggle over the particulars of that vision, however, persisted. Private and unofficial discrimination was commonplace, if complicated. Here is how African–American poet and author Langston Hughes perceived Cuba's racial hierarchy on a trip to Havana in 1930:

> [T]here exists there a sort of triple color line .... At the bottom of the color scale are the pure-blooded Negroes, black or dark brown in color. In the middle are the mixed bloods, the light browns, mulattoes, golden yellows and near whites with varying textures of Indian-Spanish hair. Then come the nearer whites, the octoroons, and the pure white of skin....
>
> But this scale is not 100% true. Occasionally a very dark Negro occupies a very high position in Cuba. That is what misleads many visitors from the United States – particularly colored visitors who are looking anixously [sic] for a country where they can say there is *no* color line – for Cuba's color line is much more flexible than that of the United States, and much more subtle. There are, of course, no Jim Crow cars in Cuba, and at official state gatherings and less official carnivals and celebrations, citizens of all colors meet and mingle. But there are definite social divisions based on color – and the darker a man is, the richer and more celebrated he has to be to crash those divisions.[38]

While race-based protest had not been seen since the 1912 massacre, the Great Depression was fueling minor uprisings and acts of violent protest by university students and their professors as well as by communist, trade unionist, and other dissident groups. President Gerardo Machado, initially revered as a war hero and elected democratically, began cracking down, eventually devolving into the familiar archetype of a Latin American dictator.

In 1933, a noncommissioned officer in the Cuban military, Fulgencio Batista, came to prominence. Batista emerged from humble origins in Oriente, the eastern region of Cuba. His ancestry is the subject of some dispute. Many of his contemporaries dubbed him *el mulato lindo* (the handsome mulatto) – supposing a mixed racial ancestry – African, Spanish, and Chinese. Others referred to him as *el Indio* (the Indian) – suggesting Taino origins – the tribe native to Cuba and surrounding islands that had been nearly extinguished by the Conquistadores centuries before. De la Fuente surmises that the latter moniker was designed by supporters to rinse away Batista's African ancestry and legitimate his ascendancy to power.[39]

Batista grew up in Banes, effectively a company town bought and paid for by United Fruit, where management lived in luxury developments complete with schools and recreational facilities while cane cutters lived in rural squalor.[40] Batista's father cut cane under the Caribbean sun. Perhaps in evasion of replicating his father's life, Batista enlisted in the military, rising to the rank of sergeant.

Aggrieved by the obvious racial hierarchy of the military, Batista delivered an address in protest to his fellow non-white service members. In it he sympathized, as well, with the civilians demonstrating in Cuba's streets, which were in political disarray. The US had been supporting President Machado, but seeing the unrest, urged him to step aside and make room for a provisional president in order to mollify the people, which he did. Batista, however, saw at that very moment an opening. Leading a group of like-minded soldiers, he pushed out the provisional president and installed a professor from the University of Havana who had protested along with his students, Dr. Ramón Grau San Martín. The US declined to intervene and after a brief battle, Batista and his military supporters put an end to any viable opposition, initiating what became known as the *second republic* (1933–58). Batista declared himself military chief of staff and proceeded to supplant the sitting president nearly a half dozen times while gripping the real reins of power behind the scenes until he was formally elected to the presidency in 1940.[41]

Batista used the presidency to line his own pockets – and they were very well-lined. In addition to taking kickbacks from government contracts, skimming off the national lottery, and maintaining a stake in *bolita* (an illegal numbers racket) and other kinds of gambling,[42] he also benefited financially from his close working relationship with leaders of the US Mafia.

The Mafia was not entirely new to Cuba; it had run bootlegging operations throughout the region during Prohibition.[43] Business conducted in Cuba was out of reach of the FBI and the IRS, which meant that the island could also serve as a base for extensive money laundering.

The powerful if unflamboyant New York mobster Meyer Lansky oversaw what was a truly ambitious undertaking. Along with associates such as Charles "Lucky" Luciano and Santo Trafficante, Lansky created in Havana a kind of heaven for organized crime and its clientele. A Jew among Italians,[44] Lansky carefully sketched a master plan for Cuba, established the necessary local political connections, and brokered deals among the various Mafia families to share in the work and the profits. The "Havana Mob" built a string of casinos along the coastline. For his cut, Batista kept a tight rein on political dissidents, cleared away legal impediments, and otherwise protected the mob's business interests.

To be fair, it is also the case that during his decade-plus of informal and formal rule, Batista oversaw real reform, including women's suffrage, workers' rights (including, as historian Richard Gott specified, "an 8-hour day, a 44 hour week and one month's paid holiday, plus a pension … and accident compensation"[45]) in addition to land reform, health and education initiatives, and public works projects.[46] A new constitution incorporated many of these reforms in 1940.

The actuality of race discrimination in Cuba and the role of the state in combatting it remained matters of dispute that surfaced in the drafting of the new constitution. "The abstract principle of equality"[47] had left rampant discrimination undisturbed. De la Fuente, in his comprehensive and extraordinary history of race in twentieth-century Cuba,[48] explains the debate:

> Those who denied the existence of racism in Cuban society supported the inclusion in the constitutional text of a general principle of equality … [while] those critical of Cuban racial realities advocated explicit antidiscrimination statements, sanctions for racist acts, and even the introduction of a quota system that would guarantee a proportional participation of blacks in all sources of employment, political candidacies, and appointments.[49]

Communist delegates to the constitutional convention generally supported the most activist version of the state in redressing racial inequality. Delegates from the other parties, who opposed an activist state on this issue, however, prevailed by appealing to racial fraternity and the need to avoid "divisions."[50]

While those seeking an aggressively anti-racist legal regime faced mostly defeats, an *Afrocubanismo* artistic movement flourished,[51] and as a matter of national consciousness, Cuba began to see itself as a characterologically mixed-race nation. "By the late 1930s and early 1940s," the prevailing view was, as one Cuban intellectual explained, "'Cuba is neither white, nor black, but *mulata, mestiza*.'"[52] While the term *mulatto* carries a negative connotation in English usage,[53] Cuban use came to represent a "celebrated … racial and cultural synthesis … the very essence" of "cubanidad" (cubanness), proudly defining the Cuban nation as racially composite.[54]

With the ratification of the new constitution, the Platt Amendment was fully and finally annulled, but with an understanding that Batista would continue to facilitate US corporate interests.[55] The White House experienced some anxiety over Batista's redistributive (read: *socialist*) tendencies, but it also felt it could work with him, and did so as an ally during World War II. In 1944, at the end of his four-year term, Batista left the presidency – voluntarily – apparently to attend to his personal life.[56]

The conclusion of World War II brought economic prosperity back to many Americans, but it also brought about a fresh set of national apprehensions. Containment of the Communist threat became a major preoccupation as the US and its wartime ally, the Soviet Union, embarked on over four decades of Cold War.

In addition to Cold War-related angst, a confluence of population changes and fluctuations in family life produced anxieties for which homophobia was a perfect expression. As historian John D'Emilio explains, "the Great Depression and World War II [had] seriously disrupted family life, traditional gender arrangements, and patterns of sexual behavior."[57] The hardships of the 1930s led to delayed marriage and falling birthrates, both of which were partially reversed with wartime prosperity. Still, the war brought increased rates of divorce and abandonment, as well as an influx of women into jobs formerly reserved to men. At the same time, single-sex military environments and women's organizations gave rise to fresh gay and lesbian opportunities and subcultures.[58] Historian Margot Canaday points to an obsessive focus in the military on rooting out lesbianism in the years immediately following the war.[59] While it had been regarded as a heroic sacrifice for women to forgo family life in favor of service to the nation during wartime, by the 1950s, women who stuck with their military careers, avoiding marriage, raised suspicions.[60]

The insecurities wrought by depression and war also teed up the anti-homosexual crusade of Senator Joe McCarthy. In a February, 1950 speech in Wheeling, West Virginia, McCarthy famously inaugurated the second Red Scare, declaring that there were two hundred and five "card carrying" communists working in President Harry Truman's State Department.[61] As the details of McCarthy's initial pronouncement emerged, it turned out that some were actually homosexuals, but McCarthy saw a connection: "[h]omosexuality," as Johnson paraphrased, "was the psychological maladjustment that led people toward communism."[62] Secretary of State Dean Acheson and Deputy Undersecretary John Peurifoy went before a congressional committee to respond to McCarthy's charge. They conceded that the State Department had discharged a number of "security risks."[63] Pushed to specify, Peurifoy testified that ninety-one "people of moral weakness" had been forced to resign, mainly, he reluctantly admitted, for homosexuality.[64]

Peurifoy's admission prompted an investigation into the State Department[65] and an intense period of scouring for homosexuals throughout the federal government, ending careers and destroying lives. McCarthy's House Un-American Activities Committee hearings ostensibly ferreted out communist infiltrators who not only lost jobs but were blacklisted from their fields for real or imagined communist connections, including for homosexuality. The presence of homosexuals in government also helped to prove the general "depravity of the Roosevelt-Truman bureaucracy."[66]

Lafayette Park, one block from the White House, had emerged as a gay cruising spot.[67] Starting in 1947, the Park and other known cruising areas were ruthlessly policed under the auspices of the "Pervert Elimination Campaign."[68] According to Johnson, "hundreds of men were arrested and charged with disorderly conduct, loitering, [and] indecency .... [T]hose against whom the evidence was insufficient were simply fingerprinted and added to the 'pervert file.'"[69] All of this was justified as preservative of national security.[70]

As Johnson thoroughly demonstrated, these dual scares, Red and Lavender, did more than coincide temporally. Their entanglement was deeply ideological. "Security principles" governing State Department personnel excluded anyone "known for 'habitual drunkenness, sexual perversion, moral turpitude, financial irresponsibility or criminal record.'"[71] Excluding such persons was premised on the idea that "'a person who has such basic weakness of character' ... might be led into an association with a subversive individual or group."[72] Homosexuals were conclusively presumed deficient in character and "emotional stability," as well as vulnerable to blackmail by Soviet spies, presenting the constant threat of espionage.[73] Meanwhile, the relentless rhetorical "pairing of 'Communists and queers' led many [Americans] to see them as indistinguishable threats."[74]

McCarthy had maintained in his Wheeling speech that communism was atheistic and anti-family, citing "collective child-care as evidence of communism's antipathy toward the patriarchal family."[75] Homosexuals, his logic suggested, would gravitate toward such an ideology. Another congressman contended that China had a history of embracing homosexuality that went back "long before the time of Confucius," and that the Soviets also supported homosexuality.[76] Conservatives urged that homosexuality was a "Communist plot," designed "'to make us 'physically weak,'" – that it was "Stalin's Atom Bomb."[77] Senator Kenneth Wherry (R-NE) asserted,

> The Russians had acquired a list of homosexuals throughout the world that had been compiled by Hitler as an espionage tool. Using this list, Russians were prying secrets out of government employees. Even worse, Soviet agents were targeting heterosexual female civil servants, controlling them by "enticing them into a life of Lesbianism."[78]

Politicians were also anxious to avoid a return to prewar economic conditions.[79] A stable economy in which women were restored to domesticity while men earned a household income was ideologically bound with containment of the communist threat. D'Emilio explains,

> When placed in [its historical] context, the Cold War era's preoccupation with the homosexual menace appears less like a bizarre, irrational expression of McCarthyism and emerges, instead, as an integral component of postwar American society and

> politics. The anti-homosexual campaigns of the 1950s represented but one front in a widespread effort to reconstruct patterns of sexuality and gender relations shaken by depression and war.[80]

Further, the new geopolitical threat of mutual annihilation increased social-psychic strain. According to Edelman, "Pressures upon the nationalistic self-image of postwar America found articulation through the portrayal of homosexual activity as the proximate cause of perceived danger to the nation at a time of unprecedented concern about the possibility of national – and global – destruction."[81]

At the very apogee of this anxiety, Evelyn Hooker conducted the study that presaged the removal of homosexuality from the Diagnostic and Statistical Manual of Mental Disorders: *The Adjustment of the Male Overt Homosexual.*[82] She administered three different personality tests to men who identified as hetero- and homosexual, and asked psychologists to differentiate between them; they could not. The homosexual personality was distinguished by precisely nothing. It was merely a bogeyman well-suited to bearing the nation's fears.

The 1950s stand out as the pinnacle for the communist homosexual archetype in the US. Postwar anxiety manifested as fear of homosexuality, perceived as a communist contaminant that had to be driven out in the name of national security. Threats to traditional family; women's financial independence; and presumed homosexual moral weakness, contempt for family, and vulnerability to blackmail; combined with rapid expansion of the federal bureaucracy to position the homosexual threat in the heart of the national body politic. The rhetorical entwinement of homosexuality with communism generated compulsions to hunt and to expel – literally from government jobs and figuratively from the US system and into its communist enemy.

Simultaneously, however, gay and lesbian constituencies were beginning their uphill climb. As Anna Lvovsky has shown, a medical narrative began to make inroads where a moral narrative had predominated. While actual and suspected homosexuals were being subjected to blacklisting and arrest, and pathologization "underwr[ote] the draconian sexual psychopath laws," the medicalization of deviance … often genuinely softened the hand of the criminal system."[83]

Moreover, the 1950s also saw the early documented "homophile" organizations, including the Mattachine Society and the Daughters of Bilitis (the former famously launched by Harry Hay, a gay communist).[84] Despite extensive surveillance, Mattachine grew into a national organization, though eventually its leadership (new people, who had replaced the founders) succumbed to the pressures of the McCarthy era and dissolved it.[85] In the 1960s, however, Frank Kameny, an astronomer who had been fired from his government position for his homosexuality, launched an independent chapter in the District of Columbia to combat the federal government witch hunts.[86]

The gay rights movement in the US also achieved its first significant legal victories in the late 1950s and early 1960s, largely – as legal scholar Carlos Ball has chronicled – under the First Amendment. Gay litigants prevailed in some key cases after being targeted by obscenity law enforcement.[87] Legal progress under the due process right to privacy or the equal protection clause was not yet feasible, nor were advances in the key of "family."

Meanwhile, Batista was enjoying a decidedly nonsocialist hiatus from Cuban politics during the immediate postwar period and the initial years of the Cold War, mostly in Daytona Beach and at the New York Waldorf-Astoria.[88] His homeland was experiencing growing political unrest. Grau (whom Batista had previously installed as president, then ousted, and who subsequently became a rival) occupied the presidency. He and his 1948 successor, Carlos Prío, oversaw a period of unrestrained sectarian violence that did not sit well with US investors. Before long, Batista returned to Cuban politics, and in 1952, he entered the presidential race. His campaign was bankrolled by Lansky, who was eager to see his business partner back in the palace. The election was scheduled for June but in March, when it looked as though Batista might lose to an anti-corruption candidate, he decided that a *coup de'etat* would be easier – and it was. His military connections eased his path back to power. It was virtually bloodless,[89] though it made hash out of the very constitution that had been such an auspicious achievement of his first administration.

In his second presidency, Batista took deft advantage of postwar boom times to bring in foreign capital investment and some diversification to Cuba's export economy, including nickel mining.[90] Still, unemployment remained high and economic inequality was stark. Batista also resumed his previous habits of graft and violent suppression of political dissent. In pursuit of the latter, he became more and more brutal.

With Batista's help, the Havana Mob continued to run Cuba's capital city as a resort for booze, drugs, gambling, and sexual adventure.[91] While rural Cubans and migratory workers exerted themselves in service of US corporate interests, men and women of the capital staffed hospitality and entertainment venues, many of them catering to the sexual appetites of US, Canadian, and European tourists, as well as US military and corporate personnel. Cuba gained "an international reputation as a whorehouse for visiting Americans and … Batista's cronies."[92]

Tourism was a profit bonanza for a host of foreign corporate investors – not just the Mob. Pan American Airlines, which held a controlling interest in the luxury Hotel Nacional (famous for a 1946 meeting of mob bosses that was fictionally depicted in *The Godfather II*) sold cheap round-trip tickets from Miami to Havana. Other airlines and cruise ship companies began offering travel deals, as well.[93]

The entertainment scene was unbeatable. Cuban music and dance, including the mambo, which had spread in popularity across the globe, dazzled visitors. In addition to Cuban performers, big American names such as Tony Bennett, Nat King Cole, Ella Fitzgerald, Benny Goodman, Frank Sinatra, and Sarah Vaughn performed at what had become world-famous nightclubs, like the Tropicana or Sans Souci. Hobnobbing about, one might encounter Marlon Brando, Gary Cooper, Ava Gardner, Graham Greene, or Spencer Tracy.[94]

The racial mingling contributed to the sense of transgression. According to one cabaret pianist, tourists from the US routinely sought his direction to the whorehouse. "'The Americans from the south wanted only black girls,'" he reported, "chuckling wryly."[95] The exotic mulatta provided much of the enticement, wielding, as anthropologist Jafari Allen has shown, an "inheritance [of] sensual and erotic power," inseparable from the act – "unsanctioned and often violent" that explains her.[96] It was only white and fair-skinned women who actually performed in the high end night clubs at the time – only they were considered beauties – but there was an exception for top-flight Black women singers.[97]

Senator John F. Kennedy made several trips in the late 1950s, including at least one where he was reportedly treated to an afternoon with three sex workers "in a special suite at Trafficante's Hotel Comodoro," courtesy of the owner who thought he might one day need a favor.[98] "Commercial sex flourished largely unfettered in and around the glitzy casinos, bars, and resort hotels."[99]

Homosexual dalliances were widely available for purchase and took place amid the purposeful absence of police attention. Americans facing profound homophobic anxiety in the US were free to sample in Cuba, where male homosexuals may even have benefitted from "preferential hiring"[100] in tourist venues to accommodate demand. Cuban men who may or may not have had homosexual desires themselves nonetheless acted as purveyors of homosexual sex in the Havana underworld due to general economic pressures as well as the specific demand for masculine, lower-class "tops" by both tourists and Cuban elites.[101] One "male hustler," Pepe, "who used to hang around the [Tropicana] bar and pick up tourists," told author Rosa Lowinger, "the house knew what we were up to, and they encouraged us to be there ... The one guy you had to watch out for was Papo Batista, the president's son. If he took a shine to you, *te ponía en candela!*"[102] (roughly, *it would put you on the hot seat*).

Notwithstanding the demand for masculine "tops" (and the racial and class-based fantasies they offered) it was the "bottoms" who came to symbolize the indignities of foreign capitalist imperialism. Sexual exploitation by Americans landed as an assault on Cuban national honor.[103] The availability of Cuban men and women – often boys and girls really[104] – for sexual consumption, ubiquitous in the "brothels, casinos, and nightclubs ... [most of which were] controlled by ... organized crime, [were] a particularly visible symbol of the American presence on the island."[105] That insult would mold the homosexual figment for Cuba in the decades that followed.

It was, without question, a period of gross inequality, as Batista and the wealthiest Cubans enjoyed the rewards of partnering with foreign capitalists, while the majority suffered extreme exploitation. Dissident groups protested, set off bombs, and attempted assassination, but Batista protected his interests ferociously, deploying his police to arrest, torture, and murder his opposition.

Fidel Castro was not the only one making himself heard, but he and his followers did eventually emerge as the greatest threat to the revelry in Havana. Born in 1926, in the Eastern province of Oriente (like Batista), his Spanish-born father Angel had managed a United Fruit plantation and acquired his own land. Angel married and sired children both in and out of wedlock. Born to Angel's cook, Fidel and his brother Raúl were reared in the servant part of the household, but nonetheless lived in relative comfort, were eventually acknowledged as Angel's sons, and attended Jesuit boarding school. Historian Jaime Suchlicki attributes some of Fidel's political development to his private school mentors.[106]

In the late 1940s, Fidel distinguished himself as a student activist and charismatic personality while studying law at the University of Havana. He participated in a number of failed rebellions, including one against the Dominican dictator Rafael Trujillo and another against the president of Colombia.[107] After graduation, he practiced law briefly, representing low-income Cubans, but armed resistance suited him better. It was justified, he believed, by Batista's illegal take-over. Over time, Fidel raised "a small group of followers for his ill-fated attack on the Moncada military barracks in Oriente Province on July 26, 1953."[108] It was the night of a carnival, so he imagined that the soldiers would be caught unprepared; they were not. Many of Fidel's comrades were killed. Fidel, his brother Raúl, and several others were arrested.

Certain that he would be convicted, Fidel delivered a political address at his trial. He later scribbled down as much of his speech as he could remember and snuck it out of jail where it was distributed in the form of a pamphlet entitled *History Will Absolve Me*.[109] It was not a communist tract but it did call for revolution and outline a list of reforms. Though Fidel was sentenced to fifteen years, he served less than two. He had married (and would divorce) the daughter of an influential member of Batista's government, who secured release for the prisoners associated with the Moncada attack.

Once free, Fidel and his small band of followers constituted themselves as the *Twenty-Sixth of July Movement*, in remembrance of the Moncada calamity. The Castro brothers decamped to Mexico, where they met the Marxist Argentine doctor, Ernesto "Che" Guevara. The three plotted, planned, trained, networked, and recruited, spent a bit of time in a Mexican prison, and raised money (via a speaking tour of the US by Fidel) to arm themselves. Finally, with an apparent (if delusional) feeling of readiness, they set sail for Cuba in 1956 with some eighty men on a rickety yacht dubbed the *Granma*. The boat was too small, the provisions insufficient, and the seas unforgiving. After an interminable and painful voyage, the inexperienced sailors made their way to the shores of Oriente, arriving ill and having left a streak of vomit along their ocean route. Their allies inside Cuba had already begun the fighting, so that by the time of the Granma's belated landing, the uprising had been largely put down and most of the rebels were already jailed or dead. The Castro brothers, Che, and small group of others managed to flee into the Sierra Maestra, a mountainous territory in the east from which they would wage their guerilla war against the Batista regime.[110]

Gradually, rural peasants began to provide them with food and other forms of support; many joined their ranks. The rebels made adroit use of propaganda. They published a newspaper, *El Cubano Libre*. Che delivered radio addresses to rouse support. Fidel permitted New York Times reporter Herbert Matthews to interview him (to the embarrassment of the regime, which had claimed he was already dead). Matthews depicted the rebels as a noble if scrappy band of young idealists battling a Goliath, sometimes without food, in the harsh wilderness, and Fidel as a heroic figure: "It was easy to see that his men adored him and also to see why he has caught the imagination of the youth of Cuba all over the island. He was an educated, dedicated fanatic, a man of ideals, of courage, and of remarkable qualities of leadership."[111]

On one occasion the rebels kidnapped forty-eight Americans – mostly employees of an American-owned nickel mining plant – in an effort to halt an air force bombing campaign. "To the anger of many Cubans, the Batista government had given the Freeport Sulphur Company a virtually tax-free arrangement to operate the Moa Bay mine."[112] The hostages were freed unharmed, but the rebels had managed to gain attention for the impact of bombing on a civilian town.[113]

University and urban dissidents waged simultaneous battle: striking, making an unsuccessful (but nevertheless bloody) assassination attempt on Batista, and setting bombs off around Havana. The soldiers who had been conscripted by Batista to fight the rebels were underpaid and lacking in dedication. Inevitably, the US lost confidence in Batista and determined that it was time for him to give up power. Pressed to concede reality, Batista fled to the Dominican Republic with three hundred million dollars. It was New Year's Eve, 1958. The Twenty-Sixth of July forces took the capital on January 1, 1959.[114]

Members of the Havana Mob made for the exits with as much cash as they could carry, but they would lose millions.[115] When the rebels from the east arrived in Havana, they made their sentiments toward the Mafia's business enterprises perfectly evident: "At the Sevilla Biltmore [a crowd] rushed up the Moorish tiled steps and through the doors of the newly renovated casino, upending tables, tearing the felts, prying open the traganickels [slot machines] and pocketing the change."[116] At Lansky's Riviera, "a truckload of pigs [was] set … loose in the lobby of the hotel and casino, squealing, tracking mud across the floors, shitting and peeing all over … one of the most famous mobster gambling emporiums in all the world."[117]

Once in power, the new regime enacted a flurry of laws, from rent and utility reductions to agrarian reform.[118] Castro also announced straightaway that "cleaning up 'vice, corruption, and gambling' [would be] among the highest priorities of the new government."[119] This spelled bad news for Cuba's homosexuals, who were understood to be intimately tied to the depravity of urban life under the now deposed regime. To further this anti-vice objective, as well as to anticipate counterrevolutionary sabotage, in 1960 the Cuban government established the neighborhood-based *Comités para la Defensa de la Revolución* (Committees for the Defense of the Revolution, *CDRs*) to maintain local eyes on alert throughout the population. CDR duties included performing "many vital roles for the health and safety of the general populace; yet, in the case of homosexuality they largely functioned as informants."[120]

Despite some early signals of amity toward its neighbor to the north, the revolutionary government promptly began nationalizing foreign assets including sugar, mining, and other interests, inevitably sinking US–Cuban relations.[121] US President Dwight Eisenhower instituted a partial trade embargo in 1960 knowing that Cuba was profoundly dependent on US commodities as well as on the US market for sugar. Former Senator, repeat-tourist, and finally President John F. Kennedy would soon make the embargo total (after sending his aides around the District of Columbia to buy up all the Cuban cigars they could find).[122] Hoping to thwart establishment of a communist foothold off the shores of Miami, Kennedy launched the disastrous Bay of Pigs invasion in 1961.[123] Fidel declared Marxism-Leninism to be official Cuban state policy and the Soviet Union quickly became Cuba's most important ally and benefactor.[124]

With Soviet guidance, Cuba developed itself into a socialist state. It dramatically raised its literacy rate to the highest in Latin America thanks to a brigade of about 100,000 young and idealistic revolutionaries who fanned out to the least educated regions of the island to teach.[125] It developed an enviable health care system, again, leading Latin America in medical education and services. It also nationalized private (including foreign corporate) holdings, divvied up ownership of large land parcels, lowered rents and utility rates as well as the cost of medicine, imposed price controls, and otherwise took command of the economy.[126]

In 1966, Castro declared racism to be officially vanquished by the equality of all under socialism. As a formal matter, race discrimination was (and is) prohibited, but of course the lived reality has always been more complicated.[127] The Twenty-Sixth of July movement had not stressed racial injustice among its concerns.[128] The movement was dominated by white Cubans, though some Afro-Cubans and mulatos did participate. "[B]lacks were not prominent in the leadership of the revolutionary war," according to Gott. "A handful, perhaps a dozen, had participated in the Moncada attack in 1953, and rather more were recruited to the Rebel Army in the Sierra."[129]

After Fidel seized power, he was faced with the tense combination of continuing racial exclusions in the private sector, widespread denial of racism's existence, resistance to full integration by white and even some mulato Cubans who hoped to hold onto whatever privileges attached to their color, and the need for national unity. Pushed in his early months of power by a Cuban writer to address racism squarely, Fidel delivered a speech declaring an end to segregation and discrimination in jobs, education, and formerly "whites only" facilities.[130] His government walked a careful line, avoiding quotas and other controversial reforms while prioritizing economic need when filling government jobs, which often accrued to the benefit of Afro-Cubans.[131]

As the 1960s progressed, the dominant discourse in Cuba held that racism had been solved by socialism, rendering the subject of racism "taboo" except in the avowal of its absence. Castro proclaimed that racism "had disappeared along with class privileges."[132] His pronouncement of racism's end effectively quieted further public complaint.

The new regime weaponized national silence about continuing racism in the international arena. Assertions of the success of socialism in eradicating racial injustice served as a rhetorical cudgel during the Cold War, and in fact Fidel cultivated political alliances with African-Americans at least in part to stick it to the US on its continuing failures to address deep racial inequality. Fidel opened this rhetorical front with his decision in 1960 to stay at the Hotel Theresa in Harlem while on a visit to the United Nations, where he met with Black luminaries including Malcolm X. As Gott observed,

> Castro held court at the Theresa for more than a week, and on one memorable evening he was visited by the Soviet leader. The symbolic significance of their meeting place was well understood by both of them. Khrushchev wrote in his memoirs that 'by going to a Negro hotel in a Negro district, we would be making a double demonstration against the discriminatory policies of hte [sic] US toward Negroes, as well as toward Cuba.' The cheering black crowds in Harlem left no one in any doubt about their support for the revolution.[133]

Cuba provided sanctuary to members of the Black Panther Party (such as Eldridge Cleaver) and the Black Liberation Army who were in flight from US law enforcement.[134] For a time, African-American militants embraced Cuba's Revolution as an alternative to racist and capitalist injustice in the US. Cuba's resistance to race-based organizing, however, as well as its gradualism in addressing racism for the sake of national unity, was bound to disappoint these activists, and it did. Gott explained, "[t]he Cuban leadership wanted to express support for American blacks, but it certainly did not want them to proselytize in Cuba, nor to allow their ideas to percolate Cuba's large black population."[135] Cleaver and others eventually became critics of the Revolution.[136]

De la Fuente posits that widespread assent to the Martí credo at its most abstract has held both advantages and disadvantages for Afro-Cubans and mixed-race Cubans. While a specific silence[137] about race pervaded Cuban discourse,[138] leaving informal but nonetheless lived inequalities difficult to address, "[t]he rhetorical exaltation of racial inclusiveness as the very essence of nationhood has made racially defined exclusion … difficult, creating … opportunities for manipulation of dominant racial ideologies by those below while limiting the political options of the elites."[139]

Advances toward the equality of women in Cuba followed a much different track because sex was the only identity category that could legally form the basis of organizing.[140] During the early years of the Revolution, according to historian Michelle Chase, while Cubans still imagined that their standard of living would "Americanize,"[141] Castro encouraged women to purchase domestically produced goods to support the national economy.[142] As souring trade relations with the US imposed food shortages and rising discontent, however, the government called on women to exercise "consumer self-restraint for the greater good of the collective," to suffer nobly, and to rebuke American consumerism.[143] Just "having 'excess' food in one's house," as Chase tells it, "was virtually considered evidence of counterrevolutionary activity."[144]

An array of early women's organizations gradually merged into the Federación de Mujeres Cubanas (Federation of Cuban Women, *FMC*). The FMC was founded in 1960 by Vilma Espín, wife of Raúl Castro. Espín staunchly resisted identification with feminism, which she deemed American and bourgeois, stressing the effects of capitalism, rather than patriarchy, on women's position in society.[145] The FMC, therefore, sought to maximize women's contribution to the Revolution. It did so initially by focusing on women as consumers, even, Chase reports, suggesting that "food lines [were] potential sites of female solidarity and consciousness raising."[146]

Espín's FMC made eradication of prostitution a top priority. It was, according to political scientist Megan Daigle, "elevated past a mere social problem to a powerful symbol of Cuba's subordination to foreign powers."[147] Fidel had promised to redeem Cuba from its reputation as a regional whorehouse. He followed through by giving former sex workers "jobs as clerks, bus drivers, and waitresses. Their 'liberation' from sex work was touted as evidence that the Revolution had eradicated the corruption and immorality associated with capitalism."[148] Recalcitrant women were sent to reeducation centers to learn honorable skills such as sewing.[149]

The FMC worked, as well, on access to contraception and abortion. The former, when available, was free.[150] The latter, according to historian Rachel Hynson, was partially decriminalized in 1965, though it remained subject to a physician determination that the abortion was medically necessary; abortion was fully legalized with the enactment of a new penal code in 1979.[151]

To encourage women's regular employment, the government provided child care and paid maternity leave, facilitated access to household appliances, and even established a service whereby "[e]mployed women could leave a list of desired items at the [grocery] store in the morning and pick the goods up after work."[152] (This was in the 1970s. In the 1980s, facing a fiscal challenge, the government would "reduce social supports for working women," even "charging on an 'ability to pay basis' for daycare."[153] More on this economic moment in Chapter 2.)

Among Cuba's most significant achievements in the arena of sex equity was its Family Code of 1975. The Family Code (discussed in detail in Chapter 3) set forth rules for marriage, divorce, child custody, and child support, but most famously, it established the requirement of equal participation between husbands and wives in household duties, including childcare.[154] While generally unenforced, this powerful symbol marked a significant departure from previously held assumptions about the respective roles of men and women, shaped in part by the legacy of *machismo*, a culturally specific ideal of Latin American masculinity, further particularized in Cuba by the iconic "New Man" of the Cuban Revolution.[155]

Cuba's "New Man," extoled and epitomized by Che Guevara,[156] was courageous, inexhaustible by physical labor, and sexually passionate yet disciplined. He was guided by family duty, honor, and morality.[157] Rebels in the Sierra Maestra had been sentenced to death for rape and even consensual sexual relations with peasant women had been discouraged.[158] Women guerilla fighters (among whom Espín was one) recall an atmosphere of "[r]espect, decency" and "discipline."[159] Chase, in her meticulous account of the role of women and gender ideology in the Revolution, devotes a chapter to how masculinity discourse shaped expectations for participation in violent resistance.[160] The *barbudos* (*bearded ones*) exuded "brashly confident hypermasculinity manifested in the will to act."[161] Those who made a call to arms "publicly manipulated allegations of cowardice to foreclose the possibility of any legitimate alternative to political violence."[162] Suggestions of homosexuality were "a quick way to politically discredit an opponent."[163] Bravery and readiness to sacrifice were central, and some believed "could compensate for the flagrant disparity in arms" between the rebels and Batista's forces.[164] "The concept of martyrdom," Chase explained, "was implicitly gendered. It was almost always young men who died, leaving women to mourn."[165]

According to historian Abel Sierra Madero, the ideal of the New Man "embodied both a model of traditional masculinity and a political ideology …. [combining] discourses on the 'authentically revolutionary' and 'being a real man' [that] were key in the production of a new communist subjectivity."[166] Indeed, Fidel testified to the incompatibility of homosexuality with Revolution when he remarked in 1967,

> Nothing prevents a homosexual from professing revolutionary ideology and, consequently, exhibiting a correct political position. In this case, he should not be considered politically negative. And yet we would never come to believe that a homosexual could embody the conditions and requirements of conduct that would enable us to consider him a true revolutionary, a true Communist militant. A deviation of that nature clashes with the concept we have of what a militant Communist should be.[167]

The image of the New Man animated revolutionary ardor throughout Latin America, coming "to represent anti-imperialism [and] third world revolution."[168] Its powerful iconography – exemplified by the famous image of a bearded Che in his beret gazing gravely into the future[169] – would continue to shape revolutionary politics well beyond the takeover of 1959.

Cultural critics note in the New Man the subtextual presence of the homosexual. Cultural studies professor Susana Peña, for example, posited that the "New Man and the homosexual became mutually constitutive categories, with the New Man representing the positive goal of revolutionary efforts and the homosexual embodying the vestiges of capitalist domination."[170] The homosexual was doomed to inhabit this position – the New Man's diacritical other – as the New Man strived to free himself of the imperialist humiliations he suffered during the Batista era.

Undoubtedly, the association of effeminacy with weakness before imperial power had begun much earlier: "Cuban national identity … [had] posited the virility of Cuban men as a measure of their ability to resist Spanish and U.S. colonization" in the late nineteenth and early twentieth centuries.[171] Later, postcolonial anti-Americanism held that "*garzonas* (mannish women) … embod[ied] U.S. colonization and … foreign contamination,"[172] as well. The association was also racially inflected: Black men, expected on one hand to be hyper-masculine, also bore a contemptuous residual association with homosexuality due to the particulars of Cuban slavery, during which many more men than women were imported and were housed in single-sex barracks.[173] Literary theorist Emilio Bejel, surveying this history, urges that the antecedents of Cuban revolutionary homophobia appear all over the place – in "[r]adical nationalism … international socialism … religion, the Eurocentric Enlightenment … and positivism."[174] In Cuba, as elsewhere, ideas about sexuality and gender have a long and multi-determined history.

Still, at the time of the Revolution, the painfully recent imperialist past reinvigorated the male homosexual figment as a specific threat to Cuban national honor. Batista had facilitated the Havana Mob's creation of a culture of extravagance and decadence, set against a backdrop of manifest suffering among the Cuban people. Bars associated with homosexual activity formed part of the same landscape as the "strip clubs, whorehouses, kinky cabarets, and live sex acts" which, if not always directly run by organized crime, certainly worked to the advantage of its business interests. Cubans who lived through the merry profiteering by mobsters and corrupt politicians of the 1950s, observed anthropologist Noelle Stout, "associated homosexuality with foreign imperialism because a large number of visitors and servicemen from the United States seeking homoerotic experiences had created a thriving gay sex trade in Havana."[175] By the time the Revolution was upon them, many Cubans had been left with the impression that "homosexuals [were] part of an urban riffraff resulting from the vices of capitalist inequality."[176] Prostitution, urban decay, capitalist exploitation, and US imperialism discursively melded into the figure of the male homosexual.[177] "Purging Cuba of [its] homosexuals," therefore, "was seen as integral to ridding the country of vice."[178]

The Cuban vocabulary of sexual identity has, in the last few decades, undergone significant evolution (see Chapter 4) but historically it reflected an idealized typology of men who engage in homosexual practices that was not uncommon in Latin America: *bugarrónes* were masculine and exclusively insertive, carrying an uncompromised heterosexual identity;[179] they were sometimes also referred to as *entendidos* (*understood*) and associated with respectable, middle-class standing. *Maricónes* (*fags*) – sometimes *locas or pájaras* (roughly *queens*) or less derisively *invertidos* (*inverts*) – were effeminate, anally receptive, and regarded as homosexuals.[180] The complementary terms *activos* and *pasivos* have also been used to describe the two archetypes.[181]

This schema is redolent of the "inversion" model of homosexuality, elaborated around the turn of the twentieth century by European sexologists such as Richard von Krafft-Ebing.[182] It predominated in various configurations in Europe and the US until roughly the time of World War II. According to George Chauncey's influential history of male homosexuality in New York City, in the decades before the war, for example, gender presentation played a much more significant role in identity categorization than it does in the contemporary US.[183] "Fairies," "faggots," "queens," and "punks," socialized in working class environments with masculine men who retained their manhood status.[184]

For Cubans, only the effeminate maricónes bore an association with the profligacy and humiliation of the Batista period.[185] The maricón was conceived as "an artifact of capitalist bourgeois decadence .... a coward and untrustworthy."[186] He had to be suppressed in the service of national pride.

In the early years of the Cuban Revolution, the young regime took steps to restore Cuba's stolen dignity. While Fidel retained the real grasp on power as Military Commander-in-Chief, the first nominal president of Revolutionary Cuba was a "puritan" named Manuel Urritia, whose top concern was "to close down casinos and brothels," which he did during his first month in office.[187] (The Tropicana, the only one among the major Havana clubs to be wholly Cuban-owned, was left intact and, though COVID-19 closed it temporarily, the Cuban government otherwise kept it in operation over the years as a spectacular tourist attraction.[188]) Brothels were legally banned in 1961.[189] "*Redades* or *recogidas* (police raids or mass arrests) were part and parcel" of the maricón experience, as was entrapment and police harassment.[190] "Operación Tres Ps" (*Operation Three Ps*), a mass arrest of "pederasts, prostitutes, and pimps," in October, 1961, stands out famously as one of the most acute incidents.[191] Homosexuals were not the only targets, but the "initial period of the revolution was characterized by a 'purging of vices'"[192] that very much included them. Accounts of abuse suffered by homosexuals in prison are harrowing.[193]

As policing increased, "[s]ocial space – the *ambiente* available to [male homosexuals] – also began to diminish .... [B]ars ... began to close because of state intervention, emigration of their owners, or unprofitability due to declining patronage. Cruising and sex became more difficult ... on account of increased police surveillance."[194] Under Batista, homosexual hangouts, while uniformly seedy, could be found by both tourists and migrants from the rural areas. Under Fidel, though, there would be no "Castro."[195]

Like US homosexuals during the Lavender Scare, maricónes were deemed morally and physically weak, and therefore vulnerable to "recruitment by the enemy." In Cuba, this translated into the need for rehabilitation through agricultural labor.[196] Revolutionary mythology idealized the archetypical *campesino*, or rural Cuban, as noble, pure,[197] and manly, as contrasted with the men from the city, where homosexuality was imagined to spread like a "contagion ... in the darkness of the cabarets."[198] Indeed, Fidel "stressed the redeeming quality of the countryside and of agricultural work ... believ[ing] that *maricones* could not emanate from the harsh conditions that had spawned Cuba's virile *campesinos*."[199]

Ironically, if one is to believe the late gay Cuban ex-pat Reinaldo Arenas, whose celebrated memoir *Before Night Falls* was made into a movie starring Javier Bardem (see Preface), rural boys and men in Cuba were highly likely to have homosexual sex[200] – many more than bore the slur *maricón*. During the Batista period, a rural maricón might well have headed for the city in search of social acceptance as well as work in the bars or brothels,[201] but those whose masculine demeanor allowed them to evade the slur remained free to engage in homosexual activity in the countryside without risk to their sexual identities. Rural boys and men were likely to have sex with farm animals, as well, as Arenas tells it,[202] apparently because the open, bucolic social space males inhabited in rural Cuba enabled a broad range of hedonic experimentation that went blissfully[203] unjudged and unlabeled.

Socialist morality demanded hard work and austerity, and male homosexuals were thought to be "concerned only with their own pleasure and unwilling to make sacrifices."[204] In keeping with socialist discipline, Cuba established in 1965 the internationally reviled work camps known as *Unidades Militares para Ayudar Producción* (Military Units to Aid Production, *UMAPs*), to reverse the consequences of capitalist corruption and instill the value of physical labor.[205] "'Work will make you men' [was] reportedly inscribed on the gate."[206]

As feminist researcher Carrie Hamilton reports, "Although the UMAP camps were reserved for men, there were also reports of women in same-sex relationships being purged from universities, mistreated in prisons, and expelled from boarding schools."[207] During this period, Cuba also removed effeminate boys from school so they would not "infect others" and established the "Yellow Brigades," where such boys would receive instruction in "sports, self-defense, and military exercises" in hopes of masculinizing them; baseball was believed to have special powers of "virilization."[208] A state newspaper defended prevailing beliefs, "No homosexual represents the Revolution, which is a matter of men, of fists and not feathers, of courage and not trembling, of certainty and not intrigue, of creative valor and not of sweet surprises."[209] Flamboyant dress attracted police attention. Long hair on men was deemed effeminate, decadent, and individualist and was sometimes treated with forced haircuts.[210]

A "Letter from Cuban Gay people to the North American Gay Liberation Movement," asserted,

> On the street we suffer persecution, aggression, and a constant abuse of authority. We are asked to produce I.D. cards. We are arrested for wearing certain clothes or using certain hairstyles, or for simple get-togethers .... Methods of psychological repression, social isolation, control by districts, neighborhoods, work places and schools, always with the aim of negating us, are commonly used by this regime.[211]

The authors are unnamed, noting at the end of their letter that "to protect ourselves, we have given a false return address."[212]

Cuba's anti-homosexual legal offensive culminated in 1971. At a roundtable organized that year by the Ministry of Public Health, one expert declared "It was the capitalist regime that fostered the corruption where the homosexual developed."[213] In addition, Cuba held its First National Congress on Education and Culture. That Congress resolved that homosexuality was "an antisocial pathology, against socialist morality."[214] Accordingly, in what became known (and reviled) as "Resolución Número 3," it "resolved that 'notorious homosexuals' should be denied employment in any institution that had an influence upon youth .... that homosexuals should not be allowed to represent Cuba in cultural activities abroad .... [and] that severe penalties should be applied to those responsible for corrupting minors, to 'depraved repeat offenders,' and to 'irremediable antisocial elements."[215] Legislation effectively ratifying the Congress's resolutions was enacted in 1974, banning homosexuals from positions of influence.[216] Purges across a range of educational, arts, and employment sectors, as well as from the military and the Communist Party, followed.

In addition to the explicitly anti-homosexual resolutions coming out of the 1971 National Congress, Fidel also announced a heightened level of attention to cultural production. "In order to win a prize in a national ... competition, one must be a true revolutionary, a true writer, a real poet .... [T]here is value in cultural and artistic creations inasmuch as they are useful for the people."[217] That year began the period commonly referred to as "el quinquenio gris" (*the five gray years*) during which the regime severely policed literary and artistic work. A number of highly regarded homosexual literary figures found themselves located at the unfortunate intersection of two carefully surveilled sectors of the population.

Meanwhile, in the US, bars had become crucial spaces for gays to congregate.[218] After decades of entrapment and raids of spaces that might otherwise have served as safe havens,[219] the Stonewall rebellion broke out in Greenwich Village in June of 1969, launching a new and ebullient phase of gay emancipation, all the more dynamic for its being situated in the larger liberatory context of second wave feminism and the sexual revolution. Things were changing – at least in the major cities – and for those most inclined to activism there was little interest in retreat.

This put many leftist gays and lesbians in the US who were sympathetic to the Cuban Revolution in a political bind. The 1960s and 1970s are widely understood to be the time of divergence between the Old and New Left, the former devoted to orthodox Marxism, the latter retaining its class commitments while expanding its attention to Black civil rights, feminism, and gay rights. Writer Allen Young's *Gays Under the Cuban Revolution*, recounts his own travels to Cuba, in 1969 and 1971, as a young, gay leftist coming into his sexual identity and politics.[220] Young was a founder of the *Venceremos Brigade*, a joint undertaking of the Cuban government and Students for a Democratic Society. The Brigade brought young US leftists to Cuba to work – typically in the cane fields – to learn from and support the Cuban Revolution, and to connect with young Cubans. Young also participated in a gay delegation of the Brigade which hoped to talk with Cuban participants about gay liberation, but the Cuban organizers forbade them from meeting.[221] Young spoke out after the 1971 anti-homosexual pronouncements contained in Resolución

Número 3, inserting himself into a painful political divide between those US leftists who were willing to overlook Cuba's persecution of homosexuals and those who were not.[222]

Also in the latter camp was famed gay Beat poet Allen Ginsberg, whom Young interviewed about a 1965 visit to Cuba to meet with Cuban poets and writers – a trip that ended abruptly after Ginsberg offered public criticism of the homophobic abuse of some of the literary figures with whom he met.[223] He also poked the regime for fun. He told Young, "Well the worst thing I said was that I'd heard, by rumor that Raúl Castro was gay. And the second worst thing I said was that Che Guevara was cute…"[224] (Ginsberg's remarks probably should not have come as a complete surprise to the Cuban authorities. In a 1961 poem Ginsberg had written "Che Guevara has a big cock/ Castro's balls are pink."[225]) For Ginsberg, communism was neither a reason to valorize nor to condemn Cuba; his concerns exceeded the bounds of political ideology. As historian Rafael Rojas recounts, it was "rigid laws and moral codes, and restricting individual freedoms by penalizing beliefs, habits, and life practices, such as homosexuality or drugs"[226] that troubled Ginsberg. "'No revolution can succeed,'" he maintained, "'if it continues the puritanical censorship of consciousness.'"[227] Ginsberg was among the international luminaries whose vocal criticism of the UMAPs hastened their end.[228]

The same year as Young's interview with Ginsberg, 1972, the Venceremos Brigade issued an official policy statement declaring gay participation in the Brigade to "have generally been destructive," citing "outright attacks" on the Revolution, "imposing North American gay culture on the Cubans (for example, parading in drag [and] acting in an overtly sexual manner)." The statement made clear that gays were not henceforth barred from the Brigade, but that they were expected to cease collaboration with the larger US "cultural imperialist offensive against the Cuban Revolution [meant to] discredit the Revolution and alienate North Americans from it."[229]

Country music singer Patrick Haggerty, also a gay caucus member of the Venceremos Brigade in the 1960s, saw things differently from Young. In 2016, he told *Out* magazine,

> I want to emphasize that American lesbians and gays were being incarcerated also. So this wasn't something unique to Cuba. Everybody likes to talk about how Fidel threw all the gays in jails and mental hospitals. Well, I wound up in a mental hospital right here in Washington [State] over the gay thing myself, so shut the fuck up. Shut up and look in your own backyard.[230]

This bitter divide would not be resolved.

***

From the outset of the Revolution through the first half of the 1970s, homosexuality – defined by male effeminacy and penetrability – represented a grave threat in the Cuban revolutionary imagination.[231] Decades of economic exploitation by the

US culminating in the corruption and indignities of the Batista era, when Havana served as "a playground for American gangsters and tourists," compounded the nation's homophobia.[232] Prostitution in particular stood for the humiliations of economic imperialism, and – discursively speaking – homosexuality entwined tightly with it. If, as Daigle maintains, the battle against prostitution waged in part by the FMC served as "an 'allegory' for the fight against capitalist exploitation,"[233] imagine how much more critical to make men out of the maricónes who submitted themselves to sexual subjugation by US capitalists.

"[P]recisely because of this institutionalized rejection of the homosexual in relation to the dominant national discourse," Bejel argues, "the category of homosexuality became … a constitutive part of the very concept of the Cuban nation."[234] Revolutionary discourse depended on homosexuality as the new socialist man's diacritical other, a line establishing the contours of Cubanness – what was inside the nation and what was outside. Scholar of Romance Languages and Literature Brad Epps observed, "homosexuality comes into focus only to signify something forever beneath, beside, or beyond"[235] Cuba's nationalist masculine ideal. Because homosexuality was imagined as irredeemably incompatible with the Revolution – an intolerable, decadent, bourgeois contaminant to be extirpated by law and labor – it stood for what was extrinsic to the Revolution, enabling the Revolution's symbolic consolidation.

Only the body of the maricón, however, and not that of the bugarrón, was so thoroughly draped in disdain. Epps surmised that what made the maricón's existence so unforgivable was his "surrender" to another man – an imperialist man – rather than to the (asexual) revolutionary brotherhood.[236] Male submission threatened the "imagined community"[237] of the Cuban nation. In this sense, the Cuban Revolution provides exemplary support to the thesis that "nationalism favors a distinctly homosocial form of bonding,"[238] in which the idea of homosociality – as elaborated by Eve Kosofsky Sedgwick – exists to "distinguish [itself] from 'homosexual[ity].'"[239] While lesbian defiance of sexuality and gender norms can expect to receive some measure of cultural excoriation, it is the male homosexual whose exclusion proved vital to Cuba's nationalist fraternity.

Women could be and sometimes were participants in this fraternity. Homosociality in its Cuban particulars favored courage and weaponry coded as masculine, but not to the total exclusion of women such as Vilma Espín, who – in spite of familial wealth associated with the Bacardi fortune – developed into a young radical and joined the guerilla war waged from the Sierra Maestra, where she fell in love with Raúl Castro.[240] Her story and others attest to the free-floating nature of fraternal solidarity. To this day, the Facebook page for the FMC is stamped with the old logo of a woman smiling, wearing army fatigues and a beret, and carrying a rifle.[241] In a variation, she carries a baby in one arm, her rifle slung over the opposite shoulder.[242]

But the inclusion of women merely illustrates the dispensability of maleness per se – as opposed to its threatened archetypical aspects. In his classic article *Raping*

Like a State, legal scholar Teemu Ruskola argued that "the injury of colonialism," can be understood "as a kind of homoerotic violation."[243] In this view, "colonized states exist effectively in a state of aggrieved masculinity …. [within which] [t]he unbearable humiliation of imperialism ultimately arouses a desire in the colonized to … become manly."[244] Following Ruskola, it would be unsurprising for ostracization of Cuba's maricón to take on new urgency in the decade or so after 1959.

Homosexuality in early Revolutionary Cuba was a domestic toxin and a rhetorical weapon, an anti–self-image that girded the national self-image. It was not a sex act or a family structure; it was not a lifestyle or a hangout. It was a *discursive figment* – conjured to assist in the production of its opposite: a nationalist fantasy of impenetrability.

2

A Tentative Embrace

1970s–1990s

The homosexual of this chapter imperfectly emerges from Cold War angst and the nationalist discourses that expressed it. Over the next several decades in the US, the homosexual grows into a rights-bearing gay subject, his emancipation evidence of progress toward the "more perfect union" promised by liberalism. The march of lgbtq civil rights comprises an astonishing compilation of formal legal achievements notwithstanding a vicious campaign of homophobic backlash. In the story told here, the combination of the AIDS crisis and a national discourse that saddled the poor with blame for sexual licentiousness and a deficit of family values pushed mainstream gay rights advocates to steer away from the New Left politics of the 1970s and build a movement consumed with partnership recognition and dominated by a discourse of privatized responsibility. This shift sharply divided the lgbtq community between those who were well-positioned to benefit from legal gains and those who were not.

How might the trajectory differ in Revolutionary Cuba? *Contra* the US, Cuba has no history of vindicating liberal rights via impact litigation brought before an independent judiciary. Government authorities have historically downplayed identitarian differences within the population (as evidenced by the "racial silence" discussed in Chapter 1). Grassroots organizing tends to be suppressed or absorbed into the state apparatus. Until recently, Cuba lacked a vigorous commercial sector that might advance lgbtq interests on a voluntary basis motivated by profit. Cuba has, however, long utilized command measures (e.g., rations, government salaries, limits on private enterprise, and prohibitions against real property accumulation) to redistribute resources across its population. How might legal advances under such systemic circumstances differ from that which took place in the US?

Cuba followed a quite different trajectory that responded to a wholly distinct set of conditions. The Cuban homosexual saw his earliest advances come not in the form of rights acquisition, but as an object of state care. A campaign across the island of progressive sex education reintroduced homosexuality to the Cuban nation as a mere "variant" rather than as a reason for nationalist scorn. Notwithstanding intermittent setbacks, Cuba's ideological turn yielded a gradual – if imperfect – transformation in the legal treatment of homosexuals. The downfall of the Soviet Union, however, presented a new set of economic conditions that brought transactional sex back into the foreground of urban life. Racial and economic stratification, as well as the emergence of a complex lexicon of sexual identity followed. This chapter traces developments in both countries beginning in the early 1970s, highlighting the political–economic circumstances that helped to shape sexual identity.

US: PROGRESS FROM THE 1970S

The US in the 1970s saw the flourishing of second wave feminism, the sexual revolution, expanding access to contraception and abortion, no-fault divorce, and the ecstasy of post-Stonewall gay liberation. These historical phenomena combined to alter dramatically the sexual landscape in exciting ways.

Not everyone, however, was equally exuberant about it. Social conservatives rallied and a powerful backlash ensued. The Save Our Children campaign, led by singer and Miss America contestant Anita Bryant, advocated repeal of a Dade County, Florida ordinance prohibiting discrimination on the basis of sexual orientation.[1] In a campaign that was technically local, but captured national attention, Bryant succeeded in 1977 in getting the law repealed in a popular referendum by arguing that "gays were 'trying to recruit our children.'"[2] Things turned out better for gays and lesbians in California the following year with the defeat of the Briggs Initiative (a.k.a. "Proposition 6") which would have banned gay and lesbian teachers and "promotion" of homosexuality in schools.[3] Still, it put Harvey Milk and his fellow activists in the position of having to push back against an image of gays as dangerous to children as laws across the country "bann[ed] lesbians and gay men from adopting … or becoming foster parents."[4]

Even as these painful battles unfolded, however, and the religious right rose to become a terrifying political force,[5] constitutional advances for gays and lesbians began to accrue. As legal scholar Carlos Ball observes, "the 1970s saw an explosion in the number and variety of LGBT organizations, spanning the gamut from political to cultural to educational to social to artistic to professional to religious."[6] Constitutional victories for these nascent organizations arrived along tracks laid by Black civil rights organizations in the preceding two decades vindicating a right to associate under the First Amendment.[7] Especially significant was *NAACP v. Patterson*, in which a unanimous US Supreme Court found that when Alabama demanded access to the NAACP's membership roster in an obvious attempt at intimidation, it violated the associational rights of the organization and its members.[8] Relying on constitutional developments such as this one, lgbtq advocates won the right to incorporate their organizations,[9] the right to form campus groups at public colleges,[10] and the right to participate in public fora.[11] These early successes enabled the organizing that was necessary to achieve future victories.

Also significant to lgbtq advancement during this decade were free expression decisions arising out of individual government employees' "coming out of the closet."[12] These cases yielded a mix of victories and defeats, but they eked out a conceptualization of freedom of expression that is, as Ball observes, grounded not only in the democratic ideal of a "marketplace of ideas" but also "in considerations of self-development and self-realization."[13] The "coming out" narrative, not entirely new but catching on in gay politics and parlance, dovetailed with the broader "self-realization" trend of the decade, as well as with the widespread quest for individual fulfillment evidenced by the sexual revolution and no-fault divorce. While the First Amendment has been wielded recently by anti-lgbtq culture warriors asserting religious and expressive exemptions from anti-discrimination protections, Ball makes evident that it once served as a crucial tool for lgbtq advancement.

In 1972, the US Supreme Court dismissed a same-sex marriage litigation "for want of a substantial federal question."[14] It was still entirely constitutional for states to criminalize sodomy and mostly permissible to overtly discriminate in employment, housing, public accommodations, child custody awards, and so on. Still, the advances of the decade laid important groundwork for what would come next.

CUBA: EARLY PROGRESS

The laws regarding homosexuality also slowly began to improve in Cuba beginning in the 1970s, but liberal rights such as expression or association played no role. Neither did impact litigation, grassroots organizing, or the individualistic "coming out" narrative. Still, gradually, the Cuban conception of homosexuality evolved from a criminal and disciplinary concern to a "medical and psychological" one.[15] As international development expert Emily J. Kirk has chronicled, public health and sex education were the keys to this perceptual transition and to conditioning Revolutionary Cuba for legal reform.[16]

Perhaps the most significant step in Cuba was the 1972 establishment by the FMC of the Grupo Nacional de Trabajo de Educación Sexual (*National Group for Work on Sexual Education, GNTES*). The FMC founder, Vilma Espín, and a physician, Dr. Celestino Álvarez Lajonchere, founded and led the group with the purpose of developing and proliferating scientifically informed sex education to the national population. They were soon joined by sexologist Monika Krause who brought expertise from her native East Germany, which had already established a progressive sex ed curriculum. The result of their collaboration was the Programa Nacional de Educación Sexual (*National Sex Education Program, ProNes*). ProNes included curricula that were targeted to every age level and to medical students.[17] A rigorous sex education was not, according to professor of education Marvin Leiner, conceived by the FMC merely "as the dissemination of technical information, but rather as part of the development of revolutionary consciousness."[18] When the First Congress of the Communist Party endorsed the FMC's program in 1975, it did so with the notion that sex ed was "an essential step in the development of the new socialist person."[19]

In 1977, convinced of the importance of sex education to the health and ideological development of the Cuban nation, the government recognized GNTES as a distinct governmental organization, separate from the FMC. The newly independent entity continued to develop its curricula and publish educational materials and began hosting conferences and discussion panels aimed at every sector of the population including "doctors, teachers, psychologists, health officials … [and] youth") on every aspect of sexuality, including the "psychological," "social," and "biological." Key themes included "respect, equality, and health" and topics included "safe and respectful sexual relations, contraception, [and] teenage pregnancies."[20]

East German experts authored many of the key texts, notably Siegfried Schnabl's best-selling[21] *Man and Woman in Intimacy* (first published in 1978, published in Spanish in 1979) which was "the first [in Cuba] to discuss homosexuality in a respectful and empathetic way."[22] Schnable's book found open minds in Cuba, perhaps because its author hailed from a socialist country.[23] According to Leiner, it "became … the hottest book in Cuba. People were passing rare copies back and forth among friends."[24] Chapter 6 addressed male and female homosexuality, characterizing each as simply "a variant" that should not be "classified as an illness."[25] The work of Schnabl and others emphasized the health aspects of sexuality, called for respect, and depicted "sexuality as an important component of the national expression of socialist ideology."[26] Marx and Engels, Schnabl stressed, viewed sexuality within the socialist context as important to human happiness. This compared favorably, he argued, with "repressive capitalist societies, which viewed homosexuality as a perversion."[27] Texts such as Schnabl's pushed Cuba toward what Kirk dubbed the "normalization" of homosexuality.[28]

The educational interventions of GNTES appear to have influenced Cuban legal authorities. Just a few years after the 1971 First National Congress on Education and Culture produced the reviled Resolución Número 3, its most oppressive provisions began to unravel. A decision of the People's Supreme Court reinstated artists who were fired for being gay.[29] Other "de facto" bans on homosexuals in the army and the Communist Party petered out slowly,[30] as purges also came to an end.

In the final year of the decade, the Cuban Penal Code took a tepid step forward. A 1979 revision decriminalized *private* homosexual acts (reversing a prohibition dating back to Spanish rule) but left the prohibition against *public* displays of homosexuality ("public ostentation" of a "homosexual condition") intact.[31] Criminalization of corrupting minors, including disparate ages of consent for homo- and heterosexual acts, were also left in place.[32]

Taking over the yeoman's work of anti-homosexual criminalization, however, was the prohibition against *peligrosidad* (*dangerousness*): "A dangerous state is considered the special proclivity in which a person is found to commit crimes, demonstrated by their conduct which is seen to be in manifest contradiction with the norms of socialist morality."[33] This provision allocates broad official discretion to arrest, jail, and/or reeducate persons violating expectations of public demeanor and resulted in arrest for same-sex affection, male effeminacy, and "transgender performance."[34] Afro-Cubans have historically been over-targeted by police under this provision.[35]

The Cuban state is not a monolith, as evidenced by the disharmony that can be observed between the improving domain of health compared to the relative intransigence in policing. Street-level inequities based on race and gender presentation occurred even as racism was officially vanquished and GNTES was creating a "multidisciplinary team" to specialize in the care of transgender Cubans and beginning to provide hormone therapy.[36]

BACKWARDS AND FORWARDS IN THE 1980S

The next decade was off to a rough start in Cuba with the Mariel boatlift – an exodus of about 125,000 Cubans from the port of Mariel whom Fidel grudgingly permitted to leave over the course of about six months in mid-1980. It all started when a small group of asylum-seekers drove headlong onto the grounds of the Peruvian embassy in Havana. When Peru granted them sanctuary, thousands of Cubans took that as their cue to follow suit. As ethnic studies professor Susana Peña discussed in her account of the Mariel migration and its aftermath in Miami, Fidel "disparaged hopeful migrants [as] undesirables, anti-social elements, lumpen proletariat … *escoria*," [scum], as well as prostitutes and homosexuals.[37] Cubans who remained on the island staged demonstrations in which they labeled the emigres "traitors."[38] Faced with few options, Fidel leaned into the departures. These undesirables, Fidel's government made clear, had succumbed to "the lure of consumerism" and were not wanted in Cuba anyway.[39]

Fidel thus flung the doors open, apparently not anticipating just how many would take him up on his offer to leave.[40] President Jimmy Carter proclaimed that the US would welcome with "open arms [these] refugees seeking freedom from communist domination."[41] Compared with the Cuban expats who fled at the time of Fidel's takeover – a time of summary executions and asset seizures – more of the Mariel-era migrants were non-white; many were also poor and some were in fact convicts.[42] Their acceptance into the Cuban expat community in Florida was less than full. Moreover, having experienced two decades of free health care and other benefits of socialism, their expectations clashed with those of the Miami Cubans who received them.[43]

While data are impossible to obtain,[44] chroniclers of Mariel claim that a significant number of the migrants were homosexual.[45] Indeed, some migrants have reported that police "rounded-up" homosexuals – especially the more flamboyant – and other "undesirables" and "forced them to leave the country"[46] or at least "facilitated their exit."[47] Peña argues that those whom the Cuban authorities ushered to the port were not deemed unwanted based on the sex acts they performed, but because they "transgress[ed] gender norms in ways associated with male homosexuality."[48] In advancing their departures, she contends, "the Cuban state would try to export the defiant cultures of gay visibility that continued to trouble its virile self-image."[49] Apparently cognizant of this state objective, some heterosexuals feigned homosexual affect to ease their way past security at the port.[50]

Lourdes Argulles and B. Ruby Rich attribute the Mariel emigration in part to visits from Cuban expats in the late 1970s "who brought gifts as well as tales of comfortable living in the United States."[51] They assert further that the CIA bribed "the homosexual intelligentsia [with] generous academic grants and publishing contracts" and also "blackmailed" homosexuals in the form of threatened exposure.[52] Pointing out that, during Mariel, the US permitted "immigration far in excess of its own quotas"[53] and "suspended laws prohibiting admission of homosexual aliens," they suggest that "the U.S. government," deep in the Cold War and having made few advances in the treatment of its own lgbtq people, "prioritized anticommunism over homophobia."[54] Indeed, the Immigration and Naturalization Service (INS) did cease automatically classifying homosexuals as medically ineligible to enter the US at about the same time as the Mariel boatlift.[55]

In large part, the attention of the US lgbtq community was focused on other matters around this time. Until AIDS made itself the community's principal preoccupation, many lesbians and feminists were in the midst of a clash over the politics of pornography, sex work, butch-femme aesthetics, sadomasochism, and strap-ons during the "Sex Wars."[56] The Sex Wars began toward the end of the 1970s and were carried out in the forms of activist groups, protests and speeches across the US (as well as in Canada and the UK), essays and pamphlets, and proposed anti-pornography ordinances. They peaked in 1982 with the controversial "Barnard Conference." This gathering resulted in the classic 1984 essay collection *Pleasure and Danger*,[57] which embraced sexual pleasure while simultaneously acknowledging the dangers associated with sex. Protesting from outside were radical feminists who believed sex to be permeated by male domination and female subordination, as well as cultural feminists who valorized non-hierarchical lesbian sexuality consistent with an ethic of care.[58] Lesbians who embraced this brand of feminism did not identify with the profligacy of gay male existence, dismissing it as reflective of masculine values.[59] (Lesbian solidarity with gay men through the staggering losses from AIDS in the 1980s, though, followed by the political shift toward same-sex marriage in the coming decades, would make room for an invigorated gay/lesbian affinity.[60])

While the Sex Wars were roiling among feminists, a broader set of national forces were at work. The election of Ronald Reagan to the presidency in 1980 represented the ascendance of neoliberal, racist "family values" used to bludgeon low-income, single mothers with moralistic condemnations of sexual licentiousness and welfare dependency. The first divorced US president capitalized on family values rhetoric to justify diminution of the social safety net and privatization of responsibility for poverty, relieving the public fisc and advancing an agenda of tax cuts.

Just as neoliberalism was capturing the political mainstream, Michael Hardwick and his male sexual partner were arrested in Atlanta in 1982 for engaging in oral sex in Hardwick's bedroom, providing an opportunity to the ACLU to mount a challenge to the state's sodomy prohibition. There was reason for optimism that the law would be struck down as a violation of the right to privacy. That right, which is not explicitly enumerated in the US Constitution, had nonetheless been expanding for fifteen years as a component of due process under the Fourteenth Amendment and seemed a solid constitutional vehicle for the ACLU's purposes.

In the years between gay rights advances under the First Amendment (outlined by Ball) and Hardwick's arrest, the right to privacy had become a powerful, if controversial, constitutional tool. It has antecedents in the early twentieth century in the protection of parental rights, but it was formally "found" by Justice William O. Douglas in the 1965 decision of the US Supreme Court in *Griswold v. Connecticut*.[61] Famously – or perhaps infamously – Justice Douglas distilled the privacy right from the "penumbras" and "emanations" surrounding a constellation of Bill of Rights provisions (including the conscience protections of the First Amendment, the right not to be forced to quarter soldiers during peacetime in the Third Amendment, and the right against unreasonable searches and seizures in the Fourth Amendment).[62] In *Griswold*, the Court refused to assign criminal liability to married couples for their use of contraception or to their prescribing physicians as accessories. Douglas's conception of the right involved two dimensions: the sanctity of the marriage *relation* and the private sanctum of the marital *bedroom*. These two aspects would evolve into the "autonomy" and "spatial" dimensions cited nearly forty years later by Justice Kennedy in a crucial gay rights decision (discussed later in this chapter).

Following *Griswold*, privacy was invoked and expanded in a flurry of subsequent decisions. The Court held the right to encompass the viewing of pornography in the privacy of one's home in 1969,[63] extended protection to unmarried persons acquiring contraception in 1972,[64] and determined that the right to privacy included the personal decision to terminate a pregnancy in 1973.[65]

At the state level, sodomy laws had already started to go by the wayside. There were a few state-level judicial developments. In Massachusetts, for example, the Supreme Judicial Court sustained the Commonwealth's sodomy prohibition in 1974, but held that it would no longer apply to consensual, private acts.[66] The New York Court of Appeals, a few years later, found its state's criminal sodomy prohibition to violate the right to privacy altogether.[67]

Judicial pronouncements, however, were infrequent. Most states that eliminated their sodomy bans in the 1970s did so legislatively, often as part of a general overhaul of their criminal codes. As law professor William N. Eskridge, Jr. reported, by 1979, "twenty-four states – almost half the states of the Union – had decriminalized consensual sodomy."[68] Some states accomplished this by adopting the Model Penal Code (MPC). The American Law Institute (ALI), which convenes field-specific experts to draft model laws and offer recommendations to state legislatures, had completed the MPC in 1962. It omitted any prohibition against acts of consensual sodomy, so that wholesale replacement by a legislature of an existing criminal code with the MPC would quietly rid a state of its sodomy ban.

Solicitation of sodomy, however, remained a crime under the MPC, enabling police stings of cruising spots to proceed unabated. The legislative differential between acts of sodomy and solicitation was consistent with an emerging conceptual distinction between public and private morality in both the US and Great Britain beginning in the late 1950s. Faced with increasing incidents of arrest for sodomy and prostitution, the British Home Secretary commissioned a study, published in 1957 and known as the *Wolfenden Report*,[69] which recommended eliminating criminal penalties against private, consensual acts of sodomy while maintaining penalties for public acts of immorality, including prostitution and solicitation. During and subsequent to the conduct of the study, two British public intellectuals, the libertarian H. L. A. Hart and the moralist Lord Patrick Devlin, sparred over the propriety of morals regulation and the role of law in promoting a community's moral cohesion. The Hart-Devlin debate provoked intercontinental commentary, including deliberations on John Stuart Mill's "harm principle."[70] The moment appeared to revitalize American libertarian instincts, manifest in the US Supreme Court's right to privacy jurisprudence in the 1960s and 1970s.

So when the US Supreme Court decided to *uphold* Georgia's sodomy prohibition against Hardwick's privacy challenge in the widely criticized 1986 case of *Bowers v. Hardwick*,[71] it was a terrible blow, not so much because gay people were routinely being arrested from the privacy of their bedrooms (they were not), but because the decision permitted tribunals – deliberating on everything from whether to pass a local anti-discrimination ordinance to whether to award custody to a gay or lesbian parent in the course of a heterosexual divorce – to treat gay and lesbian people as presumptive criminal offenders. The *Bowers* decision would be overturned seventeen years later in *Lawrence v. Texas*.[72] In the meantime, advocates turned their focus to seeking repeal or invalidation of as many of the remaining state prohibitions as possible.

The 1980s also introduced the savage destruction of the AIDS epidemic. In the US, "family only" hospital visitation and intestate death made painfully evident the benefits of partnership recognition and spurred campaigns for domestic partnership laws and equitable forms of relationship recognition that would pave the way to same-sex marriage.

AIDS also brought about fresh forms of discrimination in the US, including by insurance companies, surely related to the stigma of gay identity even if the discrimination was sometimes suffered by persons who were not gay.[73] Authorities in large cities closed gay bathhouses on public health grounds and increased arrests of sex workers.[74] All of these reactions to AIDS, combined with media and federal government indifference to gay death, precipitated a groundswell of organizing, including the founding of the highly confrontational group, ACT UP (AIDS Coalition to Unleash Power), the service organization Gay Men's Health Crisis, and the advocacy organization AIDS Action. As historian Linda Hirshman wrote, "AIDS was the making of the gay revolution."[75] Lesbians, especially those who had been active in efforts associated with the women's health movement of the previous decade, proved a crucial source of knowledge and support.[76]

Fidel blamed the US for the arrival of AIDS in Cuba, reinvigorating discursive associations among imperialism, moral decay, and homosexuality.[77] According to public health professor Mark Padilla, "Cuba's response to the AIDS epidemic, particularly in the 1980s, differed significantly from its neighbors' … [partly] because the motives behind its denial of an 'AIDS problem' were more politically oriented (and specifically anticapitalist)."[78]

In contrast to the US, where the disease went too long neglected by the federal government, but where rights such as association and expression enabled a massive wave of organizing, Cuba lacked a tradition of liberal rights to support organizing but provided universal health care to its population. The result of Cuba's distinguishing features, for both good and ill, was the establishment of a quarantine system.[79]

In addition to coercing Cubans into AIDS sanitoriums, Cuba also compelled "disclosure of sexual contacts of those who were seropositive," pressured people to submit to HIV antibody tests, and prohibited persons in "high-risk groups" from giving blood, noting such exclusion on their identity cards.[80] Unsurprisingly, given liberal human rights commitments outside of Cuba, Cuba subjected itself to international criticism for its approach to managing HIV/AIDS, notwithstanding its undeniable success in containing the virus.

According to political scientist Ian Lumsden, some of Cuba's most severe measures were given up over time.[81] Sanitoriums remained, but, Lumsden maintains, they have "become much more liberal and humanistic."[82] His impression is that they became "very comfortable, and in some cases even luxurious … by Cuban standards."[83] Patients were permitted visits with family and friends on and off grounds; gay and straight couples lived together; patients ate well, received first-rate medical care, and continued to receive their former salaries.[84]

Oddly, Cuba did not launch a rigorous AIDS education campaign at this time, despite its commitment to other areas of sex ed. Even Latin American development expert Emily Kirk, who wrote the definitive account of Cuba's public health and sex education efforts, barely mentions AIDS in the 1980s and offers no story of Cuba creating or disseminating an AIDS curriculum to the populace during that period.[85] As Lumsden proposes, the absence of pertinent curricula might be explained by a preference for control over individual empowerment.[86] He also points out the cost as well as "scarcity of condoms and the reluctance of Cuban males to use them."[87] Leiner suggests that the failure can be explained by a combination of the well-developed health care system, "fear generated by [the] epidemic," "machismo," the prevention of grassroots organizing, and homophobia.[88]

In 1986, "[t]he Cuban government launched … a campaign to 'rectify errors and negative tendencies,'"[89] or the period known as rectification. The initiative was meant to reverse experimental moves in the 1970s in the direction of markets and financial incentives, "return[ing Cuba] to a more centralized command system .... [and] reviving the Guevarist vision of a moral society."[90] Cuban rectification coincided with Mikhail Gorbachev's taking the Soviet Union in the opposite direction, to "*glasnost* and *perestroika* – the promotion of political openness and economic restructuring."[91] Though rectification focused on economic policy and did not directly address matters of sexuality, Cuba's sense of isolation, even from the Soviets, along with a mood of revanchism, could perhaps have rendered condoms, or any approach to AIDS that contained a suggestion of emasculation or imperialist influence, anathema.

GNTES nevertheless continued throughout the 1980s to provide education on other aspects of sexual health across the island. Meanwhile, evidence of attitudinal progress could be observed in the arts, where "daring homoerotic themes" were increasingly tolerated and even rewarded.[92] El Mejunje de Silverio, a state-sanctioned homosexual gathering place, opened in 1984 in the inland town of Santa Clara.[93] In 1987, the National Assembly conducted another revision of the Penal Code. The revised code eliminated the prohibition against "public ostentation" of homosexuality,[94] although the vague "dangerousness" law, remained, leaving an opening for differential treatment by police based on sexuality and gender presentation, as well as race.[95] In 1985, a new law allowed limited name changes on national ID cards for transgender Cubans.[96] This was followed three years later by Cuban physicians undertaking to perform a gender-confirmation surgery for the first time.[97]

CENESEX

At the end of the 1980s, the Cuban Minister of Public Health reestablished GNTES as an official "center" of its ministry. This raised its status and permitted it greater independence and a role in the international sphere. The entity took a new name: the *Centro Nacional de Educación Sexual* (Cuban National Center for Sex Education, or CENESEX).[98]

In the early 1990s, Mariela Castro EspÍn – daughter of Raúl Castro and Vilma Espín – joined the team at CENESEX, taking the helm at the time of her mother's death in 2007, a position that (at this writing) she still holds.[99] Mariela studied child psychology and sociology at the University of Havana, earning a PhD in 2015 after writing a dissertation on issues confronting transgender Cubans.[100] As a psychologist, a Castro, a devoted socialist whose revolutionary commitment is beyond question, and a member of the Cuban National Assembly, Mariela could hardly be better positioned to push for progress, and she has not forgone the opportunity. Under her stewardship, CENESEX has become an influential voice for equality for homosexual men and women as well as for transgender people over the last three decades.

In the years since its renaming, CENESEX has expanded its purview. It developed an HIV/AIDS education and prevention program emphasizing safe sex and condom usage. It offers workshops, lectures, and movie nights to the public, as well as support groups for lesbians, transgender Cubans, and other populations. It launched a journal of academic research, *Sexología y Sociedad* (*Sexology and Society*) and contributes as well to popular publications, including a regular column aimed at youth.[101] It draws interest beyond Cuba's shores, having hosted both the World Sexology Conference and the Latin American Congress of Sex Education.[102] It collaborates with health-oriented international NGOs and receives funding from the United Nations and other international entities to support its family planning and other public health initiatives.[103]

Since 2007, CENESEX has sponsored an annual conga celebration of the International Day Against Homophobia.[104] That day is observed in May, the month before the US-based "Pride" celebration commemorating the events at the Stonewall Inn. It celebrates the depathologization of homosexuality by the World Health Organization. "Let's," cheers Mariela at the government-sanctioned rally, "make Cuba more revolutionary!"[105]

CENESEX has also taken a strong interest in law. It maintains a staff attorney, has developed law school curricula, hosts events for lawyers and law students, and has advocated for legislative reforms, including same-sex marriage, adoption by same-sex couples, and access to assisted reproductive technologies.[106] (Chapter 3 reviews some of the reforms that have come to pass.) Cuba saw few legal advances in this area in the 1990s. Perhaps most significant was an amendment to Article 303 of the Penal Code, "taunting with a homosexual intention,"[107] so that it now prohibits sexual solicitation generally rather than homosexual solicitation specifically. Additional legal changes came about in the following decade. In 2008, the Public Health Ministry issued Resolution 126,[108] providing a range of gender confirming health services, including "diagnosis, psychological and psychiatric care, the provision of necessary medications, therapy," as well as gender confirmation surgery at no cost as part of the national health care program.[109] CENESEX successfully advocated so that those who had undergone surgery could obtain changes to their national ID cards reflecting their sex[110] and then more recently for 2025 amendments to the Ley del Registro del Estado Civil (*Law on Registry of Civil Status*) eliminating the surgery requirement.

CENESEX is not without its critics. Historian of sexuality Abel Sierra Madero has critiqued what he calls a "gender factory that obliterates the trans' subversive character," arguing that official Cuban "policy remains trapped in the binary frame of masculine and feminine."[111] Anthropologist Noelle Stout argues relatedly that "the medical and mental health discourses around homosexuality suggest new platforms for biopolitical regulation,"[112] presumably making the point that as Cuba provides medical resources it simultaneously exerts control over identities through determinations of eligibility for medical interventions and what interventions serve state purposes in the organization of gender categories. Daigle adds, "CENESEX's liberal approach to gay and lesbian couples … is based on the idea that the heteronormative model of stable, monogamous, non-promiscuous relationships can be transposed onto same-sex couples, who can then be considered as revolutionary as any other workers and citizens."[113] Taking their cue from queer critiques of heteronormativity, these writers share a concern that the reforms attributed to CENESEX should be understood as a continuation of state control, not a break from it.

Sociologist Tanya L. Saunders has also been less than entirely laudatory, though on different grounds. Saunders chronicled the rise and then precipitous fall of a CENESEX-sponsored group for Black lesbians called OREMI. A small cadre of women approached CENESEX about sponsoring the group in 2005,[114] apparently because truly independent grassroots organizing is not permitted. Lesbian social existence in Cuba is less visible and more racially divided than male homosexual or trans existence and largely consists of house parties held in secret. (They are secret because they are illegal, and they are illegal because they are conducted without a permit, and they are typically conducted without a permit because permits involve taxes if guests pay an entrance fee, which they do.[115]) The "white … parties tend to draw a femme/femme crowd, while 'black' parties tend to draw a plurality of gender representations."[116] Lesbians, according to Saunders, are among the most likely Cubans to valorize white and mulatta femininity while associating blackness with a disdained butchness.[117] The founders of OREMI sought an affirming social space in which to ameliorate the sense of ostracization that this racialization of gender produced.

The group lasted just two months.[118] Saunders attributes the collapse (in part) to what might be termed an *intersectional failure* – specifically, the failure to confront the national myth of "racelessness," by what is, in the end, an organ of the Cuban state.[119] (Saunders also reports, however, that the neighbors complained about lesbians showing up by the hundreds at the CENESEX facility and having sex around the building and on the roof, so … maybe that was the problem.[120])

NEOLIBERALISM AND VICTORY IN THE COLD WAR: THE US IN THE 1990S

The US presidency returned to Democratic control in 1993 and neoliberal ideas that had taken hold during the Reagan years continued to exert a powerful influence over national policy. The "New Democrat" in the White House, Bill Clinton, signed the 1994 crime bill (now widely blamed, along with Reagan's "war on drugs," for the devastation of mass incarceration) as well as the 1996 "welfare reform" law. Congressional findings in support of welfare reform declare "Marriage is the foundation of a successful society"[121] and among the Act's stated purposes is "end[ing] the dependence of needy parents on government benefits by promoting job preparation, work, and marriage."[122]

As legal scholar Brenda Cossman observed around that time, changes in family law, including efforts to increase participation in marriage, were a "key strategy of the privatization project of the neo-liberal state."[123] The family was "called upon to address … economic needs … at precisely the moment when the welfare state [was] being dismantled and public financial assistance [was] becoming scarce."[124] The more marriage, the better, from a perspective that prioritizes private obligations of financial support in lieu of public sector responsibility for the most needy among us.

Directing financial responsibility to the marital dyad helped to set the stage for the twenty-five-year period beginning in the 1990s during which gay rights advocates steadied their aim on the marriage objective. Same-sex marriage met with little success initially.[125] A litigation in Hawaii that spanned almost the entire decade looked for a while as if the state supreme court might actually find that same-sex couples were entitled to full marriage rights under the state constitution.[126] In the end, a 1998 state constitutional amendment thwarted the plaintiffs' efforts and the whole affair provoked state and federal backlash in the form of so-called *Defense of Marriage Acts* – that is, laws reaffirming the heterosexuality of marriage.[127]

The Hawaii case was initiated by private individuals despite reservations among mainstream lgbtq advocacy organizations, but GLAD (GLBTQ Legal Advocates and Defenders), the leading such organization in New England, launched a similar case in Vermont a few years later. That case resulted in a statewide civil unions law, providing many of the benefits of marriage to same-sex couples, but not the moniker and neither interstate portability nor federal recognition.[128] The Vermont legislature passed a civil unions law to comply with its court's requirement that the state provide the same "benefits" to same-sex-couples as it does to heterosexual married couples.[129]

Other US jurisdictions followed. The states were not ready for full marriage for same-sex couples just yet, but advocates laid the building blocks with care. In addition to continuing to reduce criminalization of sodomy (even without a federal constitutional mandate), anti-discrimination provisions were accruing at state and local levels, shielding gay and lesbian people in employment, housing, and public accommodations, as well as from homophobically motivated violence. Localities continued to enact domestic partnership ordinances, more and more private sector employers voluntarily offered their employees domestic partner benefits,[130] and courts increasingly recognized contractual arrangements between same-sex partners and conferred rights on non-biological parents on equitable bases.[131]

Anti-gay backlash was everywhere underway, as well, but in 1996, the US Supreme Court took a stand against it. In *Romer v. Evans*, Justice Kennedy led the majority in striking down as a violation of the federal Equal Protection Clause a Colorado state constitutional amendment drafted by anti-gay activists and passed by referendum that was designed to deny anti-discrimination protections to gay and lesbian people.[132] The conflicting opinions in the case perfectly embodied the debate over whether gay people should be understood as a minority group with constitutional rights or merely a group of people wishing to violate widely held social mores who lost in the to-and-fro of the culture wars.[133] *Romer* and the US Supreme Court cases that would follow[134] would press the trend in the direction of gay rights. Legal change was happening – not in isolation, of course. Popular culture and public opinion were changing, as well, and business, media, grassroots, and academic sectors each played a vital role.

The specific legal advances that US gay rights advocates made were far from random. The major organizations that plotted the course should be understood as constrained by the historical/political context in which they worked. It is no accident that legal advocacy emphasized sexual privacy, anti-discrimination, hate crimes prohibitions, partnership recognition, and – eventually – marriage. The national setting in which the law reform agenda was set was powerfully conditioned by neoliberalism's characteristic aversion to public sector responsibility for Americans' health, housing, and nutrition, as well as its tendency toward criminalization. Access to health insurance, for example, which occupied years of debate leading up to enactment of the Affordable Care Act (a.k.a. "Obamacare"), served as a key rationale for making marriage available to same-sex couples. The implication of the gay rights argument was that health insurance would continue to be predominantly provided via employment-based and otherwise privately purchased plans that could be shared with a spouse. A shift in emphasis to the public sector for health coverage for each individual would have undermined a widely appreciated, persuasive argument for permitting same-sex couples' entrance into the dominant model. That model went largely unchallenged by gay rights advocates. The resulting form of legal progress – bringing gays and lesbians into existing economic structures – largely benefited privileged sectors of the constituency, neglecting racial, regional, and economic inequalities. The principal pro-gay legal reforms from the 1990s forward were those that synced most readily with privatization trends, doing little for the most marginalized along axes of race, class, age, and region while rewarding those whose lives approximated the bourgeois family ideal.

The gay legal community's next big Supreme Court victory, *Lawrence v. Texas*,[135] would finally accomplish gay inclusion in the privacy right. When John Lawrence and Tyron Garner were arrested in Lawrence's Texas apartment for engaging in anal intercourse[136] in violation of their state's sodomy prohibition, quite a bit of progress had been made since the Court heard *Bowers*. In addition to all the state and local advances and Justice Kennedy's show of sympathy for the gay cause in *Romer*, Kennedy had also joined a troika of Republican-appointed justices to preserve constitutional protection for abortion in the 1992 case of *Planned Parenthood v. Casey*.[137] That opinion was co-authored, but these lines bear the unmistakable mark of Kennedy's hand:

> These matters, involving the most intimate and personal choices a person may make in a lifetime, choices central to personal dignity and autonomy, are central to the liberty protected by the Fourteenth Amendment. At the heart of liberty is the right to define one's own concept of existence, of meaning, of the universe, and of the mystery of human life. Beliefs about these matters could not define the attributes of personhood were they formed under compulsion of the State.[138]

The "mystery of human life" – not your usual constitutional fare outside of a Kennedy opinion – was mocked accordingly by Justice Scalia in dissent.[139] Still, Kennedy's hallmark attention to the ethereal in *Casey* managed to buttress his reasoning in *Lawrence*. While Kennedy appeared to harbor some (still befuddling) discomfort with explicit invocation of the fundamental right to privacy, he nonetheless relied on the privacy line of case law to overturn the *Bowers* precedent, attributing the same content to the "liberty" guarantee of the Fourteenth Amendment. Picking up on a dual-stranded conceptualization of privacy initially articulated by Justice Douglas in *Griswold*,[140] Justice Kennedy described the right in question as follows:

> Liberty protects the person from unwarranted government intrusions into a dwelling or other private places. In our tradition the State is not omnipresent in the home. And there are other spheres of our lives and existence, outside the home, where the State should not be a dominant presence. Freedom extends beyond spatial bounds. Liberty presumes an autonomy of self that includes freedom of thought, belief, expression, and certain intimate conduct. The instant case involves liberty of the person both in its spatial and more transcendent dimensions.[141]

Denouncing *Bowers* as wrongly decided in 1986, Justice Kennedy in 2003 held "The State cannot demean [the two men's] existence or control their destiny by making their private sexual conduct a crime."[142] The decision went on to serve as a critical building block in the equality edifice that advocates were slowly constructing. Ridding gay identity of its nearly inherent[143] criminality cleared a significant obstacle.

The first real success for the same-sex marriage campaign occurred in Massachusetts at the exact same time. Between the spring of 2003 – when the Massachusetts Supreme Judicial Court determined that same-sex couples were entitled to marriage under the state constitution[144] – and 2015 – when the US Supreme Court would make the same decision under the federal constitution – advocates grinded out a state-by-state strategy, winning some and losing some, eventually making progress in majoritarian as well as counter-majoritarian arenas. The Court's 2013 decision in *US v. Windsor*,[145] striking down the provision of the Defense of Marriage Act that denied federal recognition to same-sex couples validly married in their home states, signaled that victory was at hand. The remaining exclusions finally fell with the Court's 2015 decision in *Obergefell v. Hodges*.[146]

In the initial years of the marriage battle, defenders of heterosexual-only marriage assailed gay and lesbian people with charges of immorality, anti-family values, promiscuity, and posing a danger to children. Their arguments evolved over time, in part due to the success of activists, advocates, and the media in normalizing gay people and relationships. Those initial culture war attacks effectively demanded a retort of moral non-differentiation, or a depiction of gay and lesbian couples as essentially the same as heterosexual couples *but for* one morally insignificant difference – the nature of the private act that the couples perform in their bedrooms. That small detail, advocates implicitly argued, need not undermine gay and lesbian wholesomeness, commitment, or good citizenship. Gay and lesbian suitability for marriage established itself based on a new and only slightly revised instantiation of family values – one that was gay-inclusive, but otherwise the mirror image of the old family values, the version that prevailed throughout the debate over welfare reform, coalescing with fiscal conservatism and positing sexual virtue and privatized responsibility as the cure for poverty.

Litigations and public relations campaigns presented exemplary images of same-sex partners caring for one another through illness, caring for one another's aging parents, and otherwise demonstrating their commitment and mutual responsibility. Then-Chief Justice of the Massachusetts Supreme Judicial Court, Margaret Marshall, received the message. In describing the purposes and nature of civil marriage in her 2003 *Goodridge* decision, she stressed that it "ensures that children and adults are cared for and supported whenever possible from private rather than public funds."[147] By the time of the *Obergefell* litigation, over three hundred leading conservative and Republican figures joined together as *amici* on the side of the same-sex couples, describing themselves as believers in "traditional conservative values, including the commitment to limited government, the protection of individual freedom, and the belief in the importance of stable families."[148] They argued that marriage reduces "demands on welfare and unemployment programs."[149] Same-sex marriage was entirely consistent with fiscal conservatism.

As historian and longtime gay activist John D'Emilio observed, in the span of time between the Stonewall Uprising (1969) and HIV/AIDS (outset of the 1980s), at least some gay activism (certainly that in which D'Emilio participated) had a holistic quality. Many of the most prominent and impactful activists viewed themselves as part of the New Left and were accordingly concerned with racism, sexism, imperialism, war, and capitalist exploitation, as well as with sexual oppression and repression. D'Emilio and his fellow travelers understood these as a set of interrelated forces against which the struggle had to be simultaneously waged to be truly effective.[150] Their activism was coterminous with the work of more conservative activists who viewed gay rights as a silo, distinct from other social justice struggles, but the integrated vision looked to be prevailing in the late 1970s.[151]

In the next decade, however, despair and rage associated with the initial years of the HIV/AIDS epidemic produced intensive organizing and radicalization, particularly evident in the confrontational tactics of groups such as ACT UP.[152] D'Emilio (like Hirshman[153]) credits the terrible exigencies of the AIDS crisis with the building of the gay rights infrastructure.[154] The anguished losses of friends and lovers during the 1980s may, ironically, have fostered the *de*radicalization of the law reform effort that can be observed in the 1990s. The single-issue conception rose back to prominence, notwithstanding persistent critiques from important lefty lgbtq activists such as Urvashi Vaid[155] and scholars such as Cathy Cohen.[156] Just as the gay rights movement began to accelerate, legal advocacy turned to privacy and then to equality, specifically toward marriage. The wish for relationship recognition was understandable in the aftermath of hospitals' callously denying men access to their lovers who were dying alone in hospital beds. It was a natural reaction to the indignity of homophobic relatives of deceased men coming along sometimes after years of estrangement and claiming their intestate inheritance to the exclusion of surviving partners.

Still, the choice to chart a course for same-sex marriage as the singular most galvanizing objective beginning in the 1990s sidelined other possible law reform objectives that might have held greater benefits for the most vulnerable members of the lgbtq community – those for whom housing, nutrition, income, and criminalization were the most pressing concerns.[157] The agenda that drove the next three decades of progress for lgbtq people in the US was constituted at a moment when posing a more serious challenge to the economic order was simply not a recipe for success. It would be asking too much to argue for universal health insurance – much more realistic to seek access for same-sex couples to employer-based family plans. It was unlikely that police in tourist hubs and gentrified neighborhoods in New York and San Francisco were going to stop arresting homeless lgbtq youth for lewdness and loitering, and unlikely that they would be provided food, shelter, and medical care, but a small matter to extend privacy protections to gays inhabiting private dwellings and wishing to enjoy acts of sodomy without fear of criminalization. It would have been a major disruption to confront the deep inequality wrought by employment-at-will,[158] but a comparatively modest change to add sexual orientation to anti-discrimination law coverage. So, the top-flight lgbtq legal organizations chose the latter in each case, and that course of legal progress, driven by a teleology of equal access to marriage and conditioned by the stripping away of public sector responsibility in favor of personal responsibility, marginalized an array of possible reform projects – as well as the grassroots and direct service voices that advocated them.[159]

Finally, US victory in the Cold War also enabled the surge in gay advancement in the 1990s. The homosexual turncoat stereotype began to dissipate, experiencing its last gasps with the debate over the (now defunct) Don't Ask/Don't Tell policy regarding homosexuality in the military.[160] In 1992, the General Accounting Office (GAO) reported to Congress that the Department of Defense (DoD) "and the [armed] services have commissioned two major efforts that focused on whether homosexuals were more of a security risk than heterosexuals and concluded that there was no factual data to substantiate that premise."[161] A couple of years later, President Bill Clinton ordered a halt to all denials of security clearances for federal employees on grounds of sexual orientation.[162]

After the attacks of September 11, 2001, a new era of geopolitics brought about a new place for gay rights in US foreign policy – one reminiscent of Black civil rights half a century earlier. Legal scholar Derrick Bell famously argued that the Black civil rights victories of the 1950s and 1960s were enabled by a *convergence* of the justice imperative with US foreign policy interests.[163] Bell's convergence thesis was supported by the historical study of Mary L. Dudziak, who showed that from the announcement of the Truman Doctrine (pledging US support for democratic countries under threat by authoritarian regimes) in 1947, foreign policy experts understood that the US had to represent itself as a beacon of freedom and equality to win over formerly colonized countries that might otherwise come under Soviet influence.[164] The history of slavery and the continuing reign of Jim Crow hampered American objectives as Soviet and Chinese propaganda highlighted American racial injustice. To counter the communist narrative, the US

> revealed, rather than concealed, the nation's past failings, and it did so for the purpose of presenting American history as a story of redemption. In this story, democracy as a system of government was the vehicle for national reconciliation .... Democracy, not totalitarian forms of government ... provided a context that made ... redemption possible.[165]

Civil rights advocates pushed the US to live up to the story it was telling.[166] Starting with *Shelley v. Kraemer*[167] in the late 1940s and continuing into the mid 1960s, the US Department of Justice submitted *amicus curiae* briefs on behalf of civil rights litigants, urging that denial of racial equality was impeding American foreign policy objectives.[168]

Decades later, an echo of the Dudziak/Bell account could be heard in the context of the War on Terror. Having largely shed the association with communism, gays and lesbians now discursively serve as objects of liberal toleration, putting into relief the intolerance of unenlightened Muslim others – a new "convergence" for a new era. As Gender Studies scholar Jasbir Puar has argued, "homosexual subjects who have limited legal rights within the US civil context gain significant representational currency when situated within the global scene of the war on terror."[169]

Puar introduced the concept of "homonationalism" to stand for a limited form of gay and lesbian inclusion within the nation[170] that summons a discursive contrast with the enemy. Her term is meant to encompass the observation that "lesbian and gay liberal rights discourses ... produce narratives of progress and modernity"[171] where the flip side of gay and lesbian inclusion is "sexual othering," and "Orientalist constructions of 'Muslim sexuality.'"[172] The shift from a Cold War mentality to that of the War on Terror reconfigures, but does not eliminate, the instrumentality to which gays and lesbians might be put in foreign policy.

Coastal, urban, and predominantly white gays and lesbians in the US have begun in earnest to enjoy broad social acceptance, legally respected domesticity, and educational and professional inclusion. Trans populations, lgbtq people of color – urban and rural – lgbtq youth, and other vulnerable subpopulations, however, continue to suffer disproportionately high rates of poverty, hunger, homelessness, and criminalization.[173] The astonishingly successful march to same-sex marriage, along with hate crimes inclusion, privacy in the home, and narrowly drawn anti-discrimination protections, have neglected the wealth gap between the lgbtq *haves* and *have-nots*, leaving that gap to become even wider than in the US population at large.

In sum, same-sex marriage in the US was facilitated by a confluence of the Anglo-American privacy right in constitutional law, a privatization trend associated with the ascent of neoliberalism (wherein anti-gay moral conservatism lost out to fiscal conservatism and the racist and misogynist mantra of "personal responsibility") and the War on Terror's succession to the foreign policy space left open by the conclusion of the Cold War. This gay rights story is one of progress, but not for everyone. For those already living on the economic margins, a gay rights path forged under these discursive conditions was likely to leave its most vulnerable behind. Moreover, as some sectors of the lgbtq community wondered when the "triumphant gay revolution"[174] would reach them, the US could tout its advances in service of an anti-Muslim foreign policy.

THE SPECIAL PERIOD AND ITS AFTERMATH

Notwithstanding the flourishing of CENESEX, Cuba as a whole faced the roughest years yet of the revolutionary period in the last decade of the second millennium. The country was entirely reliant not only on Soviet military aid and protection but also on heavily subsidized trade arrangements.[175] When the Soviet Union collapsed, therefore, so did Cuba's economy. The changing world order meant not only the withdrawal of Soviet military protection[176] but also the sudden loss of favorable trade conditions.[177] As journalist and author Tom Gjelten wrote, "the socialist bloc gave Cuba virtually everything it needed .... [including] about thirteen million tons of oil each year,"[178] (some of which Cuba relied on to *re*-export[179]) while buying up "its rum ... tobacco, sugar, citrus products, and nickel,"[180] paying above-market prices.[181] Eastern bloc countries "financed and built steel mills, oil refineries, fertilizer factories, and nickel plants in Cuba and provided the island with most of its manufactured goods and half its food supply."[182] Cuba tried after the Soviet downfall to diversify its agriculture, but without sufficient fuel to distribute the food, much of it would rot.[183] Cuba was left alone to suffer "severe shortages of ... petroleum, fertilizers, spare parts, raw materials, and foodstuffs."[184] Manufacturing, transportation, and communications slowed dramatically as "imports and exports fell by 70 to 75 percent."[185] Unemployment skyrocketed while income, standard of living, and GDP dropped precipitously.[186] Electrical outages became frequent.[187] Rations became tight, long food lines became commonplace,[188] and, according to Ferrer, "daily consumption of calories dropped on average by a third," as "Russian canned meat, Bulgarian canned vegetables, [and] German sausage ... disappeared."[189] Cuba had entered what it called its *Período Especial en Tiempos de Paz* (*Special Period in Peacetime*, or just *Special Period*).

When Boris Yeltsin assumed the presidency of Russia in 1991, he showed little interest in helping Cuba, which he viewed "as a Brezhnev-era police state," the support of which was inconsistent with his reformist inclinations.[190] A bill "invalidate[d] contracts signed between the Soviet government and other countries," and arms shipments stopped altogether.[191] China tried to help Cuba on the trade front, but what it offered was insufficient to fill empty Soviet shoes.[192]

The US took the opportunity to tighten its embargo on the tiny surviving communist outpost. Due in large part to the flexing of hawkish Cuban–American political muscle, Congress passed the Torricelli Act[193] in 1992 followed by the Helms–Burton Act[194] in 1996, which together took aim at remittances, travel to Cuba, US corporate subsidiaries operating from a foreign territory and conducting trade with Cuba, and trade that touched nationalized property formerly belonging to private persons.[195] Imagining that under pressure the Cuban regime would collapse just like the Soviet satellites of Eastern Europe, the US pursued policies that purposely intensified the already severe shortages of food, soap, and other essential consumer goods, worsening the immense hardship on the Cuban people.

But Fidel's reign endured. His government took steps to ameliorate the effects of the Soviet demise. Some of these steps had a "doubling down" quality. According to historian Jaime Suchlicki, "Rations were reduced, labor brigades were organized, security and repression increased .... [and] the military was given a greater role in controlling the economy," specifically in "running agricultural and industrial enterprises."[196]

At the same time, however, Fidel permitted another wave of emigration and had little choice but to liberalize aspects of the economy. He began permitting farmers' markets, where "growers [sell] directly to the public" in order to "alleviate the critical food shortage."[197] He permitted Cuban expats to send a broader array of goods to their relatives on the island, and also granted visas more liberally so they could visit – bringing goods and spending dollars.[198] He cracked open the door to self-employment so that "hairdressers, electricians, plumbers, and mechanics," as well as shoe shiners, craftspeople, and dozens of other professions could operate independently – if registered and paying taxes.[199] In addition, "private bars and restaurants, known as *paladares*" were permitted and became extremely popular.[200]

Among the most painful ideological compromises that Fidel made to mitigate against the economic crisis was liberalization of laws constraining foreign capital investment. For the first time, Cuba actually incentivized joint Cuban-foreign ventures by exempting them from various taxes and tariffs. Foreign companies investing in Cuba were even permitted to "introduce their own management techniques, dismiss workers at their own discretion, set wages," and own property in Cuba.[201] Initially, the new enterprises were jointly held by private foreign firms – which could own up to 49 percent[202] – and the Cuban state, but in 1992 further legal revision permitted foreign companies to be majority stakeholders.[203] Cuban individuals were not eligible to participate in such ventures as owners, strictly as employees, whom foreign employers could hire and fire without government interference. Foreign investors were excited about the opportunities in Cuba, if also wary of the US embargo, the unreliability of the Cuban judiciary's commitment to contract enforcement, and the possibility that Fidel might nationalize their property interests.[204] Spanish investors predominated, but money also came in from France and Canada.[205] The new investments took hold in several longstanding Cuban industries, including nickel, tobacco, and rum, but the unrivaled number one sector attracting foreign capital was international tourism.[206]

Prying Cuba open to tourism to obtain hard currency from capitalist countries must have agonized Fidel, though he publicly minimized its significance along with that of the other deviations from socialist orthodoxy that the Special Period forced him to accept.[207] Over the last decade of the twentieth century, the tourism sector grew "approximately 20 percent annually," coming mainly from "Italy, Canada, Spain, France, and Germany …. In 1998 Cuba's tourism earnings totaled $1.8 billion, displacing the traditionally dominant sugar industry as the country's leading source of hard currency."[208] Even after the hardships of the Special Period abated somewhat in the mid- late 1990s, international tourism remained the cornerstone of the Cuban economy, as it does today. Spanish and other foreign firms operate exquisite resort hotels catering to wealthy Canadians and Western Europeans.

Finally, also in pursuit of hard currency in the midst of the crisis, Cuba altered its monetary policy. It temporarily converted itself into a dual-currency economy (the Cuban peso and the US dollar) which made it easier to receive remittances from family members in Miami and also provided Cubans in possession of dollars access to state-owned "dollar stores" – stores that had previously sold difficult-to-obtain goods exclusively to foreigners. This enabled the Cuban government to soak up currency that would otherwise have been circulating in the black market.[209]

These adaptive measures opened an aperture into which forces of global capitalism would seep, leading to a number of unintended – if entirely foreseeable – consequences. First, permission to send or carry commodities into the country combined with the introduction of the dollar renewed stratification in the Cuban population, and to a significant extent, that stratification tracked racial hierarchy. Cubans who had relatives in Miami with sufficient wealth to send remittances and goods back to the island benefited in ways that other Cubans, who lacked devoted relatives abroad with enough money to share, did not. The former could obtain goods beyond their rations as well as the currency to purchase commodities in the dollar stores. Overwhelmingly, those best positioned in this regard were white;[210] their relatives were more likely to have fled at the outset of the revolutionary period and been welcomed to the US as "good" (i.e., white, educated, anti-communist, and entrepreneurial) immigrants.[211]

The explosion of the tourism industry also contributed to racial stratification due to racist hiring by foreign-owned companies.[212] "Front of the house" jobs in the beautiful resort hotels went to workers with a *buena presencia* – a euphemism for light skin – on the assumption that European and Canadian tourists would prefer to be served by light-skinned service staff.[213] As Media and Cultural Studies Professor Amalia Cabezas reports,

> In Cuba, scholars and social observers alike have identified the absence of Black Cubans in hotel and tourism-related employment. However, the exclusion of Blacks from tourism jobs is not a monolithic form of discrimination. *Mulatos* and *mulatas*, for example, are often favored for certain jobs. Those with darker skin are less likely to be employed in frontline service positions with direct face-to-face customer contact. For instance, in the famous Hotel Nacional in Havana, all the public restroom attendants and janitors are Black, in stark contrast to the white and lighter-skinned workers who serve as receptionists and in other administrative functions in the lobby and the business center. In this sense, people of color provide the invisible "backstage" services such as working in the kitchen and in maintenance, construction, and security jobs. Black Cubans can also be found in the less prestigious, state-run hotels, where they are also more likely to be employed in the lower echelons of services. Conversely, they are widely represented in the entertainment venues of hotels and resorts, where their hypervisibility and eroticization serve to enact Cuban culture. Through Black Cubans performing in clubs as musicians and dancers, Afro-Cuban talent, music, culture, and dance are made a prominent feature of what is "folkloric" and authentic about Cuba.[214]

Because tourism work pays better than just about anything else in the above-ground economy, Cabezas found an "inver[sion of] the social pyramid" as "doctors, lawyers, economists, and engineers" left state employment to work as "taxi drivers, hotel housekeeping staff, waiters, and bartenders."[215] Afro-Cubans were effectively barred from these opportunities, including the tips they generated,[216] surfacing racial hierarchies that had been somewhat latent in previous decades. Moreover, because many of the swanky new resorts were all-inclusive, a lot of visitors barely left the grounds, eating and recreating entirely on-site and spending little-to-no money outside of the carefully cultivated corporate hotel environment.[217]

As income from state employment diminished to below subsistence level, Cuba saw a dramatic increase in all manner of black-market activity,[218] from selling shampoo to repairing cars. Additionally, many Cubans entered the tourism market – informally – by selling cigars and providing tours.[219] Unaddressed racial disparity in housing took on new importance as well-housed Cubans opened *casas particulares* (bed and breakfasts) in their private homes.[220] And perhaps inevitably, the desperation for goods and currency among the Cuban people, combined with the influx of wealthy European and Canadian tourists on a sun-drenched Caribbean island, also meant a resurgence of sexual commerce, both hetero- and homosexual.

Scholars have produced rich ethnographies of Havana's sexual economy since the changes brought about during the Special Period, several of them focusing on transactional sex between Cubans and tourists. Reading these sources together, a couple of interrelated themes rise to the surface: notably a painful ambivalence – individual and national – regarding transactional sex with foreigners and the complicated function of race in appealing to Canadians and Europeans.

To begin with, ethnographers uniformly observe the existence of a conceptual spectrum, stretching from the most commodified sex, exchanged strictly for material enrichment and devoid of affection, to sex that is genuinely about love and utterly disregards material gain. The bulk of sex transpiring between Cubans and tourists does so between these poles, "suggest[ing] that the boundaries between affection and instrumentality were difficult to discern."[221] The slipperiness of the axis can render it a matter of utmost importance to Cubans to describe their sexual exchanges with tourists as being more about love than money, though the reality of dire need makes pure, crystalline love elusive.

Cabezas urges a critical stance toward application of the term "sex work" to describe Cuban/tourist sex, offering instead "the concept of *tactical sex* … that does not rely upon essentialized notions of identity or labor."[222] Challenging the "underlying assumption that 'true love' is about untainted intimacy … [and] without monetary exchanges," she observed that Cuban "women's tales of their experiences are often riddled with contradictions that suggest agency, multivalent meanings … [and] relationships [that] can be ephemeral, amorphous, and strategic, combining affect, money, mobility, and yes, even pleasure."[223] Undoubtedly "aware of the enormous inequalities between themselves and their hosts," tourists "often bring gifts, pay for meals, or send remittances once they return home."[224] Are women who rely on "remittances and gifts from their transnational boyfriends" sex workers?[225] How should one label the muddy amalgam of affective and material ties that characterize such relationships?

An elaborate vocabulary has grown out of the uncertainty regarding this question. In Spanish, the term *puta* is an all-purpose curse word encompassing the meaning of the English slur *whore*. Due to its strongly negative valence, it is not an identity that many women are eager to adopt for themselves. The upsurge in transactional sex during the Special Period, therefore, led to the rise of a new word in the Cuban lexicon: *jineterismo*. A *jinetera* or *jinetero* is, on a literal translation, a *jockey* and *jineterismo* refers to "jockeying for advantage … but the … graphic"[226] image also contributes something to its meaning. According to Cabezas, the term (in both its feminine and masculine forms) originally came into use to capture a broad swath of people "hustling in the tourist trade at multiple income-earning schemes."[227] Cubans have done everything they can think of to capture the tourist dollars that float beyond the walls of the resort hotels: opening *paladares* and *casas particulares* and using their cars as taxis.[228] Plenty of Cubans "jockey" for cash in one way or another.

Eventually, the term *jinetera* (in its feminine form) came to refer to women engaged in sexual commerce. The figure of the jinetera has been increasingly degraded over time and also has acquired a strong racial connotation.[229] According to Nadine Fernandez, Cubans conceptualize race along a "color continuum," and the "specific nomenclature for each shade is not only descriptive phenotypically but simultaneously assesses the individual's location in a value-laden racial hierarchy."[230] Moreover, the "designations are often shaped not only by phenotype, but by education, class, refinement, or what Cubans call 'nivel de cultura' or 'cultural level.'"[231] The malleability of racial categories, history of exoticization of Afro-Cuban women, and economic pressure that pushes many Afro-Cuban women to participate in *jineterismo*, combine to produce a close association between sex work and Afro-Cuban/*mulata* identity.[232] Women who can, prefer to lay claim to the ennobling term *luchadora*, the feminine noun derived from the verb *luchar* (to struggle). "*La lucha* is understood not as sex work but as part of a communal struggle for livelihood,"[233] even for someone who employs an array of survival strategies, transactional sex among them. As Abel Sierra Madero explains it, "'*la lucha*' represent[s] a series of survival strategies designed to cope with daily hardships. To be in '*la lucha*' grants the Cuban contemporary subject a certain amount of freedom of action that transcends laws as well as ethical and moral values."[234] Another key utility of "the discourse of *la lucha*," is "as a means for avoiding the category of sex worker .... [in part because Cubans] perceive *la lucha* as a temporary condition."[235]

Daigle's research confirmed Cabezas's perception that the purely transactional "'sex worker' did not exist, was ambiguous, or at the very least was quite an unstable subject,"[236] adding that "[s]exual-affective relations between Cubans and foreigners ... rang[e] from long-term committed partnerships to fleeting encounters, none of which can be said to be purely transactional."[237] In one among Daigle's many illustrative interviews, a woman told her "I'm not looking for someone who comes for a vacation, has some fun with me, gives me money, and then leaves. No, no, no – nothing like that. I want something serious, I want him to fall in love with me – you know what I mean? I want him to take me back with him."[238] Asked about her own feelings the interviewee replied, "Look, I would really, really like to wind up falling in love with him, too. I would really like that. I don't want him to buy me clothes or a cell phone, or to fix up my house. I want to leave Cuba – that's all I want. That's my objective. When I meet a foreign man, if there isn't anything that attracts me personally to him, then I can't. I won't even consider it."[239] This winding quotation alone demonstrates just how challenging it is, psychologically, even cognitively, to distill romantic aspiration from one's wish for relief from Cuba's hardships.

Daigle also assessed the vocabulary of transactional sex and affective labor. On her reading, *jinetera* connotes an Afro-Cuban or mixed-race woman and is debased.[240] The *luchadora*, Daigle explains, carries a more respectable valence. She is "a person of great resourcefulness and integrity, one who relies on no one but herself to get by."[241] The terms are applied somewhat erratically, however, reflecting Cuban ambivalence about what one can accept from oneself under conditions of deprivation. In an interview by anthropologist Noelle Stout, a *mulata* trans woman who had fellated an Italian tourist for twenty dollars the previous evening explained, "I'm not prostituting myself or hustling .... From my perspective I haven't done either. I'm *luchando* (struggling). Struggling to survive, struggling to get ahead, do you understand me?"[242] Even activity occurring at the transactional end of the transactional/affective spectrum is cast as *luchando*, as she grapples with her own conduct and tries to articulate a self that is distinct from the *puta* or *jinetera*. The crass exchange of sex for money is subject to harsh judgment, but *la lucha* is something with which Cubans can identify and sympathize.

Some of the immense personal ambivalence that attaches to transactional sex may be a reflection of the Cuban state's own dilemma: disapproval of prostitution coexists with reliance on the allure of the accessible sexy Cuban *mulata* to draw tourists to the island. *Jinetaras* are objects of official scorn. Not even CENESEX has advocated on their behalf or sought to shed light on practices of transactional sex. Mariela, who has been known to show up at police stations "on behalf of transwomen, drag queens, and gay Cubans detained arbitrarily,"[243] persists in her condemnation of *jineterismo* as inconsistent with socialist virtue and rooted in the moral failure of consumerism. According to writer and artist Coco Fusco, Mariela's mother, Vilma Espín, as head of the FMC, "denounc[ed] *jineteras* as decadent trash whose parents had lost control of them."[244]

Prostitution is not technically illegal in Cuba,[245] though earning from another's sale of sex is.[246] Most *jineteras* work independently, that is, without a *chulo* (pimp). Police harass and arrest suspected *jineteras*, typically on charges of "dangerousness" or "bothering a tourist."[247] According to Stout, in

> 1998, the Ministry of the Interior … started 'Operativo Lacra' (Operation Vice), a special police force dedicated to eliminating prostitution around the tourist trade. As a result, many of the major nightclubs that had become popular settings for sex workers to find clients were closed …. [I]n 2003 … Castro signed a decree that ordered the confiscation of all properties used for prostitution and the making of pornography, as well as illegal discotheques and underground video stores.[248]

The police are also on the lookout for Cubans who have migrated to Havana from a rural province in a quest to meet foreigners.[249] Afro-Cubans especially, who are more likely to hail from the east, are routinely stopped and asked for proof of residency.[250] Police stops disproportionately affect dark-skinned Cubans, homosexuals, and transgender women, in part due to profiling,[251] but also because of who is (and is not) best-positioned to secure public-facing hotel jobs that enable workers to meet tourists indoors and therefore without police interference. Cabezas reports, "Access to tourists provides resort workers with opportunities that would otherwise be unattainable. The sexual and affective economies operating in the hotels effectively complement the low wages of hospitality workers."[252] As one waiter Cabezas interviewed put it, "*Camareras* [chambermaids] are the legitimate and official *jineteras*."[253] Police surveil the streets of the touristy neighborhoods, sometimes relying on vagrancy law to arrest *jineteras* who might bribe hotel guards and get inside.[254] The police do not, however, generally enter the hotels, leaving undisturbed those lucky enough to connect with foreigners on-site. Moreover, according to Cabezas, social entanglement between Cuban resort staff and tourists is not only in the interest of the workers. "Indeed, management encourages the cultivation of intimacy and affective bond …. as a corporate strategy to increase return visitors."[255]

Despite official derision toward the *jinetera*, Hamilton, Stout, and Daigle all report that Cuba "markets [itself] as an exotic paradise, often using images of Afro-Cuban women to sell this fantasy"[256] and foregrounding the "sexually voracious *mulata* in … prominent campaigns for transnational consumers."[257] In the 1990s, "the Cuban tourist board sponsored advertising campaigns featuring dark-skinned women in bikinis to lure foreigners," and even "allowed *Playboy* to photograph topless Cuban women on the beach" for a piece on "Girls of Cuba."[258] An undeniable hypocrisy comes into view as the Cuban state betrays its reliance on "the jineteras and the legions of tourists they draw," while it simultaneously "enact[s] a regime of disciplinary violence against them to preserve its own moral superiority [and] conceal its own ambiguous relation to tourism."[259] Political scientist Michael Clancy uses the phrase "the state as pimp" to capture the Cuban government's "tacit approval" of sex tourism.[260] As Daigle sums it up, "state anxieties … and conflicted engagement with the international tourism industry [are] displaced onto the bodies of young black and mixed race women."[261]

Moral ambivalence over transactional sex structures facets of Cuban male identity, as well. The masculine term *jinetero* does not convey the identical meaning as the feminine version. Its sexual dimension is not its leading edge, but rather one of a range of services that a hustling Cuban man might provide. The term *pinguero*, on the other hand, from the word *pinga* (*dick*), denotes a male sex worker, literally *a dick worker*. A flurry of connotations accompany each term and mediate the relationship of one to the other.[262] One self-identified pinguero told anthropologist Jafari Allen, "Jineteros rip tourists off."[263] They "may sell counterfeit or stolen cigars or suggest *paladares* (restaurants) and accommodations – to which they often accompany the foreign client. Sexual contact may occur, but this is incidental to other sorts of services."[264] Pingueros, by contrast "work hard offering sex in return for clothes, a good night out … or dollars."[265] Their work is coded "nonexploitive" and "masculine" according to Allen: "theirs is an interpersonal exchange that includes the mutual pursuit of leisure en la calle"[266] (*in the street*). Pingueros reject the masculine form of *jinetera* because it "would suggest that they are penetrated by tourists."[267] They further distinguish themselves from jineteras by insisting that the sexual services they provide are "a form of friendship … not just having sex but showing off the island and other such activities."[268] Pingueros are hosts, with all the magnanimity with which a good host is endowed.

Gay porn sites (e.g., "*Cruzin for Cubans*, *Havana Bananas*, *Cocks of the Caribbean*, *Cuban Cock Tales*, and *Latin Balls*") promote the fantasy of hot Cuban macho men rearing to fuck foreigners.[269] Because "Europeans and white men from the United States 'are known to be *pasivos*' ('passive' anal partners, or 'bottoms')" the *pinguero* is coded masculine – he is the penetrator.[270] Particularly those *pingueros* who identify as heterosexual can claim not to be exploited colonial subjects, bending over for first world tourist pleasure, but "studs"[271] whose prowess and domination bring pride to individual and national identities. Cuban women who engage in transactional sex with foreign men do not benefit from this depiction – their sex is necessarily understood as "a form of imperialism."[272] Cuban men who have sex with foreign men, however, "are asserting Cuban (black) masculinity by – presumably – sexually dominating" them.[273] As Daigle explained, "men's liaisons with foreigners are seen as an affirmation of Cuban masculinity, as domination of the foreign interloper; women's, on the other hand, activate nationalist fears of invasion and defilement."[274] In reality, the ideal of Cuban men dominating foreign men does not entirely hold up; once pushed to disclose specific sexual acts, some *pingueros* admit that they do in fact submit to penetration.[275] (The incongruity between the pinguero's archetype and his concrete sexual acts will be discussed in greater detail in Chapter 4.)

Pingueros are in some cases available to penetrate foreign women, as well.[276] Some understand themselves to be homosexual, others heterosexual, and – as Stout learned from her interviews – some "responded to the fantasy of cash. They told me that they focused on the money to maintain an erection"[277] – *moneysexuals*, in effect.

According to some of Allen's interviewees, foreign gay male "bottoms" typically want dark-skinned men to dominate them, and Black *pingueros* are effectively "counting on [this] racialized objectification"[278] to ensure their source of income. Allen observed that Cubans who engage in transactional sex with white foreigners are usually "savvy about [their] role in the reproduction of exotic fantasies."[279] Their enticing racial "stock in trade,"[280] however, comes with encumbrances. The police know that many rural Cubans have moved to the cities in violation of internal migration restrictions.[281] This burden tends to fall heavily on "'strong looking black men' … [who are often] picked up by national police for loitering in tourist areas and having no legitimate business in Havana."[282]

The hardship of the Special Period subsided somewhat, especially during the presidency of Hugo Chávez in Venezuela (1999–2013), who stepped in to fill some of the needs left by the Soviet demise. While life still has not been easy for Cubans (the first Trump presidency and the COVID-19 pandemic took a severe economic toll), transactional sex cannot be said to be solely about survival all the time. Wealthy tourists routinely waltz through Havana draped in enviable commodities. As Allen vividly put it, "one cannot eat a Nike shoe, a gold chain, or a designer-label T-shirt. In the late 1990s, yumas [foreigners] paid in clothing, jewelry, and other commodities much more often than in cash."[283] A "desire to consume" aroused by Cubans' contact with tourists "is a powerful enticement to sex labor."[284] Allen notes that the opening of Cuba to tourists during the Special Period "recruited black Cuban subjects to late capitalism's global market of commodities and ideas as consumers, yet global capital also requires the consumption of black bodies."[285] In Stout's telling, "Commodity desire supplanted sexual desire in a way that guaranteed virile sexual performance, as the body became at once an item on the market and a vehicle to extract cash and commodities circulating in black markets."[286] Whether under conditions of desperate need or out of a wish to be recognized as a "cosmopolitan subject" through "commodity acquisition,"[287] transactional sex between Cubans and tourists is symbiotic and functions as what Fusco aptly described as a "theatre for the playing out of colonialism's unfinished business."[288]

To complicate matters further, *pingueros* do not serve foreigners exclusively – they provide services to Cuban men, as well. Within the confines of Cuban–Cuban sexual exchange, a complex stratification emerges. Stout went to Cuba at the start of the new century to "investigate how state-sponsored initiatives to promote gay tolerance … had had an impact on the lives of gays and lesbians."[289] When she asked Cubans about the progress of gay tolerance, interviewees "redirected the conversation to … rising inequalities and the sex trade."[290] Improvements in tolerance was "overshadowed by the rise of poverty and the return of socioeconomic disparities … [as] sexual labor in Havana [became] a defining factor of queer social life."[291] Not only had "the introduction of foreign tourism split Havana's queer social worlds between 'respectable' gays involved with the arts and those tied to [hustling] and the sex trade"[292] but relationships between *pingueros* (macho studs) and effeminate homosexual men are strained by feelings of desire, resentment, and moral judgment.

Cuban men looking to be topped by a *pinguero* are, unlike their foreign counterparts, painfully aware that the *pinguero* may have a wife or girlfriend at home.[293] His love is not authentic, but part of a "game."[294] When Cuban *pasivos* are white and affiliated with more respectable work sectors, the *pinguero* nonetheless outranks his patron by maintaining his claim to heterosexuality.[295] *Pingueros* sometimes even cruelly "denigrate[] gay men and reduce[] previously affectionate … trysts into sex for pay."[296] The "true" homosexual is left feeling disdained and betrayed.

Simultaneously, however, the patron may himself "disparage" the *pinguero* for "not working."[297] *Pingueros*, unlike the more respectable homosexuals, bear the burden of moral condemnation as "materialis[t]," "self-interest[ed]," or "taking the 'easy way out.'"[298] These judgments echo the 1960s discourse of homosexual decadence and consumerism, but with a strange gender reversal: Effeminate men rebuke masculine men with the old put-downs.

****

As Chapter 1 showed, the US and Cuba each experienced anxiety related to their mid-twentieth century geopolitical positions. They managed that anxiety with a common compulsion to expel the homosexual contaminant into a despised political–economic other. In this chapter, however, global political and economic stimuli changed, shaping new forms of progress and retrenchment for sexual and gender minorities. The US and Cuban systems have both proven capable of absorbing reform as well as deploying it for nationalist purposes. Just as each system projected the homosexual onto the other during the peak of Cold War antagonism, each now exhibits its progress as testament to the superiority of its system – and does so without any apparent concern for the intra-homosexual hierarchies produced by unequal economic conditions.

For the US, pro-gay law reform and social acceptance were enabled in part by the end of the Cold War. Legal progress took specific forms that were amenable to neoliberal privatization trends and have contributed to massive racial, economic, and gendered inequalities within the lgbtq population. Highly visible advances, culminating in a constitutional right to same-sex marriage, nonetheless serve as evidence of the triumph of US liberalism as compared with rival systems.

Rights assertions had little to do with social or legal advances in Cuba, which historically lacked a liberal rights consciousness and eschewed anything resembling US-style identity-based claims. Under Cuban socialism, progress for sexual and gender minorities has not been driven by impact litigation, grassroots organizing, or corporate sector initiative. Legal reform did not rely on rights to assembly, free speech, or privacy, or occur under an equality-seeking banner of identity. Emancipatory advances were "*granted* by the benevolent state – rather than *won* … and only on the Revolution's terms."[299]

Those terms were health and education – two areas of extraordinary Cuban achievement – and they led to limited forms of depathologization, decriminalization, and inclusion. Health and education advances have been well-distributed – including by near-elimination of racial disparity in life expectancy and infant mortality – notwithstanding vestigial racial biases in Cuban culture. Moreover, sexual education programming, proliferated across the island, casts homosexual tolerance as tied to the socialist value of human fulfillment. "Inside Cuba … the Revolution is typically perceived not as a single moment or epoch, but as an ongoing process."[300] Homosexual emancipation can accordingly be trumpeted as a triumph of the Revolution.

Still, the hardships of the Special Period[301] revived inequalities that had somewhat abated during the early decades of socialism as Cuba was forced by the breakup of the Soviet Union to make ideological compromises: opening itself to new markets and introducing international tourism. That tourism, in turn, brought sexual commerce back into the foreground of homosexual existence, deepening the nationalistic need to repel the contamination that it represents. If sexual commerce went unaddressed, one young Cuban told Daigle, "our beautiful little Cuba would go back to being called the great brothel of America … because there was no whore or fag in the world more prized than the whores and fags of this country."[302]

The imperative to crack down on sexual commerce surfaced racial and other hierarchical fissures within Cuba, stratifying the Cuban population as a whole and the homosexual subpopulation specifically, and generating new anxieties about love, sex, survival, and consumerism. Even as CENESEX pursues its agenda of tolerance and care, part of the homosexual and gender-variant population continues to be fervently policed and to face official and unofficial condemnation as hopelessly contrary to socialist values. Mariela may lead congas with the slogan *Socialism yes, homophobia no!*,[303] and foreign investors may feel reassured by Cuba's increasing tolerance of its sexual and gender minorities, but a combination of economic hardship, desire for commodities, and police surveillance eclipse these positive steps for those on the bottom rungs.

Finally, law – as both governmental regulation and self-governance –proves itself a byproduct of evolving historical conditions, as the global and local mutually inflect one another. Identity, meaning, and moral struggle develop under economic and political constraints, which are themselves dynamic and inconsistent. This genealogy sets the stage upon which same-sex marriage, examined in Part II, came to Cuba.

PART II

Then Comes Marriage

3

Marriage, Property, and a Hustle

THEN COMES MARRIAGE

Fidel Castro died in Havana in 2016 at the age of ninety. The extent of his psychic dominance over Cuban political life for nearly half a century cannot be overstated. He was not just a politician but also a hero and father figure. On a trip to Cuba in the fall of 2022, I visited El Centro Fidel Castro, a museum located in the Vedado neighborhood of Havana. It is the most unrestrained and unironic paean to a single individual I have ever seen. Exhibits highlight Fidel's military prowess, including artifacts from the guerilla war he waged from the Sierra Maestra and endless cycling through video coverage of his combat acumen during the 1961 Bay of Pigs invasion (on a southwestern beach that gives the events their Cuban name: *Playa Girón*). Along with the expected photographs (e.g., Fidel with Nelson Mandela, Fidel standing before the Lincoln Memorial, Fidel welcoming home little Elián González[1]) were articles of his clothing and weaponry and a model of the Granma – the vessel by which he and dozens of other rebel fighters arrived from Mexico to launch their attack on the Batista regime. Even outside the walls of El Centro, though, Fidel's image and quotations adorn buildings, roadside signs, and other surfaces across the Cuban landscape.

Fidel served as prime minister of Cuba from 1959 until 1976, then as president until 2008. In ill-health, he then relinquished his office to his brother, Raúl, who occupied the position for a decade. Fidel remained First Secretary of the Central Committee of the Communist Party until 2011, again followed by Raúl, who served in that position until 2021. Raúl was succeeded as both president and First Secretary by Cuba's current leader, Miguel Díaz-Canel, the first person in over sixty years to rule without benefit of the mythic Castro name.

As Chapter 2 explained, the dire conditions of the 1990s "Special Period" demanded some concessions in the direction of economic liberalization in Cuba. Fidel was a reluctant liberalizer, maintaining the tightest possible reins on the economy even as he admitted some private enterprise and foreign capital into the country. But once Fidel's physical decline compelled him to yield his authority, Cuba's evolution quietly accelerated.

It was already the case that international tourism had supplanted sugar as Cuba's leading industry. It was already the case that foreign corporations were invested in luxury resort hotels along the Cuban coastline. It was already the case that everyday Cubans were running side hustles to survive, doing everything from selling shampoo and t-shirts to running *paladares* (in-home restaurants) out of their kitchens. But in the new millennium, under first Raúl's and then Díaz-Canel's stewardships, the role of private enterprise, domestic as well as international, was further legitimized and expanded. Small, native businesses – now licensed and taxed – proliferated. Foreign corporations doing business in Cuba gained increasingly favorable legal conditions. Cuba changed its housing law to permit the rudiments of a real estate market to form. As presidential decrees, legislation, judicial orders, and constitutional revisions gradually shifted Cuba in the direction of privatization and markets – and all this with the dawning of internet access – some Cubans – just *some* – began to accumulate wealth and cohere into a recognizable middle class.

At the same time that Cuba was undergoing these dramatic economic changes, gay rights were gaining rapid momentum globally. Key international documents such as the 2017 Yogyakarta Principles (setting forth human rights based on sexual orientation and gender identity) linked anti-discrimination to familial rights such as marriage.[2] Beginning with the Netherlands (2000), Belgium (2003), Canada (2005), and Spain (2005) – the latter two of which have been crucial to both tourism and investment in Cuba – same-sex marriage spread across Europe, the Americas, and beyond.[3] Argentina became the first country in Latin America to legalize same-sex marriage in 2010; Uruguay, Brazil, Colombia, Ecuador, Costa Rica, Chile, and Mexico followed over the next twelve years.[4] In 2018, both the European Court of Justice and the Inter-American Court of Human Rights (covering twenty member states in Latin America and the Caribbean – though not Cuba) determined gay marriage to be a right.[5]

As this chapter explains, marriage has long been held in relatively low esteem in Cuba, notwithstanding an ill-advised government campaign starting in the 1960s to improve marriage's appeal to its population. The plan backfired, reducing marriage to one among any number of hustles in which ordinary Cubans engage to gain access to scarce goods. Still, in 2022, Cubans voted in a national referendum by a margin of nearly 2-to-1 to join the growing number of countries that recognize marriages between two people of the same sex.

This chapter delves into the legal details of marriage in Cuba as it evolved during the revolutionary period. It also examines changes to adjacent areas of law governing housing, property, employment, and foreign investment. These legal fields all affect the potential for Cubans to acquire savings. As access to wealth among ordinary Cubans increased, it might have rendered marriage – understood as a mechanism for holding and distributing property – more important. Cuban family law, however, simultaneously evolved to treat nonmarital, cohabiting couples more or less the same as married couples (for pragmatic, if-you-can't-beat'em-join'em reasons).

This had the effect of draining marriage of much of its legal and practical import. Strange, then, that when same-sex marriage was on the ballot, marriage as an ideal suddenly recovered some of its lost force.

OVERVIEW OF CUBAN LAWMAKING AND ADJUDICATION

In Cuba, the Asamblea Nacional del Poder Popular (National Assembly for People's Power, or just National Assembly) is responsible for passing legislation. Members are elected to five-year terms. Because Cuba is a single-party system, the National Assembly is constituted entirely by members of the Partido Comunista de Cuba (Communist Party of Cuba, or PCC) which develops the policies that the legislators pursue. The National Assembly maintains the authority to interpret the Constitution for itself with no judicial check. Proposed laws are generally the product of deliberation by field-specific commissions prior to being put before the full National Assembly. Ordinary laws require a majority vote while constitutional amendments require a two-thirds supermajority. The process for amending the constitution in Cuba requires a vote of the National Assembly in all cases and a national referendum where constitutional rights are affected.[6] A subset of National Assembly members elected by the whole constitute a Council of State that can issue decree-laws while the full Assembly is out of session.[7]

From the perspective of a US-based reader, the prohibition against participation by competing political parties combined with the more general restrictions on dissent in Cuba contain a strong suggestion of authoritarianism.[8] Without minimizing the significance of these limits on political participation, the picture is more complicated. Law in Cuba is developed through a deep consultative process with the people via their trade unions, professional associations, workplaces, and (neighborhood-based) CDRs, often trickling up and down and up and down again prior to going before the National Assembly for a vote.[9]

The president can issue decrees and orders and an administrative apparatus can issue regulations consistent with laws passed by the National Assembly. A Council of Ministers composed of the heads of the executive departments can issue regulations and decrees to implement legislation.[10] Provincial and municipal bodies can enact local ordinances that conform with national legislation, as well.[11]

Cuba's judicial system utilizes a combination of professional and lay judges[12] and includes some specialized courts. It is multi-layered with the Tribunal Supremo Popular (People's Supreme Court) at the top. The top court's members are chosen by the National Assembly for five-year terms. The Court's job is to ensure uniform application of the laws both by serving as an appellate court of last resort and by issuing binding interpretations and instructions to lower courts. It cannot, however, strike down legislation passed by the National Assembly or declare laws unconstitutional; it can determine only whether administrative regulations and decrees are consistent with laws passed by the National Assembly.[13]

SAME-SEX MARRIAGE IN THE CONSTITUTION AND CODE

Same-sex marriage initially came before the National Assembly as a constitutional provision. Its defeat as Article 68 of Cuba's 2018 draft constitution attested to the then-recent rise in the influence of conservative religious forces.

In the early decades of the Revolution, Cuba, like the Soviet Union, was officially atheist; the Catholic Church was politically marginalized and associated with counter-revolution.[14] Cuba began allowing abortions in limited cases (determined necessary by physicians) in 1965 notwithstanding Church opposition, extending the general right to terminate a pregnancy to women in 1979 (soon after the establishment of GNTES – see Chapter 2).[15] Devoted Catholics were among those most inclined to flee Cuba in the early years of the Revolution,[16] weakening the Church as a contender for the people's loyalty. Santería and other African-influenced religious traditions were present, though they did not represent the rival that a large, institutional religion presents to state authority.

According to law professor José Gabilondo, "Fidel Castro and the Party softened their anti-religious stance" during the 1980s[17] (around the same time, as Chapter 2 recounts, as the Mariel boatlift and the onset of the HIV/AIDS epidemic). In 1992, after the demise of the Soviet Union, a constitutional change took Cuba from officially *atheist* to *secular*, signaling a modicum of increased tolerance.[18] A papal visit in 1998 produced something of a détente between the Church and the revolutionary regime, whereby Pope John Paul II moderated his human rights criticisms of Cuba while church officials in-country were extended greater freedom.[19] Then, in 2015, Pope Francis and Raúl Castro met at the Vatican where Raúl declared, "I promise to go to all his Masses, and with satisfaction .... I read all the speeches of the pope, his commentaries, and if the pope continues this way, I will go back to praying and go back to the church. I'm not joking."[20]

Notwithstanding this warming of relations, most Cubans do not feel obligated to follow Church doctrine when it comes to ceremonial wedlock or the injunction against divorce. According to anthropologist Heidi Härkönen, who conducted an in-depth study of life cycle events in Cuba, baptism is, by comparison to ceremonial marriage, much more prevalent, and the differential can be attributed to overlapping Santería practices as well as to a Cuban affinity for godparenting relationships.[21] In the single year 2009, Härkönen reports, Havana saw 101,755 Church-involved baptisms compared with a mere 359 Church-involved weddings.[22] The Church did perform death rituals, but Härkönen found that this, too, reflected an overlap with Santería, in which the living communicate with the dead.[23]

Should the Catholic Church care to look over its shoulder, it will see Evangelical Christianity gaining on it. "An estimated seven to ten percent of Cubans are Protestant or Evangelical."[24] Moreover, it was Evangelical forces, with the benefit of millions of dollars from US-based churches, that flexed their muscle and halted inclusion of Article 68, which would have eliminated from the constitution the sex-specificity of partners to a civil marriage as well as language restricting same-sex parenting.[25]

The 2018 draft constitution was commissioned by President Díaz-Canel; he and the Communist Party supported Article 68's inclusion.[26] Prior to the National Assembly vote, the draft was submitted to the people for consultation; it was at this juncture, reports Gabilondo, that "conflicts between churches and sexual minorities" erupted.[27] According to one report, "Methodist, Baptist, and Pentecostal churches" organized a campaign that pushed the Cuban government to remove Article 68 prior to final adoption.[28] In an unusual display of grassroots organizing, Evangelicals gathered signatures, canvassed neighborhoods, and delivered "coordinated messaging" at community meetings at which the Article was discussed.[29] The Catholic Church opposed the Article, as well. Along with references to Genesis and assertions of a divine warrant for restricting marriage to heterosexual couples, the Archdiocese of Santiago "alleg[ed] that it was foreign imperialism … behind the support for marriage equality."[30]

Article 68 of the draft was ultimately replaced in the ratified 2019 Constitution by Article 82, which, by omitting any reference to sex and stating that "[t]he law determines how [marriages] are constituted,"[31] effectively kicked the question of same-sex marriage down the road to an anticipated revision of the Family Code. While religious forces managed to prevent same-sex marriage from being guaranteed constitutionally, their influence appears to have run out as the 2022 Family Code approached referendum.

The previous version of the Family Code had been enacted in 1975.[32] Among its primary objectives was to equalize women and men, avoiding family's performance of "a counter-revolutionary role by providing the means of continuing old inequalities and impeding the acquisition of the new socialist morality and mentality."[33] Most notably, it mandated that men share in the housework and parenting.[34] As Cuban family law professor Ana María Álvarez-Tabío Albo explains,

> The principle of absolute equality between men and women governs the personal sphere of the legal-conjugal relationship. The wife does not owe obedience to the husband, nor is she obligated to follow him wherever he establishes his residence; nor is the husband protector of the woman. Both do maintain consideration and due respect, and help each other mutually. Partnership is established in domestic roles, assigning economic value to domestic work.[35]

Genuine equality between men and women in domestic responsibility is widely understood to be imperfect and largely unenforceable but nonetheless symbolically important.[36] Moreover, by formally disclaiming sex-specific domestic responsibilities, the 1975 code could be said to have laid some of the groundwork for what was to come in 2022.

The 2022 Family Code[37] does much more than legalize same-sex marriage. New provisions address matters as wide-ranging as multi-parenting,[38] progressive autonomy for youth,[39] prevention of domestic violence,[40] care for the elderly and disabled,[41] and the order of surnames.[42] Article 201, however, authorizing same-sex marriage, garnered much of the attention.[43] The new code also makes adoption newly available to cohabiting couples, whether same-or different-sex.[44] Gay and lesbian *individuals* were permitted to adopt under the old law, but a couple had to be married to adopt a child together under the 1975 Code,[45] effectively excluding same-sex couples.[46] "Stranger" adoption (as opposed to step-parent adoption) is rare in Cuba so the prohibition had little practical effect.[47] The new code also sets forth new provisions to govern surrogacy that prohibit payment or contracts between strangers and permit only those surrogacy arrangements based on altruism.[48] This section was not specifically addressed to same-sex couples though it provides a new avenue to parenting for gay men.

HETEROSEXUAL MARRIAGE AND DIVORCE IN REVOLUTIONARY CUBA

Judging by heterosexual practices, marriage is not highly valued in Cuba. For most of the revolutionary period, it has held minimal social significance and just a handful of legal benefits.

In the early decades of the revolutionary era, weddings were not uncommon, in part because when the state had more resources, it incentivized marriage by granting newlyweds a modest gift, such as brief honeymoon in one of the hotels generally reserved for tourists, some rum or beer, a cake, or an appliance at a discounted price.[49] This practice largely disappeared around 1990 as austerity became more or less the norm.

Before the Revolution, some wealthy Cubans threw lavish Catholic weddings. Those of means and religiosity, however, were the most inclined to leave the island in the early 1960s.[50] Cubans who stayed were more likely to be found in cohabiting relationships.[51] The revolutionary regime made early efforts to encourage formalization – holding "collective weddings" (in addition to granting wedding gifts)[52] – but eventually gave up and began according "long-term consensual unions the same legal status as marriage."[53] According to Álvarez-Tabío, if a "union was never legalized and one of the partners dies or abandons the relationship … it falls to the other partner to make a claim urging the court to recognize that union from its beginning to the date of termination, with the same civil effects."[54]

Among those who do undertake a ceremonial wedding, most are reluctant[55] or unable to spend the kind of money that would be required for an extravagant affair, though foreigners sometimes throw "destination weddings" in Cuba, so the extravagances have not always been unavailable.[56] A bare civil ceremony costs very little and takes a matter of minutes. Härkönen found that Cubans attributed no real significance to formalization.[57]

Though birth control is free,[58] abortion occurs at a high rate,[59] as does teen pregnancy. Like divorce, single motherhood is common and not subject to social sanction[60] perhaps in part because the Cuban guarantee of gender equality in employment combined with "subsidised child care [and] paid maternity leave"[61] reduces women's dependency on having a husband.[62] Cuban law makes no distinction between children born in and out of wedlock; a civil registry records parentage.[63]

Fear of divorce poses no barrier to marriage; divorce is easy, quick, and inexpensive.[64] The divorce rate in Revolutionary Cuba has historically been quite high, with estimates consistently coming in above 50 percent (and not reflecting the incidence of multiple divorces per person).[65] Cuba leads Latin America in divorce and places among the highest rates of divorce in the world; it is not unusual for Cubans in their thirties to have married and divorced three times already.[66] Some Cubans confess to having married multiple partners consecutively to take advantage of the incentives that the government used to provide – probably another reason that the incentive program evaporated.[67]

The 1975 Family Code used spare terms to allocate property upon divorce.[68] As is typical of a community property regime, property acquired during the marriage by earnings was joint property and divided evenly upon divorce, while property owned by one partner prior to the marriage or acquired via inheritance during the marriage was considered solely owned.[69] Article 41 (of the old code) permitted the person taking care of the children to continue *using* common property as long as the children were minors.[70] Most Cubans do not own much, so there has typically been little to fight over on divorce.[71]

The 2022 Family Code does not alter the basic community property arrangement though it fleshes it out with substantial additional detail.[72] For example, specific rules now address the liquidation and distribution of a family business.[73]

Housing in Cuba is notoriously tight. It is not uncommon for multiple generations to occupy small apartments with makeshift "walls" to create rooms. Another consequence of the housing crunch is that, while obtaining an official divorce is easy, physically separating can be difficult. "Estranged Cuban couples sometimes remain under the same roof for years or even lifetimes," because they cannot find additional housing.[74]

Historically, alimony on divorce has been extremely limited. The relevant provision in the 1975 Code provided as follows:

> If the spouses have lived together for more than one year or had children during the marriage, the tribunal will award alimony to one of them in the following cases: (1) to the spouse that does not have a paying job and lacks other means of sustenance (this type of alimony is provisional and will be payable to the other spouse for six months if there are no minor children being taken care of by the receiving spouse or for one year if there are such minor children, so that the receiving spouse can obtain a paying job); and (2) to a spouse which, as a result of incapacity, age, illness or other insurmountable impediment, is unable to work and lacks other means of [sustenance]. In this case, the alimony will continue as long as the obstacle persists.[75]

Cuba strives to keep unemployment rates low (though a government salary might be insufficient for self-support) and many Cubans reside with extended families, limiting the impact of the rule requiring alimony to an unemployed former spouse with no other means of sustenance; alimony for an unemployed former spouse would be severely time-limited in any event. The children of divorced couples typically remain with their mother and if a parent does move out, it is most often the father even though the apartment might belong to him.[76] Härkönen found that few women found it worth the hassle of seeking a court order for support of minor children.[77] With regard to Cubans with disabilities, many will already be receiving a social security payment, particularly if they became disabled as a result of work or military service, obviating the alimony requirement in that case, as well. The 2022 Family Code does not substantially alter alimony rules.[78]

Under the 2022 Code, the rules governing what Cuban law refers to as "affective de facto unions"[79] closely track those applicable to married couples. If parties who have been together for at least two years would be eligible to marry, then one party need only seek formal recognition.[80] The new law added flexibility to account for the diversity of arrangements nonmarital partners were already employing informally.[81] Partners to an affective de facto union may now set the economic terms of their partnership for the duration of the relationship or they can rely on default terms that mimic marriage.[82] Upon the death of one partner, the survivor benefits from the same inheritance rules as would a surviving spouse.[83] If the couple terminates its union while both partners are still living, the 2022 Code distributes assets according to terms that read like the functional equivalent of a standard community property regime.[84] Under the 1975 Family Code, such protections were available only to heterosexual couples because only heterosexual couples were "eligible" to marry.[85] The 2022 version eliminates this barrier. In effect, then, the 2022 Family Code not only clears the way for same-sex couples to marry but also for them to *not* marry.[86]

Cuban social provisions such as health care, education, and public salaries do not depend on marital ties. On death, surviving spouses may gain access to a survivor's pension; eligibility depends on age, the spouse's own pension, and the work history of the decedent.[87] Inheritance can be by intestacy, in which case a spouse is an heir along with descendants and forebears,[88] or by devise, in which case a spouse is a "specially protected heir" along with descendants and forebears and can take a forced share *if* that person is unable to work and was financially dependent on the decedent.[89] The meaning of "spouse" for purposes of the law of succession is determined by the Family Code, which means it includes a nonmarital partner who obtains judicial recognition of the previously informal relationship.[90]

In sum, heterosexual marriage has been of limited significance in Revolutionary Cuba. Its social meaning is insubstantial. Divorce – even multiple times – is commonplace and without stigma. Abortion is easily accessed while single motherhood is unremarkable. Legitimacy has no bearing on children's rights. Because the overwhelming number of relevant laws apply to nonmarital couples provided only they obtain recognition if and when the need arises, marriage has few implications for public benefits or private asset allocation. In fact, the most important benefit of same-sex marriage might actually be eligibility for similar treatment for couples in nonmarital, de facto affective unions. The benefits of marriage are not nil but neither do they seem an adequate explanation for the push for same-sex marriage.[91]

How much do same-sex couples in Cuba stand to gain by being granted access to an institution for which most heterosexuals have had so little regard? If the few benefits accruing to married couples were really the issue, Cuba has proven itself quite capable of redistributing resources without relying on the mechanism of marriage.

Cuba made the decision to grant same-sex couples entrance into a status that by most accounts is of little value among the majority of those who have always had access to it. It is not obvious, therefore, why same-sex marriage came about as a legal priority, especially in the context of Cubans' other needs and even exigencies.

EVOLUTION IN CUBAN PROPERTY LAW, SELF-EMPLOYMENT, AND FOREIGN INVESTMENT

In the early years of the Revolution, Fidel's new government took sweeping action to redistribute real property.[92] It confiscated the property of Batista supporters[93] and deemed the property belonging to those who fled the Revolution "abandoned."[94] With the Agrarian Reform Act, enacted right out of the gate, the new regime appropriated or broke up large farms.[95] The government nationalized US-owned businesses,[96] and soon thereafter, Cuban-owned businesses.[97]

In 1960, the government passed the Urban Reform Law, which nullified leases and divested landlords of title, awarding them compensation.[98] According to a Brookings report by Philip Peters, president of the Cuba Research Center, "private rental of housing came to an end" on the grounds "that housing is for people to live in, not live from."[99] The government slashed rents and created a "rent-to-own" system that resulted in the eventual transfer of ownership to many tenants.[100]

Seventeen years into Fidel's forty-nine-year reign, in 1976, Cuba ratified a new constitution.[101] It abandoned constitutional protections for private property and affirmed the proposition that property "belong[s] to the entire people of Cuba."[102]

A General Housing Law in 1984 granted more Cubans a rent-to-own path for state-owned housing[103] and a 1997 revision reinstituted private rental arrangements.[104] In rare instances, the government authorized private sales of homes, but this went from limited to entirely prohibited in 2003.[105] From then until 2011, the rights encompassed in the title to one's home were limited to "liv[ing] in it, improv[ing] it (with government permission), pass[ing] it to heirs, or "swap[ping] it for another" residence of similar value.[106] The housing swaps, known as *permutas* (barters), became such a cultural touchstone that a popular movie, *Se Permuta*,[107] satirized the system. According to Peters, people looking to swap homes in Havana convened at a widely known location on Paseo de Prado, a busy street and promenade on the edge of Old Havana, to arrange trades, or even "chains of transactions to satisfy multiple parties."[108] If one home were deemed more valuable than the other in an exchange, the parties were not legally permitted to agree to a cash payment on the side, though this rule was routinely circumvented and even some entirely cash transactions occurred under the table.[109] As you might imagine, this system was not going to bode well for producing a reliable chain of title.

In 2011, three years into Raúl's presidency, Decree-Law 288 put the swap-only system to rest, granting Cubans the right to buy and sell homes for a privately negotiated price or to arrange a swap with an accompanying payment to account for a value differential.[110] The government's objective was to ameliorate the housing crisis by giving people with more room than they needed an incentive to sell to those who needed more space.[111] People who downsized were in a position to pocket the difference between their sale and purchase, establishing some savings. The law instituted rules for transferring and registering title as well as for reasonable taxation.[112] This legal change enabled the rudiments of a real estate market to emerge.

Real estate brokers, who had operated illegally under the pre-2011 swap regime, are now able to function in a newly authorized form of self-employment.[113] In addition, some people still gather at Paseo de Prado to find deals, some turn to websites resembling Craigslist,[114] and some respond to signs as shown in Figure 3.1 advertising a flat available for swap. Pricing is highly variable and done without benefit of a publicly accessible record of sales.[115]

Mortgages remain illegal in Cuba,[116] resulting, according to Peters, in a limited pool of purchasers: those who have a home to sell, those who receive remittances from relatives abroad, and farmers or entrepreneurs who have managed to amass some savings.[117] Cuba does issue some loans for improvement or construction, but a home may not serve as collateral.[118]

The 2011 housing reforms make it possible for Cubans to convert their homes into savings.[119] Still, important restrictions remain. Foreigners are barred from participating; Cuba does not want individuals from wealthier jurisdictions to start buying up Cuban housing.[120] Cubans are limited to owning two homes (a primary residence and a vacation home); they may rent out a spare room but – under the 2019 constitution – this could transform the category of the property from "personal" to "private," imposing additional constraints;[121] they may not borrow against their homes; they must somehow acquire the full purchase price (a bar to market entry for many); and they must have title to make a sale.

This last requirement – after years of housing swaps and under-the-table deals – can be a difficult hurdle, but the 2011 law provided fresh incentive to homeowners to sort out title and registration. According to one Cuban attorney, before 2011, "nobody wanted to legalize their property, but now they do. The problem is, those

FIGURE 3.1 A sign in Old Havana advertising an apartment available for swap.

who bought materials illegally – before the government authorized selling them – and built their homes and now have no legal document, what do they do now?"[122] This is just one example of the kind of difficulty a homeowner may face.

The People's Supreme Court ameliorated some of the obstacles to establishing title in 2013. The facts giving rise to the case occurred in 1998. Bertha Lina Bouly Wilson married Ricardo Andux Barrueta. Bertha and Ricardo were not in love, not expecting a child, not religious, not sexual partners, not even friends. They married because Bertha wanted to buy Ricardo's home at a time when real estate purchases were severely limited. To circumvent the legal obstacles, the two arranged to marry and promptly divorce. According to their plan, Bertha would get the apartment in a staged divorce settlement and Ricardo would get the cash amount on which they had agreed as a purchase price, then they would go their separate ways having effectively concluded a sale.[123] This was apparently a common practice in Cuba prior to 2011, though it is impossible to know precisely how often it occurred. Cubans used this workaround to sell cars, as well, the sale of which was also restricted.[124]

Ricardo, however, did not follow through on his end of the deal. He attempted to force Bertha out of the apartment for which she had effectively paid. The swindled "buyer" sued. The lower courts were initially unresponsive to Bertha's plight, given her participation in a brazen scheme to evade the law. After 2011, however, she found relief in the Supreme Court, which ordered that her name replace that of the "seller" on the title document, despite the transaction having been illegal at the time it was conducted. With a follow-up missive to the lower courts, this decision effectively smoothed the way to legal title for people who had creatively circumvented the pre-2011 prohibitions.[125]

The expansion of rights in real property seen in 2011 was among the most significant changes undertaken upon Fidel's withdrawal from the seat of power, but it was not the only one. Two other areas of economic regulation have been key: legitimation of hundreds of forms of self-employment and the constantly changing rules governing foreign investment.

During Fidel's reign, the overwhelming majority of Cubans were in the employ of the state, earning a government salary.[126] Raúl, in a moment of extreme economic hardship characterized by public sector layoffs, radically expanded the permissibility of self-employment and entrepreneurship. Cubans may now apply for self-employment licenses, or *trabajadores cuentapropistas* (TCPs) enabling them to work in any among hundreds of professions.[127] More recently, Cuba has begun to allow medium, small, and microenterprises (MSMEs) to organize as Limited Liability Companies (LLCs).[128] These openings, like the real estate market, have contributed to the emergence of a Cuban middle class.

Licensure fees and some taxes remain burdensome, ensuring that many people will continue to operate in the informal market and thereby exacerbating stratification between Cubans who have access to start-up capital and those who do not. As is the case with home ownership, Cubans receiving remittances from family members living abroad are in the best position to enter the formal market, leaving others, especially Afro-Cubans who are far less likely to benefit from this income source, to struggle in the informal sector.[129] Further, while the Cuban government continues to provide social insurance for private sector workers, there is some uncertainty whether labor protections and anti-discrimination rules are uniformly applied.[130]

Government support for the nascent enterprises has been inconsistent. According to one report, "between early 2013 and 2017, Cuba had approved 439 nonagricultural cooperatives, authorizing these privately managed associations to provide construction, retail, transportation, and other key economic services," and "nonstate businesses came to account for almost a third of national employment."[131] Reversal of President Barack Obama's US-Cuban thaw by the first Trump administration, however, prompted a retreat. President Díaz-Canel imposed all sorts of hostile encumbrances on small businesses, such as a requirement that they keep three months' worth of taxes on hand in an account.[132]

After the conclusion of the first Trump presidency and in response to the economic exigencies in the tourism sector imposed by the COVID-19 pandemic, the Cuban government slackened the reins on self-employment again. Until 2021, the government maintained a finite list of *permitted* fields of self-employment; that has since been reversed: It now publishes a list of *prohibitions*.[133] A vast array of professionals, from home remodelers to hairdressers, sell their services in the formal economy. The biggest sectors, according to Cuban professor and business consultant Riury Rodríguez Lorenzo, are "[c]ooperatives and independent farmers," who "are responsible for around 80% of the country's agricultural production,"[134] along with bed-and-breakfasts (*casas particulares*), in-home restaurants (*paladares*), private taxi services, and small construction businesses.[135]

Small regulatory changes have granted private firms some breathing room.[136] For example, because so many of the supplies needed to engage in commerce are obtained informally, accounting to the government for their procurement can be a challenge. One modestly helpful measure permits "justification of [only] 80% of those expenses,"[137] effectively recognizing and accommodating the difficulty of acquisitions in the above-ground economy.

Entrepreneurs have long been stymied by the prohibition against accepting foreign investment.[138] Foreign capital has been pouring into Cuba for decades now – since the adaptations of the Special Period – but it has been confined to joint ventures with state-held operations.[139] Over the years, the Cuban government has evidenced ambivalence between trying to foster favorable conditions for foreign investment and maintaining its grip on matters such as hiring and how long contracts with investors should run before requiring renewal.[140] Still, foreign corporations (European, Asian, Canadian, and Latin American) are now invested not only in tourism, but also in rum, tobacco, nickel mining, biotech, and other industries. Individual Cuban entrepreneurs, however, have generally been ineligible to benefit from this inflow[141] … until recently.

In 2022, Cuba issued new rules redefining who is an eligible domestic investor.[142] The new rules represent a slight relaxing of constraints, though they do not quite fling the doors open. The government permits investment selectively, distinguishing between retail and wholesale, joint ventures and whole ownership, and so on. Cuban economist Omar Everleny told Reuters that the "announcements were full of words such as 'exceptions, control, conditions.'"[143]

Still, the changes have the potential to bring Cuban entrepreneurs more capital, business "know how," supplies, and export markets.[144] This business growth, according to Professor of International Political Economy Richard Feinberg, is yet another factor fostering the development of a middle class.[145]

In sum, Cuba's economic changes, halting to be sure, have accelerated since Fidel's exit and some segments of the Cuban population have genuinely begun to experience the benefits of economic liberalization. Cubans are establishing businesses, buying and selling real estate, accruing new forms of property, and formalizing title.

These increasing opportunities for wealth accumulation could lead one to surmise that marriage in Cuba would naturally acquire new significance as a mechanism for holding and distributing real estate, savings, and other ownership interests. Marriage is many things (an expression of love and commitment, a religious sacrament, etc.) but to the dispassionate legal mind, it is foremost a distributive mechanism, variously aiding in public welfare systems as well as private asset allocation. The combined changes affecting property ownership, self-employment, entrepreneurship, and foreign investment, as well as the consequent formation of a nascent middle class, set a stage upon which marriage *could* stand to gain new relevance.

MARRIAGE AS A HUSTLE

Then again, why would it? Under some legal regimes, one might sensibly assume that increasing property interests would foster a renewed regard for marriage and the felt need for same-sex couples to gain access to it. In Cuba, however, same-sex couples did not require access to marriage to manage new wealth. On the contrary; the connection between asset allocation and marriage is not a necessary one in fact in Cuba; post hoc recognition of affective de facto unions and the application of marital protections to the unmarried suffices as a technical matter. This strongly suggests the involvement of other, perhaps less obvious, factors behind the push for same-sex marriage.

The last section of this chapter proposes a partial theory. (A second partial theory follows in Chapter 4.) Even where marriage is not technically necessary for property management, it could nevertheless accumulate discursive meaning. In particular, the Cuban government, wittingly or unwittingly, used law to promote the perception of an association between property and marriage, and that perception outlived its accuracy.

To formulate this argument, the work of law professor and expert in family law, sexuality, and the Caribbean Aníbal Rosario-Lebrón proves helpful. Rosario-Lebrón wrote a 2013 article to shed light on marriage's astonishing resilience (in general, not specifically in the Cuban context).[146] He proposed that "family-normativity" with the preeminence of the marital couple at its core functions as a "hegemonic discourse,"[147] in the Gramscian[148] sense – that is, as an example of ideological domination internalized as "common sense."[149] Application of the Gramscian conception means considering the power of marriage as an *ideal*, notwithstanding its negligible distributional load in Cuba.

The theory is difficult, perhaps impossible, to prove empirically, but a key episode in the history of Cuban marriage law and practice not only renders it plausible but makes the Gramscian model especially salient. Starting in the 1960s, the revolutionary regime tried, against the country's cultural tide, to incentivize formal marriage. It offered immediate, tangible rewards, but eventually gave up on the futile practice as the end of the 1980s brought austerity to the island. The incentives had effects, just not the ones the government likely intended.

As Chapter 2 explains, the term *la lucha* (literally, *the fight* or *the struggle*) has come to stand in Cuba for a life of perpetual hustle: a kind of nationalist pride in resourcefulness, including broad acceptance of the need to circumvent or exploit the law to survive waves of economic hardship. The campaign to encourage marriage was expertly metabolized by this trademark national capacity.

In response to state marriage incentives, Cubans married – often multiple times – to obtain an appliance, dishware, a few nights in a hotel, or even a case of beer. They married to effectuate an otherwise illegal sale of real estate or a car. Hamilton tells the story of a woman who maintained a relationship (unclear whether it was formalized) with a prison inmate as part of a deal whereby she could live in his house in exchange for regular conjugal visits, including the provision of sex and home cooked food.[150]

The material incentives were effective in propelling Cubans to enter into marriages, but not quite as the government anticipated. The measures were meant presumably to spur proliferation of formal, stable unions for a mixture of moral and administrative reasons, but instead they lent Cubans tools that they could deploy as part of la lucha – that is, *instrumentally*, and (*contra* the marriage ideal) *repeatedly*, undermining the very stability the regime sought to produce. Economic concerns no doubt animate marriage decisions the world over, but Cubans raised the gaming of these enticements to an art form, draining marriage of ideals such as sanctity and permanence. The material benefits, from washing machines to beer, de-romanticized and de-sacralized marriage for at least some Cubans even while temporarily producing concrete legal ties between marriage and property.

Such an incentive program would have entrenched a perception of marriage as a regime of property or benefits and could easily lead sympathetic Cubans to imagine that access to marriage was critical to treating gays and lesbians equally. If there is anything to the theory, same-sex marriage would have scaled the priority list for advancing the interests of gays and lesbians due at least in part to the Cuban government's having effectively fastened marriage to a fresh array of benefits, reenforcing a discursive association that would outlast the benefits' themselves.

Complicating this theory, however, is the fact that whatever hegemony marriage might have attained as a result of the incentive campaign, it coexists with marriage's popular *de*valuation. That is, the incentive campaign simultaneously furthered the association between property and marriage (i.e., sending the message that marriage is important) *and* diminished marriage's prestige (i.e., it's just a temporary hustle; once the incentives become unavailable, who needs it?).

Turning back to Rosario-Lebrón's broader discussion of marriage's nonregulatory force, he explains that in the Gramscian framework, an "interregnum" period occurs when a "hegemonic discourse … start[s] to lose its supremacy and [a] counter-hegemonic discourse" emerges.[151] A hegemony and counter-hegemony, therefore, can co-exist, and struggle. One version of "common sense as domination" does not supplant another in a single swoop.[152]

Moreover, a specific dynamic occurs between the competing forces. The "counter-hegemon"[153] functions as an agent of "demystification,"[154] undermining the existing hegemon. One possible form of demystification, Rosario-Lebrón notes, is "irony towards one's local practices and institutions."[155]

Irony as a form of anti-hegemonic resistance is familiar to readers in queer and postmodern social theory. A classic example is feminist theorist Judith Butler's endorsement of drag.[156] Drag functions in Butler's work to dramatize femininity, serving it up for critique. Drag queens are not trying to "pass" as women; their feminine accoutrements are intentionally exaggerated and parodic. They "operate within the matrix of power"[157] (i.e., within predominating discourses of gender), but they reiterate femininity in such an extravagant way as to provide their audience access to its constructedness. Drag, for Butler, is repetition and critique in simultaneous action.

For about three decades of Cuba's revolutionary era, while the state was offering marriage incentives, Cubans got married while at the same time demystifying marriage, taking advantage of the material benefits offered by the state only to turn around and divorce and repeat the series. These Cubans (not all, of course) turned marriage into a parody – of the institution itself as well as of the regime's apparent wish to preside over a nation of ideal families. Marriage became a hustle, just another instance of *la lucha* when Cubans wanted a few nights in a nice hotel or needed a stove.

Evacuated of its noble purposes, of a piece with selling shampoo on the street, stripped even of the modest governmental wedding gifts as the futility of the incentive campaign disclosed itself, and ultimately associated with few substantial benefits that de facto affective couples could not equally access, what remained that same-sex couples really needed from such a vacant institution? The domination of marriage internalized as "common sense," ironically, might be at a peak in the same-sex context even as it lingers at its nadir in the heterosexual context. The move to legalize same-sex marriage looks like an old hegemony reasserting itself against its parodic critique.

Still, why did marriage *specifically for same-sex couples* seem important? Why did marital hegemony rear its head *in the gay context* amid so much counter-hegemonic stimuli among heterosexual Cubans? It was no coincidence that marriage gained seeming importance once newly animated by the powerful and increasingly global norm of gay and lesbian equality.

As Chapter 4 argues, the pressures of global capitalism not only pushed Cuba to extract itself from socialist economic orthodoxies. Cuba was forced to admit new discourses of identity, as well. Cuba's old homosexual is metamorphizing into a global gay subject. Same-sex marriage, as the ultimate triumph of that identity, took root in the soil of Cuban economic liberalization.

While at first blush, same-sex marriage might seem like an important legal advance for managing new forms of ownership that have become available to Cubans especially since the end of Fidel's time in office, marriage was not actually doctrinally necessary for this purpose. This chapter, combined with the next, shines a spotlight on alternative explanations for Cuba's legalization of same-sex marriage, specifically, a combination of discursive factors –shaping the consciousness of legal and nonlegal actors. These factors surely are not the sole determinants bringing same-sex marriage to Cuba, but because they are hard to see, they are worth illuminating here. The struggle between the hegemon of marriage and the counter-hegemon of marriage-as-a-hustle joins with a global discourse of gay identity discussed in Chapter 4. The mystique of marriage – including the fantasy of a nation composed of ideal families well-ordered for property management – met the international charisma of gay identity and equality to facilitate the seeming importance of same-sex marriage, even in the minds of those heterosexuals who do not take marriage seriously for themselves.

4

Queer Encounters

GENDERED LOGICS

It is probably intuitive that a national jurisdiction characterized by a lot of homophobia would be likely to stand fast against legal recognition of same-sex marriage, but that as its homophobia abated, the jurisdiction would gradually come around. It is a simple equation: a lot of homophobia = no same-sex marriage; diminishing homophobia = growing possibility of same-sex marriage. Self-evident as that proposition might seem, it is *not* the theory presented here.

This chapter instead proposes a change in the *conception of* – not merely the *attitude toward* – the homosexual that enabled the advent of same-sex marriage in Cuba. It picks up on a suggestion made by historian of US marriage Nancy Cott: specifically, that something had to change in order for same-sex marriage to *make sense*.

In the US case of *Perry v. Schwarzenegger*,[1] plaintiffs, same-sex couples suing the state of California for the right to marry, called Cott as an expert witness at their 2010 trial. Cott told a compelling story about the evolution of marriage in the US.[2] The story begins in colonial America with coverture, the common law doctrine according to which husbands and wives performed highly differentiated and legally specified roles within a marriage. The husband was required to support his wife and children and represent the family in most legal matters. The wife owed her husband a duty of obedience and effectively folded her legal personality into that of her husband, so that during the marriage she could not manage her own property or exercise contractual capacity.[3]

This all changed over the course of about a hundred years, beginning in the mid-to-late nineteenth century. The Married Women's Property Acts (state laws granting married women limited authority over property derived from their families of origin) instigated the track to coverture's demise. Meanwhile, the agrarian homesteading economy evolved into an industrial one, entailing an evolution in economic and domestic roles.[4] Later, military demands on men during World War II opened up a new array of workplaces to women. The 1960s and 1970s ushered in important legal changes, including the passage of Title VII (prohibiting employment discrimination on the basis of sex and other protected categories) and a cluster of constitutional decisions granting women something approaching formal equality with men.[5]

In our current historical moment, explained Cott, there is no longer any legal requirement that spouses organize their lives in a manner consistent with traditional gender roles. Marriage in the early US was legally premised on economic complementarity, structuring the household to enable its survival. Contemporary marriage, though, rests on ideals of companionship and legal egalitarianism.[6] Same-sex marriage would have made no sense in the era of coverture: If a couple consisted of two men, who would obey? If it consisted of two women, who would represent the couple in contract? Now, though, Cott concludes, there is no longer any reason to exclude same-sex couples from marriage because economic complementarity is no longer one of marriage's defining features.[7]

Cott's testimony, like the identical contentions she made in affidavit form in other gay marriage litigations, was tailored to satisfy the kind of inquiry plaintiffs' counsel surely anticipated from the likes of Justice Antonin Scalia, who, when the case reached the US Supreme Court as *Hollingsworth v. Perry*,[8] put this question to former Solicitor General Theodore B. Olsen during his argument on behalf of gay and lesbian couples in California:

> I'm curious, when – when did – when did it become unconstitutional to exclude homosexual couples from marriage?
>
> 1791?
>
> 1868, when the Fourteenth Amendment was adopted?
>
> Sometimes – some time after Baker, where we said it didn't even raise a substantial Federal question?
>
> When – when – when did the law become this?[9]

Cott's theory about what exactly did change is meant to justify an interpretation of the Fourteenth Amendment that would not have been plausible in the nineteenth century. Her story effectively renders marriage compatible with the *sameness* of the same-sex couple because it tells a story of the decline of role differentiation since the Amendment was ratified. Importantly, Cott's account is limited to the decline of *formally* distinct gender roles in marriage. Whether couples actually organized their lives in such a fashion is a separate question, but what matters for the argument in this chapter is the logic of legal archetypes rather than anyone's lived reality. The archetypes of husband and wife, over the course of years, were rendered formally the same in terms of their legal marital obligations such that the sameness of the same-sex couple is no longer incongruent with marriage.

But what precisely is the "same" about gay or lesbian partners in a same-sex couple? Before trans and nonbinary constituencies achieved political traction, the easy answer would have been sex, biologically defined. In the US, for about the last eighty years, masculine or feminine gender expression in dress, mannerisms, and so forth, has not been germane to a determination that a person was gay or lesbian or that persons in a couple were of the same sex. The dominant model in the contemporary US is *sexual orientation*: Gays and lesbians are defined entirely by their sexual object choice. If a man experiences relatively consistent sexual desire and romantic affinity for other men, he is gay. Of course, in lived reality subcultural semiotic variations certainly exist,[10] but again, what is important here is the dominant archetype, and for that it does not matter whether a man presents as masculine or effeminate, nor does it matter whether he primarily "tops" or "bottoms." Gay and lesbian identities in the contemporary US are linked principally to same-sex desire, and while the categories of men and women are currently undergoing critical reevaluation, the terms *gay* and *lesbian* generally assume underlying cis identities.[11]

For most of the history of Revolutionary Cuba, however, the logic has run differently – at least for male homosexuals.[12] As discussed in Part I, only effeminate men – derogatorily known as *maricónes* (or less so as *invertidos*) – presumed to be anally receptive, were conceptualized as homosexual. The term came with stereotypes of weakness and decadence and was also burdened by the legacy of US imperialism, specifically the penetration of male sex workers by men from the US wielding economic power. *Bugarrónes*, on the other hand, presumed to penetrate, were not forced to bear the homosexual stigma. They might have girlfriends or wives, and so long as they were held to be the penetrator, their claim to heterosexuality remained intact. Surely, some Cuban men were versatile in their proclivities to top or bottom, but the archetypes were not derived from research about anyone's actual practices. This is the *inversion* model, more recently prevailing in a number of Latin American, Caribbean, and some other global south contexts. Gender presentation and accompanying presumptions about which role a man performs in same-sex intercourse, *activo* or *pasivo* in Spanish parlance, is definitional according to that model.

Famed gay Cuban ex-pat writer and poet Reinaldo Arenas observed the contrast, disparaging his experience of gay sameness in the US:

> [I]n exile, I found that sexual relations can be tedious and unrewarding. There are categories or divisions in the homosexual world. The queer gets together with the queer and everybody does everything .... How can that bring any satisfaction? What we are really looking for is our opposite. The beauty of our relationships then [i.e., back in Cuba] was that we met our opposites. We would find that man, that powerful recruit who wanted desperately to fuck us.[13]

Since Arenas's death in 1990, in New York City, Cuba's inversion model of homosexuality has eroded – as indeed it had to for same-sex marriage to *make sense*. It takes two gays to make a gay marriage, so for a society to pursue a same-sex marriage agenda, it would have to contemplate two gay people to enter into it. They could be a masc/top and a femme/bottom, but then the masc/top would lose his status – he would have to be reconceptualized *as gay*. Alternatively, one or both men could be versatile in the performance of acts and/or androgynous in gender expression, but again, that would diminish the contrast and alter the typology. Two femmes/bottoms – the *only* homosexuals under the fading rubric – would make no sense any more than two husbands or two wives would have made sense under coverture.

A rubric, however, can change. Cott's narrative, historicizing the institution of marriage in the US, is a perfect example. Her narrative illustrates the interwovenness of marriage – *as an idea* – with its political–economic environment. Under a particular set of pre–twentieth century economic conditions, highly differentiated sex roles seemed essential to marriage and to each family's economic viability. As the conditions around marriage evolved (e.g., the rise of industry, World War II, and the passage of Title VII) the necessity of gender-specific economic complementarity within marriage fell away rendering same-sex marriage fathomable.

Following Cott, this chapter proposes a theory unique to Cuba about one site at which same-sex marriage accumulated not merely favor, but *intelligibility* within an ever-evolving discursive system. That discursive system followed circumstances that befell the Cuban economy in the wake of the Soviet demise, prompting a hard turn in the direction of international tourism. With tourism, came foreign capital – from tourists, business managers, and other points of contact between local and international discourses of identity.

TOGETHER AND APART: THE ECONOMY AND THE SEXUAL SYSTEM

To set the stage for the details of the story, we take a brief detour into anthropologist Gayle Rubin's foundational article from 1975, *The Traffic in Women*.[14] Ultimately, the argument here will be about how changes in the Cuban economy could facilitate adaptations in its sexual logics, so that same-sex marriage would come to "make sense." Rubin's deep dive into the relationship between the economy and sexuality, therefore, will be of use in affording us a vision of how economic change can enable sexual reorganization.

Rubin considered the question of the relationship between the economy (defined as "the system by which elements of the natural world are transformed into objects of human consumption")[15] and the "sexual system," (i.e., that "set of arrangements by which the biological raw material of human sex and procreation is shaped by human, social intervention and satisfied in a conventional manner"[16]). Are they one and the same? Does one cause or enable the other? If so, by what mechanism?

Rubin urged that the two systems are autonomous; "analogous," she contended, but "not isomorphic."[17] Her argument, however, suggests a bit more than analogy. The economy and the sexual system are, in Rubin's account, deeply – but *not* inextricably – entwined. Her article, then, searches for a theory of how to extricate them so that the latter might be reconfigured in service of feminist aims.

Rubin begins with a reading of Claude Lévi-Strauss, specifically his "theory of primitive reciprocity,"[18] according to which marriage in a premodern society[19] functions as a gift exchange in which men trade their daughters and sisters for the purpose of forming alliances with men in other kinship groups.[20] Women are, in this context, objects of commerce. The importance of this observation for Rubin is in the quest to identify the roots of women's oppression – crucial, therefore, to feminism.[21] Alliances, the very rudiments of society, rely on the traffic in women.

The imperative of building alliances, with the traffic in women as its principal means, necessitates, in turn, a sex-based division of labor: "The division of labor by sex can, therefore, be seen as a 'taboo': a taboo against sameness of men and women, a taboo dividing the sexes into two mutually exclusive categories, a taboo which exacerbates the biological differences between the sexes and thereby creates gender."[22]

Societies may vary in which tasks they assign to men and which to women, but it is the division itself that maintains the discreteness of the trafficked as distinct from the traffickers. The sexual division of labor functions to accentuate sex differences, which in turn enable forms of exchange necessary for a kinship group to thrive.[23] A sex system requiring stark differentiation, then, arose to sustain an early economy of exchange.

Rubin turns next to psychoanalysis, in particular Lacan and Freud. Lacan, observes Rubin, "suggests that psychoanalysis is the study of the traces left in the psyches of individuals as a result of their conscription into systems of kinship."[24] How are individuals so conscripted? That is the function of the Oedipal struggle.

> In Lacan's scheme, the Oedipal crisis occurs when a child learns of the sexual rules embedded in the terms for family and relatives. The crisis begins when the child comprehends the system and his or her place in it; the crisis is resolved when the child accepts that place and accedes to it .... Before the Oedipal phase, the sexuality of the child is labile and relatively unstructured. Each child contains all of the sexual possibilities available to human expression. But in any given society, only some of these possibilities will be expressed, while others will be constrained. When the child leaves the Oedipal phase, its libido and gender identity have been organized in conformity with the rules of the culture.[25]

"[T]he Oedipal complex," Rubin concludes, is "a machine which fashions the appropriate forms of sexual individuals."[26] These appropriately formed individuals will grow to fulfill their distinct roles in Lévi-Strauss's system of exchange.

For the Oedipal machine to operate successfully and serve its economic purpose, boys and girls must resolve their crises in antipodal terms. Herein lies the centrality of the phallus, or the vesting of the penis with the symbolic power to array the sexes, assign their places in the system of kinship, and establish male dominance.[27] A boy accepts the power of the phallus and the right to a woman[28] by ceding his mother to his father. "The girl," though, not only "concludes that the 'penis' is indispensable for the possession of the mother" but that lacking the phallus, she must cede all women; this is "the rule of obligatory heterosexuality."[29] The girl's only access to the phallus is through sexual intercourse with a man or through giving birth; it is never really hers.[30] Her acceptance of these terms gives rise to the "ascendance of passivity" (which Freud associated with vaginal, as opposed to clitoral, eroticism).[31] It is easy to see how passivity would make for a good quality in a trafficked object.

Some girls will "cling to [their] desire," refuse to "sign the social contract," and become "'masculine' or "homosexual."[32] The majority, however, who acquiesce to the demands of sexual organization, submitting to the "psychic brutality" exacted upon them and adopting the feminine role, are left with "immense resentment of the suppression to which they were subjected."[33] Rubin summarizes Freud's pertinent writings as his explanation of how girls are "prepared psychologically … to live with … oppression."[34]

Together, Rubin's readings of Lévi-Strauss, Freud, and Lacan provide the beginnings of an explanation for the inequality that feminism exists to challenge. Women are the products of a socialization process that, when successful, trains them for their role in a premodern economy of exchange – that of trafficked objects. "Kinship systems," she derives from Lévi-Strauss, "require a division of the sexes. The Oedipal phase divides the sexes,"[35] producing women as passive and prepared to serve their function as objects in an economy of exchange.

Rubin's combined reading of these texts advances her argument that the sexual system supports an exchange economy but that the two systems are not one and the same. This schematic positions her to observe that in "modern" societies, while we continue to live with the old sexual system (bear in mind, she wrote this essay a half a century ago already) the economy it once served has been transformed.

> The organization of sex and gender once had functions other than itself – it organized society. Now, it only organizes and reproduces itself. The kind of relationships of sexuality established in the dim human past still dominate our sexual lives, our ideas about men and women, and the ways we raise our children. But they lack the functional load they once carried. One of the most conspicuous features of kinship is that it has been systematically stripped of its functions – political, economic, educational, and organizational. It has been reduced to its barest bones – sex and gender.[36]

Much like Cott's marriage story, according to which sex-differentiation is no longer needed because the economy no longer relies on complementary roles, Rubin's story has modern economies no longer requiring the dramatic sex-differentiation that arose in service of alliance-formation among kinship groups. This divergence between the sex system and the economy it once girded presents an "opportunity to seize control of the means of sexuality, reproduction, and socialization."[37] Now that the economy does not require the old sex system we can deliberately intervene, bringing "conscious choice"[38] to bear.

Rubin proposes one such intervention. In the Oedipal struggle, as Rubin reminds us, the girl's

> love for the mother is induced by the mother's job of child care. The girl is then forced to abandon this love because of the female sex role – to belong to a man. If the sexual division of labor were such that adults of both sexes cared for children equally, primary object choice would be bisexual. If heterosexuality were not obligatory, this early love would not have to be suppressed and the penis would not be overvalued .... [T]he entire Oedipal drama would be a relic. In short, feminism must call for a revolution in kinship.[39]

As it happens, Cuba's 1975 Family Code, enacted the same year that Rubin's essay was published, attempted precisely the rearrangement Rubin envisions (for adult gender equity reasons – not with the purpose of producing bisexual or gender non-differentiated children). As Chapter 2 describes, the Code mandated that husbands and wives equally share the burdens of domesticity, including childcare.[40] Whatever expressive significance this legal reform may hold, no one seems to think, even combined with the subsequent Cuban prohibition against employment discrimination based on sex,[41] that the law actually eradicated the sexual division of labor, so one cannot quite say that Rubin's theory was tested in Cuba.

Moreover, it seems a bit narrow to suppose that gender is produced at just one site (i.e., child-rearing) while neglecting, for example, gender-based violence, legal impediments to reproductive autonomy, or the treatment of nonnormative genders. Abel Sierra Madero points out, for example, that Cuba has been steadfast in its commitment to a binary model of gender in its approach to transgender health care, providing gender affirming surgery and ID changes, but so far foreclosing any space for nonbinary identities (see Chapter 2).[42] Practices at this site arguably work against the rule that equally distributes household responsibilities. It is difficult to quantify a particular jurisdiction's commitment to disrupting its sexual system; one policy might point in one direction (e.g., gender differentiation) and another policy in the opposite direction (e.g., gender non-differentiation).

Rubin's predictions in the excerpted paragraph about what "would" happen if kinship were rearranged must be regarded as highly speculative. She revisited her predictions in an interview conducted by Judith Butler and published in 1997.[43] To invite Rubin's reconsideration, Butler asks her to recall a moment at which British feminists imagined "that if you could reconfigure and change your kinship arrangements that you could also reconfigure your sexuality and your psyche" but, alas, were forced to give up on this dream.[44] Was this a test of the theory that reveals its failure? Rubin responds,

> Leaving aside such issues as how much these social and kinship relations have actually been transformed at this point, the magnitude of such changes and the time spans required to make them, and the fact that most of our psyches were long since formed and are resistant to such swift reeducation, what is the something

> that is intractable? One of the nifty things about psychoanalytic approaches is that they explain both change and intractability. But there is something about the particular intractability of the symbolic that I don't understand. Is there supposed to be something in the very nature of the structure of the brain and the way it creates language?[45]

Butler proposes that the "speaking subject" emerges "through sexual differentiation."[46] Rubin sounds dissatisfied: "There is something intrinsically problematic about any notion that somehow language itself or the capacity for acquiring it requires a sexual differentiation .... A specific symbolic relation that precedes any social life whatsoever – I have a problem with that."[47]

This exchange suggests Rubin's continuing commitment to the idea that social life structures the brain, which presumably implies that changes in one would facilitate changes in the other, leaving open exactly how that might happen and how long it would take. Rubin's prediction in *The Traffic in Women* might have been a bit overstated, but the increase in the incidence of queer and nonbinary identifications in locations where one could also point to increasingly involved fathers, mothers working in the marketplace, and the rise of same-sex parenting, might suggest that she was on to something. In any event, the near-infinity of variables caution against regarding these correlations as a natural experiment.

It should not go without mention that Rubin relied on a contested reading of the Oedipal story according to which men are defined by their genitalia and the literal penis is inextricable from the symbolic phallus. The extent to which the penis and the phallus are extricable is a live debate within psychoanalysis.[48] It is not established, as far as I am aware, whether same-sex parented children (a booming population since Rubin's paper was published[49]) psychically assign maternal and paternal roles to their parents consistent with the Oedipal order. If researchers were to conclude that they do, it would require further inquiry still to determine whether that assignment is based on the parents' gender presentations, care responsibilities, or something else. If a man can function in the child's psyche as the "mother" or a woman as the "father," then it might follow that the Oedipal structure is resilient enough to withstand reconfiguration of household labor assignments, precluding a real rearrangement of the sexual system, that is, the sexual system is here to stay regardless of social or economic changes. Then again, it could instead follow that the Oedipal structure's resilience comes from its elasticity, and that the child's struggle could, therefore, be disentangled from its rigidly heterosexual objectives. The malleability of the Oedipal construction serves as a reminder of its being less an empirical truth than a metaphor, useful here for facilitating exploration of sameness and complementarity as conjugal possibilities.

Amid all the unknowables, we can extract from Rubin's essay the argument (this is perhaps a cautious, or minimalist, reading) that a sexual system that arises in service of an economy can diverge from that economy over time, rendering itself available for reconfiguration. The economy might evolve, shedding its reliance on the sexual system, while the latter remains stagnant. This creates the possibility of putting conscious deliberation to the task of rearranging the sexual system, now detached from the original economic imperative, so that it is more desirable from a feminist, queer, or gay perspective.

Presumably, though Rubin does not say it, a revised sexual system must be feasible within the constraints of the current economy. Perhaps if Rubin had written another few pages, she would have speculated on the range of possibility for feminist, queer, and gay reformers within a modern economic context. It cannot be that once the premodern economy evolves, loosening its bonds with the sexual system, which stays behind, that feminist, queer, or gay pioneers are free to design *anything*.

Cott's account, in which same-sex marriage became intelligible only in the aftermath of more than a century of economic changes in the US, exemplifies the lesson. A same-sex marriage litigation such as *Perry* could be understood as gay rights advocates doing exactly what Rubin called for: putting the sexual system before the courts for conscious deliberation and reorganization, but again, not inventing a wild utopia of sexual innovation; rather, a modest reform that is entirely consistent with the trend favoring privatization in the contemporary US economy.

In one sense, Cuba long ago laid the groundwork for the sameness of the same-sex marital couple by promoting (as a formal legal matter) sex-based equality at work and in the home. The requirements of workplace equality and equal domestic responsibility combine to render the same-sex couple intelligible as an *economic* unit … just not as a *sexual* one.

For the conjugality of the same-sex couple to "make sense," the conception of the homosexual as effeminate and available for penetration by a man who is *not* coded homosexual, had to change. The sexual complementarity between two highly differentiated male types for which Reinaldo Arenas felt such nostalgia, where only one partner inhabits the degraded identity, had to give way to a reorganized sexual typology. A version closer to that which predominates in the US (i.e., the "sexual orientation" model) according to which gender presentation and role in intercourse are irrelevant in favor of object choice, had to displace, and now is displacing, Cuba's old definitional order.

This observation is at a high level of abstraction – *concepts* had to change, not necessarily sex itself (though I do not mean to preclude that possibility). Nothing here is meant to assert that at any historical moment or in any national setting two effeminate men or two masculine men could not or would not couple in actuality; this is about the *logic of archetypes*. Under the old logic in Cuba, sex between two men occurred between a homosexual (read: effeminate and anally receptive) and a heterosexual (read: masculine and penetrative). For same-sex marriage to take hold in Cuba, Cubans would have had to start thinking about homosexuality in a different way. They would have had to shift – gradually, of course, almost imperceptibly, not suddenly – to a model in which *two men*, regardless of effeminacy or masculinity and associated assumptions about respective roles in intercourse, *could legibly be gay* and constitute a couple.

The remainder of this chapter offers a partial theory of how this happened. It is partial in the sense that identity surely evolves in more than one way. What is important here, drawing from Cott and Rubin, is that economic change in Cuba enabled a departure from the old definitional order. A new order is emerging, and it is consonant with the economic conditions Cuba is facing as well as the adaptive measures it has taken. For Cuba to become amenable to same-sex marriage, the key enabling condition was not merely fortuitous declining homophobia (though that might have occurred epiphenomenally) but rather a conceptual transformation in which the male homosexual gradually sloughs off previously definitional qualities of effeminacy and humiliation and metamorphizes into the new gay man. It is that metamorphosis that permits him to form a legible sexual couple with another gay man, each defined by his object choice rather than his gendered traits. The law, specifically the recognition of same-sex marriage as part of the 2022 Family Code, can be understood then to consolidate this reorganization.

TRAVELING IDENTITY

At the highest level of generality (and carrying colonial baggage which will be thoroughly addressed) Cuba's ratification of same-sex marriage reflects gay identity's globalization. The gay man is not marked principally by failed masculinity and exclusion from the nationalist project, but by minoritarian identity – the emergence of which is typically accompanied by political opposition; indeed, churches in the US and other parts of the Americas are exporting financial and moral support for anti-gay, Evangelical culture warriors in Cuba, because a culture war requires (at least[50]) two sides.

Gradually, the old archetype of the effeminate, anally receptive homosexual, that humiliating reminder of imperialist domination who must be expelled from the revolutionary ideal, is disintegrating. The globally legible gay subject is emerging in his stead. In Cuba, the gay subject does not need marriage to obtain health coverage or protections in the event of divorce. He does not need marriage because it is a vital institution of social inclusion. He wants it (and others want it for him[51]) because marriage has fastened itself to an historically specific instantiation of the gay subject and full recognition of that subject is no longer possible without it. As minoritarian gay identity has circulated globally, so has same-sex marriage, gay equality's ultimate vindication. Marriage has materialized among those rights that, as Gayatri Spivak put it, "we cannot not want."[52] Rendered the zenith of gay recognition and equality by same-sex marriage proponents and actualized over the preceding two decades in country after country, it had to be had.

In Cuba, global capital flows contributed to the conceptual transformation. Recall that beginning in the 1990s, Cuba had little choice but to pry itself open to obtain desperately needed foreign currency. This meant that tourism, family visitors, and foreign investment (sometimes accompanied by corporate managers from wealthier jurisdictions) were pouring into Cuba at new levels, each an instance of economic and discursive contact between the local and the global. While in the prerevolutionary era, sex tourism especially by travelers from the US, added insult to the degraded homosexual archetype, in more recent decades, gay identity, along with its virtually inseparable claim to same-sex marriage, entered Cuba by piggybacking on new forms of traveling capital.

Before proposing one of the routes by which this occurred, an acknowledgment: Such stories, observing correlations between circulating capital and circulating gay identity, impose discursive costs in the key of lingering coloniality. The sexual orientation model of gay identity, coded *modern*, is regularly opposed to the inversion model of homosexuality, coded *primitive*. The former, predominant for many decades in the global north, enters a post-colony making an implicit claim of advancement and often bringing along liberal conceptions of rights as well as markets. English professor Neville Hoad has sent up a warning signal about this: While conceding "that gay identity follows capitalism,"[53] he nonetheless expresses wariness of temporalizing colonized spaces as "primitive."[54]

Temporalizing in precisely this fashion is a hazard of observing Cuba's shift from the inversion model to the sexual orientation model. I take the point. Is there an anti-colonial mode in which to observe gay identity's habit of sneaking into a post-colony with the tourism, foreign investment, and other forms of capital? Are we left either to deny the connection between the movement of capital and that of sexual identity or to fall into "predigested," "evolutionary narratives"?[55]

Recapitulation of such narratives might be inextricable from the task of shedding light on the emergence of gay marriage as a revolutionary priority in Cuba. Notwithstanding that concession, though – that a cost accompanies the benefit – one can still do one's best to mitigate the damage. Not to rebut Hoad's argument but to ratify it while also trying to diminish the harm he identifies, we can turn to one of feminist theorist Judith Butler's insights about discursive power. To continue exerting force, Butler argues, discourse requires repetition, but each repetition is *inexact*.[56] While the Cuban story told herein reiterates a colonial narrative at a general level, in its particularity it does so inexactly and it is in that inexactitude, following Butler, that the possibility of resistance – here, unsettling the colonial narrative – lies.[57]

Moreover, describing the relationship between identity and capital simultaneously contributes to an effort to "interrogat[e] both the preconditions of identity and its effects"[58] – a principal object of queer theory, as Annamarie Jagose has explained. Queer theory offers "analytical models which dramatise incoherencies in the allegedly stable relations between chromosomal sex, gender and sexual desire."[59] The dual projects of historicizing sexual identity and examining it comparatively – two principal undertakings of this book – can be fertile exercises in the pursuit of queer ends. While the Cuban story as it is told here, therefore, risks reproducing narrative patterns, it has the potential to disrupt them, as well.

In short, I propose to palliate rather than eliminate the narrative injury and to do so using the mechanism of *particularity*. Cuba is not every other post-colony. While recognizable patterns may surface at disparate postcolonial locations, the effort herein is to highlight the localized details of the Cuban experience. The Cuban story might generate familiar echoes but is also unique.

Law professor Ivana Isailovic illustrates what might be sacrificed by over-generality in a comparative analysis. In her article comparing the ratification of same-sex marriage in the US and France, Isailovic recounts the differences between the two national debates (the US focusing on equal rights and "social marginalization" and France preoccupied with psychoanalytic "filiation rules").[60] She critiques what she dubs the "conventional universalist approach," – an approach that sets its attention at a high level of generality – charging its adherents with "thin description of how same-sex reforms came to be, what their effects on the ground are, and what meanings they have for the various interpretive communities."[61] While the "universalist view may well capture a trend [such as same-sex marriage recognition] at the global level," Isailovic argues, it nonetheless fails to "account for the underlying different social and cultural dynamics that bring about these reforms and invest them with meaning."[62] The close up detail of Isailovic's analysis, in contrast, yields a rich depiction that enables the reader to comprehensively appreciate the dynamics of reform in its unique cultural context.[63]

Not every legal comparativist is so careful. Soon after the Netherlands became the first national jurisdiction to secure the right to same-sex marriage in 2001, the Dutch legal scholar Kees Waaldijk, a specialist in the comparative law of sexual orientation, proposed his influential theory "the law of small change,"[64] purporting to lay out a sequence of legal reforms that would gradually take a jurisdiction from zero to same-sex marriage. The chronology proposed by Waaldijk begins with decriminalization of (private, consensual) same-sex sexual activity, proceeds through anti-discrimination reform, and culminates in recognition of intimate partnerships and family relationships. The theory breaks each step down into subparts – equalizing the age of consent for homo- and heterosexual activities, enacting anti-discrimination measures in a range of employment and nonemployment sectors, equalizing treatment in taxation, immigration, and foster parenting – each a stone laid along the path to the garden of marriage equality.[65]

Proceeding incrementally in the order set forth by Waaldijk accords with what he called "the law of standard sequences."[66] His use of the term "law" in this phrase does not refer to positive law (such as a statute or regulation) but rather to his apparent belief that, when it comes to pro-gay reforms, *this is just how things work*. He made his view explicit that this is the pattern by which "same-sex marriage can be achieved in other countries,"[67] going so far as to claim that he could glean from the Dutch experience, as well as from progress underway at the time in other European jurisdictions, that "this process is governed by certain trends, that can tentatively be formulated as if they were 'laws of nature.' At the very least," he contended, "there is a clear pattern of *steady progress* according to *standard sequences*."[68]

Waaldijk's paper has been multiply translated and globally consumed. In the US, William N. Eskridge, Jr., another leading legal academic proponent of same-sex marriage, picked up on Waaldijk's argument in his own work.[69] According to Eskridge, a comparative legal analysis reveals "the likelihood of pluralism's progressing, slowly but surely, to state recognition of same-sex unions."[70] Citing Waaldijk, Eskridge asserted that "legal recognition of same-sex unions – or, ultimately, marriages – comes through a step-by-step process. Such a process is *sequential* and *incremental*: it proceeds by little steps that are taken in a particular order."[71]

The small steps theory typifies a certain immodesty that is familiar to readers in postcolonial studies. It assumes that sexual identities are uniform everywhere and that the gradual acquisition of liberal rights for a sexual identity group is what lies ahead. Some national cultures simply lag behind others in the sequence, evoking what Dipesh Chakrabarty dubbed "an imaginary waiting room of history"[72] in which global south countries dawdle until they are developed enough to adopt the norms of the global north.

Striving for particularity in telling the Cuban story not only diminishes the hazard of an uncritical colonial narrative; it is also a form of humility. What hubris it is to propose a law of nature unaffected by the wild array of natural, economic, and cultural conditions through which identities and legal reforms swirl, as well as the differently situated subpopulations variously affected on arrival! What we can do, more modestly, is theorize plausible explanatory factors and enabling conditions by studying context closely, eschewing assertions of universal or determinate patterns.

The Cuban story told in Part I does not repeat in its particulars anywhere else in the world. No other country shared the uniquely fraught relationship with the US during and after the Cold War, including decades of quasi-independence under the Platt Amendment, serving as a sexual playground run by the US Mafia after World War II, and a long embargo tightened over and over again at the behest of hawkish and politically influential ex-pats living in Florida or New Jersey. No Latin American country can boast the educational or health systems Cuba built during its early years as a Soviet benefactor, and neither did any country in Eastern Europe stick to its ideological guns quite the way Castro-led Cuba did after the dissolution of the Soviet Union. Quite a few Caribbean nations rely on tourism generally and sex tourism specifically, but none is inflected with the resentments of socialist identity standing against the capitalist tide the way Cuba is. The Cuban story is the Cuban story. While it may include motifs recognizable in, say, the Dominican Republic or Vietnam, the variations are many and crucial to fully understanding pertinent legal developments in their national context.

What exactly happens when gay identity arises at a new location? Here again, Cuba's experience can only be fully appreciated in its particulars. International

Relations scholar Rahul Rao imagines capital and knowledge "travel[ling] across distance and becom[ing] practically effective through friction" – a term he borrows from anthropologist Anna Tsing to describe "'the awkward, unequal, unstable, and creative qualities of interconnection across difference' … [through] 'contingent and botched encounters.'"[73]

THE PINGUERO-TOURIST ENCOUNTER

For Cubans, some of those encounters have been helpfully traced by anthropologist Derrick Hodge and historian Abel Sierra Madero in their separate ethnographic studies of Cuban pingueros. As explained in Chapter 2, the word *pinguero*, on a literal translation, refers to someone who works with his *pinga*, or *dick*. While the pinguero distinguishes himself with a label designed to signal that his work is penetration rather than anal receptivity,[74] this is an ideal, not an empirical truth. As one of Sierra Madero's informants told him, "Even though *pingueros* allowed themselves to be penetrated, they say they are active and always try to hide the fact that they are passive because if they accept it, they would be admitting that they are homosexuals."[75] Said another, "Some say that they don't do this or that but in the end, they do everything although they pretend to be tough men."[76]

The category of the *pinguero* is effectively "a marketing tool that announces to the sex tourists … who they are and what they are about."[77] It "let[s] the traveler know what to ask for, where to get it, and what to expect."[78] This is not to suggest that pingueros are necessarily gay; on the contrary, they might bring any set of personal desires. One informant told Hodge (for a separate article on the social significance of name-brand clothing) "'A pinguero has a better chance of having more girlfriends than anybody else. Because girls like a cute guy, one who dresses well, according to the latest fashions.'"[79] Anthropologist Noelle Stout found further that some pingueros "introduce gay foreigners to their parents, their siblings, and even their wives and girlfriends" in an effort to cultivate a sense that the foreigner is part of the family, creating a sense of obligation to contribute financially.[80]

The information gap in the sex tourism market that the pinguero arose to fill opened, Hodge asserts, because "the bugarrón was not a category that could withstand the transition to capital market relations."[81] By virtue of the very conception of the bugarrón – that he maintains his heterosexual status – a gay sex tourist arriving in Havana looking to be topped would have difficulty identifying him; the bugarrón would be illegible to a foreigner hailing from a jurisdiction in which the sexual orientation model of gay identity predominates. The pinguero, on the other hand, represents himself as just the man the tourist is looking for.

Moreover, as the years have passed, the pinguero has not remained stagnant, but has accommodated the semiotic structure of his market niche. In his 2001 account, Hodge reports,

> I have heard more than one pinguero talking to a tourist, and when asked, '*Eres gay?*' ['Are you gay?'] the Cuban answered in the affirmative. But the Cuban did not mean the same thing by 'gay' as did the tourist;' for the latter, often from Europe or Canada, gay is a concrete category of sexual identity and preference. But Cubans are accustomed to defining themselves sexually in terms of what they do, not who they are....
>
> [U]nder the pressure of the market, [though,] even this is changing ... [Y]ounger Cuban men, whose puberty had come after the onset of the Special Period, tended to speak of pinguerismo and gay as ontological categories; language of doing gives way to language of being."[82]

Hodge concludes, "the pinguero killed the bugarrón."[83] Importantly, as I read Hodge, it is the *archetype* of the pinguero that "killed" the *archetype* of the bugarrón. Stated otherwise, the advent of sex tourism in Cuba – a consequence of the Soviet demise and the hardships that arose during the Special Period – ushered in identitarian developments. European and Canadian visitors, as bearers of traveling capital, facilitated a street-level reconfiguration of identity categories by entering the sex tourism market and prompting service provider adaptations to purchaser expectations. While Hodge appears to describe this process as an empirical claim, my reference to his ethnographic data is intended to generate theory: The pinguero-tourist encounter stands as one among multiple sites at which the global and local, as well as the material and discursive, collide, capturing a snapshot along the genealogical course of Cuban sexual identity.

NATIONAL PRIDE/SHAME IN THE PINGUERO-TOURIST ENCOUNTER

To the extent that the pinguero shares with the bugarrón the ideal trait of performing exclusively the penetrative role, he allays anxieties over the humiliations of the Batista period. "[I]n a pinguero-tourist sex act, the Cuban has invaded the tourist, 'screwed' him, as it were,"[84] says Hodge. Or as Sierra Madero explains it, "*pingueros* embody the anti-imperialist, decolonizing power of the Cuban phallus, symbolically conquering the bodies of the foreigners and defending Cuba from its would-be invaders."[85]

Cuba's sex tourism economy is heavily laden with imperialist baggage. During the prerevolutionary period, especially under President Batista, Cuba functioned as a regional brothel. The revolutionary regime's initial prioritization of eradicating sex work was not merely for prudish reasons; it was to cleanse itself of the indignity associated with the sexual exploitation of Cuba's sons and daughters by wealthy *yumas* (*foreigners*). These early years were the most brutal for maricónes, due at least in part to their being a visible reminder of imperialist humiliation. It is easy to see how the idealized reversal of that dynamic in an individual sex act wherein a Cuban man penetrates a tourist could offer a psychic reward in a nationalist key.

For a moment, set aside the fact that pingueros do not in actuality always perform the penetrative role when they have sex with tourists and just contend with the archetype on its own terms. Even if we provisionally accept the exclusively penetrative ideal, the pinguero inhabits a power relation that is a little harder to sum up than who is penetrating whom.

The complexity of that deceptively simple relation is addressed by queer theorist Leo Bersani in his classic essay, *Is the Rectum a Grave?*,[86] written during the first decade of the AIDS crisis in the US. Bersani aimed in part to disabuse readers of any easy assumptions they might make regarding a correlation between gay identity and left politics. "To want sex with another man," Bersani maintained, is not "a credential for political radicalism."[87] Observing a continuing capacity among white, middle class, gay men to cling to racism and otherwise reactionary politics, Bersani refuted the view expressed by some gay writers and activists that gay minority status leads inexorably to radical leftism.

He believed that male homosexuality does indeed have political significance but that significance is not so easily discerned. "[T]here has been a lot of confusion about the real or potential political implications of homosexuality," he argued. "While it is indisputably true that sexuality is always being politicized, the ways in which *having sex* politicizes are highly problematical."[88]

Bersani asserted a surprising theory of "the extremely obscure process by which sexual pleasure *generates* politics,"[89] leaning – even more surprisingly – on famed dominance feminists Catharine MacKinnon and Andrea Dworkin, specifically on their contentions regarding women's subordinate position in heterosexual intercourse. MacKinnon and Dworkin decried the "eroticization of dominance and submission" and its "fusi[on] … with the social construction of male and female."[90] In Dworkin's book *Intercourse*, she makes the (entirely plausible) claim that prohibitions against male homosexuality have had as their central purpose the protection of men against penetration and its inherent humiliation, an effect reserved for women.[91] Indeed, even in societies that have been more or less tolerant of male same-sex eroticism, Bersani notes that male anal receptivity has nevertheless been frowned upon. Cuba is no exception. The ideal of impenetrability that characterizes the pinguero archetype conveys this sensibility. "*To be penetrated is to abdicate power*," says Bersani.[92] Like Dworkin, Bersani concludes that "the moral taboo on 'passive' anal sex … [is therefore] a kind of hygienics of social power"[93] meant to protect men against humiliation and preserve their dominance.

To further his argument, Bersani turns to Freud's suggestion that orgasm is a moment at which, pushed past a threshold of tolerance for pleasure, one relinquishes one's intact self (however transitorily) to psychic disaggregation.[94] In this limit-passing moment, one loses one's identity – presumably including name, gender, sexual orientation, race, and so forth – along with the self's "will to dominate."[95]

Bersani carries this insight over to the physical conditions of anal receptivity: By submitting themselves to penetration, gay men – even (and I embellish a bit here) white, Republican, Wall Street bankers – fleetingly relinquish the struggle for dominance. Male submission to anal penetration – the shame, the surrender, the suicidality – therefore, "gestures"[96] toward a politics of "*jouissance* as a mode of ascesis,"[97] or, as Janet Halley explains, "[s]exual abjection with its momentary disorientation of the self offers to interrupt [the] generation of social dominance through the self, and constitutes a vast critique of political and social power."[98]

Bersani's theory is a stunning reversal of MacKinnonite feminism's moral presuppositions. Sexual subordination is not merely a structural evil to be opposed,[99] but a brief reprieve from the perpetual struggle for domination that characterizes political and social life. The radical politics Bersani envisions comes not through a "pastoralizing"[100] equality in sex, but through the very annihilation of the self that draws critical fire from MacKinnon and Dworkin. Bersani's startling insight (even today it reads that way) incisively narrates a turn-about of dominance feminism by *embracing* the humiliation represented by penetration. It is a spectacular analytical flip ... but we can extract another.

Anally receptive male pleasure has also been figured as a hopelessly bourgeois species of libertinism, a shameless excess of the privileged, exemplary of status-based domination exercised as leisure.[101] The figment of the privileged, pleasure-seeking bottom coexists with the degraded homosexual archetype of Cuba's early revolutionary years, bent over in service of imperialist penetrative pleasure; the former socially dominant, the latter socially dominated.

Indeed, today's pingueros earn their living (ostensibly) penetrating European and Canadian tourists, often drawing on the exotic allure of race to appeal to white men seeking to be topped by dark-skinned machos.[102] Must this be read in Bersani's terms, that is, as a surrender of white/imperialist power and a fleeting break from political domination? Or is it better read as a luxury that gay male tourists from the global north can afford? Put another way, can the context of global hierarchy effectively reverse what Bersani (following MacKinnon and Dworkin) understood to be the physical positions of domination and subordination? And put one more way: Bersani contended that when women are on top in heterosexual intercourse, they are just playing at dominance; men remain the real tops.[103] When a pinguero tops a Scottish male sex tourist, is the Scot's a "real" surrender, signaling the kind of radical politics Bersani imagined, or is it just a game, one that does nothing to ruffle actual north-south relations of domination?

As mentioned in Chapter 2, Teemu Ruskola has argued that colonialism inflicts a homoerotic violation – a metaphorical rape – in which one state is coded masculine and the other emasculated.[104] That metaphor probably does some of the work of explaining why lesbians do not figure as prominently as gay men do in stories such as the one told here: Emasculation is the injury, and women (following MacKinnon) are always already violated.[105] It is also why the image of the macho pinguero penetrating the yuma is tolerable while the image of the maricón opening himself to imperialist invasion is more fraught. If, however, a sex tourist submits to penetration as an act of leisure, then physical positioning does not reliably correlate with relations of domination and subordination and the penetrative pinguero is merely a cover story for the same old imperialist humiliation that rendered the maricón intolerable to the Revolution's nationalist project.

Bersani's argument, turning away from gay minoritarian identity as a reliable correlative to radical politics, considers instead the implications of sexual positioning. But the physical act of penetration also might not get the final say. Act and identity *both* fail as stable indicia of political meaning. Deriving politics from the act of intercourse requires operating in the domain of metaphor and metaphors are labile.[106]

In her essay on the politics of analogy, *Queers Are Like Jews, Aren't They?*,[107] queer theorist Janet R. Jakobsen illustrates the need for caution in just this kind of analytical environment. When A is described as being *like* B, the lesson to be derived regarding the first term depends on the meaning of the second term. "We will call the [term] which is the object of the discourse the *thème* and the second, thanks to its effecting the [metaphoric] transfer [of meaning,] the *phore*."[108] The phore provides the "ground" of the analogy, and "the ground … must be kept stable in order to shift our understanding of the *thème*."[109] But if B – the phore – is *not* stable, what does that mean for the message we are to take regarding A? The structure of the analogy implies the phore's stability where it might not be so. An attempt to bind penetration as a set of physical relations to the social relation of domination and subordination suffers from precisely this fallacy.

In the street, additional complexity accrues. In addition to taking deft advantage of white desire for black and brown bodies, one pinguero told Sierra Madero, "I always say that I am active and when I let them penetrate me I just make something up … that it is my first time and that I do it as a token of affection. I pretend to be nervous at first and reject them because afterwards I can get them to eat from the palm of my hand."[110] As Sierra Madero observes, this informant effects yet another power reversal and he does so by reference to aspects of himself that are typically understood as powerless.[111]

Endless contradictions and reversals are embedded in the figure of the pinguero, vesting him with a capacity to negotiate complex power relations with wealthy tourists from foreign jurisdictions. Moreover, his encounters serve to mediate the conceptual clash over sexual identity that separates him from his benefactor under material conditions where, as one pinguero put it to Sierra Madero, "If homosexuality did not exist, I would starve to death."[112]

The pinguero can be understood as a transitional figure, his sex a site (just one) at which the gradual shift from an inversion model of homosexuality to a sexual orientation model and gay identity occurs. "Eres gay?" the tourist asks. "Sí," answers the pinguero. It is precisely one of those "awkward, unequal, unstable, and creative" moments "of interconnection across difference" – the kind of "contingent and botched encounter" to which Tsing and Rao allude.[113]

To the charge that a story of traveling discourses of identity denies Cuban agency in its recognition of same-sex marriage, effectively crediting all of Cuba's ideas to outsiders, my response is to return to the comparative legal scholars cited in the introduction whose work frames my own: "laws neither fall from heaven, as lawmakers' ingenious insights, nor do they grow organically from the soil of local culture."[114] Instead, they are often best "understood as products of the confluence of information – some local, some … from elsewhere."[115] Further, it was the adaptations of the Cuban government amid global economic pressures as well as of Cuban individuals struggling to survive that produced the encounters out of which changing conceptions of identity emerged. Identifying conditions that shape our consciousness and the array of options available to us is not the same as denying agency.

The old homosexual, defined by his actions, is yielding to his gay successor, defined by his identity – an identity that is never distilled, rigid, or immutable, but nevertheless salient and increasingly predominant. He slipped into Cuba with the flow of capital like a stowaway, as the pinguero's emergence and adaptations exemplify.

Of course, male-male sexual commerce could not possibly be the *only* site at which foreign discourses of identity arrive in Cuba. Cuba accepts capital from foreign investors who might place a few managers in-country, or who might wish for assurances regarding a gay-friendly business environment; gay relatives from Miami, New York, and elsewhere might return to visit the island seeking acceptance of their identities, partners, or even marriages; individual Cubans in search of resources or contacts on the internet might be forced to make concessions to identity-related search terms. Myriad sites could host encounters between discourses from the outside and discursive conditions on the ground, producing altered conceptions.

***

In the US, same-sex marriage was made possible by an array of national and international factors. The Cold War was in the rear-view mirror, while the War on Terror became a central US foreign policy preoccupation. The specter of the communist homosexual infiltrator had faded, giving way to exhibit A of the progressive virtues of liberal rights as compared with the presumed illiberal stagnation and repression of Islamic countries. Moreover, the privatization of financial responsibility within the marital dyad climbed to prominence during the Reagan administration and peaked in the welfare reform bill signed into law by President Bill Clinton. The turn to partnership recognition as a result of AIDS, the rhetorical value in the war against Islamic adversaries, and the moralized pressure to privatize support within families in order to reduce welfare expenditures and cut taxes, paved the way to same-sex marriage in the US. The lgbtq movement could have gone in other directions (e.g., sexual liberty and non-monogamy, poverty alleviation and racial equality) but historical factors guided the movement leaders' sights toward marriage and converging national interests prepared the US to absorb that once unthinkable legal reform.

The end of the Cold War also delivered serious and substantial effects on sexual identity in Cuba, but they played out quite differently. Collapse of the Eastern Bloc left the tiny surviving socialist outpost to endure on its own against intentional deprivations inflicted by a hostile neighbor. To carry on without Soviet food, energy assistance, or trade subsidies, Cuba was forced into concessions to the global marketplace, which were reluctant and lurching, and chafed against its identity and ideology.

As Chapter 3 recounts, Cuba legalized new forms of home ownership as well as business entrepreneurship and self-employment. Some Cubans amassed savings for the first time. Additionally, Cuba pried open doors to tourists and investors, who brought much needed currency into the country. As tourism grew to become Cuba's leading industry, with many Cubans leaving government employment for its superior pay (and even Cubans still in the employ of the government providing services to foreigners as a side hustle), Cuba subjected itself to external influences that it could not completely control, including a transformed notion of sexual identity and the virtually entailed claim to marriage equality.

Marriage has long been a weak institution in Cuba, minimally pertinent to the workings of public or private distributive systems and largely devoid of social or religious meaning for the majority of Cubans. As gay identity crept into Cuba along with the much-needed capital, however, marriage gained new meaning. That gay and lesbian Cubans needed marriage in order to be treated equally under a regime of few benefits (especially when compared with affective de facto unions) makes little sense as a technical legal matter. Even as an issue of social inclusion, Cubans invest little importance in marital status. The best explanation for the emergence of same-sex marriage, supported even by heterosexual Cubans for whom marriage has long been regarded as trivial, lies in a less conscious realm. Unspoken assumptions about the role of marriage as necessary to a nation composed of ideal families well-ordered for property management joined with the globally circulating gay subject to open Cuba to the spreading imperative of same-sex marriage.

The factors facilitating the advent of same-sex marriage that are highlighted here do not preclude co-determinacy by other factors. Marriage always held *some* concrete benefits under Cuban law that gay and lesbian people and their allies might wish to see become more widely available. It is also possible that while the Catholic Church wields less direct influence in Cuba than it does in other former Spanish colonies, Catholicism nonetheless echoes through Cuban culture, subtly shaping moral and familial ideals, and paradoxically producing a gay desire for inclusion. Moreover, as Revolutionary Cuba's ardent critics suspect, gay marriage might function as a diversion from an array of liberal rights (notably expression and assembly) that Cubans effectively lack.[116] In the aftermath of the 2021 demonstrations[117] protesting shortages of food, medicine, and utilities, as well as the resultant arrests, crackdowns, and internet interruptions, Cuban eyes may be meant to follow the shiny object of same-sex marriage and be temporarily satisfied that progress is afoot.

Mariela Castro, whether with an intent to distract, a genuine dedication to equality, or some combination of the two, was undoubtedly instrumental to the gay, lesbian, and trans legal advances in Cuba during this century. Her backing ensured that same-sex marriage would come down from above, delivered by the hand of Cuba's somewhat obscure internal politics. But while Mariela's influence tells us something about *how* same-sex marriage became the law in Cuba, it does not tell us *why*. Why, in a country that has largely devalued the institution? Why, in system where – notwithstanding restrictions on dissent – major legal changes are sent out through the population for local discussion and feedback? Mariela surely played an important role, but to stop there is to give up on the question of why she used her power as she did.

It also overlooks the fact that Cuba is not an island – not in the figurative sense anyway. Mariela herself tours the world promoting the successes of CENESEX and engaging with international sex educators. What might have influenced the influencer? Perhaps a perceived association between same-sex marriage and modernity or justice acquired during her travels led her to believe that Cuba must not be left out of what has become an increasingly global imperative.

Moreover, CENESEX itself is extensively engaged with the lgbtq community within Cuba, providing health services, education, support groups, and so on. Even from a legally and socially marginalized subpopulation such as pingueros, evolving practices, conceptions, and vocabularies are bound to seep through the broader sexual economy, reaching the psychologists, educators, and lawyers at CENESEX.

Gay identity does not cross an ocean on its own zephyr. Its journey is observably correlative with capital flows. This adds something to the project of explaining same-sex marriage in Cuba, because for same-sex marriage to *make sense* in the Cuban context, categories of identity *had* to change. In the US, something had to change for marriage to make sense, as well, as Cott attested in her story of women's increasing formal equality in the workplace and household. Of course, the two nations' stories differ as widely as their geopolitical positions have differed over the last century and a quarter. In both cases, however, evolving political–economic conditions facilitated discursive and regulatory change.

PART III

Legal Consciousness

5

"Dentro de La Revolución"

METHOD

To gain insight into how Cuban lawyers thought about the advent of same-sex marriage and related matters, I traveled to Cuba in the fall of 2022 with my then-research assistant, Annery Miranda.[1] Our hope was to get a sense of the capacities and limits of Cuban law when it comes to social change – in general and for the benefit of lgbtq constituencies specifically.

Through some remote connections, I was able to obtain two invitations to the IX Conferencia Internacional Mujer, Género y Derecho (Ninth International Conference on Women, Gender, and Law) in the seaside resort town of Varadero. The conference was sponsored by the Unión Nacional de Juristas de Cuba (a professional development organization established by the 1976 Constitution) and chaired by its vice president, *Dra. Yamila González Ferrer*. It was attended mostly by law professors and lawyers from around the island along with a few international guests, mainly from Spanish-speaking countries, as well as by some social scientists, psychologists, and public health experts who specialize in fields pertinent to family law. Many of the attendees had played some role in the drafting and/or adoption of Cuba's 2022 Family Code. For three days, panelists delivered informative talks about various aspects of the new code, relevant constitutional provisions, and related sociological phenomena.

We learned an enormous amount substantively at the conference, but another principal benefit to us was recruiting interviewees to talk to us about Cuban law and social change.[2] We met individually with six lawyers, one of whom introduced us to five law students whom we interviewed as a group. We limited our discussions to lawyers and law students and confined our questions to issues of law and its possibilities. Because we did not engage any vulnerable populations and did not inquire about personal matters (beyond why our interviewees chose to attend law school and what kinds of legal careers they were pursuing or intended to pursue), our university granted us a waiver from IRB (Institutional Review Board) requirements with the exception of obtaining informed consent.

Our objective was to probe the contours of Cuban legal consciousness, especially in the context of social change for the benefit of lgbtq people. Duncan Kennedy explains, "The idea of legal consciousness is that people who practice legal reasoning do so within a pre-existing structure of categories, concepts, conventionally understood procedures, and conventionally given typical legal arguments."[3] Or, in the words of law professor Ugo Mattei,

> The notion of legal consciousness refers to a set of premises about the salient features of the legal order, especially the historical background of the legal process, the institutional apparatus, and the conceptual tools devised by lawyers, judges, and commentators. A number of those shared premises are so deeply embedded in the actors' minds that they are seldom acknowledged .... [L]egal consciousness is a cluster of beliefs held by the legal profession as a social group.[4]

The idea of legal consciousness in this chapter holds that legal advocates are constrained by a network of shared cultural assumptions at least as much as, and perhaps more than, by any positive law. These assumptions compose an unarticulated conceptual ambit within which some legal possibilities readily present themselves and others are difficult to see. They suggest to lawyers what legal tools are at our disposal and what law can or cannot accomplish. Legal consciousness is, in short, the legal profession's unspoken beliefs about the nature and extent of the possible.

Our primary objective in the interviews was not, therefore, to accumulate factoids about Cuban law, such as what some code provision requires or whether a particular act is illegal, though we did acquire some information of this nature. Instead, we were trying to gain insight into how Cuban lawyers and law students think about law. How do they make sense of its workings? What do they believe it can and cannot legitimately achieve? What avenues to change become obvious and why?

The largely unacknowledged nature of legal consciousness means that it is not a straightforward proposition to glean its contours from interviews. One cannot expect to gain much of value by asking directly "what are the contours of your legal consciousness?" or "what legal avenues has your training and professional culture placed beyond your imagination?" In an effort to elicit useful answers, we conducted interviews that largely proceeded as follows:

First, we invited interviewees to tell us about their own educational and professional trajectories. This not only brought each person into conversation and told us something about the specific interests of the individual before us but also familiarized us with some of the norms governing Cuban legal education, practice, and academia. Second, we asked questions designed to reveal whether they had an idea about what it means to "think like a lawyer." Wary of the biases instilled by our own training, we opened this topic by asking what, apart from the specifics of legal doctrine, they understood about law now that they did not understand before becoming lawyers; what (again, beyond doctrine) they were trying to get their students to understand about law (for students, what did they think their professors were trying to get them to understand) and what misconceptions their nonlawyer friends and family had about how law works. Third, we asked whether law was a good profession in Cuba for someone who wants to work for social justice, following up with questions about what law could and could not accomplish. And fourth, we drew attention to lgbtq populations specifically, asking what Cuban law had achieved, what it had not, and what it still might accomplish for the benefit of this constituency.

The interviews were "semi-structured,"[5] in that while we maintained this basic progression, we also tried to create a conversational tone, asking follow-up questions that pushed where we did not feel we got a satisfying answer or, alternatively, that traced an interesting thread from an initial answer. We framed most of our questions in an open-ended manner and engaged in dialogue, making an effort to be explicit about our own positionality.[6] For example, if we did not initially elicit much substance about "thinking like a lawyer," I sometimes shared my own experience trying to facilitate first year law students' shift from seeking answers to legal questions to producing arguments with the hope that this would provoke discussion of some similar or contrasting experience.

Toward the end of each interview, our questions became a bit more pointed. We sometimes gave specific prompts regarding reform possibilities in an interviewee's field of expertise. Based on my reading in the ethnographic literature, for example, I was particularly interested in whether criminal law enforcement by the police figured as an untapped area that could benefit lgbtq populations and asked about that specifically. (In the US, the policing of sex work imposes a burden on those sectors of the lgbtq population who are struggling to survive in the underground economy and are not always visible to law reformers focused on anti-discrimination and partnership recognition. I have asserted in past work that a discourse of equal rights has made formal equality measures the most obvious course of reform despite their limits when it comes to advancing the interests of people living on the economic margins.[7]) Going into the interviews, I predicted that marriage – as the now globally self-evident answer to the question "what does gay equality demand?" – might edge criminal enforcement by the police conveniently out of the frame.

Also toward the end of each interview, I prodded the possibility that the US and Cuba have historically valued marriage differently based in part on the number of public and private distribution schemes that rely on marriage in the US as compared with Revolutionary Cuba, where, for example, everyone has health insurance. I predicted that interviewees would agree and not regard the suggestion as an especially startling insight.

In listening to interviewees' answers, we were attentive to what lay beyond the information they directly provided; we listened for *narratives*[8] that might suggest underlying assumptions about what lay within or beyond law's capacities.[9] We also took note of questions that went unanswered and of moments in which we detected tension.

Almost all answers were delivered in Spanish. English excerpts below were translated by Annery.

The nature, scope, and number of interviews we conducted command humility. The interviewees should not be understood as a sample – that is, I have not relied on the data gleaned from the interviews as a basis for generalizing about populations.[10] Nor were we testing the effect of a particular variable.[11] The purpose of the interviews was to generate theoretical possibilities[12] about the contours of Cuban legal consciousness and the extent to which it might shape reform possibilities for the benefit of sexual and gender minorities in Cuba.[13]

The pages that follow advance extracts from our interviews in conjunction with complementary sources (conference presentations, informal conversations, environmental observation, and published primary and secondary materials). It is all assembled into a single narrative here to convey as fully as possible the inductive process.

CUBAN CONVERSATIONS

We arrived in Varadero on a sweltering afternoon at a *casa particular* owned by a cheerful and welcoming older couple where we would stay for the duration of the conference. Most of the other attendees stayed at the conference site, a huge hotel with swimming pools and other amenities, but the hotel was on the US State Department blacklist – a list of places in which US travelers are forbidden to stay by our own government,[14] presumably because the income generated by the hotel supports the Cuban military. It was an inconvenience to be sure, but it also gave us an opportunity to spend time in a quiet residential neighborhood.

Annery turned on the TV in her room. Flipping channels, she landed on footage from the Bay of Pigs invasion.

The next morning, at the start of the family law conference, the chair (the same person who invited us to attend) delivered a welcome address – mostly touting the achievement that is the new Family Code, reciting its highlights, and crediting many of the people in the room with its success. In a startling non sequitur, she concluded her remarks by referring to the US blockade, characterizing it as a "genocide," and adding "we denounce this crime against our people. Solidarity and love will win."

These two experiences occurring at the outset of our visit conveyed straightaway an impression that the specter of the US as an antagonist looms over everything in Cuba. That impression, of which we were never disabused, influenced my interpretation of what we heard in the interviews, as the following paragraphs will show.

The shadow of enmity between Cuba and the US did not, however, manifest as wariness toward us as individuals. On the contrary, most everyone was warm and generous with us, extending themselves in support of our learning and to make our visit easy and enjoyable. We were invited to join our new colleagues for lunch, go out for drinks and dancing, go to the beach, and be introduced to more people who might advance our work.

My own panel presentation (which I delivered in Spanish after some practice) reviewed recent developments in relevant areas of US law (especially the *Dobbs*[15] decision), explained a bit about federalism and the right to privacy, and lamented the US Supreme Court's hard rightward turn. Annery's flawless Caribbean Spanish and my best effort went a long distance toward cultivating trust and credibility, with one co-organizer letting me know that she was moved by my remarks.

Most of the Cuban scholars and professionals who spoke focused on efforts to address gender inequality, promote child well-being, or curb domestic violence. Several speakers emphasized multi-disciplinarity and how the new law responded to specific social problems. Our first interviewee, a law professor at Universidad de Camaguey, in an inland area of eastern-central Cuba, maintained a special expertise in children. Her conference presentation highlighted the important role performed by psychologists, noting specifically that in some tribunals a child's interests may be explored through picture drawing.

Several speakers introduced a social phenomenon (e.g., family violence) with a phrase such as "we don't like to talk about this, but …" or with acknowledgement of machismo or patriarchy as an obstacle to progress. This need for increased awareness or attitudinal transformation was echoed throughout the conference as well as in our interviews. When we asked about the role of law in advancing the interests of lgbtq people, the children's legal issues expert responded, "I don't think it's about changing laws. Law doesn't have a big role to play. The problem is really changing the mentality and the formation of values of people," adding that this required "confronting a patriarchal conception."

A significant contrast between the US and Cuban systems is the extent to which the legal process itself plays a role in attitudinal transformation.[16] In the US, the representational system, including regular election cycles, lobbying, public debate, and legislative deliberation, is the substance of the democracy in the legislative arena. Notwithstanding Cuba's single-party system and low tolerance for dissent, the Cuban government cannot fairly be said to have simply imposed the new Family Code on its citizens without vigorous public conversation. Neighborhoods and workplaces were charged with debating the proposed provisions, and the results of those discussions filtered their way up to the lawmakers, then back down with revisions, then back up. It was precisely because of this process that the Evangelicals were able to defeat the same-sex marriage provision contained in the 2018 draft constitution despite the president's and Communist Party's support for it. It took a few more years and a further campaign to win over enough Cubans to pass the Family Code via referendum (see Figure 5.1).

One nonlawyer with whom we spoke informally about the new Family Code expressed gratification about the referendum. He pointed out that the vote in favor

FIGURE 5.1 Roadside sign encouraging a *yes* vote in the referendum on the 2022 Family Code (#códigosí).

of the code was around 60 percent, not the near-100 percent by which some referenda have succeeded in the past. This was a positive indicator to him that the vote was real.

CHANGING LAWS, CHANGING ATTITUDES

The children's law expert from Camaguey, however, did not see law as important in the process of social change; it was mostly "mentality" and "cultural," she thought. Yet, she also described how the code was extensively based on citizen input, going through twenty-four drafts since 2006, much of it in response to public discussion. I asked her whether the process of adopting the law was itself a way of achieving attitudinal change. Reconsidering, she revised her answer: Law serves "both a regulating and an educational function."

Another of the interviewees was a notary and law professor specializing in civil rights and the law of obligations at Universidad de Matanzas (on the northern coast, a little bit east of Havana). A notary in the Roman–French tradition, she hastened to explain, plays a much more substantial role than in the Anglo system. A notary is a highly trained civil servant who functions as a delegate of the Ministry of Justice, presiding over a wide array of actions, with an emphasis on civil rights.

She stressed the importance of attitudes and "stereotypes" particularly in areas that are "very controversial." It came up in response to a question about what deeper lessons (than doctrine) she was trying to convey to her students. She explained,

> I don't like to teach in a way that I am above the student and they have to listen to me. I'm about an exchange, but sometimes you try to explain in different ways and people are unable to undo a formation they bring from their homes ... It's a social science, one where you bring your experiences, what your friend, your parent, said and that's what you apply. What we have to have clear is that human dignity has to feature prominently.

A few minutes later the notary added,

> It's important to work not just in the legal space. It's also important to work through the media, classrooms, from the moment of formation pre-university and from the point of view of psychological development .... What's taught to you in the first stages of life remains like a rock...

In the last segment of the interview, I told the children's law expert that I had read that gay men and trans women were often targeted by police, excessively suspected of solicitation. I felt the tension rise a bit in this moment, as she labeled my suggestion "a myth," correcting me by explaining that people who approach foreign tourists do so to extract money. (Her tone suggested that this was a nefarious motive.) It might turn out, she thought, that a person who "calls attention" to themselves in this way (i.e., by soliciting) is transgender, but she disclaimed the notion that the police targeted trans people. If I had had the wherewithal to follow the thread, the next question would have pushed on the apparent contradiction between her view that cultural attitudes were the problem while simultaneously dismissing the suggestion that some police may harbor transphobic attitudes; I missed the opportunity.

The notary readily pointed to the connection between transphobic attitudes and economic need that leads to sex work. When I asked specifically about the outstanding legal needs of lgbtq populations, she indicated that the needs were sweeping. In her scholarship, she analyzed the results of a 2017 survey of the trans population, explaining that the "psychological burden" of living in a "society that doesn't accept them" has the effect of "drag[ging down] the rest of their social relationships from social, educational, and family points of view." As a group, for example, "trans people had less educational achievement, and an extremely high drop-out rate. Very few go to university." She added that the survey participants "did not achieve stability in their socio-sensual, affective relationships."

The notary also indicated that societal attitudes toward same-sex marriage were lagging. "It was one of the aspects of the code that has the least comprehension or support," she said.

A law professor from Universidad de la Habana who had what he conceded was an unusual combination of specialties – environmental and family law – answering a question about law's limits, echoed this theme: "What can't law do? Law can often do more but law has to accompany society in its regulation functions and ordering functions. Society has values, has a determined sensibility that law can trigger but it can't go much further than what society requires."[17] He proceeded to give an example about trying to inculcate an appreciation for biodiversity – among ordinary people as well as police, prosecutors, and judges – in a culture in which many people keep birds as pets. A prohibition against the practice is "in the law formally, but the possibility of those laws are limited precisely because we have not gotten to the place in terms of education or awareness to touch that space of the Cuban soul." The state, he concluded, "needs to be concentrated on education and socialization – more so than repression."

That example, I suggested, made a good segue into laws regarding lgbtq people. Answering with specific reference to same-sex marriage he said "there is a part of the population that isn't in agreement because of things like traditional machismo or religion … maybe it could have been introduced more gradually." Still, he thought "the change in 2022 was a justifiable change."

Unlike the children's law expert, the environmental/family law professor frankly acknowledged the phenomenon of excess police attention to gay men and transwomen for possible involvement in the sex trade. He conceded that while no formal law directs this, the underlying attitude will not disappear overnight.

One interviewee was a former judge, now a family law professor at Universidad de la Habana who also serves as in-house counsel to Mercedes-Benz in Cuba. She was an especially interesting personality; she was the only person who at first seemed bothered by our request for an interview, but she was also the one who later said she had been moved by my remarks at the conference which seemed to cause her to warm up to us considerably. To interview her, we traveled to Mercedes-Benz local offices, located in a repurposed mansion in a pretty Havana neighborhood about twenty minutes from the university by car. She met us at the front door and led us up a flight of stairs and down a hallway to a conference room. Proceeding along the hallway, we passed large photographic portraits of Fidel and Che – hanging there unironically as far as I could tell. I was a bit stunned to see their images glorified in that particular setting, but I was being hustled along and failed to snap a photo.

The former judge echoed the concern about transforming attitudes, including in the legal profession.

> There are … lawyers who are very conservative. That's one of our battles we have now, that lawyers have to shed all of these traditional ideas that they've been dragging through generations to offer a service in accordance with what's being asked

> [by the new law]. I can't represent someone in a conflict that is intrinsically connected to questions of gender while being a homophobe, a machista person, a retrograde person who isn't sensitive about gender.

Like some of the conference speakers, she emphasized that when she was a law student, some topics were simply not discussed. "Violence is something people didn't talk about and regarding gender especially. CENESEX has been vital in transforming society. It has been a long journey but they have been instrumental in changing mentalities. Lots of machista conceptions and patriarchal preconceived notions that are difficult to change…"

She did see law as important to social change, though progress, to her mind, depended heavily on who was making the decisions. Interestingly, she had a family lineage in the law.

> Another thing that has a big influence is that I come from a family of jurists. My grandfather was one of the most well-known magistrates in the pre- and post-revolutionary eras. He played a great role in denouncing some of the scariest parts of the Batista dictatorship. Young boys would turn up in the mornings at the doors of [unintelligible], tortured and very mistreated and that moved him. They expelled him from judicial power in '57 or '58 and then he was one of the greatest constitutionalists [presumably after the 1959 Revolution] and that's why I say education is so important. I would see my grandfather come in with the records and go into his office and I would hear the typewriter going and he'd go to the discussions at the tribunals and it was something fantastic … And that humanist vision can come from your formation as a lawyer but it can also come from your formation as a doctor. A psychologist has to have a humanist vision. I think any of these can mark you.

NORMS VERSUS APPLICATION

The former judge volunteered a story about a case she decided back in 1997. A trans woman had emigrated but returned to Cuba to be with her dying parents. To reenter, the government required her to use her assigned male birth sex, "because in Cuba they only recognized who she was at birth." The woman lost initially, but as a judge at a higher level in a provincial tribunal, our interviewee reversed the lower court. The positive law ("norms") did not provide anything specifically on point, but the judge strung together an array of general provisions and "recognized the right of the person in light of the registry to change their name and sex … and provide a new document." She described the decision as "explosive" at the time but seemed proud to have made it and believed it helped set the course for subsequent advances.

This story was consistent with something that a number of interviewees stressed: The distinction between positive law (which they referred to as "norms" in the Kelsenian sense[18]) and its application, or what an American Legal Realist, following Roscoe Pound (a friend and admirer of Kelsen[19]) would refer to as Law in Books versus Law in Action.[20] The notary, for example, responding to a question about the role of lawyers in social justice, said,

> I think it has more to do with the person than with the law. It's the mode that you practice ... is what makes the difference. The way we put ourselves in the shoes of the person looking for legal counsel .... I tell our students that we have people's lives in our hands like doctors .... A correct solution that leads to solutions and consensus I think is sometimes better than the cold application of the law.

In response to a prompt about the limits of what law can do, the notary stated, "The limits are established by the law and you have to have the common sense to not overstep them, but not being the cold jurist who applies a blind law without particularities." And addressing the needs of transgender people specifically, she explained,

> What needs to happen is understanding ... you have to know what it's about and that's what's missing. When I talk about lack of comprehension and understanding from the population, the generality of the people, the people in their homes and families where someone is having a different experience of gender than what they were taught ... that's where I'm seeing a great problem ... the understanding that anyone in that situation may feel ... isolated, without needing to have that experience themselves. That's where we're seeing the barrier. The barrier is not the norms; there's total support at the policy level, but...

She went on to refer to an unfortunate story we had heard at the conference about an individual working at a civil registry who had exhibited zero understanding or compassion for a trans person seeking a name change and how this manifested as inflexibility in the enforcement of technical rules.

Another interviewee, the only Afro-Cuban lawyer with whom we met and one of just a small handful present at the conference, did some law teaching at Universidad de la Habana but primarily worked as counsel at CENESEX. She drew the same distinction between norms and their application. In response to a question about what law can do for the lgbtq population, a population very much at the center of the CENESEX mission, she replied, "It's not so much legislation or law, but implementation or application," adding "If we're talking about state responsibility, it's guaranteeing training and raising awareness of those who apply the law: judges, lawyers, prosecutors, assessors." When pressed about whether you can go to court and get a law enforced, she replied, "Yes, but we can't guarantee the success of the process. If the judge is prejudiced, what do rights resolve?"

Legal education in Cuba appears to be quite attentive to illumination of the gap between law in books and law in action. We met with a small cadre of third year law students at Universidad de la Habana. They explained that they will all do a practicum during their four years. One student said that she saw a real difference between doctrine and practice. Her professors, she said "open our minds ... application doesn't come out perfect," but you must "keep going." Another student said it was a lawyer's job to think critically, "not all the rules are great," but it is important to "be brave and look for justice and equality."[21] Several of the students emphasized law's role in protecting vulnerable people, such as minors, the disabled, and the elderly.

We had a hurried (but not too hurried for coffee) interview with a property law professor at Universidad de la Habana. He also saw implementation as the crucial thing, not what the rules say, opining that it is "better to have good judges and bad norms than bad judges and good norms."

The notary reported that some of her fellow notaries have indicated an unwillingness to formalize same-sex marriages. This issue, she said, prompted a national meeting to convey the message that "you can have your own beliefs … but you are working in service of the public."

The CENESEX lawyer noted a recent procedural change allowing judges to recuse themselves if they recognize that they might discriminate. Obviously "the problem is whether the judge will recognize that they will discriminate …. but at least it's something," she said, adding "[t]hose who are applying the laws did not make them nor did they study them" (because they are so new).

Similarly, the environmental/family law professor observed,

> Sometimes the vision that the public has of law is normativist, and as a result, the legal professional is someone who understands all the laws. And you have to explain that law is actually much more complicated. It includes principles and values. Just as important as the letter of the law is what is applied.

By way of further explanation, he said, "If you want to understand Cuban law and you just read what the law says you'll have a very partial view."

The former judge agreed.

> [A] lot of what I know now I acquired later [after law school] through practice, through confrontations with specific cases and that led me to go deeper into questions that you normally think are [answered] like a machine – the judge enters the lawsuit through a machine and it comes out on the other side exactly how the law says. All the awareness you need … you start acquiring over time.

ON MARRIAGE AND DISTRIBUTION

Near the end of each interview, I proposed that marriage might be more important in the US than in Cuba in part because of the vast array of distributive regimes, public and private, that rely on it – everything from employment-based health insurance to social security to loss of consortium to probate. In Revolutionary Cuba, I suggested, perhaps marriage has just not proven as important because of the limits on private ownership and the prevalence of social insurance programs that stream directly from the state to the individual.

The CENESEX lawyer completely rejected the theory. While she admitted that the "opening of the economy" meant that "there are people with money … [and] someone may have a business, car, or home," she felt that my theory could only be vindicated if I had data about home ownership and marriage with dates to see about correspondences. She did not seem intrigued.

The former judge did not respond directly. "Cubans don't like to get married. That's not new," she reported, dating the lack of interest in marriage back to the early 1900s. She explained that the 1975 Family Code took steps to protect survivors of deceased nonmarital cohabitating partners. She acknowledged some economic benefits to marriage but reduced them to "economic things ... if we divide the assets ... if I stay with the house." She reported that about half of Cubans do not marry and thought that those who did were not as interested in the property angle as with the idea that marriage was the ideal way to form a family, with other forms of union being "inferior." This, she thought, also explained why some Cubans have been slow to accept same-sex marriage: They do not think same-sex couples should be admitted to the ideal. Ironically, it seemed that those heterosexual Cubans who value marriage least are the same people who supported extending its availability to same-sex couples, while those who regard marriage as a morally significant, ideal family form were the most likely to have opposed its extension. With a sigh the former judge concluded, "Cubans get married and get divorced and get married and get together..."

The environmental/family lawyer also observed Cuba's cultural predisposition against marrying. "There is a lot of cohabitation .... [and] since the beginning of the twentieth century we have had a very divorce-friendly regime. Today in Cuba you can get divorced in front of a notary if there is agreement." He did not seem put off by my theory, but turned toward his view of the relationship between non-marital cohabitation and marriage:

> I do agree in part with the theory because now with the code we have given a bunch of rights to that affective union, cohabitation, including rights over certain common goods, inheritance rights ... law is similar between marriage and civil union [i.e., non-marital cohabitation] .... The more you give equal rights to people in civil unions and matrimony, matrimony becomes less important .... And that explains a bit of the statistics we've seen after the code. There have been celebrations of matrimony between members of the same sex but not as much as we thought. This kind of thing might explain why.

Toward the end of the visit, I slightly reworded my last question to focus more on recent changes in Cuba and less on the contrast with the US. Is it possible, I asked near the conclusion of the interviews, that marriage in general, and consequently same-sex marriage, becomes important as property becomes more important to more Cubans? The property professor did not think so, though it was not clear why. He mostly responded by speaking to the evolution of property law and the increasing number of Cubans who own property but did not seem inclined to tie these changes to marriage.

One of the law students struggled to explain that protecting vulnerable populations was more challenging where there was "private conflict between people," stammering a bit: "there are places where law doesn't go." He cited the prohibition against mortgages, but the connection was not evident to us. Pushed to clarify he said, "the private sector is growing ... it's not regulated yet because it's new."

Confounding our inquiry is the fact, as the environmental/family law professor noted, that two legal trajectories are running in contrary directions. Property is becoming more widespread, which could make marriage seem more important (though none of the interviewees confirmed this outright). As nonmarital cohabitation catches up with marriage, however (in the sense that the legal ramifications differ less and less), the effects of one trend offset the effects of the other. In other words, it may be that while marriage could gain significance as a vehicle for managing property, it is not sufficiently distinct from nonmarital cohabitation to produce a real rise in formalization. Marriage became more and less important at the same time.

Our last night in Cuba, Annery and I met up with a small group of queer activists at a bar in Old Havana. All favored the legalization of same-sex marriage. This came as somewhat of a surprise to me, due in part to the biases I bring from my own national lgbtq culture. In the US, the queer left tends to be skeptical of same-sex marriage, often because it is heteronormative[22] though that issue is not central to my own critique. I briefly explained my view that when gay rights advocates in the US pushed an agenda of same-sex marriage they effectively collaborated with the privatization propensities of neoliberalism and the moralization of containing financial responsibility within the marital dyad, thereby relieving the public sector of its responsibilities for the poor, elderly, and infirm. Could recent changes to property law in Cuba, especially new rights to buy and sell real estate, inject marriage with fresh significance and make this moment opportune for same-sex marriage? They paused to consider, then nodded, conceding that I could be right.

BACK TO BOSTON

I left Havana ruminating about why my professional colleagues did not agree. Back home, reviewing notes from the trip, some of the dimensions of the legal consciousness I wanted to understand began to materialize. The themes that surfaced most readily in the interviews and during the conference presentations were multidisciplinarity (especially reliance on psychological and public health expertise), the importance of education and attitudinal transformation within both Cuban officialdom and the general populace, and the gap between the written rule (the "norm") and its application. Every interviewee lamented law's limitations, gesturing toward machismo, the attitudes one learns from one's parents, or an encounter with some retrogressive official, as obstacles to progress. Each conveyed a belief that the legal letter cannot achieve its objectives without judges, civil servants, and the Cuban people evolving in their thinking. The lawyers with whom we spoke all seemed to view code changes as relatively ineffectual in the absence of attitudinal transformation.

In some respects, these themes sound familiar to a US-trained lawyer: We are, after all, all Realists now.[23] The introduction of empiricism to legal analysis and the critique of formalistic linear deduction where a single "general proposition" can yield more than one possible case outcome due to some element of judicial disposition, have been standard fare since around turn of the twentieth century.

Strikingly, though, the interviewees' cognizance of the gap between the codes and their application sat alongside regular invocation of high ideals such as equality, dignity, and humanism. As a US-trained lawyer, I generally envision a longer distance to lie between that sort of ideal and a case outcome than between a concretely drafted code provision and a case outcome. This is not to say that I hold either to be reliably determinative, just that the chain of reasoning might be a bit shorter in the latter case, permitting a tribunal fewer decision points and therefore creating less opportunity for political or cultural values to seep into the analysis. The Cuban lawyers and law students with whom we spoke, however, appeared to perceive the greater distance to lie between codes and their application, while imagining very lofty ideals such as equality, dignity, and justice to provide real direction. I had difficulty making sense of their skepticism when it came to short chains of reasoning combined with their apparent belief in the determinacy of the longer chains.

To appreciate what I had heard, I had to get past assumptions ingrained by my legal training regarding the aspiration to objective, linear, deductive, legal analysis. In interviews and conference presentations, our interlocutors made repeated references to the "spirit" of the law or the Cuban "soul."[24] The humanism to which they referred did not necessarily function as a starting principle from which case outcomes were to be deduced, but something less familiar: a living mandate, a form of compassion that – if it has reached a jurist's soul – guides that jurist toward justice. It did exactly this for the Batista-era magistrate – the grandfather of the former judge we interviewed. As the granddaughter told us, however, this humanistic spirit is not confined to the law; it is bigger than that. It is also there to guide the physician and the psychologist.

As a US-based legal thinker, I regard positive law as typically the outcome of struggle between conflicting (often but not always left/right) possibilities available within a shared legal consciousness. Based on what I could glean from our interviews, however, the trajectory of Cuban law did not read as a continuous partisan tussle between liberal and conservative political combatants. Instead, individual Cubans (a transphobic magistrate, or a law student's parents who hold patriarchal views) might fail to appreciate the law's spirit. It is the job of the lawyer or judge to pursue justice in the face of retrogressive thinking or bad norms – to do better than to give the law a "cold" reading.

The CENESEX lawyer told us that a recent change in the law allows judges who are aware that they might discriminate to recuse themselves – not for having a personal stake in a litigation, but for not being disposed to apply norms in a manner consistent with the law's spirit. Likewise, the students told us that their professors taught them to set their gaze beyond norms, toward justice in its manifold applications.

Add to this what was *not* said. None of our interlocutors fretted over judicial neutrality – a virtual holy grail in US legalism.[25] None appeared to share John Adams's aspiration to a government "of Laws, not of Men."[26] They understood right-thinking judges and ministry personnel to be *more* valuable and *more* predictable than codified mandates. These are the people whose souls have been reached by the humanistic spirit, guiding them toward justice.

Moreover, there was not much mention of gay, lesbian, or trans people being entitled to "rights." Rights are central to the progress of identity-based constituencies in the US. As explained by law professor Duncan Kennedy, the unique power of rights is that they exhibit both normative and "factoid" dimensions. "[T]hey are 'universal' in the sense that they derive from needs or values or preferences that every person shares or ought to share .... [T]hey follow from values but are neither arbitrary nor subjective because they are universal."[27] Then, "once you acknowledge the existence of the right," Kennedy explains, "you have to agree that its observance *requires x, y,* and *z.*"[28] In the US, a universal right serves as a starting place in a linear deductive analysis. It is supposed to take us from a general abstraction to a specific entitlement. Advocates of same-sex marriage have argued, for example, that gay and lesbian people have an equality right and are therefore entitled to access marriage on the same terms as heterosexuals.[29]

My Cuban colleagues, however, did not describe improved legal treatment of lgbtq people in this manner. Equality certainly came up, but it was not used as a starting point for the kind of analysis Kennedy describes. Improved treatment of lgbtq people came from something less deductive and more inspired.

The law of Revolutionary Cuba, if I listened well to my Cuban colleagues, is not the sum-total of its *norms*. It is constituted instead by an evolving humanistic consciousness. The lawyer's gaze is trained on the spirit of the ongoing Revolution as the source of and guidance toward progress. Because the lawyers we interviewed conceptualize things this way, they had no difficulty seeing a through-line from the Revolution to the extension of marriage to same-sex couples – notwithstanding some extremely homophobic legal mandates during the early revolutionary years. *The norms were never the thing.* It was the humanistic spirit that brought them to their pro-gay, lesbian, and trans position, and that spirit would bring along the rest of society – "touch the Cuban soul" – in time. Castro's maxim, "Dentro de la Revolución, todo; contra de la Revolución, nada" ("*Within the Revolution, everything; against the Revolution, nothing*")[30] captures an effective tautology: Legal progress is always revolutionary because the revolutionary spirit is what brings it into being.

CONSCIOUSNESS AND CONSTRAINT

To a US-trained lawyer, the absence of any aspiration to deductive neutrality and the deemphasis on rights reasoning are striking. One consequence of such tendencies, to the extent that they predominate within Cuban legal consciousness, is that they completely deflate what scholars of Critical Legal Studies (CLS) call the *indeterminacy* or – less sweepingly and more precisely[31] – *under-determinacy critique*. The critique is a case-by-case attack on linear deduction – not because logic has no value, but because it can be overvalued and put to ill use.[32] When effective, a critique of determinacy shows that a decision was not logically required by the legal materials upon which a decision-maker purported to rely.[33] It peels back the cover of objectivity in a specific analysis and exposes gaps and decision points[34] into which political, moral, or personal preferences might have seeped.

The reason for the delegitimating impact of an in/under-determinacy critique in the US is that the legal culture places a premium on apolitical neutrality. This is especially the case in the domain of counter-majoritarian decision-making because judges in our federal system are not elected and are therefore unaccountable to the voting public for their policy preferences. Non-motivated expertise (typically scientific or social scientific) is also prized,[35] and just as lawyers sharply distinguish *law* from *policy*, policy experts analogously distinguish *policy* from *politics*.[36] In either dichotomy, the offender is *desire* – a contaminant in what is supposed to be a chaste process of apolitical rationality. (More on this is coming in Chapter 6.)

It was the American Legal Realists of the late nineteenth to early twentieth century who pioneered the under-determinacy critique.[37] Most famously, Justice Oliver Wendell Holmes, Jr., in his dissent in *Lochner v. NY*,[38] illustrated the falseness of the majority's claim that the due process clause of the Fourteenth Amendment *required* that a maximum hour law for bakers be struck down as a violation of contractual freedom. He did so in part by identifying instances in which contractual freedom was infringed without constitutional interference and by musing at the absence of a principled distinction between the case at bar and those other instances.[39] The Realists (excepting Holmes, actually) were mostly Progressives,[40] and while they led the way to this critique of judicial reasoning, some key players put their faith in empiricism, expertise, and policy analysis as a more reliable foundation for legal outcomes.[41] Writers associated with Critical Legal Studies (CLS) built on the work of the Realists in part by extending the under-determinacy critique to policy, as well.[42]

The interviews suggest the possibility that Cuban legal culture may not prize objectivity over competing values. On the contrary, the best decisions, according to my interlocutors, come when the humanistic spirit reaches the soul of the decision-maker. A Cuban legal actor considers norms, but might have to move beyond them, striving for justice. There was no valorization of neutrality evident in the interviews as far as I could detect, nor do norms seem to function as starting principles in an idealized deductive process insulated from extrinsic considerations. A critique aimed at exposing the failure of neutrality then, would have no delegitimating effect.

Cuba is, however, noticeably engaged in a broader nationalist discourse, not confined to legal actors: that of the unremitting specter of the capitalist, imperialist menace to the north, and the determined stiff-arm against any suggestion that Cuba has slackened its resistance to US economic pressure. This was evident everywhere we looked. One cannot miss the posture of defiance. All around were constant references to US antagonism and its failure to defeat the Cuban Revolution. Bay of Pigs footage was running on daytime television as if it were breaking news. The chair of the family law conference, in her welcome address, abruptly turned from extoling the new Family Code to passionately condemning the US blockade as genocidal.

I came to suspect that the obscured significance of economic change in the advent of same-sex marriage was related to this defiance, partly due to the difference between the queer activists, outsiders to the Cuban power structure, and the lawyers, who were relative insiders. The activists had no difficulty acknowledging the global circulation of gay identity, possibly because they were party to it. The lawyer-interviewees, however, were either steadfast in their denial of such influence or just blasé about the suggestion. Their apparent confidence in the humanistic spirit as the primary force moving the law forward seemed to join with the affective residue of US imperialism and bullying to produce their sense of what did and did not play a role in lgbtq advancement.

Cuba's discourse of defiance converges with, and bolsters, its resolute identification with socialism as a discrete political–economic system. In the midst of all the changes to Cuban law governing real estate, entrepreneurship, and foreign corporate partnerships, the preamble to Cuba's 2019 Constitution[43] reads in part,

> WE, THE PEOPLE OF CUBA,
>
> inspired by the heroism and patriotism of those that fought for a free, independent, sovereign, and democratic homeland of social justice and human solidarity, forged through the sacrifice of our ancestors …
>
> by those that fought for over fifty years against imperialist domination, political corruption, the lack of rights and liberties, unemployment, the exploitation imposed by capitalists, landowners, and other social evils;
>
> by those who promoted, participated in, and developed the first organizations of laborers, farm workers, and students; disseminated socialist ideas; and founded the first revolutionary, Marxist, and Leninist movements…
>
> GUIDED
>
> by the most advanced revolutionary, anti-imperialist, Cuban-Marxist, Latin American, and universal thought, in particular by the ideal and example of Martí and Fidel, as well as the social emancipation ideas of Marx, Engels, and Lenin;
>
> SUPPORTED
>
> in proletariat internationalism…
>
> DETERMINED
>
> to carry forward the triumphant Revolutions of Moncada and Granma, of the Sierra, of the underground struggle, and of Girón that, sustained in the contribution and unity of the principal revolutionary forces and the people, conquered full

> national independence, established revolutionary power, realized the democratic transformations and initiated the construction of Socialism;
>
> COMMITTED
>
> to Cuba never returning to capitalism as a regime sustained by the exploitation of man by man, and that it is only in socialism and communism that a human being can achieve his or her full dignity;
>
> CONSCIOUS
>
> that national unity and the leadership of the Communist Party of Cuba, born through the unitary will of the organizations that decisively contributed to the triumph of the Revolution and legitimized by the people, constitute fundamental pillars and guarantees of our economic, social and political order…
>
> WE ADOPT
>
> by our free and secret vote, through a popular referendum … the following.…

Then the "following" (notwithstanding the foregoing!) includes Title II, Art. 22(d), newly recognizing "private ownership," including by foreigners.

In an even more recent example, in October 2022, President Díaz-Canel delivered a speech to the 22nd International Meeting of Communist and Workers' Parties in which he pronounced the arrival of a global crisis resulting from "declining capitalism that pushes the world toward barbarity."[44] He proclaimed,

> Our horizon continues to be socialist, even after the tragic disappearance of the socialist bloc in Europe and the disintegration of the Soviet Union, and despite the ferocious anti-communist campaigns that the powers of transnational capitalism have turned into a single thought dogma through powerful global media.[45]

Increasing privatization, marketization, and foreign capital investment are unmistakable hallmarks of the post-Fidel economic order in Cuba, yet Díaz-Canel does not waver in his representation of Cuba's socialist national identity or capitalism's barbarity and decline. The photographic portraits of Fidel and Che hanging on a wall at Mercedes-Benz struck me similarly: as if nothing at all were exploding with contradiction.

Examples such as these point to a resilient belief in a crisp socialist/capitalist dichotomy, each side of which corresponds tightly with a self/other (Cuba/US) national identity. It is de rigueur to observe that Cuba could not diverge too far from Fidel's ideological commitments while he was still alive, but even now, amid the dramatic economic shifts, a deep official investment in socialist identity persists.

The original question that generated this research was whether and how socialist Cuba might "do" lgbtq legal advancement differently from the capitalist and neoliberal US, and whether the Cuban socialist approach would leave less economic stratification in its wake. On the one hand, Cuba's early progress for lgbtq constituencies came in the form of public health and sex ed initiatives. Both were (and are) socialized resources in Cuba and both are universal and destratifying. Those approaches, however, do not *entirely* distinguish themselves from the US system, which also socializes health and education to *some* extent. The US has Medicaid and other welfarist programs to support the health of its poor, elderly, veterans, and so forth, though the programs are stingy, to be sure. The US also has sex education classes in public schools, though their nature and quality vary widely from state to state and school district to school district.

As Erik Olin Wright observes, "actual economic systems are messy combinations of capitalist and noncapitalist relations."[46] While Cuban and US stories of lgbtq progress differ in many respects, the differences cannot be comprehensively explained on the basis that one is socialist and the other capitalist. Wright argues, "No economy has ever been – or ever could be – purely capitalist."[47] He effectively says the same of socialism when he urges, "the contrast between capitalism and socialism should not be regarded as a simple dichotomy, in which an economy is either one or the other. Instead, we can talk about the *degree* to which an economic system is capitalist or socialist."[48]

Wright defines *capitalism* in terms that involve markets, private property, and class relations.[49] *Socialism*, he explains, was once widely thought to refer to "an economic system in which private ownership was replaced by state ownership of the principal means of production, and markets were replaced by some form of comprehensive planning oriented to meet needs rather than maximize profits."[50] The failures and "repressive character[s]," of the Soviet Union and China, however, prompted some rethinking.[51] Wright proposes an improved vision of socialism as an "idea [about] the way power is organized within economic structures, particularly power over the allocation and use of economic resources."[52]

The Cuban conception of socialism, however, looks to be fixed in the earlier definition, despite the undeniable existence in Cuba of private property and markets. This was the case even prior to the Special Period. Just review the rules governing property on divorce under the 1975 Family Code,[53] or the dimensions of ownership set forth in the 1984 Housing Law,[54] to say nothing of the (prohibited but nevertheless pervasive) underground markets that have existed in Cuba for decades. The mixedness of the Cuban economy exemplifies Wright's point on the socialist side just as surely as everything from national parks to public assistance benefits within the US economy exemplify it on the capitalist side. In each case, there is an emphasis that reflects the systemic identity, but neither system is unified behind a singular characterization.

To the extent that an unrelenting devotion to the socialist ideal provides Cuba with a sense of unified political–economic and national identity, concessions to the economic pressures imposed by the US blockade or by global markets are bound to be difficult to acknowledge. It is unclear how far in the direction of private property and markets Cuba could go without its leadership feeling the nation's socialist identity to be jeopardized. This could partially explain Cuba's constant loosening, tightening, loosening, and tightening of economic controls. Cuban policy vacillates between the Scylla of economic despair and the Charybdis of loss of self.

The visit to Cuba did not enable me to return to the US armed with a cache of specific law reforms of a socialist nature that could advance the interests of lgbtq people living on the economic margins. Instead, the visit provided me with a glimpse into how the Cuban lawyers and law students I met understand the capacities and limitations of law and the role of legal professionals in advancing social justice. It opened me up to the idea that a contemporary legal culture could aspire to something other than apolitical neutrality, as well as to the interrelated possibility that something other than political desire could be suppressed by predominating discursive forces. The suggestions about legal consciousness that I extracted from the interviews are situated within a broader, stalwart, political–economic and nationalist identity, one of standing strong against the deliberate pressures of a regional antagonist and the prevailing winds of the global economy.

Part II asserted that Cuba's legalization of same-sex marriage was, for at least two reasons, improbable: The low degree of religious or social significance that a majority of Cubans attribute to marriage and the minimum of formal legal benefits attached to marriage as distinct from its de facto alternative. It went on to ask what, then, might explain the sudden importance of extending marriage to same-sex couples? Chapters 3 and 4 point to converging discursive conditions as under-recognized factors. Chapter 3 draws attention to the revolutionary regime's ill-conceived promotion of marriage in the 1970s and 1980s and its unintended and contradictory effects: production of marriage as hegemonic and simultaneously parodic. Chapter 4 adds the impact of gay identity (and marriage as its essential form of recognition), entering Cuba by way of the very channels by which desperately needed foreign capital arrives on its shores (tourism, expat visits, managers from foreign firms, and the internet).

If I have listened well and interpreted fairly the lawyers and law students who generously sat for interviews, the perspectives they shared suggest a theory about some of the "premises" or "pre-existing structure of categories," that could be "deeply embedded," and "seldom acknowledged" among these practitioners of legal reasoning – that is, their legal consciousness. The notion that gay identity and equality in the form of marriage sprouted naturally out of the revolutionary spirit, and its commitments to broad ideals such as humanism and justice could easily suggest itself to the exclusion of outside forces. At the same time, a nationalist discourse resistant to acknowledging imperialist influence or concessions to capitalist elements that contravene socialist identity would make it harder to see the relevance of the factors that stood out to me as a lawyer shaped by quite a different legal culture and very distinct nationalist assumptions.

I propose this as a theory, developed from a particular vantage point and a fecund encounter with Cuban legal thinkers, all of us shaped by our histories. The purpose is to open up theoretic possibilities in Chapter 6. What I gathered from my Cuban colleagues' offerings will serve as a mirror, providing fresh insights into the under-recognized conditions establishing contours around my own legal culture, and specifically around leftist approaches to law reform generally and for the benefit of lgbtq populations in particular.

6

Reflections in a Cuban Mirror

Under-interrogated assumptions circumscribing the legal imagination can come into greater relief after investigating another legal culture. Indeed, studying Cuba and dedicating specific focus to the trajectory of its sexuality and gender minorities surfaced some of the presuppositions animating this project at its outset. Notwithstanding my own methodological rootedness in the highly variable distributional minutia of legal rules, standards, and degrees of enforcement within the US legal system, I nevertheless permitted myself to imagine that a socialist country would offer specifically socialist ideas for lgbtq legal advancement that might curb economic stratification in the wake of US liberal rights gains under capitalism. The nature of legal change, however, turns out to be far more obscure. Rather than growing out of systemic imperative, the law governing sexuality and gender minorities takes a wild ride through global and local interfaces and is shaped by material and discursive forces that do not consistently align with any systemic frame.

This chapter gazes into the mirror of Cuba in pursuit of what lessons can be found there for legal thinkers situated in the US (or a similar Anglophonic jurisdiction that foregrounds markets and legal liberalism). It identifies two: excessive confidence in the determinative power of meta-systems and underestimation of the importance of discursive power to the dynamics of law.

After exploring these twin lessons, the chapter turns directly to an inquiry at the heart of the book: How can we best understand the role of political economy in the evolution of sexual and gender identities and the law that governs them? It reviews possibilities ranging from the idea that gay emancipation envisioned in communist terms could end capitalist alienation to the proposition that gay liberation comes with expanding markets. Finally, it concludes with a genealogical vision of a richly contextualized and nonsystemic mode of comprehending political economy and governance of sexual and gender identities.

ALL SYSTEMS GO

Cuba's unique history of defiantly maintaining its socialist identity against global tides, read together with snippets from the interviews (in Chapter 5) regarding the revolutionary spirit reaching the Cuban soul, suggests the possibility of a distinctive facet of legal consciousness: a belief that socialism and revolutionary spirit drive legal advances. If this theory has any purchase it would make it easy for Cubans like our interlocutors to view a legal development such as same-sex marriage as a natural outgrowth of socialist ideology and the ongoing Revolution. Discourses of identity that accompany the inflow of global capital, on the other hand, would be less visible to someone prone to reject a narrative of pervasive imperialist or capitalist influence. The mirror, then, consists of a high degree of confidence in the determinative capacity of a political–economic system, including a tendency to perceive that system (in the context of a concomitant nationalism) as the force behind progressive legal change.

What, then, is reflected back to the legal left in a setting such as the US? It would not be attribution of determinative power to Cuba's socialist and revolutionary spirit, but its obverse: attribution of determinative power to capitalism.

In 2023, law professor Matthew Dimick contributed a post to the Law and Political Economy (LPE) Project blog entitled *Is Capitalism 'a Thing'?*[1] His post was one in a series published on the blog that fall in which contemporary legal scholars addressed a longstanding debate among social theorists regarding the relationship between law and political economy. Although less fully elaborated than long form material, the LPE series in which Dimick's essay appeared provides a recent, succinct, and handy representation of a cluster of longstanding arguments about whether political–economic systems have an existence separate and apart from their legal constitution. The following paragraphs, therefore, treat the series as a text from which key points in a contemporary debate among left-legal academics can be gleaned.

Dimick's own answer, explicitly reliant on his reading of Marx's conception of *capital* as investment to accrue more capital, is that *capitalism* is indeed a *thing*: The term refers to "a society subordinated to the process of accumulation."[2] Capitalism has a trans-contextual essence for Dimick, a structural logic untethered to any particular legal configuration. To those who would maintain that "economies are just a 'mushy continuum' between capitalist principles and non-capitalist ones," Dimick retorts that under capitalism, even "across … many different [legal] arrangements, money is still used to make more money."[3]

Dimick's post and the other installments in the series were prompted by law professor Samuel Moyn, who in September, 2023 posted a provocative essay entitled *Does LPE Need Theory?*[4] In it, Moyn offered a friendly critique of recent scholarship published under the LPE banner (not necessarily on the blog, but associating itself with the surging LPE school of thought in which the blog plays a major role) and in so doing, he contrasted LPE with Critical Legal Studies (CLS). According to Moyn, CLS (about which he writes as if it were an historical relic rather than a thriving tradition with adherents generating first-rate scholarship around the globe[5]) had an excess of theory, while LPE suffers from a theory deficit. LPE, Moyn maintains, "treats such words as 'democracy' and 'equality' favorably, though they are contested," but "has shown essentially no interest in articulating the general social theory of law on which its pluralistic normative claims rest."[6] A certain amount of "theoretical quietism," Moyn conceded, is unobjectionable, but that "shouldn't mean that we don't know what we are signing up for."[7]

Moyn attributes LPE's reluctance to announce a theory, or even to undertake the difficult process of sorting it out, to "a deferential attitude towards grassroots movements, and … a strategic postponement of potentially divisive controversy."[8] As to the former, he appreciates the wish to avoid subordinating movements "to bloviating theory-heads who will not shut up," but asks whether we ought to "envision law schools … as nothing more than staging grounds for practical servants of the masses?"[9] As to the latter, Moyn observes that LPE is indeed growing in its appeal among left legal academics but "wonder[s] … at what point the advantages [of silence] begin to be outweighed by the drawbacks."[10]

Moyn provoked Dimick and others by posing the question whether "there is such a thing as the 'capitalism' that we attack most consistently,"[11] effectively suggesting, at least as Dimick reads him, that capitalism is "nothing more than a contingent jumble of various legal rules."[12] Dimick complains that while "Moyn encourages us to eschew the detour of capitalism and view all economic arrangements as 'only legal and more broadly political arrangements in which inequality improves or … worsens,'" Dimick wants us to stop "deny[ing capitalism's] existence."[13]

Law professor Yochai Benkler closes the series, also addressing the question of capitalism's "thingness."[14] Benkler's definition of capitalism, however, which he uses interchangeably with "market society," gets him off to a less dogmatic start: Under capitalism, Benkler explains,

> (a) most people live in households that depend on commodity exchange in markets to satisfy their basic needs and wants; (b) most organizers of production depend on commodity exchange in markets for access to labor, material and knowledge resources, and credit or finance to deal with time and uncertainty; and (c) the political military formations depend primarily on taxing market activity or selling public debt as commodity exchange in markets to satisfy their fiscal needs.[15]

So, Benkler, too, sees a *thing* called *capitalism*, but he describes it using a couple of "mosts" and a "primarily" rather than defining it by a single driving purpose. Still, Benkler appears sympathetic to Dimick's viewpoint when he says, "Power seeking – pursuing the capacity to impose transactions and prices one wants on counterparties to produce a steady flow of rents – is the animating spirit of capitalism."[16]

After interviewing Cuban lawyers who made periodic references to law's "spirit," it was curious to see that word in Benkler's description. He does not seem to be referring to Weber ("spirit of capitalism")[17] or Montesquieu ("spirit of the laws").[18] I took Benkler to mean instead that seeking power for the purpose of maximizing rent-extraction is a current that runs through the whole of capitalism, not in a mystical sense, but in a unifying one.

What is the role of law in Benkler's capitalism?

> [Law] has played a large role as a terrain of struggle over the institutionalization of market dependence for subsistence, production, and protection .... By structuring access to natural resources ... access to knowledge ... and access to means of payment and credit, as well as the forms of coordination and cooperation in labor and investment processes, law structured social relations of production creating a distinct combination of freedom and coercion, opportunity and imperative, that has been the driving dynamic of capitalism.[19]

Specific legal rules are born of "power struggles" for Benkler, and they "structure asymmetric power in social relations of production along dimensions of class, gender, and race."[20] All along, legal "academics and judges [have] harnessed legal theory" to both "legitimate and contest ... emerging ... relations."[21]

Benkler's account is more dynamic and conflictual than Dimick's, but not enough to account for myriad practices incompatible with capitalism's "animating spirit" by being indifferent to or inconsistent with rent-extraction (think national parks, Social Security, etc.[22]). Socialized resources in an economy widely understood to be capitalist form a mirror image of socialist Cuba's ubiquitous private property and markets. Both Dimick and Benkler see a unity that is regularly belied.[23]

Sociologist Fred L. Block refers to this kind of systemic vision as an "illusion;" specifically, "the idea that capitalism is a system that has its own logic."[24] In Block's view, "capitalism, whether conceptualized in global or national terms, is not a coherent and unified system. On the contrary, successful market economies depend on a complex combination of conflicting institutions and motivations; they are contradictory and unstable, and they periodically require major structural reorganizations."[25]

To build his argument, Block relies on economic sociologists (such as Karl Polanyi) but also on legal writers, particularly those in the American Legal Realist (ALR) and CLS traditions.[26] These two schools of legal thought tend to eschew systemic thinking in favor of granular analysis and the search for levers of redistribution that might be located in the "background."[27] The political–economic (so-called) *system* is actually a constantly shifting *assemblage*[28] of rules, rules gaps, standards, zones of discretion, prohibitions and permissions, as well as degrees of enforcement. Sometimes what looks to be a minor change can effectuate a significant redistribution.[29]

If capitalism were a *thing*, that is, a unified system with a trans-contextual logic, then we might expect it to have relatively stable structural features that reliably produce outcomes – but it does not. Retired South African jurist Dennis Davis and law professor Karl Klare (a major figure in CLS) explain,

> [P]articular 'types' of society – whether capitalist, socialist, or other – do not possess an inbuilt structure that tightly determines the legal regime .... A social or economic institution – say, a market for the purchase and sale of labor power in a capitalist society – can be legally structured in a wide variety of ways based on

> different foundational rule sets … These rule sets may have quite different distributive consequences …. In a general way, one might attribute the content and distributive effects of a particular rule set – for example, the law of contractual offer and acceptance in late nineteenth century England – to the type of society in which it appears (industrial capitalism, in this example). But the attribution would tell us very little about the shape and content of the rules or possible alternative configurations.[30]

Labor law and practices in a given context could be extremely oppressive (e.g., poverty wages, no maximum hour rule, absence of workplace safety regulations) or comparatively generous (e.g., lengthy paid parenting leaves, paid training opportunities, on-site childcare and fitness facilities). The contrasting legal arrangements would look quite different as would the distributive landscapes, including the prevalence (or not) of dire life circumstances for working people. A systemic label does not help us much to understand conditions as they are lived on the ground.

But more conceptually, as Davis and Klare argue, characterization of the system "would be circular. One cannot provide a coherent description of late nineteenth century English industrial capitalism … without discussing the legal rules that partially construct and constitute that social order."[31] It is difficult to describe a political–economic system without reference to law. What renders a system *capitalist*? Could we answer the question without explaining private ownership of property or distribution via markets? Even if we were to define capitalism using a summative principle (e.g., Dimick's *everything is subordinated to accumulation*) this would lead inexorably to the follow-up question: How exactly would one recognize that subordination? At that point, we are back to property and markets, which are, as we learned from ALR, creatures of law. Markets are massive constellations of various rights in property and contract, enforced (and thereby also defined) by courts and other tribunals (e.g., zoning boards, regulatory agencies, etc.). The "system," therefore, does not "have" law; it is *constituted by* law and social practice in all their variability.[32] No single rule renders the system *capitalist*; millions of legal features vary across nominally capitalist systems. At the same time, however, to explain a system *as capitalist* one would likely resort quickly to its legal features.

None of this is to say that *capitalism* is entirely devoid of meaning. Davis and Klare again: "the claim about indeterminacy in the law/society relationship is modest …. [It is only that] we cannot identify core social structures … that tightly determine legal institutions, and … that legal rules, practices, and cultures are central to identifying what we mean by a given social order and its characteristic arrangements."[33]

We could say, then, that capitalism lies somewhere between a system with a transcontextual logic (i.e., a "thing") and nothing but an utterly disconnected assortment of rules. It is perhaps best understood as a heuristic that stands for an emphasis on markets and private property (each of which is also highly variable and, therefore, not a "thing") rather than as a structural logic that yields predictable outcomes. Even where a national economy leans in a capitalist direction, the actual variety of legal arrangements that can be contained under the term is quite vast, and so, therefore, are the possible resulting distributions.

Finally, laws do not stand still. Lawmaking (including law-interpreting and law-enforcing) continuously evolves to solve and create new problems, serve and produce new interests, and adapt to and generate new circumstances. Every small or large adjustment (in family law, tenancy, criminal law, labor law, immigration, antitrust, taxation, zoning, environmental regulation, etc.) is potentially redistributive. To sum up this perpetual motility in any one national (or local, or regional, or global) economy, therefore, as statically capitalist or socialist, is not all that useful. Rather than imagining capitalism and socialism to be antipodal, expect to see arrangements under each that resemble the tendencies associated with the other.

If systemic logic predictably determined all the injustice in a particular context, whole-system solutions would readily suggest themselves. In her celebrated 2023 law review article on "non-reformist reforms,"[34] law professor Amna Akbar[35] reasons, "If capitalism is the problem, then abolition rather than reform should be the goal."[36] This if/then formulation illuminates potential drawbacks to the recent spate of abolitionist movements (though each should be assessed on its own terms). Promotion of an abolitionist solution performatively establishes the nature of the problem. The if/then implicitly reverses itself: *If* abolition is the only real solution, *then* a unified and determinate system must have been the problem. Abolitionism implicitly accepts that the root of bad outcomes lies with a system as a whole. It accords capitalism far too much credit, overlooking the sense of false necessity that provides alibis to so many specific injustices. While the turn to abolition is understandable in the face of pervasive violence and dramatic inequality, make no mistake: It is a unifying move. In the context of capitalism, abolitionism takes for granted the trans-contextual logic of the system and eclipses opportunities that the system's indeterminacies afford. As Block put it, the "illusion" that capitalism is a unified system with a consistent internal logic "mak[es] it far more difficult to see what kinds of changes [could be made] in institutions at the local, national, and global level."[37]

It is equally possible, however, that a legal thinker who adheres to a systemic mindset, attributing undesirable legal conditions to capitalism's consistent internal logic, *does* see the variability that Block wants everyone to see; it is just that the thesis is poorly matched to the analysis.

Take, for example, a piece by law professor Ntina Tzouvala,[38] that provides an analysis of international trade law and its facilitation of what anti-capitalist economist Thorstein Veblen referred to as *sabotage*, or capital's "conscientious withdrawal of efficiency" (e.g., the oil industry's "deliberate reduction of production" to control prices).[39] As Tzouvala explains, the sabotage thesis is a rejoinder to "the ideal that capitalism [is] a fundamentally dynamic and innovative system" in which competitors strive to outdo one another by improving their products or increasing efficiency.[40]

Law, Tzouvala tells the reader, enables forms of sabotage, and she gives the example of tariffs. "[D]omestic capitalists [might enlist] the power of the state in order to sabotage their foreign competitors and acquire a competitive edge without the need to produce cheaper or better products."[41] For Tzouvala, this is *textbook capitalism*:

> [P]rivate property rights allow the owner not only to enjoy their property, derive an income from it, or exclude others from its enjoyment. They also allow owners to under-use, misuse, or not use at all socially valuable resources insofar as their fulsome use would cause their profits to decline. The combination of *unrestricted* private property rights and production for profit makes sabotage endemic, and not aberrational, in capitalist societies.[42]

"Unrestricted" is a peculiar word to use to describe property rights, as lawyers well know. Property is circumscribed by innumerable restrictions; that is why it is sometimes described as "a bundle of rights" where an owner has some, but not all, the sticks in the bundle. Can you legally open an all-night pub in your living room? Probably not, even if you own your home. Rules on commercial versus residential use are likely to be in the zoning code governing your neighborhood and there is likely also an applicable liquor licensing scheme. Your property rights are not, therefore, unrestricted. In the context of international trade, a different array of restrictions governs. The Doha Declaration (now enshrined in Article 31bis of the Agreement on Trade-Related Aspects of Intellectual Property, or TRIPS), for example, establishes that a country experiencing a public health emergency can compel a pharmaceutical patent holder to license another producer in order to ensure access to needed medicine.[43]

The regulatory details governing property holders engaged in international trade are beyond the scope of this book (and my expertise) but the fact that there *are* such details is the point. Picture them as just a few among thousands of tiny levers distributing the costs and benefits of trade to various parties (manufacturers, retailers, laborers, consumers, carriers, exporting countries, importing countries, etc.).

Tzouvala's own work amply demonstrates that she is cognizant of the broad array of rules and regulations at play. She points to "quantitative restrictions" and "regulatory barriers," as well as "intellectual property rights," associated with the World Trade Organization (WTO) as facilitating increased international sabotage, observing that pertinent arrangements set a "specific balance" of what is "permissible, mandatory, and impermissible."[44] She notes how the rules "shift production and … its associated risks [from large multinationals] to mid-and lower-tier firms" and explains

> [f]or this model to work, international trade law had to ensure that products could cross borders multiple times before hitting the consumer market …. WTO law made this possible by requiring low tariffs, generally prohibiting quantitative restrictions, and offering strong protection of intellectual property rights and rigorous scrutiny of regulatory barriers.[45]

It is plain that Tzouvala is well attuned to how treaty rules yield a calibrated degree of efficiency/sabotage. But what if the rules changed? What if tariffs were permitted to inch up or border-crossing of some goods were restricted? It is not Tzouvala's characterization of the system as capitalist that tells us where we might intervene to redistribute gains and losses; it is her observance of the specific rules and their effects.

This summary is of a short-form piece by Tzouvala for reasons of space, but lest you fear the assessment sets too high an expectation for a blog post (even in such a high caliber operation as the LPE Project blog) her book, *Capitalism as Civilisation*, also contends that rules emanate from systemic imperative and that legal variation does not undermine that contention.[46] The question that Tzouvala does not (and I suspect *cannot*) answer is: *At what point could the rules change enough that they could no longer fairly be considered to flow from capitalism as an independent force?* How much variability is too much for the systemic logic to sustain? The WTO, like any ordinary governmental or intergovernmental agency, makes marginal rule adjustments routinely and larger changes more periodically. Technology and other contextual factors change around even the longstanding agreements, redistributing effects.

What does the idea that everything is pre-determined by capitalism add to our observation of the hydraulics of the rules and their enforcement? In her book, Tzouvala's answer is, "[t]hinking through structures enables us to embed legal analysis into broader considerations about the synergies between our discipline [of international law] and global patterns of profoundly unequal distribution of wealth, power and pleasure," adding, "[i]f the law [were] wholly indeterminate, fluid and contingent … it [would be] impossible to argue that it 'did' anything, that it somehow constituted, or even influenced relations of domination, exclusion, or exploitation."[47] The problem with this argument is that the "structure" cannot be said to be doing much without resort to its constitution through law (Moreover, *indeterminacy* does not mean that law does not do anything, but we will get to that later).

Benkler's contribution to the LPE Project series, too, acknowledges the endless array of legal forms that can be characterized as *capitalist* as well as the role of law as a "terrain of struggle" over resource distribution. His invocation of an "animating spirit of capitalism," then, is odd; the idea of an independent driving force is unsupported by what he himself has characterized as variable and contradictory.

Why not let go of the fantasy of the independent force? Perhaps credulity regarding a trans-contextual logic, or animating spirit, of capitalism betrays a longing to identify a soul of oppression that, if struck, would transform our unjust social world into one that is fair and equitable. Excessive reliance on systemic characterization, however, faces a serious circularity problem. A system is plausibly described as *capitalist* largely by virtue of its legal dimensions, but those dimensions are so variable that there is no point at which a legally effectuated redistribution converts the system to one that is noncapitalist. Benkler and Tzouvala effectively acknowledge that the struggle over the rules is where all the distributive action occurs, but then pull back, as if a gravitational force is at work and the only real possibility for justice is its wholesale eradication, ultimately rendering human agency, hard at work in the minutiae, worthless – just tinkering that can never defeat the all-powerful "system."

Further, the analytical problem forces a political quandary: Can legal reform lead us to a better world – one of social democracy and distributional fairness? If not, does that leave us with a choice between violent revolution and reformist futility?

Akbar proposes that "non-reformist reforms" can ameliorate this dilemma, helping leftists to think through alternatives to "liberal reformism" on the one hand and "armed insurrection" on the other.[48] This is an excellent objective, but it would best be furthered by giving up on the notion, contained in abolitionism, of the capitalist system as a seamless and determinate whole in favor of a turn toward mounting delegitimation of the system's purported constraints. Those constraints are not intrinsic; they are perceptions filtered through the consciousness of its players.

Klare explains in his response to Akbar, "[t]he non-reformist reformer does not hope to accumulate enough reforms to miraculously 'tip' the system from authoritarian capitalism to egalitarian post-capitalism. The goal … is to induce a revolution in political consciousness … [to] undermine the "common sense" of capitalist culture."[49] To do this demands a constant eroding of hegemony, or what Duncan Kennedy has labeled "viral" critique.[50]

The difference may sound like internecine left-legal academic pablum, but there are *stakes*. Systemic thinking can curb the legal imagination, making it more likely that attention will be diverted away from opportunities for progressive change and political consciousness-raising. These opportunities require a critical eye, on the lookout for the myriad internal contradictions that can be pushed or pried to achieve redistributive ends and can also help to reveal the falseness of narratives of necessity. Concession to the existence of systemic logic has the potential to unwittingly aid in legitimation of the unjust distributions that leftists seek to challenge. Preoccupation with wholesale transformation undermines confidence in possibilities for real change.

This is a hazard that exists for left-legal thinkers situated in the US and other Anglophonic jurisdictions characterized by liberal legalism and a market orientation. It came into relief, however, in the mirror produced by listening to Cuban lawyers and law students (in Chapter 5). What I heard as an apparent faith in a humanistic spirit, tied to Cuban socialist ideology, as a principal determinant of progressive change, brought left-legal faith in the unity of capitalism into view.

Let's return now to the topic of *indeterminacy* (or, more judiciously, *under*-determinacy), a critique not only of determinist claims regarding capitalism but also regarding judicial reasoning – and for a homologous reason: to guard against inadvertent legitimation of unjust legal outcomes by taking the logic of the system for granted. Consider the example of lgbtq advocacy in the US. Widespread social acceptance and a long list of legal advances could easily lead one to conclude that gays and lesbians (not so much transgender persons) have "made it" as national subjects, going practically mainstream in politics and culture. Economic data, however, continue to show elevated rates of poverty,[51] homelessness,[52] and food insecurity[53] among gay and lesbian people while simultaneously showing slightly above-average incomes.[54] You read that correctly: Gays and lesbians in the US are both poorer *and* richer than the general population. Stated another way, the data reflect a dramatic wealth gap.

As I have argued elsewhere,[55] that wealth gap is at least partially a consequence of law reform strategies that have predominated within lgbtq legal advocacy in the US over the past few decades. Specifically, such advocacy has too often participated uncritically in a discourse of equal rights that excludes from its purview a broad array of legal conditions shaping life on the ground for the most marginalized members of the community. The acquisition of formally equal legal status can itself legitimate dramatically unequal lives.

Consider the 2019 US Supreme Court case of *Bostock v. Clayton County*.[56] This case presented the question whether Title VII of the 1964 Civil Rights Act, which prohibits employment discrimination "because of … sex,"[57] effectively prohibits discrimination on the bases of sexual orientation and gender identity. The Court consolidated three cases that arose from three separate circuits of the US Court of Appeals, two of which involved the explicitly discriminatory discharge of gay men and one of which involved the explicitly discriminatory discharge of a trans woman. Confident that they would have four votes from the liberal side of the Court, attorneys for the fired employees designed their arguments to woo at least one of the conservative justices who adhere to a *textualist* interpretive method. According to this method, the statutory words should be read as they would have been widely understood at the time the law was enacted, in this case, 1964, when it was unlikely that the term *sex* was commonly understood to entail sexual orientation or gender identity.

Relying on a strategy generated by law professor Katie Eyer,[58] legal advocates framed their argument in textualist terms.[59] The strategy worked; Justice Gorsuch wrote the majority opinion and Chief Justice Roberts also came over to the employees' side for a surprising 6–3 victory over the discriminatory employers. Gorsuch's reasoning represents the pinnacle of formality:

> The employer hosts an office holiday party and invites employees to bring their spouses. A model employee arrives and introduces a manager to Susan, the employee's wife. Will that employee be fired? If the policy works as the employer intends, the answer depends entirely on whether the model employee is a man or a woman. To be sure, that employer's ultimate goal might be to discriminate on the basis of sexual orientation. But to achieve that purpose the employer must, along the way, intentionally treat an employee worse based in part on that individual's sex.[60]

An analogous line of reasoning supported the outcome on the trans case.[61]

> [T]ake an employer who fires a transgender person who was identified as a male at birth but who now identifies as a female. If the employer retains an otherwise identical employee who was identified as female at birth, the employer intentionally

> penalizes a person identified as male at birth for traits or actions that it tolerates in an employee identified as female at birth.[62]

To win over Gorsuch and Roberts, advocates could not propose to expand the definition of *sex*; they had to rely on the definition as it would have been understood at the time the legislation was passed. Because both sexual orientation and gender identity, as the Court understood them, rely on an underlying conception of *sex* as simply male or female, the Court was able to reason its way to this outcome without changing the meaning of the term.

Bostock is a colossally important case for several reasons. First, Title VII is a federal law, so an anti-discrimination provision now blankets those parts of the country that had not yet enacted state laws explicitly protecting sexuality and gender minorities in employment. Second, trans people especially face immense obstacles to above-ground employment, forcing many into the underground economy where they are subject to an excess of police attention resulting in high rates of incarceration. Third, this was the US Supreme Court's first time addressing a specifically transgender issue on the merits, so it is encouraging to see that transphobia did not overwhelm methodological commitments for two of the Court's conservative members. And fourth, this was the Court's first merits decision on sexual orientation since the retirement of Justice Kennedy, a pro-gay conservative who swung the majority and authored the main opinions in most of the gay rights decisions of the last three decades, so it is encouraging to see this outcome without him.

At the same time, the *Bostock* case cannot help but legitimate fallacious formal logic that could do some real damage down the line. In Justice Alito's characteristically cranky dissent, he writes,

> [S]uppose we add two more individuals [to the employee holiday party, so we] have the four exemplars listed below …
>
> **Man attracted to men**
> Woman attracted to men
> **Woman attracted to women**
> Man attracted to women….
>
> The discharged employees have one thing in common. It is not biological sex, attraction to men, or attraction to women. It is attraction to members of their own sex – in a word [sic], sexual orientation.[63]

Alito flips Gorsuch's reasoning on its head, taking advantage of the indeterminacy of the statutory language. On the US Supreme Court, where political neutrality continues to be prized, majority and dissent each present their analysis as chastely deductive. A Martian, landing on earth without any particular investment in lgbtq politics, could be forgiven for thinking Gorsuch and Alito presented equally persuasive cases about whether the term *sex* in Title VII encompassed the *Bostock* plaintiffs' distinguishing traits.

Gorsuch's formalistic approach also legitimates reasoning we might anticipate about scenes that do not appear in the office holiday party hypothetical. A future case, for example, might concern who, under Title VII, can use the women's restroom at a workplace. If an employer denies access to a transwoman, *Bostock* provides all that a transphobic court requires to legitimate rejection of her discrimination claim. If the court considers the transwoman's sex to be that which was assigned at birth, that is, male, and other males are denied access to the women's restroom, not only would the requirements of Title VII be satisfied, but the outcome would be legitimated by the very reasoning that gave us *Bostock*.

Moreover, the *Bostock* Court artificially stabilized sexual and gender identities. How will Gorsuch's formalism work for a nonbinary person? Imagine that a sympathetic court awards a trans victory in a bathroom access case based on acceptance of the idea that a transwoman *is* a woman. What of the person who does not so identify, but – given only two options – would prefer to access the women's restroom at work rather than the men's room? Or, imagine if, in establishing the definition of *woman*, the court determines that the most relevant factor is that the plaintiff had surgically changed her body to conform to expectations of femaleness. What then of the employee who identifies as a woman but has not undergone surgery, whether for reasons of preference or financial inability? The textualist interpretation of *sex* in *Bostock* worked for a basic "fired just for being trans" case, but its presuppositions are way too formalistic and binary to accommodate the internally variegated categories within the trans and gender-nonconforming population.

Lastly – and in my view both most important and least appreciated – even after *Bostock*, lgbtq constituencies continue to disproportionately perform sex work and other labor in the underground economy. Anti-discrimination laws, after all, do not *eradicate* discrimination. We can expect, therefore, to continue to see obstacles to above-ground employment for a minority that is (at this writing) under severe political assault. *Bostock*, like other formal equality rulings for the benefit of marginalized identity-bearers, by pronouncing the group equal in the realm of employment, effectively legitimates the carceral response, as well as any adverse consequences in employment or public assistance that follow from having a criminal record.

This is simply a downside of anti-discrimination law: The fact of its existence suggests that continuing inequalities are outside the reach of the law. Among the progressive critiques of *Brown v. Board of Education*[64] is that once the law declared the races formally equal, continuing de facto segregation in schools and its resultant inequalities in wealth, educational and professional attainment, and encounters with the criminal law appeared to be a result of the failures of African-Americans.[65] Similarly, once *Bostock* formally extends Title VII's employment protections to trans people, any remaining unemployment, poverty, and criminalized survival activity appear to be the fault of trans people themselves. *They could have just gotten a job, right? Employment discrimination against trans people is, after all, illegal.* As a group approaches formal legal equality, responsibility for its lived inequalities increasingly look to reside with the group rather than the law.

Bostock presented a specific legal question to a Court with a particularly challenging composition; to win the case might well have required the strategy that the plaintiffs deployed, and there is no doubt that the victory comes with important benefits. The decision to bring the case, however, was not required. Legal advocates sometimes put a straightjacket on gay and trans identities even when they win. Those cramped identities in turn have the potential to produce a false sense of necessity for a gross maldistribution of resources. A honed instinct for indeterminacy and some foresight about the costs of formal equality pronouncements *might*, after getting everything into the calculus, have steered advocates away from the case and toward a different overall strategy.[66] An alternative,[67] one attentive to a broader set of legal conditions facing lgbtq subpopulations, would necessitate attention to the thousands of rules and regulations governing everything from labor to ID to zoning to credit and more. In other words, it would require retraining the lgbtq advocacy gaze toward the myriad levers of distribution affecting and constructing lgbtq constituencies.

Two key reasons support advancing an in/under-determinacy critique such as this one in the context of judicial reasoning even where the outcome, on its own, benefits a constituency of concern: First, one might foresee the likely application of the reasoning to hurt the same or another vulnerable constituency. Second, the outcome of this case, the acquisition of formal equality in employment, has the potential to legitimate *distributive inequality* (i.e., rampant unemployment and the consequences that flow therefrom).

The in/under-determinacy critique, then, is a tool of delegitimation. Its aim is to divest an asserted logic of its force by demonstrating that even on its own terms a resulting unjust distribution – which was ostensibly impersonal and apolitical – was not necessary. Ideally, the critique should erode faith in the supposed neutral correctness that fortifies large-scale inequality, empowering those with a redistributive agenda. The point applies to both capitalism *and* judicial reasoning.

DISCOURSE AND AESTHETICS

My Cuban interlocutors, though, did not appear committed to an ideal of neutral correctness. When we asked them questions such as what nonlawyers do not understand about law and what law can and cannot accomplish, their answers invoked broad, aspirational ideas about justice and the need to look past "norms" (i.e., positive law) to achieve it. The law students reported being explicitly encouraged by their professors to train their eyes on justice, even where the norms did not easily lead them there. The best reading of a rule, we gleaned from the interviews, would be that which most comports with the humanistic spirit associated with the Revolution. This is not to idealize Cuban legal thought, which made plenty of allowances for homosexual persecution in years past, but merely to highlight a contrast on the value of apolitical deduction. None of our Cuban interlocutors said anything that suggested a remote interest in or aspiration to apolitical reasoning or a neutrality ideal. In fact, a "cold" reading, as one interviewee put it, would be contrary to her conception of how to do legal interpretation and application.

Such articulations by our interviewees reflected back a quite contrasting aspect of US legal consciousness. In the US, even as the possibility of neutral judicial reasoning becomes less and less believable (to lawyers and laypeople alike) initiation into professional legal culture nevertheless still requires training in a discourse of neutrality, chaste rationality, and the exiling of political desire. The apparent contrast with our Cuban interviewees puts US devotion to neutral rationality into stark relief.

Impersonal interpretation is the discourse in which US lawyers present their arguments and in which judges explain their decisions. This can be explained in part by the conceptual constraints imposed by a counter-majoritarian federal judiciary as set forth in the US constitution; judges in the federal system are not elected, so (the theory goes) it would be anti-democratic for them to rule from their values or politics. Neutrality discourse, however, exceeds the domain of federal litigation, inflecting law more broadly with an ideal of neutral correctness.

This section returns to the LPE series launched by Moyn's provocative essay to work through a related but nevertheless separate point regarding the discourse of rationality. Two rather pugnacious posts in the series took exception to Moyn's characterization of CLS as substantially theorized in comparison to LPE. One embittered installment, entitled "Legal Theory in the Lowercase," was contributed by Tzouvala, who condemned CLS for being (1) "grounded in … Marxism-related anxieties," (2) drawing from "non-legal literatures ((post)structuralism, linguistics, psychoanalysis)," and (3) "gravitat[ing] toward an aesthetic sensibility."[68] The overall effect of these lamentable CLS attributes, Tzouvala contended, is to "marginalize[] materialist inquiry within law" and forget "what legal theory … is for."[69] The way to understand CLS, she maintained, is "as an attachment to certain avant-garde aesthetics and a commitment to paradox-uncovering as its opening and closing move," and – Tzouvala's *coup de grace* – as "suggesting that trying to explain anything at all besides vague references to contingency was a sign of lacking nuance and, even worse, of being uncool."[70]

An equally dyspeptic post came from law professor Talha Syed, entitled, "Did CLS Have (Much of) Any Theory?"[71] His answer … well, you probably guessed. Syed twists the knife in the wound: "for many within CLS, the aim of theory seemed less to be the cognitive one of explain[ing legal outcomes,] than an aesthetic one of celebrating complexity for its own sake."[72] Syed condemns the resort to complexity as "a sign of defeat … masquerading as sophistication."[73] The "*entire point* of … analysis," Syed asserts, is "to wrestle that complexity into generative insight. To end an analysis with 'it's all very complex' is simply to put up one's hands."[74]

Notwithstanding their evident hostility, they are not entirely off-base as a descriptive matter. It is true that some leading CLS writers borrow from post-structuralism, linguistics, and psychoanalysis, which *I think* is related to the charge that CLS is consumed with "aesthetics." Neither of the two authors explain exactly what they mean by "aesthetics," but I take them to refer to aspects of CLS critique that are oriented toward the discursive or affective.

The main reason for the interest of many CLS writers in "aesthetics" is that legitimacy can be facilitated aesthetically. Reading in post-structuralism, linguistics, psychoanalysis, and (I would add, though they did not mention them) queer, critical race, and postcolonial theory, helps one to appreciate the power of discourse, narrative, subtext, affect, and whatever else might be collected under the umbrella of "aesthetics" in legal analysis.

Foucault contributes a key insight here in the second of his Two Lectures,[75] specifically in his observation that "[t]here can be no possible exercise of power without a certain economy of discourses of truth."[76] In the Foucauldian formulation, "discourses of truth" legitimate acts of the sovereign by assuring subjects that the sovereign's conduct is constrained, and therefore, his rule is not sheer "domination," but instead is "right."[77]

CLS writers have taken this insight on board in the service of leftist projects. "Leftism," as Duncan Kennedy has written, "is aimed at transformation of existing social structures on the basis of a critique of their injustice …. The goal is to replace the system, piece by piece or in medium- or large-sized blocs, with a better system."[78] While some injustice is perpetrated by sheer force, offering no alibi, that which is perpetrated in the name of The Law relies on legitimacy, or what David Kennedy describes as an "alchemy of prestige and fear."[79] In the US, legitimation is facilitated by a discourse of apolitical rationality – using an ostensibly neutral deductive process and "express[ing] power as right."[80] This discourse of rationality *is itself an aesthetic*. It exerts legitimating power by obscuring political desire. An indeterminacy critique, when effective, gives lie to an apolitical and impersonal linear deductive process, damaging the legitimacy of the outcome that the deduction girds. Tzouvala and Syed regard the indeterminacy critique, or "paradox uncovering," as a kind of recreational mental gymnastics, a logic game with no particular politics or consequences. The dangers of *Bostock's* discourse of crystalline rationality, especially the legitimation of poverty, incarceration, and other concrete injustices that flow from formal equality, are invisible to them.

CLS writers employ critique in service of delegitimation not only by using an uber-rational exercise that exposes the limits and gaps in a specific deductive process, but also by rupturing the aesthetic of neutrality. Duncan Kennedy refers to critique as a "transgressive artifact,"[81] that "'shatters' the forms of 'proper' expression in order to express something that those forms suppressed."[82] The objective is to

> loosen the sense of closure or necessity that legal … analyses try to generate. But rather than putting a new theory in place, it looks to induce, through the artifactual construction of critique, the modernist emotions associated with the death of reason – ecstasy, irony, depression, and so forth.[83]

Critique is meant to, and often does, produce what might be an unwelcome and, as Duncan Kennedy describes it, "intense experience in the interstices of a disrupted rational grid."[84] Dislike of this "intense experience" could be behind the rancor of some CLS detractors. Those detractors probably also suspect (and not without cause) that some CLS writers take pleasure in irrational affective experiences, as well as in provoking those experiences in others. I concede it; it is much like the exhilaration of blowing your students' minds. The gratification is in reaching someone deeply, making the kind of impact that a powerful piece of music might make, but ideally with a political pay-off.[85] I suspect it is characterological for some people to feel distressed by such a disorienting experience and others to get a thrill. For those of the latter disposition, the disruption can provide not only excitement, but fresh confidence that rationality discourse in service of a particular injustice is misleading and vulnerable. It saps the discourse of its authority and capacity to intimidate. Successive efforts to induce that experience are meant to achieve exactly what Klare calls for in his response to Akbar: "induc[ing] a revolution in political consciousness ... [to] undermine the "common sense" of capitalist culture."[86]

Redistribution is also a goal, but there is no expectation that it happen all at once. The strategy is to erode the pretense to objectivity, hopefully effectuating a partial redistribution as well as a moment of awakening. Foucault aligns himself with this strategy when he speaks of "conduct[ing] an *ascending* analysis of power, starting, that is, from its infinitesimal mechanisms."[87]

Targets of CLS critique typically include "the central ethical/theoretical concepts of bourgeois culture, including the autonomous individual choosing self [along with the market], conventional morality, the family, manhood and womanhood, the nation state ...."[88] Each of the targets Kennedy cites supplies alibis for injustice. But so have "the proletariat, class solidarity, party discipline and socialist realism, and... sexual and racial identity,"[89] so they, too, have been targets of CLS (as well as of queer theory, critical race theory, and postcolonial theory).

Syed admonished CLS for failing to adequately engage with critical (as opposed to orthodox) Marxism to develop a "genuine theoretical alternative to the naturalizations of liberal individualism."[90] The consequences of CLS failures, Syed concludes, are "critical blinders, as if nothing can be wrong with laws apart from internally unstable meanings ('indeterminacy') or market processes apart from the role of the state ('legal constructivism')."[91] Injustice can occur under conflicting nominal systems and theoretical banners, hence, the resistance to reconstruction among (at least a strand of[92]) CLS writers. This could also be a breaking point for left-legal detractors of CLS who read the CLS allergy to reconstructive theory as "throwing up one's hands" or "forgetting what theory is for." It is true that refusal of reconstruction can produce an epistemological crisis in which one must confront one's normative commitments without the security of a theoretical foundation. This can be scary, but there is an alternative: shake off the wish for validation of abstract rightness and acknowledge political desire. Put otherwise, shift away from putting one's faith in theory and redirect it to "balancing ... conflicting ethical and practical considerations."[93]

The apparent lack of concern with neutrality among the Cuban lawyers and law students we interviewed, along with what was (for me) a startling discourse of the spirit and the soul, highlighted by way of contrast a profoundly powerful aesthetic that pervades US legal consciousness. In the US, apolitical, deductive neutrality is *our* elusive ideal. Even as legal thinkers disclaim belief in its plausibility, the quest for a totalizing theory of "right" hangs on. Attending to the power of discourse yields another important benefit of in/under-determinacy critique. Its function in "paradox uncovering," and disclosure of "complexity" can produce a deep experience of disenchantment in the aesthetic of rationality that legitimates unjust distributions. The power of this aesthetic becomes visible in the mirror held up by our Cuban interlocutors, for whom deductive neutrality appears not to play a significant role.

HOMOPHILIC DESIRE

In the field of sexuality and gender, attention to discourse (or the "aesthetic," if you prefer) is vital – and not only to critique rationality. Identities form and reform, sometimes inviting regulatory transformations, which in turn might transfigure identities. As Part I showed, the male homosexual acquired meaning – not denotation, but subtextual valence – in Cuban and US political imaginations during and after the Cold War. While Revolutionary Cuba cast him as a remnant of capitalist depravity, in the US he represented the threat of communist infiltration. Each of these homophobic but nevertheless diametrical discourses arose out of an anxiety specific to the geopolitical position of a nation in a particular historical moment. The figments are more than random, but not exactly a product of careful deliberation.

Homophilic writers, however, have devoted serious thought to vindicate their intuitions that gay/homosexual emancipation is especially compatible with their political–economic ideologies. Is there any basis for believing that emancipation of sexual and gender minorities attaches readily to a specific political–economic arrangement? This section reviews a sampling of efforts by homophilic writers of contrasting political–economic ideologies to secure an elusive connection between two deeply felt parts of themselves. Not unlike the "big system" approach discussed earlier, however, the connections they identify will prove unreliable, indeterminate, and wishful.

Take Mario Mieli, a leading voice in the early movement for gay emancipation in Italy who died in 1983, young and by his own hand. Rejection of commodity capitalism was, Mieli thought, essential to sexual liberation. In his most well-known book, *Towards a Gay Communism*, Mieli picked up on Freud's *Civilization and Its Discontents* as follows: "the process of civilisation [is] the conversion of powerful libidinal forces, their deviation from the sexual aim into labour and culture ... labour [is] the sublimation of Eros."[94] From this premise he deduced, "Civilisation, therefore, is seen as having repressed those erotic tendencies that are subsequently defined as 'perverse', in order to sublimate this libidinal energy into the economic sphere."[95] (This piece of his argument shares a sensibility with Gayle Rubin's in Chapter 4; the sexual system supports the economy in both accounts.) Invoking Herbert Marcuse, Mieli went on to contend, "the perversions uphold sexuality as an end in itself" and societies must therefore "ostracise" them "because they threaten to reverse the process of civilisation which turned the organism into an instrument of work."[96]

While Mieli treats Marcuse favorably, he insists that *Eros and Civilization* requires an update: "Today," Mieli explains, "it is clear that our society makes very good use of the 'perversions' .... 'Perversion' is sold both wholesale and retail; it is studied, classified, valued, marketed, accepted, discussed. It becomes a fashion .... The unconscious is sold in slices over the butcher's counter."[97] In other words, while the perversions (understood as sex strictly for pleasure rather than for reproducing laborers) once condemned in service of maximal productivity, now find greater acceptance, but only to advance commodity capitalism (e.g., in movies, apparel, and – alas, it must be conceded – gender and sexuality studies).

A crucial change has occurred according to Mieli's telling. The perversions were at one time *suppressed*, but now they are *liberalized*, in the service of capitalism:

> If for millennia, therefore, societies have repressed the so-called 'perverse' components of Eros in order to sublimate them in labour, the present system liberalizes these 'perversions' with a view to their further exploitation in the economic sphere, and to subordinating all erotic tendencies to the goals of production and consumption. This liberalization ... is functional only to a commodification in the deadly purposes of capital. Repressed 'perversion', then, no longer provides simply the energy required for labour, but is also to be found, fetishized, in the alienating product of alienated labour, which capital puts on the market in reified form.[98]

From this dismal appraisal, a specific project follows: "The struggle for the liberation of Eros is today ... the rejection of a sexuality that is liberalized and packaged for sale ... it is the refusal of sexual consumerism."[99]

Mieli's diagnosis means that it is not sufficient to limit one's analysis to class conflict. "The struggle for communism today must manifest itself also in the negation of the heterosexual Norm founded on the repression of Eros and essential for maintaining the rule of capital over the species."[100] This is offered by Mieli as a corrective to the Marxist framework which casts sexuality as *superstructural*: "labour ... and hence, the entire economic structure of society, depends on the sublimation of Eros .... Eros is *substructural*."[101]

This is a peculiar conclusion for Mieli to reach. If, as he argues, the perversions threaten capitalism at one moment and sustain it at another, then their relationship to capitalism is not structural at all. Just as Mieli himself uncovers the indeterminacy of the relationship, he proclaims its determinacy.[102]

Foucault also opined on the absence of a structural relationship between capitalism and sexuality. Here, he is refuting the attribution of repression of infantile sexuality to a bourgeois interest in preserving sex for the reproduction of laborers:

> These kinds of deduction are always possible. They are simultaneously correct and false. Above all they are too glib, because one can always do exactly the opposite and show, precisely by appeal to the principle of the dominance of the bourgeois class, that the forms of control of infantile sexuality could in no way have been predicted. On the contrary, it is equally plausible to suggest that what was needed was sexual training, the encouragement of sexual precociousness, given that what was fundamentally at stake was the constitution of a labour force whose optimal state … was to be infinite: the greater the labour force, the better able would the system of capitalist production have been to fulfil and improve its functions.[103]

Foucault perhaps overstates the diagnostic case when he contends, "I believe that anything can be deduced from the general phenomenon of the domination of the bourgeois class," but his prescription is nonetheless a good one: "One needs to investigate historically, and beginning from the lowest level."[104]

I detect a hint of gay supremacism in Mieli (which I do not share). Mieli betrays such tendencies when he offers, for instance, this retort to the old charge that homosexuality is a manifestation of narcissism: "it is in this very capacity to recognise ourselves in others that [homosexual] relations can bring about a markedly revolutionary disruption, a revolt towards the attainment of communist intersubjectivity and the overcoming of that shimmering illusion of atomized individuality."[105] So it is not just that the perversions were sublimated to the cause of capital, but also that same-sex eroticism has a unique capacity for bringing about communist intersubjectivity. Homosexuality, Mieli suggests, might just be the key to ending the alienation Marxists associate with life under capitalism.

I read Mieli to be expressing feelings of longing – a profound wish to identify a deep-seated, even innate, connection between his sexuality and his politics – two things he perhaps experienced with emotional intensity and believed *must* bear some relation to one another.

In his introduction to the foundational volume of queer theory, *Fear of a Queer Planet*, American Studies professor Michael Warner conveyed something similar, albeit not specifically Marxist.

> Every person who comes to a queer self-understanding knows in one way or another that her stigmatization is connected with gender, the family, notions of individual freedom, the state, public speech, consumption and desire, nature and culture, maturation, reproductive politics, racial and national fantasy, class identity, truth and trust, censorship, intimate life and social display, terror and violence, health care, and deep cultural norms about the bearing of the body. Being queer means fighting about these issues all the time.[106]

Warner's use of the term *queer* (rather than *gay* or *homosexual*) imports a signal of his normative commitments into his sexual identification. It is effective for purposes of communicating his politics to his reader, but it embodies, rather than resolves, the problematic of the relationship between sexuality and politics.

The socialist feminists of the 1970s and 1980s in the US and UK complement Mieli with their theory of capitalism's reliance on the heterosexual nuclear family. As law professor Cynthia Grant Bowman explains,

> While socialist feminists in the [early twentieth century] had repeatedly pointed to the immense amount of labor in the home performed by women, second-wave socialist feminists returned directly to Marx's theory of surplus value and articulated the ways in which women's work in the home was also a form of surplus labor essential to capitalism, by feeding, clothing, and caring for the workforce without pay and producing, caring for, and educating the workers of the future.[107]

According to leading socialist feminist Zillah Eisenstein, therefore, "capitalism and patriarchy [are] interdependent."[108] A "Wages for Housework movement" proposed a strategy of "pay for domestic labor performed in the home as a way to make this interdependence visible."[109]

Feminist theorist Judith Butler has maintained that the implication of socialist feminism is that any disruption to traditional gender and sexuality arrangements constituting the nuclear family would disrupt capitalism.[110] It is not at all clear, however, that this cause-and-effect functions as she predicted. If one takes the advent of same-sex marriage as a natural experiment, for instance, one would have to conclude that capitalism has been shown not to depend on heterosexuality or gender normativity. The heterosexual nuclear constellation might have been important to the functioning of capitalist relations under particular historical conditions, but it was not immutably essential.[111] Some socialist feminists nonetheless sought to vindicate the intuition of an essential link.

A homophilic capitalist, by contrast, would see instead a correlation between gay emancipation and markets. Lee Badgett, perhaps the most prominent US economist working specifically in lgbtq issues, argues in her book *The Economic Case for LGBT Equality* that countries lose "as much as 1 percent of [their] gross domestic product (GDP) because of homophobia and transphobia."[112] A big piece of Badgett's argument regards the advantages that accrue to companies that treat their lgbtq employees fairly by minimizing the costs of employee turnover and increasing productivity by means of improving employee health, loyalty, and job satisfaction.[113] She also, however, touts the benefits of lgbtq "buying power," observing with approbation that US "companies discovered the gay consumer."[114]

> In the 1990s, the US marketplace began to see couples selling dining room tables in IKEA ads, sexy men modeling Calvin Klein underwear on big city billboards, and ads for financial planning services for same-sex couples. Companies bought ad

space in gay and lesbian publications, sponsored LGBT organizations' events, and marched in Pride parades.

Attention to LGBT consumers grew as gay entrepreneurs launched new marketing companies to help corporate clients better target this allegedly affluent but untapped niche market. And while later research uncovered the inconvenient fact that LGBT people are *not* an affluent elite overall … enough affluent LGBT people existed … to reinforce the stereotype. Thus, was born the pink dollar – and later the pink pound, pink euro, and pink yuan.

Gay consumers were also a juicy carrot that LGBT employee groups dangled in front of their employers … [when seeking] nondiscrimination protections and healthcare benefits for same-sex partners.

Today, [Badgett rejoices,] images of LGBT people appear in ads for everyday products …. Burger King celebrated the San Francisco Pride Parade with a rainbow wrapper for a "Proud Whopper" [and] Honey Maid featured two gay dads and their kids in an ad for graham crackers.[115]

Finally, same-sex weddings, Badgett reports, generate substantial revenue, more than $1.5 billion in a single year after the *Obergefell* decision.[116] "That's a lot of new business for hotels, caterers, restaurants, bands, photographers, jewelers, florists, and other parts of the wedding industry that have eagerly expanded into this new market."[117]

Ideas about the corporate benefits of nondiscrimination against lgbtq people have been influential. The Fortune 200 company Altria Group, Inc., parent company of Philip Morris USA, submitted an *amicus* brief in the *Bostock* litigation on the side of the employees.[118] Relying on numerous empirical studies, Altria argued that "diverse and inclusive companies experience better average growth than, and otherwise outperform, their peers,"[119] and that "confident employees who are comfortable expressing their true selves are more productive and less likely to leave, thereby reducing employee turnover."[120]

Homophobic state legislation has even been scuttled by threats from pro-lgbtq, big money, private entities that local lawmakers usually want to attract. The National Football League, for example, hinted in 2014 that it might change its plans to hold Super Bowl XLIX in Arizona because of pending legislation that would have effectively legalized discrimination against gays and lesbians in public accommodations. The prospect of that loss apparently motivated the Republican governor to veto the bill.[121] Of course, this kind of pressure does not always work. North Carolina passed, and its governor signed, its notorious "bathroom bill" known as HB2 in 2016 notwithstanding PayPal's decision to cancel plans to build a large campus in Charlotte that would have employed 400 people.[122] Still, the willingness of the company to spend its clout to ally itself with lgbtq rights suggests a striking understanding of its own business interests.

The argument that business benefits from lgbtq rights is not limited to the US. Badgett also offers it as an international development strategy.[123] Rahul Rao's critique of the strategy forms the basis of his concept *homocapitalism*.[124] According to Rao, *homocapitalism* "[h]old[s] out the prospect of a rosy future redolent with growth and productivity should a state embrace LGBTQ rights."[125] It is an enticing promise – one that compares favorably with instances of merely brow-beating developing countries in need of economic support. Sociologist Cindy Patton decries the imposition of gay rights as a "prerequisite to securing funds from … supranational monetary and development bodies,"[126] effectively spreading the lgbtq gospel at knifepoint. *Homocapitalism*, though, contemplates a softer touch. The "business case" for lgbtq "diversity and inclusion"[127] uses persuasion rather than threats. A case such as the one made by Badgett, "deploy[s] arguments grounded in [economic] self-interest … rather than in the language of human rights."[128]

Indeed, the business case pointedly eschews normative claims. We can certainly guess at Badgett's normative preference, but she leaves those arguments to the human rights NGOs. This deliberate separation of economic growth from social justice rationales causes Rao to express concern about what happens when the two objectives collide and also to wonder "what queer adivasis [indigenous people of the Indian subcontinent] might make of a [World] Bank project that hailed their participation as queers in the very processes that destroyed their lifeworlds as adivasis."[129]

But that is not Badgett's wheelhouse. Her skillset goes to combatting anti-lgbtq discrimination on the grounds that it is not in anybody's financial interest and in fact we would all fare better without it. It is an explicitly market-based argument. Why is it in a country's interest not to discriminate against lgbtq people? Because that will make lgbtq people into better employees and consumers. As Rao suggests, however, marketizing initiatives are neither inherently all good nor inherently all bad for sexual and gender minorities.

As will be discussed, gay and lesbian consumerism has maddened some left/progressive scholars in the US. After presenting their concerns, the chapter's final section highlights a way to think about the issue genealogically. What is important about gay consumerism for the moment, though, is as a facet of gay emancipation's conceptual malleability so that it can be made to correspond with Mieli's virulent contempt for consumer markets or Badgett's sunny optimism for them. Considered together, the instability of sexual categories and the gaps and contradictions in any political–economic system, make it difficult to imagine that any arrangement of these fitful ideals could possibly offer useful corollaries (Table 6.1).

The availability of homosexuality for contradictory ideological projects, whether homophobic (e.g., Cold War nationalism) or homophilic (e.g., Mieli and Badgett) and whether thinly or richly theorized, should be instructive. The relationship of homosexual or gay emancipation to political economy is more obscure than a supposition of rational entailment. (To be fair, Badgett's claims are more empirical than theoretical. For theoretic corroboration, we might have to look beyond the lgbtq sphere to someone like economist Friedrich A. Hayek, who tied free markets to liberal rights more generally, warning that state interference in the market would

TABLE 6.1 *Four failing corollaries.*

	Sexual system	Political–economic system
Corollary #1	Compulsory heterosexuality	Capitalism
Corollary #2	Homosexual/gay emancipation	Socialism (or communism)
Corollary #3	Compulsory heterosexuality	Socialism (or communism)
Corollary #4	Homosexual/gay emancipation	Capitalism

lead to totalitarianism,[130] or perhaps to John Locke, on the right to property as foundational to a rights-based order.[131]) Developing a lucid picture of the relationship between sexuality and political economy demands grappling at an earthbound level with histories of imperialism, racial hierarchy, capital flows, and more.

CONSUMING GAYS: A GENEALOGICAL APPROACH

Those of us on the fortunate side of the economic divide within the US lgbtq community now enjoy inclusion not only in the above-ground employment market, lending, housing, and other sectors where discrimination has been curbed. We also, as Badgett shows, have come to constitute a consumer market niche. Companies large and small market directly to lgbtq purchasers. I confess that I personally am a major customer – platinum status if it existed – of a cottage industry of small businesses that sell masculine-style apparel for butch lesbians, nonbinary folks with curves, and transmen (e.g., Kirrin Finch, Androgynous Fox, HauteButch, Dapper Boi, and Peau de Loup).

Understandably, left/progressives who would prefer to see lgbtq advancement come in a form that is more broadly distributed across race, class, age, and other hierarchies of privilege, have sounded an alarm about consumerism. Their complaint is that lgbtq progress has become so entangled with lgbtq consumption that is difficult to identify where social and political inclusion ends and market participation begins.

In her aptly entitled book *Selling Out*, with a rainbow-colored barcode on the cover, Alexandra Chasin laments that "the market eventually undermines the radical potential of identity-based movements for social change," focusing on the lgbtq movement as a case study.[132] Tracing the relevant ideological conditions all the way back to John Locke, Chasin observes the entwinement of rights and liberties with "economic freedoms" and property.[133] Much of the book, though, regards the political consequences of marketing. "[A]dvertising," she argues, "hails … individuals as subjects."[134] The concept of *hailing* (a.k.a. *interpellation*), proposed by the French Marxist theorist Louis Althusser, stands for the idea that "In the very act of addressing … people, a variety of social institutions with ideological projects – school, church, and the media among them – actually shape people's identities.

Through this process of hailing, institutions call into being, or constitute, 'subjects' of ideology, people who recognize themselves in the way they are addressed."[135] If advertising has the "power to hail (and thus bring into being) people with gay or lesbian identity, [what, Chasin asks, is] … the exact character of that constitution"?[136] Her contention is that it is one of a consumer, "subject[ing] gay men and lesbians to the idea that emancipation could be achieved through the market, particularly in the mode of assimilation, especially through consumption."[137] In other words, ads address gays and lesbians, who learn to recognize themselves according to the terms of the hail – that is, as consumers in a market niche.

Thus constituted, gay and lesbian subjects begin to understand "consumption [as] a form of political participation, perhaps supplanting other, more direct models."[138] Chasin views this as "inimical to progressive political change."[139] Her ultimate concern is that a politics so rooted in consumption "fail[s] to address the systemic disadvantages faced by gay men and lesbians who are not economically privileged." Chasin calls instead for a more racially, economically, and otherwise inclusive movement, "focused on economic justice."[140]

This is not quite the same as Mieli. Chasin wants increased attention devoted to economic justice, but her book reads as a course-corrective for a liberatory movement that has been corrupted, or at least distracted, by the temptations of consumerism. Mieli, on the other hand, wrote from an explicitly Marxist position. He conceptualized the economic and the sexual as mutually sustaining through a structural relation. Chasin is looking for a more distributive focus but her argument is not embedded in a larger political–economic theory.

Liz Montegary's *Familiar Perversions*, echoes some of Chasin's themes, but focuses specifically on the "family equality" strand of gay and lesbian advocacy.[141] Montegary's argument invokes the concept of "homonormativity," a term that Lisa Duggan used to describe the threat of "a demobilized gay constituency and a privatized, depoliticized gay culture anchored in domesticity and consumption."[142] *Familiar Perversions* devotes an entire chapter to "lesbian mom icon Rosie O'Donnell's attempt to capitalize on the popularity of … family-centric pride events by starting a vacation company catering exclusively to lesbian and gay parents and their children," where families can "engage publicly in wholesome leisure activities."[143] Another chapter critiques the marriage equality movement, particularly the pursuit of "legal and financial protections" and the "white supremacist logics of private property."[144] Montegary's animating concern, not unlike Chasin's, is that the "individualizing rhetoric of financial security effectively displaced collective demands for economic justice."[145]

Ann Pellegrini too, has observed a discomfiting link between gays and lesbians as consuming subjects and as national subjects bearing equal rights, but she takes a quite different attitudinal tack: resignation.[146] Facing the correlation head-on she asks, "[r]ather than nostalgically yearning for lesbian and gay identities unmarked by commodity capitalism, what if we acknowledged that lesbian and gay identities have always been in some way marked by capitalism?"[147] Such a turn would not mean "the end of politics … but [would simply be] among its operating conditions and constraints."[148] Pellegrini accepts the correlation between lesbian and gay identities and the consumerism decried by Chasin and Montegary because her impression is that it has been that way for a long while and she got tired of trying to imagine it otherwise. Indeed, there is some rich genealogical work to substantiate Pellegrini's impression.

By *genealogy*, I mean to invoke Nietzsche and Foucault,[149] and specifically their rejection of "origins," or any "attempt to capture the exact essence of things, their purest possibilities … because this search assumes the existence of immobile forms that precede the external world."[150] A genealogist studies history, but her objective "is not the erecting of foundations: On the contrary, it disturbs what was previously considered immobile; it fragments what was thought unified; it shows the heterogeneity of what was imagined consistent."[151] A genealogical method reveals the noninevitability of prevailing assumptions. Just as legal reasoning and capitalist logic can be delegitimated by indeterminacy critique, so sexuality and gender identities can be denaturalized by a genealogical approach. A discourse of nature, like a discourse of rationality, can serve a legitimating function, but genealogy takes "the development of humanity [to be] a series of interpretations [and directs itself to] the history of morals, ideals, and metaphysical concepts."[152]

Over four decades ago,[153] John D'Emilio was perhaps the first, in his groundbreaking and utterly indispensable article *Capitalism and Gay Identity*,[154] to articulate how industrial capitalism, by releasing individuals in the US from the homestead into a system of free labor, created conditions that made gay identity, community, and long-term relationships possible.[155] By historicizing gay identity – including separating it conceptually from homosexual acts – D'Emilio illustrated gay identity's contingency – that is, its instability as well as its dependence on material circumstance.

D'Emilio's paper avoids claiming that capitalism *determined* how gay identity would form in the US. His argument was that the shift away from the homestead economy *enabled* it to form as it did. The language in these paragraphs is representative:

> In divesting the household of its economic independence and fostering the separation of sexuality from procreation, capitalism has created conditions that allow some men and women to organize a personal life around their erotic/emotional attraction to their own sex. It has made possible the formation of urban communities of lesbians and gay men and, more recently, of politics based on sexual identity….
>
> There was, quite simply, no "social space" in the colonial system of production that allowed men and women to be gay. Survival was structured around participation in a nuclear family. There were certain homosexual acts – sodomy among men, "lewdness" among women – in which individuals engaged but family was so

> pervasive that colonial society lacked even the category of homosexual or lesbian to describe a person. It is quite possible that some men and women experienced a stronger attraction to their own sex than to the opposite sex – in fact, some colonial court cases refer to men who persisted in their "unnatural" attractions – but one could not fashion out of that preference a way of life….
>
> By the second half of the nineteenth century, this situation was noticeably changing as the capitalist system of free labor took hold. Only when individuals began to make their living through wage labor, instead of as parts of an independent family unit, was it possible for homosexual desire to coalesce into a personal identity – an identity based on the ability to remain outside the heterosexual family and to construct a personal life based on attraction to one's own sex.[156]

Notice words such as "allowed" and "possible." D'Emilio is talking about enabling conditions.

Recall Gayle Rubin's argument (in Chapter 4) that a sexual system could arise in service of an economic system, but that the former might outlive its utility as the latter evolved. In other words, the economy cannot be said to causally determine the sexual system. If the relationship were that determinate, then the sexual system would be expected to keep up, adapting to economic change, but in Rubin's version of events, it has not. If Rubin has that much right, then D'Emilio goes the exact right distance by speaking to enabling conditions rather than determinative factors. An assertion that gay identity *necessarily* follows the progress of capitalism would exceed the warrant. Instead, D'Emilio's story has capitalism creating room for new identity formations but stops short of announcing a causal chain.[157] His analysis can be understood as genealogical, as he traces the evolution of identity in its material context resisting attribution of an origin or essence, and *queer*, in the sense of revealing through historicism how sexual identity is conditional rather than universal, natural, or timeless.

D'Emilio also offers some insight into the association of gays and lesbians with consumption, a bane to writers such as Chasin and Montegary.

> [I]n the early twentieth century, large cities contained male homosexual bars …. [D]rag balls brought together large numbers of black gay men. Public bathhouses and YMCAs became gathering spots for male homosexuals. Lesbians formed literary societies and private social clubs. Some working-class women 'passed' as men to obtain better-paying jobs and lived with other women – forming lesbian couples who appeared to the world as husband and wife. Among the faculties of women's colleges, in settlement houses, and in the professional associations and clubs women formed, one could find lifelong intimate relationships supported by a web of lesbian friends. By the 1920s and 1930s, large cities such as New York and Chicago contained lesbian bars. These patterns of living could evolve because capitalism allowed individuals to survive beyond the confines of the family.[158]

Noting that sexologist Alfred Kinsey had identified "a strong positive correlation between years of schooling and lesbian activity," D'Emilio observed, "[c]ollege educated white women, far more able than their working-class sisters to support themselves, could survive more easily without intimate relationships with men."[159] Higher education did not *create* lesbians, but it did *enable* the financial self-sufficiency that rendered it feasible to live without a male earner.

D'Emilio effectively makes the case that "gay men and lesbians have not always existed. Instead, they are a product of history."[160] Writer Jeffrey Escoffier takes the existence of gay people as a given, but it is perhaps because he begins his account a bit later. His work provides a vivid glimpse into the development of the association of gay identity with consumption. Escoffier illustrates in his "economic history of homosexual communities" the deep entwinement of gay (mainly male) life with specific forms of consumption in the aftermath of World War II. He periodized the economics of gay life as follows:

> The first period was the *Closet Economy*. Its primary economic institutions were bars, baths, adult bookstores and heavily coded mail order services, most of which operated on the margins of legality. The second period was initiated by Stonewall and might be called the *Liberation Economy*. Its dominant economic institutions were the proliferating retail business – bars, bookstores, baths and consumer services that emerged from the confines of semi-legality. Political and other voluntary organizations also provided previously unavailable public services. The third phase of the homo/economy was the *Territorial Economy* of the late seventies, marked by the spread of gentrification and neighborhood development. This process was cut short by the emergence of AIDS and development of the *AIDS Economy*, a period in which the largest economic institutions of the homo/economy are those that provide AIDS services as well as educational and other non-profit organizations. Currently, [Escoffier published this paper in 1997] gay communities are in transition to a new phase – one of hyper-commodification, as mainstream corporations target the homo/market niche with consumer goods and advertising.[161]

Escoffier elaborated on the economics of each period, for example, the "high transaction costs ... of concealing one's homosexuality" for closeted homosexuals who expended resources on "transportation, liquor, multiple sets of clothing, and even ... maintaining separate households," the legal expenses resulting from arrest, the cost of blackmail to conceal one's identity or arrest record, and the inflated cost of liquor due to bars' having to pay protection money to police or organized crime.[162]

Escoffier's analysis is compelling due in part to its rootedness in ethnographic reality. One can almost follow in the footsteps of a man making expenditures associated with his sexuality through the decades. The method illustrates a common feature of genealogical study: if "traditional history ... is given to a contemplation of distances and heights: the noblest periods, the highest forms, the most abstract ideas," Foucault instructs us that genealogy "shortens its vision to those things nearest to it: the body, the nervous system, nutrition, digestion, and energies .... It has no fear of looking down."[163]

Warner, in a slightly more normative exposition, has observed that gay people as a political and identitarian group have been forced to rely heavily on places of consumption by their exclusion from the kinds of nonmarket institutions that support and consolidate racial/ethnic/religious identities.

> In the lesbian and gay movement, to a much greater degree than in any comparable movement, the institutions of culture-building have been market-mediated: bars, discos, special services, newspapers, magazines, phone lines, resorts, urban commercial districts. Nonmarket forms of association that have been central to other movements – churches, kinship, traditional residence – have been less available for queers. This structural environment has meant that the institutions of queer culture have been dominated by those with capital.[164]

Sexual identity in the US has, therefore, evolved through its entwinement with political economy, though not in the sense of meta-systemic determination. Instead, it has happened through quotidian run-ins with changing material and discursive conditions that make room for new possibilities.

The same is true for Cuba, as shown in Parts I and II. A close examination of variable historical conditions (e.g., exploitation of Cubans by the US mafia and large corporations before the Revolution, the subsequent revolutionary and nationalist refusal to bear the lingering humiliations of US imperialism, the demise of Cuba's Soviet benefactor and the hardships imposed by that loss, the spreading global appeal of gay identity) illuminates some of these evolutions. Both the US and Cuba have legalized same-sex marriage, but their paths to that particular legal factoid could hardly be more divergent. A genealogical account such as the one contained herein offers no origin, no nature, no truth, and no structural determinacy. Instead, it produces a narrative of inconsistent encounters between the global and the local, and of the effects of discursive and the material factors on each other.

* * *

By its very nature as a constellation of unacknowledged, shared assumptions, legal consciousness is difficult to critically examine from the inside. A comparative study, though, has the potential to offer fresh perspective, holding up a mirror that renders the assumptions of one's own legal culture more visible. The statements of aspiration (as well as the discursive silences[165]) of the Cuban lawyers and law students we met shed fresh light on aspects of US legal consciousness – including aspects that I thought I had exceeded before realizing that they had formed the initial premises of my own inquiry. My method therefore changed as I came to understand that a study of Cuban law and identity that accepted meta-systemic premises about socialism and capitalism risked eclipsing more insight than it might yield. As Foucault admonished:

> When I see you straining to establish the scientificity of Marxism I do not really think you are demonstrating once and for all that Marxism has a rational structure

> and that, therefore, its propositions are the outcome of verifiable procedures; for me you are doing something altogether different, you are investing Marxist discourses and those who uphold them with the effects of a power which the West since Medieval times has attributed to science and has reserved for those engaged in scientific discourse.[166]

An array of "critical" Marxisms has no doubt arisen to correct orthodox claims to "scientificity." Still, "[w]hat types of knowledge do [they] disqualify?"[167] The purpose of the genealogical method is to "emancipate historical knowledges from … the coercion of a theoretical, unitary … discourse."[168] And it is the very rejection of such an inquiry that provides "a good reason to continue to pursue it."[169]

Producing a comparative and genealogical encounter between the Cuba and the US dedifferentiates their political–economic systems at a meta-level, reorienting the eye to the elements on the ground. It highlights the significance of discursive power in the formation of identity under changing social and economic conditions and reminds one of the immense power of the discourse of unmotivated rationality in which US lawyers are trained.

Conclusion

On a 2019 visit to the Peabody-Essex Museum in Salem, Massachusetts, I happened upon the astonishing sculpture shown in Figures C.1 and C.2. The sculpture is entitled *Immanence* (2015) and is the creation of Cuban artist Yoan Capote. Capote constructed Immanence by welding together rusty door hinges collected from fellow Cubans. According to the sculpture's page on the museum website, Capote made trips abroad and returned to Cuba with new hinges that he could exchange for old ones.[1] The hinges join to form a bust of Fidel Castro, though from the side it appears incomplete, as if disintegrating. Fidel's head sits atop a pedestal composed of a haphazard-looking pile of frayed and broken doors.

The description posted next to the exhibit referred in general terms to the Cuban people's struggle for change under dictatorship and the museum webpage proposed that the "image of the Cuban leader becomes a collective portrait of Cuba's resilient citizens."[2] I took Capote's choice of materials to refer at least in part to Cuba's housing shortage and the decomposition of its physical infrastructure, brought on by some combination of the US embargo and the leadership's failures. The rust, as I read it, along with the worn doors and the fact that the sculpture is dated the year before Fidel's death when he was known to be in ill-health, cannot help but refer also to the passage of time. Further, the artist's decision to construct the sculpture out of objects that would ordinarily serve as an entry to a dwelling, a traversable boundary between inside and outside, I took to be a reference to spatial liminality. The inside of a home (perhaps because it is filtered through my US eyes) is ideally a space of privacy, for family and sexuality, while the image of Fidel stands for nothing less than the state itself. The public and private mutually suffuse one another in the ten-foot form. The title *Immanence* evokes this mutual suffusion, and perhaps also nods to the Frankfurt School tradition known as *immanent critique*,[3] which would suggest that Cuba is being or ought to be judged according to its own professed ideals.

As Yishai Blank and Issi Rosen-Zvi observed in 2012, municipalities can have a significant "impact [on] the daily lives of gays and lesbians by using their districting, zoning, land use, business licensing, public health, education, spending, and law

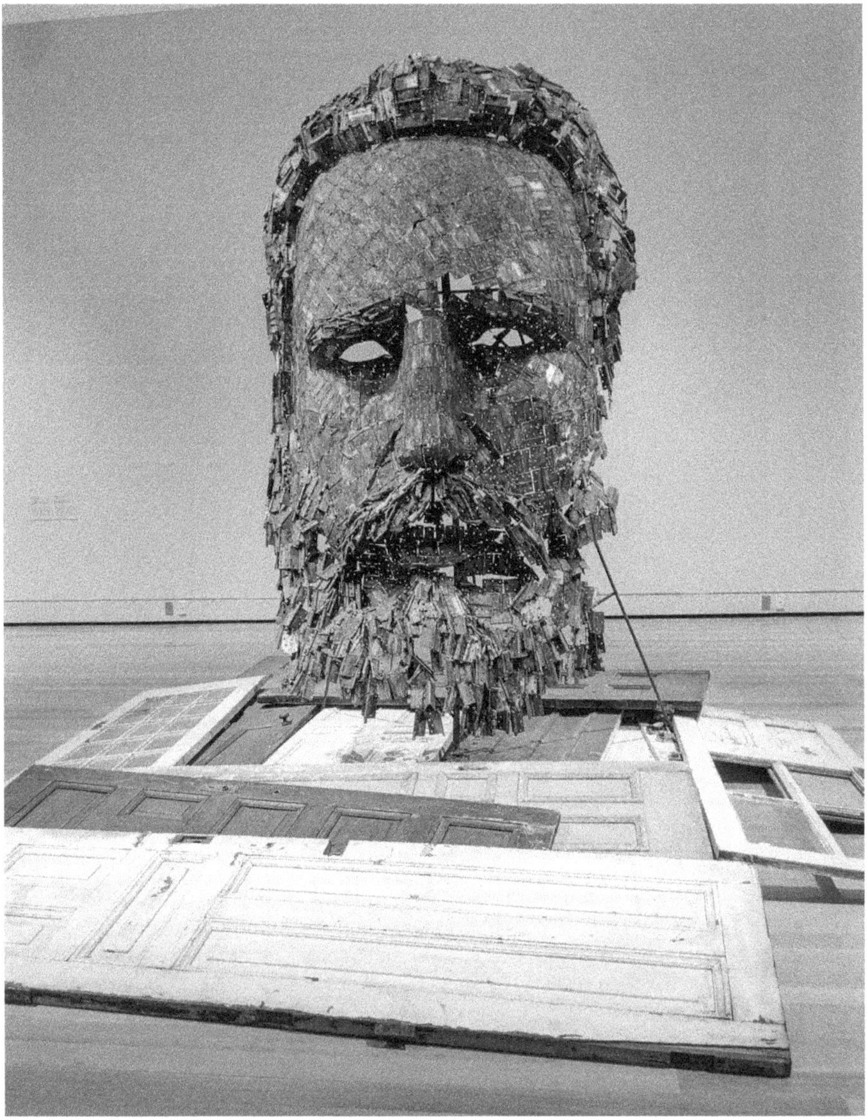

FIGURE C.1 *Immanence* (2015), by Yoan Capote. Front view. On exhibit at Peabody-Essex Museum, Salem, Massachusetts, 2019.

enforcement power."[4] Physical boundaries and the passages between them, however, are also instruments of governance in the broad sense of the term as it is understood in this book (see Preface). Boundaries, such as those between the inside and outside of the home, might be enforced internally (i.e., via a deeply assumed sense of where we are, where we belong, and how we ought to conduct ourselves) as well as by state actors (i.e., the police). This does not necessarily mean that police officers

FIGURE C.2 *Immanence* (2015), by Yoan Capote. Corner view. On exhibit at Peabody-Essex Museum, Salem, Massachusetts, 2019.

are standing beside our front doors, but that, for example, in jurisdictions such the US, property owners as well as tenants are protected by trespassing laws and many types of conduct (sex, urination, sleeping) are largely prohibited outside while they are entirely permissible inside. As philosopher Elizabeth Grosz has argued,

> The city orients and organizes family, sexual, and social relations insofar as the city divides cultural life into public and private domains, geographically dividing and defining the particular social positions and locations occupied by individuals and groups .... These spaces, divisions, and interconnections are the roles and means by which bodies are individuated to become subjects .... Finally, the city's form and structure provide the context in which social rules and expectations are internalized or habituated in order to ensure social conformity, or positions marginality at a safe or insulated and bounded distance (ghettoization). This means that the city must be seen as [a] concrete locus for the production and circulation of power.[5]

Approaching Cuba as an outsider rendered spatial governance, which might escape my notice at home, quite visible. Anyone who has even a passing familiarity with Havana is cognizant that housing is in both short supply and decaying condition. Crowded apartments hamper sexual access for everyone, but perhaps especially for same-sex couples. Sharing a tight living space with multiple extended family members or an excess of roommates can push sex out of the home, notwithstanding the legal rules discussed in Part I such as prohibitions against "dangerousness" and "ostentatious displays of homosexuality."

In the 1993 documentary film *Looking for Space*,[6] depicting gay and lesbian life in Cuba, one of the interviewed subjects, a gay man, explains, "People have to see us every day in the streets, even in public spaces like the bathrooms. Among the ruins. In the abandoned houses. Because nobody accepts them, they have nowhere to have sex."[7] Similarly, as Chapter 2 recounts, the Afro-Cuban lesbian group OREMI drew complaints from neighbors because its members were having sex behind and around the meeting space; those complaints may have played a role in precipitating OREMI's swift dissolution.

When available, some people looking for sexual privacy resort to *posadas*, rooms that can be rented by the hour.[8] According to one report, customers include "tourists in search of very cheap sex, people having affairs or giving in to forbidden passions, low-class prostitutes denied admission at luxury hotels, young couples or humble folk who do not have a place where they can spend a few hours together."[9] Some posadas are state-run,[10] but there are also

> tenement buildings ... where nearly all the tenants live off the rent of such rooms. Often, it is the livelihood of entire families who, after renting a room out to a couple, must leave their homes and wait out on the street until the time needed by the couple has passed.
>
> Then, in a hurry, without thoroughly cleaning the room, they prepare the bed for the next two strangers, the same bed where perhaps the owners of the house, or their children, must sleep in [sic] every day....
>
> In the larger hovels, sometimes the family stays in the adjacent room while the other is being used. If there are children in the house, some parents force them to sit in front of the television and raise the volume to drown out the moans of pleasure, the dirty talk and all other noises.[11]

Overnight hotels are more expensive, of course, but the bigger obstacle may be that not everyone is allowed into them. Police and hotel security typically guard the entrances, blocking Cubans from going up to tourist rooms.[12]

One of the reasons that jobs in the resort hotels are so coveted (as discussed in Chapter 2) is the opportunity they afford to engage in transactional sex with tourists on-site.[13] Landing a hotel job effectively immunizes the employee from police interference. On the streets of Havana, police regularly stop Cubans, disproportionately Afro-Cubans, suspected of being nonresidents, migrating without permission from the east to solicit tourists.[14] There is no specific prohibition against prostitution in Cuba; instead, the conduct is policed by a combination of cognate laws against "vagrancy,"[15] "bothering a tourist" or entering the tourist-only hotels. While the government makes an effort to separate Cubans from foreigners, anthropologist Noelle Stout reports interviewing "queer tourists," for whom "transgressing state-imposed boundaries added an air of adventure and discovery to their experiences and provided a sense of superiority over other tourists."[16] The constellation of rules and evasion of them manage the interplay of the global and the local, very much along a racial axis because of who is most likely to be stopped by police and who is most likely to find work in the resort hotels.

Additional examples of spatial governance surfaced during my research. Comités de Defensa de la Revolución (Committees for the Defense of the Revolution, or CDRs) served as neighborhood watchdogs keeping an eye out during the 1960s and '70s for anyone engaged in homosexual or other counterrevolutionary activity. Lesbian house parties are subjected to a tax that, if unpaid, could lead to a raid; this prompts the parties to move from place to place; information regarding the next location is transmitted on the down-low.

Some queer theoretic work on the subjects of time and space[17] points to embedded domestic norms (i.e., settle down and have children) and the disruption of such norms that is presented by queer life. Professor of English and gender studies Jack Halberstam, for example, explains in the opening of his book on the subject, "[q]ueer uses of time and space develop, at least in part, in opposition to the institutions of family, heterosexuality, and reproduction;" Halberstam proposes that queerness be conceived "as an outcome of strange temporalities, imaginative life schedules, and eccentric economic practices."[18] Professor of architecture Aaron Betsky in his book *Queer Space* notes that architecture played a key role in the production of middle class culture by organizing "[t]he city and the suburb, the domestic environment and the place of work, the promenade and the bar"[19] and by "order[ing] … the nuclear family (the single-family house and the suburb), the regimented and defined body (the gymnasium and the boys' school, but also prisons), and the notion of a correct way of public behavior through which one might present oneself (public squares and boulevards)."[20] But, Betsky observed, "[n]one of these worked too well for queer men. They did not have families at the cores of their life, the disciplining of the body turned into its reverse, i.e., the satisfaction of desire, and public space was where the queer man had to hide his desire."[21] In these accounts, queerness can be understood as oppositional, or it could be conceptualized more subtly, as something that disturbs or unsettles a prevailing cultural norm. I prefer the latter reading because it is less predetermined – its character more variable and unstable.

This is the sense in which political economies, like space, might be studied through a queer lens. As Amy J. Cohen and Stephen Healy explain in their discussion of J. K. Gibson-Graham (who, in turn, referred to the work of Eve Kosofsky Sedgwick), a queer approach to political economy would entail a preference for "weak theory," characterized by a "descriptively and ethnographically rich" account, over "strong theory," characterized by systemically determined and "paranoid certainties."[22]

Space is merely one facet of governance, though a powerful one to be sure, in part because physical barriers can be internalized as natural and obeyed without conscious deliberation. Because sexuality is entangled with the privacy ideal, anyone seeking to understand the regulation of sex in a particular jurisdiction might benefit from devoting a measure of attention to spatial aspects. In particular, when and where does one encounter a line purporting to circumscribe the private domain?[23] Under what conditions is the line permeable? What economic factors (e.g., a housing shortage) and what politics (e.g., a sustained embargo radically reducing the availability of building supplies) constitute or compromise the line? How have specific forms of homophobia or racism emerged in their spatial context and how have they affected morality or identity?

This line of inquiry benefits from a methodology that comprehends law expansively, so that it encompasses not only codes, constitutions, and cases, but also an array of interrelated, circulating assumptions that shape our identities and perceptions, directing both governance by external rule and self-governance by an internalized sense of order. It eschews systemic determinacy in favor of fragmentation and discrepancy, taking broad account of how identity, morality, and rationality evolve under heterogenous conditions. It attends to the power of the aesthetic, inclusive of the discursive, to make governance appear natural and legitimate. And finally, it benefits from comparison, which – if approached with humility – can be an instrument of denaturalization and self-reflection.

***

Remember Clandestina from the Introduction, the little lgbtq-themed gift shop in Old Havana? What precisely is "clandestine" about it? The store itself is not hidden away – it is a tourist attraction. I had no trouble finding its brightly painted storefront with a big sign out front shaped like a T-shirt, buzzing inside with the languages of international customers. It maintains English and Spanish websites[24] and a social media presence, all of which invite foreign patronage.

The name refers, one can surmise, to a past of surreptitious encounters, private but in public spaces, a strange nostalgia for the furtive and perilous existence of the old homosexual, in the years before same-sex marriage was imaginable. Yet now,

Clandestina functions openly as a site for the inflow of capital that comes along with visitors from the global north.

What remains of Clandestina's secret, it seems, is the small but not insignificant role the shop plays in a dynamic process, neither systemically determined nor utterly idiosyncratic, by which law travels. Traveling law shape-shifts under new conditions, responding to peculiar market niches, unstable racial hierarchies, sugar yields, dance crazes, oil subsidies, sunshine, and more.

Construction of a political–economic account of lgbtq law in Cuba demands that we not imagine we know too much in advance. By opening ourselves to surprise – that is, to conditions that may not be consonant with the expectations associated with any meta-system – we stand not only to gain a rich appreciation for the lived complexity within a single locale but also help in scouting for the opportunities that the law affords to delegitimate injustices and advance positive change.

At this writing, autocratic and oligarchic figures predominate across the international political landscape, exploiting every mechanism at hand to redistribute resources upward. Global capital appears as an impenetrable monster. Precisely at such a moment it is crucial to regard the monster as we might a high-resolution image, comprising innumerable pixels, each an opportunity.

Notes

PREFACE

1. Edwin McDowell, "Reinaldo Arenas, 47, Writer Who Fled Cuba, Dies," *The New York Times*, December 9, 1990, www.nytimes.com/1990/12/09/obituaries/reinaldo-arenas-47-writer-who-fled-cuba-dies.html.
2. Reinaldo Arenas, *Before Night Falls*, trans. Dolores M. Koch (Penguin Books, 1993), 87.
3. *Before Night Falls*, directed by Julian Schnabel (Grandview Pictures, 2000).
4. *Before Night Falls*, directed by Julian Schnabel (Grandview Pictures, 2000).
5. Arenas, *Before Night Falls*, 87.
6. Michel Foucault, *The Birth of Biopolitics: Lectures at the Collège de France 1978–1979*, trans. Graham Burchell (Palgrave Macmillan, 2008), 186.
7. Foucault, *The Birth of Biopolitics*, 186. "[P]rocedures of governmentality" are equated here with "micro-powers."
8. Janet Halley, "Introducing Governance Feminism," in *Governance Feminism: An Introduction*, ed. Janet Halley et al. (University of Minnesota Press, 2018), ix. Halley et al. relied on Foucault's governmentality in the development of their analysis of "governance feminism," or "every form in which feminists and feminist ideas 'conduct the conduct of men,'" though they explicitly limited themselves to "efforts feminists have made to become incorporated into *state, state-like, and state-affiliated* power." Halley, "Introducing Governance Feminism," ix, x.
9. Duncan Kennedy, "The Stakes of Law, or Hale and Foucault!," in *Sexy Dressing etc.: Essays on the Power and Politics of Cultural Identity* (Harvard University Press, 1993), 90.
10. Michel Foucault, "Two Lectures," in *Power/Knowledge: Selected Interviews & Other Writings 1972–1977*, ed. & trans. Colin Gordon (Pantheon Books, 1980), 93–94.

INTRODUCTION

1. KF was founded by a lesbian couple in 2015 and markets its products to butch lesbians and trans-masc and nonbinary people who are looking for masculine style clothing that fits their bodies. https://kirrinfinch.com/pages/our-story.
2. https://kirrinfinch.com/blogs/dapper-scouts/dapper-scouts-clandestina?utm_source=Klaviyo&utm_medium=email&utm_campaign=2024.06.06_Clandestina&utm_id=01HZFNB6WN7CZD4VPGR1FC7T8Y&_kx=lvvR-XNwp5N6JAE2fgvoNovf-_99_qbRiMAL1R-H9Y0.QkCWPk.

3. https://kirrinfinch.com/blogs/dapper-scouts/dapper-scouts-clandestina?utm_source=Klaviyo&utm_medium=email&utm_campaign=2024.06.06_Clandestina&utm_id=01HZFNB6WN7CZD4VPGR1FC7T8Y&_kx=lvvR-XNwp5N6JAE2fgvoNovf-_99_qbRiMAL1R-H9Y0.QkCWPk.
4. Sarah Marsh, "Scrappy Cuban Clothing Line Exemplifies Ingenuity with U.S. Online Store Opening," *Reuters*, October 26, 2017, www.reuters.com/article/lifestyle/scrappy-cuban-clothing-line-exemplifies-ingenuity-with-u-s-online-store-opening-idUSKBN1CV3JO/.
5. The week before the KF email blast, on May 28, the Office of Foreign Assets Control (OFAC) within President Joe Biden's Treasury Department amended its regulations to permit limited banking in the United States for business entrepreneurs located in Cuba. "Cuban Assets Control Regulations," *Code of Federal Regulations*, Title 31, Part 515 (2024), www.ecfr.gov/recent-changes?search%5Bhierarchy%5D%5Bpart%5D=515&search%5Bhierarchy%5D%5Btitle%5D=31&search%5Blast_modified_after%5D=2024-05-26. Under the new rules, § 515.585, even wholly Cuban owned private businesses could, for the first time since the outset of an embargo that began during the Eisenhower administration, open bank accounts in the US and sell goods to purchasers using US-based credit cards through online platforms. See also David C. Adams, "Biden Moves to Open U.S. Banks to Cuba's Private Sector," *The New York Times*, May 28, 2024, www.nytimes.com/2024/05/28/world/americas/biden-us-banks-cuba.html; Kylie Atwood, "US Gives Cuban Private Business Owners Access to US Online Payment Systems," *CNN*, May 28, 2024, www.cnn.com/2024/05/28/politics/us-cuba-online-payment-systems/index.html. The Biden rule could be repealed by the (second) Trump administration but has not been at this writing.
6. Clandestina designers had the opportunity to dress Michelle Obama and the two Obama daughters in 2016 when President Barack Obama made himself the first US president to visit Cuba since Calvin Coolidge in 1928. Wilfred W. Labiosa, *The LGBT Cuban Revolution* (Deletrea, 2023), 77.
7. Tragically, it seems necessary to acknowledge that while the US has long understood itself to be a liberal democracy notwithstanding its many failings, that form of government is very much imperiled at this writing.
8. See, e.g., Libby Adler, *Gay Priori: A Queer Critical Legal Studies Approach to Law Reform* (Duke University Press, 2018); Libby Adler, "Life at the Corner of Poverty and Sexual Abjection: Lewdness, Indecency, and LGBTQ Youth," in *Research Handbook on Gender, Sexuality and the Law*, ed. Chris Ashford and Alexander Maine (Edward Elgar Publishing, 2020).
9. Obergefell v. Hodges, 576 U.S. 644 (2015).
10. David Kennedy, *A World of Struggle: How Power, Law, and Expertise Shape Global Political Economy* (Princeton University Press, 2016), 4.
11. Kennedy, *A World of Struggle*, 11.
12. Fernanda G. Nicola and Günter Frankenberg, *Comparative Law: Introduction to a Clinical Practice* (Edward Elgar Publishing, 2024), 9.
13. Günter Frankenberg, *Comparative Law as Critique* (Edward Elgar Publishing, 2016), 15.
14. Frankenberg, *Comparative Law as Critique*, 11, 82.
15. Jorge L. Esquirol, "The Fictions of Latin American Law (Part I)," 1997 *Utah Law Review* 425 (1997): 433–36, https://ecollections.law.fiu.edu/faculty_publications/330.
16. Ugo Mattei, "Comparative Law and Critical Legal Studies," in *The Oxford Handbook of Comparative Law*, ed. Mathias Reimann and Reinhard Zimmermann (Oxford Academic, 2019), 821–25, https://doi.org/10.1093/oxfordhb/9780198810230.013.26.
17. David Kennedy, "Law and the Political Economy of the World," *Leiden Journal of International Law* 26, no. 1 (2013): 10, https://doi.org/10.1017/S0922156512000635.

18. Nathaniel Berman, "Aftershocks: Exoticization, Normalization, and the Hermeneutic Compulsion," 1997 *Utah Law Review* 281 (1997): 282, https://heinonline.org/HOL/LandingPage?handle=hein.journals/utahlr1997&div=22&id=&page=.
19. Berman, "Aftershocks," 282 ("What critical resources exist both within one's 'own' frame of reference and within the 'Other's' that can be deployed for emancipatory purposes?").
20. Nicola and Frankenberg, *Comparative Law*, 18–23.
21. Frankenberg, *Comparative Law as Critique*, 11.
22. Adler, *Gay Priori*, 128; Adler, "Life at the Corner," 80.
23. Frankenberg, *Comparative Law as Critique*, 13.
24. Berman, "Aftershocks," 282–83.
25. Frankenberg, *Comparative Law as Critique*, 230.
26. Frankenberg, *Comparative Law as Critique*, 232.
27. Nicola and Frankenberg, *Comparative Law*, 22.
28. Nicola and Frankenberg, *Comparative Law*, 22.
29. George Chauncey, *Gay New York: Gender, Urban Culture, and the Making of the Gay Male World 1890–1940* (Basic Books, 1994), 8–9, 358–59.
30. This view could alternatively be attributed not to sexism, but to dominance feminism à la Catharine MacKinnon wherein the structure of heterosexual intercourse is dominance/subordination. Catharine A. MacKinnon, "Feminism, Marxism, Method, and the State: An Agenda for Theory," *Signs* 7, no. 3 (Spring 1982): 533, www.jstor.org/stable/3173853.
31. Nicola and Frankenberg, *Comparative Law*, 21.

1 EXPULSION OF THE HOMOSEXUAL FIGMENT: 1898–1970S

1. Hundreds of years of Spanish colonialism, Catholicism, slavery, labor migration, and Santería have each contributed to the evolution of Cuban cultural attitudes regarding sex. Cuba's reputation as a commercial sex hub dates back nearly to the European conquerors. This chapter nonetheless begins its brief sketch of the relevant Cuban history with the end of Spanish rule and the beginning of US influence. While homophobia is obviously not unique to Cuba, the specific valence of Cuban regard for homosexuality finds important roots in the relationship of exploitation between it and the US during the twentieth century.
2. Tom Gjelten, *Bacardi and the Long Fight for Cuba: The Biography of a Cause* (Viking, 2008), 78. Cuba was not a party to the Treaty of Paris and the Spanish–American War took its name without notice of Cuban participation.
3. Richard Gott, *Cuba: A New History* (Yale University Press, 2004), 99; Gjelten, *Bacardi*, 72. See also Michael Beschloss, *Presidents of War: The Epic Story, from 1807 to Modern Times* (Crown Publishing, 2019), 259. Thanks to Zach Gale for this source.
4. Gott, *Cuba: A New History*, 104.
5. Ada Ferrer, *Cuba: An American History* (Scribner, 2021), 177–80.
6. "President Roosevelt Proclaims the Platt Amendment" in *The Cuba Reader: History, Culture, Politics*, ed. Aviva Chomsky et al. (Duke University Press, 2019), 145–46.
7. Alejandro de la Fuente, *A Nation for All: Race, Inequality, and Politics in Twentieth-Century Cuba* (The University of North Carolina Press, 2001), 27.
8. De la Fuente, *A Nation for All*, 23.
9. The debate took place not only in Cuba but was a larger hemispheric debate. See, e.g., Gilberto Freyre, *The Masters and the Slaves: A Study in the Development of Brazilian Civilization* (University of California Press, 1986); Tanya K. Hernández, *Racial*

Subordination in Latin America: The Role of the State, Customary Law, and the New Civil Rights Response (Cambridge University Press, 2013); Marilyn G. Miller, *Rise and Fall of the Cosmic Race: The Cult of Mestizaje in Latin America* (University of Texas Press, 2004); Yeidy M. Rivero, *Turning Out Blackness: Race and Nation in the History of Puerto Rican Television* (Duke University Press, 2005).

10. Ferrer, *Cuba: An American History*, 208.
11. De la Fuente, *A Nation for All*, 66.
12. Jafari S. Allen, *¡Venceremos?: The Erotics of Black Self-Making in Cuba* (Duke University Press, 2011), 52.
13. Allen, *¡Venceremos?*, 52.
14. De la Fuente, *A Nation for All*, 66–78.
15. Ferrer, *Cuba: An American History*, 210.
16. Gjelten, *Bacardi*, 73.
17. Gott, *Cuba: A New History*, 92, 109, 122; Ferrer, *Cuba: An American History*, 209. The reference is to uprising of the Black people of the French colony of San Domingo that led to the establishment of the independent nation of Haiti. See generally C. L. R. James, *The Black Jacobins: Toussaint L'Ouverture and the San Domingo Revolution* (Vintage Books, 1989).
18. De la Fuente, *A Nation for All*, 49–50.
19. Ferrer, *Cuba: An American History*, 187.
20. Ferrer, *Cuba: An American History*, 191.
21. Ferrer, *Cuba: An American History*, 192.
22. *The Cuba Libre Story*, episode 2, "War and Sugar," directed by Emmanuel Amara, Kai Christiansen, and Florian Dedio, released December 11, 2015, on Netflix, www.netflix.com/watch/80117386?trackId=14277281.
23. Gjelten, *Bacardi*, 103.
24. Gjelten, *Bacardi*, 98, 168. According to Tom Gjelten, the American journalist who wrote the authoritative history of the Bacardi rum company, US iron mine workers in the town of Daiquirí in Eastern Cuba received an allotment of rum as part of their compensation and were the first to drink it in the cocktail that took the town's name.
25. Megan Daigle, *From Cuba with Love: Sex and Money in the Twenty-First Century* (University of California Press, 2015), 47.
26. David K. Johnson, *The Lavender Scare: The Cold War Persecution of Gays and Lesbians in the Federal Government* (The University of Chicago Press, 2004), 95.
27. See, e.g., American Liberty League Pamphlet No. 90 "The American Constitution – Whose Heritage? The Self-Reliant or Those Who Would Be Wards of the Government?" Speech of Frederick H. Stinchfield before the Fifth Annual Meeting of the Utah State Bar Association, January 18, 1936. ("We used to be a virile, self-reliant people … Has there been a change, that the theory of paternalism could have received so much support…?" Pamphlet No. 90, 6. "I HAVE no doubt that the Constitution of the United States was written with the hope of developing strength and self-reliance, and that it was not made with the notion of promoting utter dependence upon the powers of government …. It is for you to say whether our Constitution shall retain in it the spirit of our forefathers, or this new spirit of weakness, paternalism, and utter dependence on government." Pamphlet No. 90, 19.) https://exploreuk.uky.edu/fa/findingaid/?id=xt7wwp9t2q46#fa-heading-collection-overview. The League was composed of wealthy businessmen and high-ranking politicians opposed to the New Deal on constitutional, economic, and philosophical grounds.
28. Johnson, *The Lavender Scare*, 95.

29. Lee Edelman, "Tearooms and Sympathy, or, The Epistemology of the Water Closet," in *Nationalisms and Sexualities*, ed. A. Parker, M. Russo, D. Sommer, and P. Yaeger (Routledge, 1992), 276.
30. Johnson, *The Lavender Scare*, 95. See also D. J. West, "Parental Figures in the Genesis of Male Homosexuality," *International Journal of Social Psychiatry* 5, no. 2 (1959): 85–97, https://doi.org/10.1177/002076405900500201 expressing the predominant psychoanalytic view of the early–mid twentieth century.
31. Johnson, *The Lavender Scare*, 42.
32. Johnson, *The Lavender Scare*, 92.
33. Johnson, *The Lavender Scare*, 93.
34. Pierre Birnbaum, "Political Antisemitism, 'State Jews' and Roosevelt's New Deal," in *Antisemitism before and since the Holocaust: Altered Contexts and Recent Perspectives*, ed. Anthony McElligott and Jeffrey Herf (Springer International Publishing, 2017), 149–181.
35. Johnson, *The Lavender Scare*, 43.
36. Johnson, *The Lavender Scare*, 44.
37. Johnson, *The Lavender Scare*, 43.
38. Langston Hughes, *I Wonder as I Wander: An Autobiographical Journey* (Octagon Books 1956, 1981), 10–11.
39. De la Fuente, *A Nation for All*, 208.
40. The novel *Telex from Cuba* (Scribner, 2008) by Rachel Kushner is set in a town very much resembling Banes. The residential arrangement in the novel reflects the one in Banes, based on United Fruit's employee hierarchy, from managers down to cane cutters. The novel takes place not during Batista's childhood, but during his presidency.
41. Gott, *Cuba: A New History*, 136–46; Jaime Suchlicki, *Cuba: From Columbus to Castro and Beyond* (Brassey's Inc, 2002), 95–100.
42. T. J. English, *Havana Nocturne: How the Mob Owned Cuba … and Then Lost It to the Revolution* (HarperCollins, 2009), 64.
43. Hemingway's novel *To Have and Have Not* (1937) tells the story of a ship's captain in dire financial need who smuggles rum and other contraband between Cuba and Key West.
44. In the 2005 movie *The Lost City*, written by Cuban ex-pat novelist G. Cabrera Infante and directed by Andy García, Dustin Hoffman portrays Lansky as friendly and unassuming, babbling on about the secret to a good egg cream, but with a subtly threatening manner.
45. Gott, *Cuba: A New History*, 144.
46. Suchlicki, *Cuba: From Columbus to Castro*, 104–05.
47. Ferrer, *Cuba: An American History*, 254.
48. De la Fuente, *A Nation for All*, 208.
49. De la Fuente, *A Nation for All*, 214.
50. De la Fuente, *A Nation for All*, 218–20.
51. De la Fuente, *A Nation for All*, 180.
52. De la Fuente, *A Nation for All*, 183.
53. The English word is derived from the Spanish and Portuguese. It is related to the word *mula*, meaning *mule*. A mule is the product of a male donkey and a female horse and is unable to produce offspring. www-oed-com.ezproxy.neu.edu/view/Entry/123402?redirectedFrom=mulatto&.
54. De la Fuente, *A Nation for All*, 183.
55. Washington had by then shifted to its "Good Neighbor Policy" toward Latin America, a friendly and diplomatic form of influence. Susan Eva Eckstein, *Back from the Future: Cuba under Castro* (Princeton University Press, 1994), 17.

56. English, *Havana Nocturne*, 65.
57. John D'Emilio, "The Homosexual Menace: The Politics of Sexuality in Cold War America," in *Making Trouble: Essays on Gay History, Politics, and the University* (Routledge, 1992), 65.
58. D'Emilio, "The Homosexual Menace," 65.
59. Margot Canaday, *The Straight State: Sexuality and Citizenship in Twentieth-Century America* (Princeton University, 2009), 175, 180.
60. Canaday, *The Straight State*, 177–78.
61. Johnson, *The Lavender Scare*, 15.
62. Johnson, *The Lavender Scare*, 16.
63. Johnson, *The Lavender Scare*, 16.
64. Johnson, *The Lavender Scare*, 17.
65. D'Emilio, *Making Trouble*, 59.
66. Johnson, *The Lavender Scare*, 18.
67. Johnson, *The Lavender Scare*, 47.
68. Johnson, *The Lavender Scare*, 59.
69. Johnson, *The Lavender Scare*, 59.
70. Johnson, *The Lavender Scare*, 62.
71. Johnson, *The Lavender Scare*, 21.
72. Johnson, *The Lavender Scare*, 21.
73. D'Emilio, "The Homosexual Menace," 59–60. See also the senate committee report concluding that sex perverts were not suitable for employment by the government due to their poor moral character and vulnerability to blackmail. U.S. Congress, Senate, *Employment of Homosexuals and Other Sex Perverts in Government*, 81st Cong., 2d session, Sen. Doc. no. 241, 1950, https://web.archive.org/web/20120402035757; https://ecf.cand.uscourts.gov/cand/09cv2292/evidence/PX2337.pdf.
74. Johnson, *The Lavender Scare*, 31.
75. Johnson, *The Lavender Scare*, 36.
76. Johnson, *The Lavender Scare*, 36. The Bolsheviks decriminalized sodomy in 1918, but Stalin reversed that move in 1934. Linda Hirshman, *Victory: The Triumphant Gay Revolution* (HarperCollins Publishers, 2012), 29.
77. Johnson, *The Lavender Scare*, 37.
78. Johnson, *The Lavender Scare*, 80.
79. D'Emilio, "The Homosexual Menace," 67.
80. D'Emilio, "The Homosexual Menace," 68.
81. Edelman, "Tearooms and Sympathy," 277.
82. Evelyn Hooker, "The Adjustment of the Male Overt Homosexual," *Journal of Projective Techniques* 21 (1957): 18–31, https://doi.org/10.1080/08853126.1957.10380742.
83. Anna Lvovsky, *Vice Patrol: Cops, Courts, and the Struggle over Urban Gay Life before Stonewall* (University of Chicago Press, 2021), 11. "Prevailing historical accounts understandably tend to portray the medical model as a source of profound social stigma," though Lvovsky's telling reveals both advantages and disadvantages to medicalization. Lvovsky, *Vice Patrol*, 11.
84. John D'Emilio, "Dreams Deferred: The Birth and Betrayal of America's First Gay Liberation Movement," in *Making Trouble: Essays on Gay History, Politics, and the University* (Routledge, 1992), 17–56; Lillian Faderman, *Odd Girls and Twilight Lovers: A History of Lesbian Life in Twentieth-Century America* (Penguin Books, 1991), 148–49.
85. D'Emilio, "Dreams Deferred," 37–52.
86. Johnson, *The Lavender Scare*, 179–84.

87. Carlos A. Ball, *The First Amendment and LGBT Equality: A Contentious History* (Harvard University Press, 2017), 15–49.
88. English, *Havana Nocturne*, 49.
89. Suchlicki, *Cuba: From Columbus to Castro*, 116.
90. Suchlicki, *Cuba: From Columbus to Castro*, 118–19.
91. Carrie Hamilton, *Sexual Revolutions in Cuba: Passion, Politics, and Memory* (The University of North Carolina Press, 2012), 27. See also Kamala Kempadoo, "Continuities and Change," in *Sun, Sex, and Gold: Tourism and Sex Work in the Caribbean*, ed. Kamala Kempadoo (Rowman & Littlefield, 1999), 12.
92. Coco Fusco, "Hustling for Dollars: *Jineterismo* in Cuba," in *Global Sex Workers: Rights, Resistance, and Redefinition*, ed. Kamala Kempadoo and Jo Doezema (Routledge, 1998), 151–166, 153.
93. English, *Havana Nocturne*, 153, 163, 238–43; *The Godfather Part II*, directed by Francis Ford Coppola (Paramount Pictures, 1974).
94. Gjelten, *Bacardi*, 169; English, *Havana Nocturne*, 155.
95. Rosa Lowinger and Ofelia Fox, *Tropicana Nights: The Life and Times of the Legendary Cuban Nightclub* (Harcourt, 2005), 206.
96. Allen, *¡Venceremos?*, 58–61.
97. Lowinger and Fox, *Tropicana Nights*, 239.
98. English, *Havana Nocturne*, 211.
99. Daigle, *From Cuba with Love*, 48.
100. Lourdes Arguelles and B. Ruby Rich, "Homosexuality, Homophobia, and Revolution: Notes toward an Understanding of the Cuban Lesbian and Gay Male Experience, Part I," *Signs* 9, no. 4 (1984): 686, www.jstor.org/stable/3173617.
101. Arguelles and Rich, "Homosexuality, Homophobia, and Revolution: Part I," 686–87.
102. Lowinger and Fox, *Tropicana Nights*, 222.
103. Daigle, *From Cuba with Love*, 50.
104. Kempadoo, "Continuities and Change," 12. See also Allen Young, *Gays under the Cuban Revolution* (Grey Fox Press, 1981), 9.
105. Hamilton, *Sexual Revolutions in Cuba*, 27.
106. Suchlicki, *Cuba: From Columbus to Castro*, 111.
107. Suchlicki, *Cuba: From Columbus to Castro*, 113.
108. Suchlicki, *Cuba: From Columbus to Castro*, 123.
109. Fidel Castro, "History Will Absolve Me," in *The Cuba Reader: History, Culture, Politics*, ed. Aviva Chomsky et al. (Duke University Press, 2019), 283–91.
110. Suchlicki, *Cuba: From Columbus to Castro*, 129.
111. Herbert L. Matthews, "The Cuban Story in the *New York Times*," in *The Cuba Reader: History, Culture, Politics*, ed. Aviva Chomsky et al. (Duke University Press, 2019), 306.
112. English, *Havana Nocturne*, 275.
113. English, *Havana Nocturne*, 275–76.
114. *The Cuba Libre Story*, episode 4, "A Ragtag Revolution," directed by Emmanuel Amara, Kai Christiansen, and Florian Dedio, released December 11, 2015, on Netflix, www.netflix.com/watch/80117388?trackId=200257859.
115. English, *Havana Nocturne*, 301.
116. Lowinger and Fox, *Tropicana Nights*, 317.
117. English, *Havana Nocturne*, 305.
118. "Bay of Pigs" is the name given to a failed attempt by a group of 1,400 Cuban exiles, trained by the CIA, to invade Cuba and incite a rebellion against the revolutionary regime. Ferrer, *Cuba: An American History*, 323–25.

119. English, *Havana Nocturne*, 310.
120. Emily J. Kirk, *Cuba's Gay Revolution: Normalizing Sexual Diversity through a Health-Based Approach* (Lexington Books, 2017), 17, EBSCOhost; Hamilton, *Sexual Revolutions in Cuba*, 39; Young, *Gays under the Cuban Revolution*, 22. The CDRs were instituted in 1960 to assist various parts of the state with governance at the neighborhood level. They have had a broad remit over the years, from watching out for counterrevolutionary activity, to carrying out public health initiatives, to running seminars on matters such as US imperialism and the need for sacrifice. Suchlicki, *Cuba: From Columbus to Castro*, 173.
121. Eckstein, *Back from the Future*, 31–32.
122. *The Cuba Libre Story*, episode 6, "Of Soviets and Saviors," directed by Emmanuel Amara, Kai Christiansen, and Florian Dedio, released December 11, 2015, on Netflix, www.youtube.com/watch?v=c1spoI7ND10.
123. Ferrer, *Cuba: An American History*, 354–68.
124. Suchlicki, *Cuba: From Columbus to Castro*, 142–49; Eckstein, *Back from the Future*, 5.
125. Gott, *Cuba: A New History*, 189.
126. Gott, *Cuba: A New History*, 170.
127. De la Fuente, *A Nation for All*, 4; Allen, *¡Venceremos?*, 63.
128. Gott, *Cuba: A New History*, 173.
129. Gott, *Cuba: A New History*, 173.
130. Allen, *¡Venceremos?*, 63; Gott, *Cuba: A New History*, 174.
131. De la Fuente, *A Nation for All*, 274.
132. De la Fuente, *A Nation for All*, 279.
133. Gott, *Cuba: A New History*, 185, 225.
134. De la Fuente, *A Nation for All*, 296–99.
135. Gott, *Cuba: A New History*, 227.
136. De la Fuente, *A Nation for All*, 300–01.
137. Michael Foucault, *The History of Sexuality*, Vol. 1, trans. Robert Hurley (Vintage Books, 1990), 27.
138. Allen, *¡Venceremos?*, 66.
139. De la Fuente, *A Nation for All*, 8.
140. Sarah J. Seidman, "Angela Davis in Cuba as Symbol and Subject," *Radical History Review*, no. 136 (2020): 25, https://read.dukeupress.edu/radical-history-review/article-abstract/2020/136/11/148070/Angela-Davis-in-Cuba-as-Symbol-and-Subject?redirectedFrom=fulltext.
141. Michelle Chase, *Revolution within the Revolution: Women and Gender Politics in Cuba, 1952–1962* (The University of North Carolina Press, 2015), 137.
142. Chase, *Revolution within the Revolution*, 139.
143. Chase, *Revolution within the Revolution*, 147.
144. Chase, *Revolution within the Revolution*, 151.
145. Seidman, "Angela Davis," 25.
146. Chase, *Revolution within the Revolution*, 165.
147. Daigle, *From Cuba with Love*, 50.
148. Fusco, "Hustling for Dollars," 153.
149. Daigle, *From Cuba with Love*, 51–52; Hamilton, *Sexual Revolutions in Cuba*, 27.
150. Fusco, "Hustling for Dollars," 156.
151. Rachel Hynson, *Laboring for the State: Women, Family, and Work in Revolutionary Cuba, 1959–1971* (Cambridge University Press, 2019), 14, 27.
152. Eckstein, *Back from the Future*, 43–44.
153. Eckstein, *Back from the Future*, 49.

154. Hamilton, *Sexual Revolutions in Cuba*, 33.
155. Daigle, *From Cuba with Love*, 54.
156. For one exposition of this vision, see Che Guevara, "Socialism and Man," in *The Cuba Reader: History, Culture, Politics*, ed. Aviva Chomsky et al. (Duke University Press, 2019), 343–47.
157. Chase, *Revolution within the Revolution*, 52. See also Ana Serra, *The "New Man" in Cuba: Culture and Identity in the Revolution* (University Press of Florida, 2007), 166 on the centrality of "masculinity" to the "New Man."
158. Chase, *Revolution within the Revolution*, 74.
159. Chase, *Revolution within the Revolution*, 74.
160. Chase, *Revolution within the Revolution*, 44–76.
161. Chase, *Revolution within the Revolution*, 45.
162. Chase, *Revolution within the Revolution*, 50.
163. Chase, *Revolution within the Revolution*, 52.
164. Chase, *Revolution within the Revolution*, 50.
165. Chase, *Revolution within the Revolution*, 59.
166. Abel Sierra Madero, "The Sex of Nations: An Interview with Abel Sierra Madero," interview by Frances Negrón-Muntaner, *CSER Newsletter*, Vol. 1 (2011): 12.
167. Marvin Leiner, *Sexual Politics in Cuba: Machismo, Homosexuality, and AIDS* (Westview Press, 1994), 26. Castro apologized for the UMAPs and generally for his homophobia in 2010. Noelle M. Stout, *After Love: Queer Intimacy and Erotic Economies in Post-Soviet Cuba* (Duke University Press, 2014), 39; Allen, *¡Venceremos?*, 73.
168. Chase, *Revolution within the Revolution*, 45.
169. The image, entitled *Guerrillero Heroico (Heroic Guerilla)*, is credited to Cuban photographer Alberto Korda (1960).
170. Susana Peña, *¡Oye Loca!: From the Mariel Boatlift to Gay Cuban Miami* (University of Minnesota Press, 2013), 3.
171. Stout, *After Love*, 35.
172. Stout, *After Love*, 35, citing Abel Sierra Madero, Del otro lado del espejo: La sexualidad en la construcción nación cubana (Casa de las Americas, 2006), 95.
173. Ian Lumsden, *Machos, Maricones, and Gays: Cuba and Homosexuality* (Temple University Press, 1996), 50–51.
174. Emilio Bejel, *Gay Cuban Nation* (The University of Chicago Press, 2001), 96.
175. Stout, *After Love*, 36.
176. Stout, *After Love*, 36.
177. Bejel, *Gay Cuban Nation*, 100.
178. Allen Young, "Cuba: Gay as the Sun," in *Out of the Closets: Voices of Gay Liberation*, ed. Karla Jay and Allen Young (New York University Press 1972, 1992), 214.
179. Stout, *After Love*, 27; Allen, *¡Venceremos?*, 75. The Caribbean Spanish term "bugarrón" shares an etymology with the English term "bugger." Both derive from the Medieval Latin word for "Bulgarian," used derogatorily by the Crusaders who considered the Bulgarians' Orthodox Church heretical. Wiktionary, s.v. "bugarrón," https://en.wiktionary.org/wiki/bugarrón. Thanks to Kaiponanea Matsumura for pointing me to this.
180. Leiner, *Sexual Politics in Cuba*, 22.
181. In the modern era, according to Lumsden, "more and more gays are *completo* (reciprocal in sex)." Lumsden, *Machos, Maricones, and Gays*, 30.
182. His key work was *Psychopathia Sexualis: eine Klinisch-Forensische Studie*, or *Sexual Psychopathy: A Clinical-Forensic Study*, first published in 1886.
183. Chauncey, *Gay New York*, 99–111.

184. Chauncey, *Gay New York*, 65–97.
185. Lumsden, *Machos, Maricones, and Gays*, 58. Indeed, Castro's "[g]uerrillas … taunted [Batista's] government soldiers with, ¡Ríndanse, maricones! (Surrender, queers!)." Lorraine Bayard de Volo, *Women and the Cuban Insurrection: How Gender Shaped Castro's Victory* (Cambridge University Press, 2018), 90.
186. Allen, *¡Venceremos?*, 68. See also Julio César González Pagés, *Macho Varón Masculino: Estudios de Masculinidades en Cuba* (Editorial de la Mujer, 2010), 69–70. "Los homosexuales son juzgados como flojos, débiles, femeninos y amanerados. Tales atributos denotarían poca confiabilidad para ejercer determinadas profesiones, sobre todo las relacionadas con decisions de poder" (describing stereotypes of homosexual men as weak, untrustworthy, and unsuited to positions of power). González Pagés goes on to cite a letter in a newspaper asking "¿Quién podrá contener la risa cuando ve á un hombre barbado gastar la mayor parte de una mañana en peinarse, ataviarse y env er copiada su hermosura en un Espejo, cuál lo practica la Dama más presumida?" (the letter asks who can contain their laughter at seeing a bearded man beautifying himself and gazing at his own reflection in a mirror). González Pagés, *Macho Varón Masculino*, 70.
187. Gott, *Cuba: A New History*, 167, 170. "The first steps taken by the new government were to conduct a census of the prostitutes and pimps and then to establish medical clinics for special health examinations, rehabilitation programs for 'pimps', and reeducation programs for former sex workers." Kempadoo, "Continuities and Change," 13 (internal citation omitted).
188. Lowinger and Fox, *Tropicana Nights*, 88, 233.
189. Daigle, *From Cuba with Love*, 52.
190. Lumsden, *Machos, Maricones, and Gays*, 57.
191. Lumsden, *Machos, Maricones, and Gays*, 58; Kirk, *Cuba's Gay Revolution*, 16; Bejel, *Gay Cuban Nation*, 97.
192. Bejel, *Gay Cuban Nation*, 97.
193. Kirk, *Cuba's Gay Revolution*, 16; Arenas, *Before Night Falls*, 177–201.
194. Lumsden, *Machos, Maricones, and Gays*, 62.
195. It is too hard to resist pointing out the name of perhaps the world's most well-known "gayborhood" in San Francisco, California.
196. Bejel, *Gay Cuban Nation*, 100–102.
197. Hamilton, *Sexual Revolutions in Cuba*, 152–53.
198. Leiner, *Sexual Politics in Cuba*, 12.
199. Lumsden, *Machos, Maricones, and Gays*, 67.
200. Arenas, *Before Night Falls*, 19.
201. Lumsden, *Machos, Maricones, and Gays*, 34, 57.
202. Arenas, *Before Night Falls*, 18–19.
203. My use of the word "blissfully" here refers to the experience of the boys and men; I cannot speak for the farm animals.
204. Allen, *¡Venceremos?*, 68.
205. Religious dissidents such as Jehovah's Witnesses and other nonconformists were also sent to the UMAPs, which closed in 1968 under pressure domestically from the Cuban Writers and Artists Union as well as from international celebrities such as Graham Greene, Jean-Paul Sartre, and Allen Ginsberg. Hamilton, *Sexual Revolutions in Cuba*, 40; Bejel, *Gay Cuban Nation*, 101–102.
206. Allen, *¡Venceremos?*, 69. (Yeah, I know.)
207. Hamilton, *Sexual Revolutions in Cuba*, 41. There was one women's UMAP whose inmates included lesbians as well as sex workers who "refused to enter government retraining programs." Stout, *After Love*, 37.

208. Leiner, *Sexual Politics in Cuba*, 33–34; Hamilton, *Sexual Revolutions in Cuba*, 39; Bejel, *Gay Cuban Nation*, 103.
209. Hamilton, *Sexual Revolutions in Cuba*, 39.
210. Lumsden, *Machos, Maricones, and Gays*, 72; Leiner, *Sexual Politics in Cuba*, 32.
211. Young, "Cuba: Gay as the Sun," 245–46.
212. Young, "Cuba: Gay as the Sun," 246.
213. Jennifer L. Lambe, "Historicizing Sexuality in the Cuban Revolution: The Spectral 'Before,'" *Radical History Review*, no. 136 (2020): 224, http://dx.doi.org/10.1215/01636545-7857392.
214. Kirk, *Cuba's Gay Revolution*, 19.
215. Lumsden, *Machos, Maricones, and Gays*, 71, 73.
216. Kirk, *Cuba's Gay Revolution*, 19.
217. Serra, *"New Man" in Cuba*, 16.
218. Michael Warner, introduction to *Fear of a Queer Planet: Queer Politics and Social Theory* (University of Minnesota Press, 2000), xvi–xvii.
219. See generally Lvovsky, *Vice Patrol*.
220. Young, *Gays under the Cuban Revolution*, 71–78.
221. Young, *Gays under the Cuban Revolution*, 31.
222. Young, *Gays under the Cuban Revolution*, 78–79.
223. Rafael Rojas, *Fighting over Fidel: The New York Intellectuals and the Cuban Revolution* (Princeton University Press, 2016), 159.
224. Young, *Gays under the Cuban Revolution*, 20.
225. Allen Ginsberg, *Collected Poems 1947–1980* (Harper & Row, 1984), 265. See also Rojas, *Fighting over Fidel*, 146.
226. Rojas, *Fighting over Fidel*, 151.
227. Rojas, *Fighting over Fidel*, 152, citing Allen Ginsberg, *Deliberate Prose: Selected Essays 1952–1995* (HarperCollins, 2000), 144.
228. Rojas, *Fighting over Fidel*, 159.
229. Young, *Gays under the Cuban Revolution*, 98–99.
230. Matt Baume, "A Gay American Revolutionary Remembers Queer Life in Fidel Castro's Cuba," *Out*, December 3, 2016, www.out.com/news-opinion/2016/12/03/gay-american-revolutionary-remembers-queer-life-fidel-castros-cuba.
231. Bejel, *Gay Cuban Nation*, 96.
232. Lumsden, *Machos, Maricones, and Gays*, 57.
233. Daigle, *From Cuba with Love*, 146.
234. Bejel, *Gay Cuban Nation*, 103.
235. Brad Epps, "Proper Conduct: Reinaldo Arenas, Fidel Castro, and the Politics of Homosexuality," *Journal of the History of Sexuality* 6, no. 2 (1995): 231, www.jstor.org/stable/3704123.
236. Epps, "Proper Conduct," 251.
237. Benedict Anderson, *Imagined Communities: Reflections on the Origin and Spread of Nationalism* (Verso, 1991), 6.
238. Andrew Parker, et al., "Introduction," in *Nationalisms and Sexualities*, ed. A. Parker, M. Russo, D. Sommer, and P. Yaeger (Routledge, 1992), 6.
239. Eve Kosofsky Sedgwick, *Between Men: English Literature and Male Homosocial Desire* (Columbia University Press, 2016), 1.
240. Gjelten, *Bacardi*, 161, 171–72, 187, 201. Vilma's father was an attorney for Bacardi. Bayard de Volo, *Women and the Cuban Insurrection*, 104.
241. www.facebook.com/FMCdeCuba/.

242. https://thinkglobalcentralamerica.wordpress.com/2015/03/16/blog-7-the-federation-of-cuba-women/.
243. Teemu Ruskola, "Raping Like a State," *UCLA Law Review* 57, no. 5 (2010): 1479, https://heinonline.org/HOL/P?h=hein.journals/uclalr57&i=1487; www.uclalawreview.org/raping-like-a-state/.
244. Teemu, "Raping Like a State," 1497.

2 A TENTATIVE EMBRACE: 1970S–1990S

1. Michael Bronski, *A Queer History of the United States* (Beacon Press, 2011), 219.
2. Bronski, *Queer History*, 220.
3. Bronski, *Queer History*, 220.
4. Bronski, *Queer History*, 223.
5. Bronski, *Queer History*, 221.
6. Ball, *The First Amendment and LGBT Equality*, 50.
7. Ball, *The First Amendment and LGBT Equality*, 51.
8. NAACP v. Alabama ex rel. Patterson, 357 US 449 (1958).
9. Ball, *The First Amendment and LGBT Equality*, 73–74.
10. Ball, *The First Amendment and LGBT Equality*, 75–83.
11. Ball, *The First Amendment and LGBT Equality*, 83–86.
12. Ball, *The First Amendment and LGBT Equality*, 92–122.
13. Ball 2017, 95.
14. Baker v. Nelson, 409 US 810 (1972).
15. Leiner, *Sexual Politics in Cuba*, 43. As Chapter 1 notes, homosexuality was medicalized in the US in the 1950s, with mixed consequences. See Lvovsky, *Vice Patrol*, 11.
16. Kirk, *Cuba's Gay Revolution*, chapter 2.
17. Kirk, *Cuba's Gay Revolution*, chapter 2.
18. Leiner, *Sexual Politics in Cuba*, 68.
19. Leiner, *Sexual Politics in Cuba*, 69.
20. Kirk, *Cuba's Gay Revolution*, chapter 2.
21. Bejel, *Gay Cuban Nation*, 107.
22. Kirk, *Cuba's Gay Revolution*, chapter 2.
23. Bejel, *Gay Cuban Nation*, 107.
24. Leiner, *Sexual Politics in Cuba*, 44.
25. Kirk, *Cuba's Gay Revolution*, chapter 2.
26. Kirk, *Cuba's Gay Revolution*, chapter 2.
27. Kirk, *Cuba's Gay Revolution*, chapter 2.
28. Kirk, *Cuba's Gay Revolution*, Introduction.
29. Cuba, Gaceta Oficial de la República de Cuba, September 24, 1973, http://hdl.handle.net/2047/D20509347.
30. Hamilton, *Sexual Revolutions in Cuba*, 42.
31. Lumsden, *Machos, Maricones, and Gays*, 82. Cuba. Código Penal, art. 359 (1979) is the version in which homosexual sodomy is decriminalied but "ostentation" remains criminal.
32. Lumsden, *Machos, Maricones, and Gays*, 85; Age of consent is equalized in Cuba. Código Penal, art. 310 (1997).
33. Daigle, *From Cuba with Love*, 119 (translating *Código Penal, Ley No. 21 de 15 de febrero de 1979, Art. 73*).

34. Allen, *¡Venceremos?*, 72.
35. De la Fuente, *A Nation for All*, 315.
36. Emily J. Kirk, "Setting the Agenda for Cuban Sexuality: The Role of Cuba's Cenesex," *Canadian Journal of Latin American and Caribbean Studies* 36, no. 72 (2011): 151, https://doi.org/10.1080/08263663.2011.10817018.
37. Peña, *¡Oye Loca*, 28.
38. Hamilton, *Sexual Revolutions in Cuba*, 44.
39. Gott, *Cuba: A New History*, 267.
40. Gott, *Cuba: A New History*, 268.
41. Gott, *Cuba: A New History*, 268.
42. Gott, *Cuba: A New History*, 268; Ferrer, *Cuba: An American History*, 416.
43. Gott, *Cuba: A New History*, 269.
44. Peña, *¡Oye Loca!*, 48, 57.
45. Bejel, *Gay Cuban Nation*, 107.
46. Hamilton, *Sexual Revolutions in Cuba*, 128; Lumsden, *Machos, Maricones, and Gays*, 79.
47. Peña, *¡Oye Loca!*, 27.
48. Peña, *¡Oye Loca!*, 6.
49. Peña, *¡Oye Loca!*, 10.
50. Peña, *¡Oye Loca!*, 30.
51. Arguelles and Rich, "Homosexuality, Homophobia, and Revolution: Part I," 695.
52. Arguelles and Rich, "Homosexuality, Homophobia, and Revolution: Part I," 695.
53. Arguelles and Rich, "Homosexuality, Homophobia, and Revolution: Part I" 695.
54. Lourdes Arguelles and B. Ruby Rich, "Homosexuality, Homophobia, and Revolution: Notes toward an Understanding of the Cuban Lesbian and Gay Male Experience, Part II," *Signs* 11, no. 1 (1985): 128, https://doi.org/10.1086/494203.
55. Peña, *¡Oye Loca!*, 34, 55.
56. Ummni Khan, *Vicarious Kinks: S/M in the Socio-Legal Imaginary* (University of Toronto Press, 2014), 57–64.
57. Carole S. Vance, *Pleasure and Danger: Exploring Female Sexuality* (Routledge, 1984). See also *Signs: Journal of Women in Culture and Society*, Vol. 42, no. 1 (2016), for a special issue revisiting the themes of the famous Vance collection.
58. Alice Echols, *Daring to Be Bad: Radical Feminism in America 1967–1975* (University of Minnesota Press, 1989), 244, 256.
59. Khan, *Vicarious Kinks*, 66–67. Echols, *Daring to Be Bad*, 244.
60. "Women took on the cause of AIDS for many reasons – because the homophobia it triggered threatened them as well, because their friends were dying, and because they really are just good human beings.... AIDS was the remaking of the [gay/lesbian] alliance." Hirshman, *Victory*, 180.
61. Griswold v. Connecticut, 381 U.S. 479 (1965).
62. Griswold, 381 U.S. at 484.
63. Stanley v. Georgia, 394 U.S. 557 (1969).
64. Eisenstadt v. Baird, 405 U.S. 438 (1972).
65. Roe v. Wade, 410 U.S. 113 (1973), *Overruled in* Dobbs v. Jackson, 597 U.S. 215, 292 (2022).
66. Commonwealth v. Balthazar, 318 N.E.2d 478 (1974).
67. People v. Onofre, 415 N.E.2d. 936 (1980).
68. William N. Eskridge, Jr., *Dishonorable Passions: Sodomy Laws in America 1861–2003* (Viking, 2008), 201.
69. John Wolfenden et al., *Report of the Committee on Homosexual Offences and Prostitution* (London: Her Majesty's Stationery Office, 1957).

70. "That principle is, that the sole end for which mankind are warranted, individually or collectively, in interfering with the liberty of action of any of their number, is self-protection. That the only purpose for which power can be rightfully exercised over any member of a civilized community, against his will, is to prevent harm to others." John Stuart Mill, "On Liberty" in *Three Essays* (Oxford University Press, 1975), 15.
71. Bowers v. Hardwick, 478 U.S. 186 (1986) *overruled in* Lawrence v. Texas, 539 U.S. 558, 578 (2003).
72. Lawrence v. Texas, 539 U.S. 558 (2003).
73. Bronski, *Queer History*, 225.
74. Bronski, *Queer History*, 227.
75. Hirshman, *Victory*, 170.
76. Aziza Ahmed, *Risk and Resistance: How Feminists Transformed the Law and Science of AIDS* (Cambridge University Press, 2025), 19–20; Bronski, *Queer History*, 229.
77. Hamilton, *Sexual Revolutions in Cuba*, 194.
78. Mark Padilla, *Caribbean Pleasure Industry: Tourism, Sexuality, and AIDS in the Dominican Republic* (University of Chicago Press, 2007), 255n6.
79. Padilla, *Caribbean Pleasure Industry*, 255.
80. Lumsden, *Machos, Maricones, and Gays*, 168. Gay and bisexual men were also banned from donating blood in the US for years, but the FDA relaxed restrictions in 2020 and proposed a case-by-case assessment in 2023. Christina Jewett and Emily Anthes, "New Blood Donation Rules to Loosen on Gay and Bisexual Men," *New York Times*, January 27, 2023. www.nytimes.com/2023/01/27/health/blood-donation-gay-bisexual.html.
81. Lumsden, *Machos, Maricones, and Gays*, 169.
82. Lumsden, *Machos, Maricones, and Gays*, 171.
83. Lumsden, *Machos, Maricones, and Gays*, 172.
84. Lumsden, *Machos, Maricones, and Gays*, 172.
85. Kirk, *Cuba's Gay Revolution*, chapter 2.
86. Lumsden, *Machos, Maricones, and Gays*, 170.
87. Lumsden, *Machos, Maricones, and Gays*, 171.
88. Leiner, *Sexual Politics in Cuba*, 123–24.
89. Eckstein, Susan. "The Rectification of Errors or the Errors of the Rectification Process in Cuba?" *Cuban Studies* 20 (1990): 67–85, www.jstor.org/stable/24486987.
90. Gott, *Cuba: A New History*, 275.
91. Gott, *Cuba: A New History*, 275.
92. Bejel, *Gay Cuban Nation*, 110; *Fresa y Chocolate*, directed by Tomás Gutiérrez Alea and Juan Carlos Tabío (Miramax, 1993). The film *Fresa y Chocolate* (*Strawberry and Chocolate*) featured a friendship between two men, one homosexual and one heterosexual. The homosexual character is overtly dissatisfied with the oppression of homosexuals and with artistic censorship under the Castro regime. This was the first Cuban film to be nominated for an Academy Award. Cuban masculinity studies scholar Julio César González Pagés notes that the movie was significant for depicting a homosexual character as "nacionalista y valiente" ("nationalist and brave"). González Pagés, *Macho Varón Masculino*, 75.
93. Wiilfred W. Labiosa, *The LGBT Cuban Revolution* (Deletrea, 2023), 62–63.
94. Lumsden, *Machos, Maricones, and Gays*, 82.
95. Lumsden, *Machos, Maricones, and Gays*, 87; Daigle, *From Cuba with Love*, 124.
96. Kirk, *Cuba's Gay Revolution*, chapter 1.
97. After the initial surgeries, there was an almost twenty-year gap before more surgeries were performed, likely due to resource constraints. Emily J. Kirk and Robert Huish, "Transsexuals' Right to Health? A Cuban Case Study," *Health and Human Rights Journal* 20, no. 2 (2018): 215–22, https://pmc.ncbi.nlm.nih.gov/articles/PMC6293354/.

98. Kirk, *Cuba's Gay Revolution*, chapter 1.
99. Labiosa, *The LGBT Cuban Revolution*, 67.
100. Kirk, *Cuba's Gay Revolution*, chapter 3.
101. Kirk, *Cuba's Gay Revolution*, chapter 3.
102. Kirk, *Cuba's Gay Revolution*, chapter 3; Tanya L. Saunders, "Grupo OREMI: Black Lesbians and the Struggle for Safe Social Space in Havana," *Souls* 11, no. 2 (2009): 169, https://doi.org/10.1080/10999940902910198.
103. Kirk, *Cuba's Gay Revolution*, chapter 3.
104. Kirk, "Setting the Agenda," 151–57. In 2019, as the government attempted to manage growing conflict between the lgbtq community and anti-gay religious forces, the governmentally sponsored event was canceled, but an extra-legal demonstration occurred anyway. "Cuba Cancels Annual Conga against Homophobia March" BBC, May 8, 2019. www.bbc.com/news/world-latin-america-48199835. As a consequence of COVID-19, the regular, government-sponsored conga did not resume until 2023.
105. *Mariela Castro's March: Cuba's LGBT Revolution*, directed by Jon Alpert (HBO, 2016).
106. Kirk, *Cuba's Gay Revolution*, chapter 3.
107. Kirk, *Cuba's Gay Revolution*, chapter 4. Cuba. Ley No. 87 de 16 de Febrero de 1999, amending Código Penal art. 303.
108. Resolución Ministerial No. 126. República de Cuba, Ministerio de Salud Pública 2008.
109. Kirk and Huish, "Transsexuals' Right to Health?" 220.
110. Kirk and Huish, "Transsexuals' Right to Health?" 220.
111. Sierra Madero, "The Sex of Nations, 13.
112. Stout, *After Love*, 51.
113. Daigle, *From Cuba with Love*, 157.
114. Saunders, "Grupo OREMI," 168.
115. Saunders, "Grupo OREMI," 177.
116. Saunders, "Grupo OREMI," 179.
117. Saunders, "Grupo OREMI," 176–79.
118. Saunders, "Grupo OREMI," 170.
119. Saunders, "Grupo OREMI," 170, 175.
120. Saunders, "Grupo OREMI," 183.
121. *Personal Responsibility and Work Opportunity Reconciliation Act of* 1996, Pub. L. No. 104–93, 110 Stat. 2105 (1996).
122. 42 U.S.C. § 601(a)(2) (1997).
123. Brenda Cossman, "Family Feuds: Neo-Liberal and Neo-Conservative Visions of the Reprivatization Project," in *Privatization, Law, and the Challenge to Feminism*, ed. Brenda Cossman and Judy Fudge (University of Toronto Press, 2002), 169. Cossman directed her analysis primarily to Canada, but it applies with even greater force in the historically stingier US.
124. Cossman, "Family Feuds," 169.
125. For review and analysis of much earlier efforts, see Michael Boucai, "Glorious Precedents: When Gay Marriage was Radical," *Yale Journal of Law & Humanities*, 27 (2015): 1, https://ssrn.com/abstract=2543686.
126. Baehr v. Miike, 910 P.2d 112 (Haw. 1996).
127. The federal Defense of Marriage Act, Pub.L. 104–199, 110 Stat. 2419 (1996), was struck down in United States v. Windsor, 570 U.S. 744 (2013) and Obergefell v. Hodges, 576 U.S. 644 (2015). State analogues fell as a consequence of *Obergefell*, as well.
128. Baker v. VT 744 A.2d 864 (Vt. 1999).
129. Vermont statutes Title 15, Ch. 23, § 1201.

130. Carlos A. Ball, *The Queering of Corporate America: How Big Business Went from LGBTQ Adversary to Ally* (Beacon Press, 2019): 95–125.
131. Douglas NeJaime, "Marriage Equality and the New Parenthood," *Harvard Law Review*, 129(5) (2016): 1196–230, https://harvardlawreview.org/print/vol-129/marriage-equality-and-the-new-parenthood/.
132. Romer v. Evans, 517 U.S. 620 (1996).
133. *Romer*, 517 U.S. at 636, 652 (Scalia, J., dissenting).
134. *Lawrence*, 539 U.S. 558; *Windsor*, 570 U.S. 744; *Obergefell*, 576 U.S. 644.
135. *Lawrence* 539 U.S. 558.
136. According to Dale Carpenter, the legal scholar most well-known for having investigated the circumstances leading to the case, the sexual act probably never occurred. Dale Carpenter, *Flagrant Conduct: The History of Lawrence v. Texas* (Norton, 2012), xii.
137. Planned Parenthood v. Casey, 505 U.S. 833 (1992) *overruled in* Dobbs v. Jackson, 595 U.S. 215, 292 (2022). The plurality opinion in *Casey* was co-authored by Justices Kennedy, O'Connor, and Souter.
138. *Casey*, 505 U.S. at 851.
139. *Casey*, 505 U.S. at 980 (Scalia, J., dissenting).
140. *Griswold*, 381 U.S. at 485–86.
141. *Lawrence*, 539 U.S. at 562.
142. *Lawrence*, 539 U.S. at 578.
143. I say "nearly" because there were advocacy efforts to disentangle gay identity from homosexual acts. The conceptual separation of identity from act enabled the *Romer* Court to apply equal protection sexual orientation categories. Sonia K. Katyal, "Exporting Identity," *Yale Journal of Law & Feminism* 14(1) (2019), 102–14, https://lawcat.berkeley.edu/record/1108613?v=pdf.
144. Goodridge v. Department of Public Health, 440 Mass. 309 (2003).
145. *Windsor*, 570 U.S. 744.
146. *Obergefell*, 576 U.S. 644.
147. *Goodridge*, 440 Mass. at 322.
148. Kenneth B. Mehlman et al., *Brief as Amici Curiae Supporting Petitioners, Obergefell v. Hodges* (No. 14-566) at 1 (U.S. 2015), https://lambdalegal.org/legal_document/henry_oh_20150306_amicus-mehlman-et-al/.
149. Mehlman, *Amicus Brief*, 11.
150. John D'Emilio, "A Meaning for All Those Words: Sex, Politics, History and Larry Kramer: Sex, Politics, History and Larry Kramer," in *The World Turned: Essays on Gay History, Politics, and Culture* (Duke University Press, 2002), 68.
151. Bronski, *Queer History*, 211.
152. D'Emilio, "A Meaning for All Those Words: Sex, Politics, History and Larry Kramer," 76.
153. Hirshman, *Victory*, 180.
154. D'Emilio, "A Meaning for All Those Words: Sex, Politics, History and Larry Kramer," 76.
155. Urvashi Vaid, *Virtual Equality: The Mainstreaming of Gay and Lesbian Liberation* (Anchor Books, Doubleday, 1995). See also Libby Adler, "Distributive Justice for LGBTQ People," in *The Oxford Research Encyclopedia of Politics*, ed. Donald P. Haider-Markel (Oxford University Press, 2021), https://oxfordre.com/politics/view/10.1093/acrefore/9780190228637.001.0001/acrefore-9780190228637-e-1235.
156. See generally Cathy J. Cohen, "Punks, Bulldaggers, and Welfare Queens: The Radical Potential of Queer Politics?" in *Black Queer Studies: A Critical Anthology*, ed. E. Patrick Johnson and Mae G. Henderson (Duke University Press, 2005): 21–51, https://doi.org/10.1515/9780822387220-004.

157. Adler, *Gay Priori*, 100–106.
158. Thanks to Karen Engle for this insight.
159. Adler, *Gay Priori*, 212–15. See also Lenore Carpenter, "Getting Queer Priorities Straight: How Direct Legal Services Can Democratize Issue Prioritization in the LGBT Rights Movement," *University of Pennsylvania Journal of Law and Social Change*, Vol. 17 (2014): 123, https://scholarship.law.upenn.edu/jlasc/vol17/iss2/2.
160. The policy known as Don't Ask/Don't Tell was enacted in 1993, becoming effective in 1994. National Defense Authorization Act for Fiscal Year 1994, Pub. L. No. 103–160, 107 Stat. 1670 (1993), www.congress.gov/bill/103rd-congress/house-bill/2401/text. Repealed by Don't Ask, Don't Tell Repeal Act of 2010, Pub. L. No. 111–321, 124 Stat. 3515, www.congress.gov/bill/111th-congress/house-bill/2965/text.
161. GAO Report to Congressional Requesters. United States General Accounting Office, *Defense Force Management: DOD's Policy on Homosexuality* (1992), www.gao.gov/assets/nsiad-92–98.pdf.
162. Exec. Order 12968, 60 Fed. Reg. 40245 (August 2, 1995), www.dni.gov/files/NCSC/documents/Regulations/EO_12968.pdf.
163. Derrick Bell, *Silent Covenants: Brown v. Board of Education and the Unfulfilled Hopes for Racial Reform* (Oxford University Press, 2004), 59–68.
164. Mary L. Dudziak, *Cold War Civil Rights: Race and the Image of American Democracy* (Princeton University Press, 2002).
165. Dudziak, *Cold War Civil Rights*, 49.
166. Dudziak, *Cold War Civil Rights*, 67–77.
167. Shelley v. Kraemer, 334 U.S. 1 (1948).
168. Dudziak, *Cold War Civil Rights*, 91, 203–240.
169. Jasbir K. Puar, *Terrorist Assemblages: Homonationalism in Queer Times* (Duke University Press, 2007), 4.
170. Puar, *Terrorist Assemblages*, 2.
171. Puar, Jasbir. "Rethinking Homonationalism." *International Journal of Middle East Studies* 45, no. 2 (2013): 337, www.jstor.org/stable/43302999
172. Puar, *Terrorist Assemblages*, 4.
173. Bianca D. M. Wilson et al., *LGBT Poverty in the United States: Trends at the Onset of COVID-19* (The Williams Institute, UCLA School of Law, February 2023), https://williamsinstitute.law.ucla.edu/wp-content/uploads/LGBT-Poverty-COVID-Feb-2023.pdf; Bianca D. M. Wilson et al., *Homelessness among LGBT Adults in the US* (The Williams Institute, UCLA School of Law, May 2020), 2, https://williamsinstitute.law.ucla.edu/wp-content/uploads/LGBT-Homelessness-May-2020.pdf; Brad Sears, Andrew R. Flores, and Jet Harbeck, *LGBT Adults, Food Insecurity, and Reliance on SNAP* (The Williams Institute, UCLA School of Law, June 2025), 7, https://williamsinstitute.law.ucla.edu/wp-content/uploads/SNAP-Reliance-Jul-2025.pdf; Winston Luhur, Ilan H. Meyer, and Bianca D. M. Wilson, *Policing LGBQ People* (The Williams Institute, UCLA School of Law, May 2021), https://williamsinstitute.law.ucla.edu/wp-content/uploads/Policing-LGBQ-People-May-2021.pdf.
174. Hirshman, *Victory*.
175. Suchlicki, *Cuba: From Columbus to Castro*, 192, 195.
176. Gott, *Cuba: A New History*, 286.
177. Suchlicki, *Cuba: From Columbus to Castro*, 195.
178. Gjelten, *Bacardi*, 319.
179. Eckstein, *Back from the Future*, 91.
180. Gjelten, *Bacardi*, 319.

181. Ferrer, *Cuba: An American History*, 436.
182. Gjelten, *Bacardi*, 320.
183. Eckstein, *Back from the Future*, 96–97.
184. Suchlicki, *Cuba: From Columbus to Castro*, 195.
185. Suchlicki, *Cuba: From Columbus to Castro*, 195.
186. Suchlicki, *Cuba: From Columbus to Castro*, 195; Amalia L. Cabezas, *Economies of Desire: Sex and Tourism in Cuba and the Dominican Republic* (Temple University Press, 2009), 61–62.
187. Cabezas, *Economies of Desire*, 61–62.
188. Eckstein, *Back from the Future*, 98–99.
189. Ferrer, *Cuba: An American History*, 439.
190. Eckstein, *Back from the Future*, 91.
191. Eckstein, *Back from the Future*, 92.
192. Eckstein, *Back from the Future*, 93.
193. U.S. Congress, *Cuban Democracy Act of 1992*, Pub. L. No. 102–484, 106 Stat. 2315 (1992), codified at 22 U.S.C. ch. 69 § 6001 et seq.
194. U.S. Congress, *Cuban Liberty and Democratic Solidarity (LIBERTAD) Act of 1996*, Pub. L. No. 104-114, 110 Stat. 785 (1996), codified at 22 U.S.C. §§ 6021–91.
195. Gott, *Cuba: A New History*, 303.
196. Suchlicki, *Cuba: From Columbus to Castro*, 196.
197. Suchlicki, *Cuba: From Columbus to Castro*, 196.
198. Suchlicki, *Cuba: From Columbus to Castro*, 197.
199. Gott, *Cuba: A New History*, 292; Gjelten, *Bacardi*, 321.
200. Gott, *Cuba: A New History*, 292.
201. Suchlicki, *Cuba: From Columbus to Castro*, 197–98.
202. Gott, *Cuba: A New History*, 290.
203. Ferrer, *Cuba: An American History*, 443.
204. Suchlicki, *Cuba: From Columbus to Castro*, 199.
205. Gott, *Cuba: A New History*, 290.
206. Gjelten, *Bacardi*, 322.
207. Gott, *Cuba: A New History*, 293.
208. Nadine Fernandez, "Back to the Future: Women, Race, and Tourism in Cuba," in *Sun, Sex, and Gold: Tourism and Sex Work in the Caribbean*, edited by Kamala Kempadoo (Rowman & Littlefield, 1999), 81–89, 83 (internal citations omitted).
209. Ferrer, *Cuba: An American History*, 443.
210. Allen, *¡Venceremos?*, 120; Cabezas, *Economies of Desire*, 80. See also Fernandez, "Back to the Future," 85.
211. Allen, *¡Venceremos?*, 120.
212. Ferrer, *Cuba: An American History*, 445.
213. Cabezas, *Economies of Desire*, 80; Hamilton, *Sexual Revolutions in Cuba*, 77.
214. Cabezas, *Economies of Desire*, 98–99.
215. Cabezas, *Economies of Desire*, 65–66. See also Ferrer, *Cuba: An American History*, 444.
216. Allen, *¡Venceremos?*, 121.
217. Cabezas, *Economies of Desire*, 92.
218. Cabezas, *Economies of Desire*, 61–62, 65.
219. Ferrer, *Cuba: An American History*, 445.
220. Ferrer, *Cuba: An American History*, 446.
221. Stout, Noelle. "When a *Yuma* Meets Mama: Commodified Kin and the Affective Economies of Queer Tourism in Cuba." *Anthropological Quarterly* 88, no. 3 (2015): 665–91, 667, https://dx.doi.org/10.1353/anq.2015.0040.

222. Cabezas, *Economies of Desire*, 117.
223. Cabezas, *Economies of Desire*, 118.
224. Cabezas, *Economies of Desire*, 123.
225. Cabezas, *Economies of Desire*, 8.
226. Daigle, *From Cuba with Love*, 60.
227. Cabezas, *Economies of Desire*, 121.
228. Daigle, *From Cuba with Love*, 59.
229. Cabezas, *Economies of Desire*, 121.
230. Fernandez, "Back to the Future," 86.
231. Fernandez, "Back to the Future," 86–87.
232. Fernandez, "Back to the Future," 87; Fusco, "Hustling for Dollars," 155.
233. Cabezas, *Economies of Desire*, 121.
234. Abel Sierra Madero, "Bodies for Sale: Pinguerismo and Negotiated Masculinity in Contemporary Cuba," trans. Lillian Guerra and Roberto Garcia, *J. of the Assoc. of Soc. Anthropologists* no. 10 (2015): 6, www.theasa.org/downloads/asaonline/PDF/asaonline0110.pdf.
235. Sierra Madero, "Bodies for Sale," 6.
236. Daigle, *From Cuba with Love*, 15.
237. Daigle, *From Cuba with Love*, 15.
238. Daigle, *From Cuba with Love*, 82.
239. Daigle, *From Cuba with Love*, 82.
240. Daigle, *From Cuba with Love*, 5.
241. Daigle, *From Cuba with Love*, 102.
242. Stout, *After Love*, 77.
243. Daigle, *From Cuba with Love*, 152.
244. Fusco, "Hustling for Dollars," 161.
245. Daigle, *From Cuba with Love*, 26.
246. Código Penal, Ley No. 151, art. 302 (prohibiting "procuring and trafficking in persons") (Cuba 2022).
247. Stout, *After Love*, 139.
248. Noelle M. Stout, "Feminists, Queers and Critics: Debating the Cuban Sex Trade," *Journal of Latin American Studies* 40 (2008): 725, https://doi.org/10.1017/S0022216X08004732.
249. Decreto-Ley No. 217, Regulaciones Migratorias Internas para La Habana y sus Contravenciones (Cuba 1997) (prohibits internal migration without permission).
250. Cabezas, *Economies of Desire*, 76; Stout, *After Love*, 139.
251. Daigle, *From Cuba with Love*, 5.
252. Cabezas, *Economies of Desire*, 108.
253. Cabezas, *Economies of Desire*, 108.
254. Fusco, "Hustling for Dollars," 165.
255. Cabezas, *Economies of Desire*, 95.
256. Hamilton, *Sexual Revolutions in Cuba*, 47.
257. Stout, *After Love*, 161.
258. Stout, *After Love*, 163.
259. Daigle, *From Cuba with Love*, 219.
260. Michael Clancy, "The Globalization of Sex Tourism and Cuba: A Commodity Chains Approach," *Studies in Comparative International Development* 36 (2002): 80, https://doi.org/10.1007/BF02686333.
261. Daigle, *From Cuba with Love*, 180.

262. Yet a third term for a male sex worker in the tourist economy is *fogatero*, who provides services to heterosexual women, typically from Europe, "who visit the island to consume the sexual myth of the Cuban lover." Sierra Madero, "Bodies for Sale," 2.
263. Allen, *¡Venceremos?*, 175.
264. Allen, *¡Venceremos?*, 175.
265. Allen, *¡Venceremos?*, 175.
266. Allen, *¡Venceremos?*, 174–75.
267. G. Derrick Hodge, "Colonization of The Cuban Body: The Growth of Male Sex Work in Havana," *NACLA Report on the Americas* 22, no. 5 (2001), https://doi.org/10.1080/10714839.2001.11722597.
268. Allen, *¡Venceremos?*, 174.
269. Stout, *After Love*, 163.
270. Allen, *¡Venceremos?*, 176.
271. Allen, *¡Venceremos?*, 163.
272. Daigle, *From Cuba with Love*, 69.
273. Daigle, *From Cuba with Love*, 97.
274. Daigle, *From Cuba with Love*, 173.
275. Allen, *¡Venceremos?*, 176.
276. Allen, *¡Venceremos?*, 177–78.
277. Stout, *After Love*, 135.
278. Allen, *¡Venceremos?*, 160.
279. Allen, *¡Venceremos?*, 160.
280. Allen, *¡Venceremos?*, 160.
281. Sierra Madero, "Bodies for Sale," 9, 15.
282. Allen, *¡Venceremos?*, 162.
283. Allen, *¡Venceremos?*, 164.
284. Allen, *¡Venceremos?*, 165.
285. Allen, *¡Venceremos?*, 157.
286. Stout, *After Love*, 135.
287. Allen, *¡Venceremos?*, 157.
288. Allen, *¡Venceremos?*, 180 (citing Coco Fusco).
289. Stout, *After Love*, 7.
290. Stout, *After Love*, 7.
291. Stout, *After Love*, 7.
292. Stout, *After Love*, 10.
293. Stout, *After Love*, 107.
294. Stout, *After Love*, 94.
295. Stout, *After Love*, 107.
296. Stout, *After Love*, 106.
297. Stout, *After Love*, 98.
298. Stout, *After Love*, 15.
299. Daigle, *From Cuba with Love*, 66.
300. Hamilton, *Sexual Revolutions in Cuba*, 13.
301. Venezuela functioned as an economic partner to Cuba in the 2000s but eventually it, too, devolved into crisis. The US President Donald J. Trump reversed steps taken by Barack Obama's administration to normalize relations with Cuba. Moreover, the COVID-19 pandemic radically impaired Cuba's tourism sector. Shortages were so severe that some analysts compared conditions to the Special Period. See, e.g., Tony Perrottet, "Cuba Is Staying Strong," *WSJ Magazine*, September 7, 2020, www.wsj.com/articles/cuba-is-staying-strong-11599481303.

302. Daigle, *From Cuba with Love*, 177.
303. Bex Wade, "'Socialism Yes, Homophobia No!': A Day at Cuba's LGBTQ Rights March," *Vice*, June 6, 2016, www.vice.com/en_us/article/wnwwd4/socialism-yes-homophobia-no-a-day-at-cubas-lgbtq-rights-march.

3 MARRIAGE, PROPERTY, AND A HUSTLE

1. Elián was a six-year-old boy whose mother attempted to emigrate with him from Cuba to the US but she did not survive the voyage. The boy's relatives in Florida wanted to raise him but his father in Cuba wanted him returned, giving rise to an international custody dispute. In the end, the Clinton administration used force to retrieve Elián from his Florida family and send him back to his father. For a timeline of events see "The Elian Gonzalez case: Chronology; Custody tug of war over Cuban boy," *The New York Times*, April 14, 2000, www.nytimes.com/2000/04/14/us/the-elian-gonzalez-case-chronology-custody-tug-of-war-over-cuban-boy.html. For analysis, see Lillian Guerra, "Elián González and the 'Real Cuba' of Miami" in *The Cuba Reader: History, Culture, Politics*, ed. Aviva Chomsky et al. (Duke University Press, 2019).
2. "The Yogyakarta Principles," ARC International, https://yogyakartaprinciples.org. "Take all necessary legislative, administrative and other measures to ensure that in States that recognise same-sex marriages or registered partnerships, any entitlement, privilege, obligation or benefit available to different-sex married or registered partners is equally available to same-sex married or registered partners" (Principle 24 (e)). The Yogyakarta Principles should be understood merely as guidelines, not as binding obligations.
3. Josephine Roselle, Brianna Navarre, and Megan Trimble, "Same-Sex Legalization by Country," *U.S. News and World Report*, February 15, 2024, www.usnews.com/news/best-countries/articles/countries-where-same-sex-marriage-is-legal.
4. Roselle et al., "Same-Sex Legalization by Country."
5. "Marriage Equality around the World," Resources, Human Rights Campaign, www.hrc.org/resources/marriage-equality-around-the-world.
6. Constitution of the Republic of Cuba of 1976, ch. XV, art. 137 (in effect at the time of the 2019 ratification).
7. Marjorie S. Zatz, *Producing Legality: Law and Socialism in Cuba* (Routledge, 1994), 53–97; www.cubahora.cu/politica/claves-para-entender-la-estructura-del-estado-cubano.
8. As I write this, the US is over a year into the second presidential term of Donald J. Trump. Efforts by his administration to suppress dissent and punish political enemies using criminal prosecution have prompted debate over whether the US is headed down the road to authoritarianism or has already arrived.
9. Zatz, *Producing Legality*, 53–97. Lawmaking is also, according to Zatz's findings and my own (as discussed in Chapter 5) conceptualized as an educational process. Zatz, *Producing Legality*, 60.
10. Zatz, *Producing Legality*, 53–97.
11. Zatz, *Producing Legality*, 53–97; www.cubahora.cu/politica/claves-para-entender-la-estructura-del-estado-cubano.
12. The purpose of the lay judges is to include a "non-technical" perspective. Zatz, *Producing Legality*, 164.
13. Zatz, *Producing Legality*, 53–97, 163–84, www.ecured.cu/index.php/Sistema_Judicial_en_Cuba.

14. José Gabilondo, "Whither the Revolution? Framing Political Animosities between Sexual Minorities and Churches in Cuba's New Constitution," *Harvard Latin American Law Review* 23 (2020): 43, 50, https://law.fiu.edu/wp-content/uploads/2020/06/WHITHER-THE-REVOLUTION_Gabilondo.pdf.
15. Hynson, *Laboring for the State*, 14. Women gained the general right to terminate their pregnancies with adoption of the 1979 Penal Code. Hynson, *Laboring for the State*, 27.
16. Joanne P. Cavanaugh, "Cuba's Wedding-Go-Round Custom: What Favorite Cuban Pastime Takes 15 Minutes and Is Frequently Done More than Once? Answer: A Wedding," *The Baltimore Sun*, March 11, 1997, www.baltimoresun.com/news/bs-xpm-1997–03–11-1997070117-story.html.
17. Gabilondo, "Whither the Revolution," 53.
18. Rebecca Bodenheimer, "How American Evangelicals Helped Stop Same Sex Marriage in Cuba," *Vice*, August 20, 2019, www.vice.com/en/article/qvg8pw/how-american-evangelicals-helped-stop-same-sex-marriage-in-cuba.
19. Bodenheimer, "American Evangelicals."
20. Jim Yardley, "Raúl Castro Meets with Pope Francis at Vatican," *The New York Times*, May 10, 2015, www.nytimes.com/2015/05/11/world/europe/raul-castro-meets-with-pope-francis-at-vatican.html.
21. Heidi Härkönen, *Kinship, Love, and Life Cycle in Contemporary Havana, Cuba: To Not Die Alone* (Palgrave Macmillan, 2016), 76.
22. Härkönen, *Kinship, Love, and Life Cycle*, 183.
23. Härkönen, *Kinship, Love, and Life Cycle*, 184.
24. Bodenheimer, "American Evangelicals." It is difficult to get a solid take on the religious data for Cuba. It seems to depend on whether one measures self-identification, baptism, or practice. According to the GroundTruth Project of the MacArthur Foundation,

    > Only 13 percent of Cuban residents practice Santería while 27 percent identify as Catholic, according to a 2015 poll conducted by Univision and Fusion in collaboration with The Washington Post. A large proportion of Cubans – 44 percent – indicate they don't follow any religion.
    >
    > But 80 percent of Cubans practice Santería in some way, said Tomás Fernández Robaina, the primary investigator of the Department of Historical Cultural Investigations at the National Library. Meanwhile, Walker said around 60 to 65 percent of the population is baptized Catholic, but less than 1 percent of Cubans attend Sunday Mass regularly.

    Paxtyn Merten, "In Cuba, Santería Flourishes Two Decades after Ban Was Lifted," *The GroundTruth Project*, July 31, 2018, https://thegroundtruthproject.org/cuba-santeria-catholicism-religion-flourish-two-decades-freedom-granted/.
25. Bodenheimer, "American Evangelicals."
26. Gabilondo, "Whither the Revolution," 62.
27. Gabilondo, "Whither the Revolution," 62.
28. Bodenheimer, "American Evangelicals."
29. Bodenheimer, "American Evangelicals."
30. Gabilondo, "Whither the Revolution," 63.
31. Constitution of the Republic of Cuba of 1976, Chapter III, art. 82.
32. Cuba, Council of Ministers, Family Code, Ley No. 1289, February 14, 1975, https://oig.cepal.org/sites/default/files/1975_ley1289_cub.pdf.
33. Anton L. Allahar, "Women and the Family in Cuba: A Study across Time," *Humboldt Journal of Social Relations* 20, no. 1 (1994): 87, 104, www.jstor.org/stable/23262643.

34. Allahar, "Women and the Family in Cuba" 103; Código de las Familias, arts. 24–28 (1975).
35. Ana María Álvarez-Tabío Albo, "General Overview of Cuban Family Law Legislation," *Florida Journal of International Law* 29, no. 1, Art. 3 (2017): 19, 26, https://scholarship.law.ufl.edu/fjil/vol29/iss1/3. In addition, the 1975 code rendered common law (or de facto) marriages retroactively formalizable, instituted a community property rule with multiple exceptions, and made divorce available on a no-fault basis. Legal status differential based on legitimacy was eliminated by a separate Civil Registry Law. Álvarez-Tabío Albo, "Cuban Family Law Legislation," 23–28. See also Código de las Familias, art. 24 (1975).
36. Chase, *Revolution within the Revolution*, 44–76.
37. Cuba, National Assembly of the People's Power, Family Code, Ley No. 156, July 22, 2022, https://legaliscuba.org/normativa/ley-156-de-2022-de-asamblea-nacional-del-poder-popular.
38. Código de las Familias, arts. 56–59 (2022). See also Liz Conde Sánchez, "Adoption or the Right to a Family," *Granma*, April 7, 2022, https://en.granma.cu/cuba/2022-04-07/adoption-or-the-right-to-a-family.
39. Código de las Familias, art. (2022). See also Susana Antón, "A Code Consistent with the Development of the Family," *Granma*, July 12, 2022, https://en.granma.cu/cuba/2022-07-12/a-code-consistent-with-the-development-of-the-family.
40. Código de las Familias, art. 13 (2022).
41. Código de las Familias, arts. 421 et seq. (2022).
42. Código de las Familias, art. 51 § 3 (2022). In Spain and former Spanish colonies, the convention is to put the father's name before the mother's but then to drop the mother's name in daily use. According to Dr. Álvarez-Tabío, the new version will "establish that parents determine by mutual agreement, before civil registry authorities, the order of surnames, which once determined would be applied to all of the couple's children. Maintaining preference for the paternal surname reproduces a custom imposed by patriarchal culture." Yudy Castro Morales, "The New Families Code, Much More than Marriage," *Granma*, January 14, 2020, https://en.granma.cu/cuba/2020-01-14/the-new-families-code-much-more-marriage.
43. Art. 201 authorizes same-sex marriage by eliminating sex-based terms and describing marriage as "the voluntarily agreed union of two people … on the basis of mutual affection, love and respect."
44. Código de las Familias, arts. 100, 102 (2022).
45. Código de las Familias, art. 101 (1975).
46. Liz Conde Sánchez, "Adoption or the Right to Family," in *Granma*, August 2, 2022, https://en.granma.cu/cuba/2022–04-07/adoption-or-the-right-to-a-family.
47. The fact that "stranger" adoption is rare in Cuba is not surprising given Cuba's relatively compressed economic strata. Adoption in general is an economically upward redistribution of children, so less pronounced stratification would be expected to result in less adoption; cf. Dorothy Roberts, *Shattered Bonds: The Color of Child Welfare* (Basic *Civitas* Books, 2002): 103–4.
48. Código de las Familias, arts. 130–31 (2022); Claudia Pis Guirola, "Cubans to Approve or Reject the Family Act in September," *Havana Times*, July 28, 2022, https://havanatimes.org/features/cubans-to-approve-or-reject-the-family-act-in-september/.
49. Cavanaugh, "Cuba's Wedding-Go-Round Custom"; Nicolas Montano, *The Death, and Rebirth, of the Cuban Wedding Ceremony*, Brown University: Beyond the Sugar Curtain: Tracing Cuba-US Connections since 1959, December 2017, on file with author.
50. Cavanaugh, "Cuba's Wedding-Go-Round Custom."

51. Cavanaugh, "Cuba's Wedding-Go-Round Custom." See also Härkönen, *Kinship, Love, and Life Cycle*, 4.
52. Härkönen, *Kinship, Love, and Life Cycle*, 4.
53. Härkönen, *Kinship, Love, and Life Cycle*, 4. See also Art. 18 of the 1975 code and Código de las Familias, art. 308 (2022).
54. Álvarez-Tabío Albo, "Cuban Family Law Legislation," 26. See Código de las Familias, art. 18 (1975) and Código de las Familias, art. 308 (2022).
55. Härkönen, *Kinship, Love, and Life Cycle*, 95.
56. Cavanaugh, "Cuba's Wedding-Go-Round Custom."
57. Härkönen, *Kinship, Love, and Life Cycle*, 5.
58. Coco Fusco, "Hustling for Dollars," 156.
59. Härkönen, *Kinship, Love, and Life Cycle*, 53.
60. Härkönen, *Kinship, Love, and Life Cycle*, 70.
61. Stout, "Feminists, Queers and Critics," 721–42, 724.
62. Montano, *The Death, and Rebirth, of the Cuban Wedding Ceremony*; Cavanaugh, "Cuba's Wedding-Go-Round Custom."
63. Álvarez-Tabío Albo, "Cuban Family Law Legislation," 23. In the 2022 Family Code, the relevant provisions are Código de las Familias, arts. 48–50 (2022).
64. Yardley, "Raúl Castro;" Cavanaugh, "Cuba's Wedding-Go-Round Custom."
65. Álvarez-Tabío cites a divorce rate of 55.3 percent in her 2017 article. Álvarez-Tabío Albo, "Cuban Family Law Legislation," 29.
66. Cavanaugh, "Cuba's Wedding-Go-Round Custom."
67. Montano, *The Death, and Rebirth, of the Cuban Wedding Ceremony*.
68. Código de las Familias, arts. 29–42 (1975).
69. Álvarez-Tabío Albo, "Cuban Family Law Legislation," 27. Article 29–32 of the 1975 Family Code establishes a marital community property regime, but "[s]pouses, once the marriage has been terminated, retain all property acquired before the marriage, any gifts or inheritance received during the marriage, or any lucrative title, exchange or substitution of personal property, or those acquired with their own money, or those of exclusive personal use." Álvarez-Tabío Albo, "Cuban Family Law Legislation," 27. The 2022 code does not change this. Código de las Familias, arts. 227–229 (2022).
70. Código de las Familias, art. 41 (1975). This rule is confirmed in The General Housing Law Art. 66.1 as amended by Decree-Law no. 288, discussed further below. Cuba, Council of State, Decree-Law no. 288 amending Law no. 65, the "General Housing Act" of December 23, 1988, October 28, 2011, https://legaliscuba.org/normativa/decreto-ley-288-de-2011-de-consejo-de-estado.
71. Yudarkis Veloz Sarduy, "Getting a Divorce in Cuba Is Routine," *Havana Times*, February 15, 2018, https://havanatimes.org/features/getting-a-divorce-in-cuba-is-routine/.
72. Código de las Familias, arts. 226–290 (2022).
73. Código de las Familias, art. 262 (2022).
74. Yardley, "Raúl Castro."
75. Código de las Familias, art. 56 (1975).
76. Härkönen, *Kinship, Love, and Life Cycle*, 14.
77. Härkönen, *Kinship, Love, and Life Cycle*, 56.
78. Código de las Familias, art. 275 (2022).
79. 2022 Family Code, tit. VII ch. I.
80. Código de las Familias, arts. 306–309 (2022). This can be done on an uncontested basis before a notary or judge, but if the facts are in dispute, evidence must be presented to a judge, who will determine whether to declare the existence (along with its start and end dates) or nonexistence of the union. Código de las Familias, arts. 313–315 (2022).

81. István Ojeda Bello, "Family Code a Year Later: People's History Is Not Only Written with DNA," *Periódico 26*, October 2, 2023, www.periodico26.cu/index.php/en/special-reports-2/15337-family-code-a-year-later-people-s-history-is-not-only-written-with-dna.
82. Código de las Familias, arts. 310–311 (2022).
83. Código de las Familias, art. 328 (2022).
84. Código de las Familias, art. 325 (2022).
85. Código de las Familias, art. 19 (2022).
86. In an article on the debate over same-sex marriage in South Korea, Rama Hyeweon Kim discusses how de facto marriage "destabilizes" marriage and thereby has the potential to provide advantages to same-sex couples that the extension of formal marriage would not. Rama Hyeweon Kim, "Historicizing Same-Sex Marriage Debate in the Legal Periphery: Savigny, Nakagawa, and the Korean Marriage" *Minnesota Journal of International Law* 33, no. 2 (2024): 102–13, https://scholarship.law.umn.edu/cgi/viewcontent.cgi?article=1003&context=minn-jrnl-intl-law.
87. "Social Security Programs throughout the World: The Americas, 2019," Social Security, Office of Research, Evaluation, and Statistics, August 4, 2025, www.ssa.gov/policy/docs/progdesc/ssptw/2018-2019/americas/cuba.html.
88. Código Civil, Ley No. 59, art. 510 (Cuba 1987).
89. Código Civil, Ley No. 59, art. 493 (Cuba 1987).
90. Código Civil, Ley No. 59, First Special Provision (Cuba 1987) and Código de las Familias, arts. 306–309 (2022). It was Art. 18 of the 1975 Family Code.
91. A Cuban same-sex marriage enthusiast whom I met at a conference directed my attention to the matter of family reunification. I believe he was referring to emigration from Cuba and consequent confrontation with the destination country's rules regarding admittance of a partner. In the US, for example, while a *citizen* can petition for admittance of a spouse *or* fiancé, a *permanent resident* can only petition for a spouse (8 USC § 1101(a)(15)(K)(i) (2022)). This is not strictly speaking a benefit under Cuban law but is nonetheless the only kind of benefit of marriage – recognition in a foreign jurisdiction – of which I am aware that could not be secured to same-sex couples by Cuban law without granting access to marriage.
92. I use the term *real property* here in the sense that common law lawyers do, to refer to land and attachments, but real estate is categorized as *personal* property in the Cuban system if it is used entirely for personal consumption, not for production. Cuba Const. of 2019, art. 22.
93. Ley No. 112, Confiscación de Bienes Malversados (Cuba 1959).
94. Ley No. 989. Gaceta Oficial de la República de Cuba, 1961. Confiscation from emigrants remains a sore point for Cuban-Americans. The quest for restoration of title continues to appear in scholarly work produced in the US, though it is not clear that Cubans in Cuba are as interested in the issue. See, e.g., Jose A. Ortiz, "The Illegal Expropriation of Property in Cuba: A Historical and Legal Analysis of the Takings and a Survey of Restitution Schemes for a Post-Socialist Cuba," *Loyola of Los Angeles International and Comparative Law Review* 22, no. 3 (2000): 321, https://digitalcommons.lmu.edu/cgi/viewcontent.cgi?article=1497&context=ilr.
95. Renee Monzon, "Introducing Private-Property Rights to Cuba: How Cuba's New Constitution Paves the Way for Economic Growth," *Case Western Reserve Journal of International Law* 52, no. 1 (2020): 642, https://scholarlycommons.law.case.edu/jil/vol52/iss1/28. Cuba, *Primera Ley de Reforma Agraria* [First Agrarian Reform Law], May 17, 1959.
96. Ley No. 851, de 6 de julio de 1960, Nacionalización de Propiedades Estadounidenses (Cuba); Monzon, "Private-Property Rights," 642.
97. Ley No. 890, de 13 de octubre de 1960, Nacionalización de Corporaciones Extranjeras (Cuba). See also Monzon, "Private-Property Rights," 642.

98. Cuba. *Ley de Reforma Urbana del 14 de octubre de 1960* [Urban Reform Law of October 14, 1960]. *Gaceta Oficial de la República de Cuba*, October 14, 1960.
99. Philip Peters, "Cuba's New Real Estate Market," Latin America Initiative Working Paper (Brookings, February 2014), 1 (emphasis added).
100. Peters, "Cuba's New Real Estate Market," 1.
101. Cuba, *Constitución de la República de Cuba* [Constitution of the Republic of Cuba], February 24, 1976.
102. Monzon, "Private-Property Rights," 642, citing Constitución de la República de Cuba (1976), translated by Albert P. Blaustein and Gisbert H. Flanz, eds., *Constitutions of the Countries of the World* (Oceana Publications, 1996), Vol. 5, 1.
103. Ley General de Vivienda de 1984, Conversión de Arrendatarios en Propietarios (Cuba).
104. Decreto Ley 171, art. 1 (amending Art. 74 of Ley No. 65, the 1988 General Housing Law).
105. Peters, "Cuba's New Real Estate Market," 2.
106. Peters, "Cuba's New Real Estate Market," 2. US-based lawyers will be accustomed to more rights in the bundle than seen here. US property law disfavors restraints on alienation, which would ordinarily include a right to transfer the property (along with rights to use or enjoy, to exclude, and to be compensated for a governmental taking, unless subject to some limitation). "Restraints upon alienation are generally void as against public policy." Andrew R. Gelman, Todd J. Schneider, and David Shayne, "Perpetuities and Accumulations," in *Horner Probate Practice and Estates*, edited by Michael P. McElroy, Vol. 4, § 78:7 (June 2025).
107. *Se Permuta*, directed by Juan Carlos Tabío (ICAIC, 1983), www.youtube.com/watch?v=XaRzgyKJRkI.
108. Peters, "Cuba's New Real Estate Market," 2–3.
109. Peters, "Cuba's New Real Estate Market," 3.
110. Monzon, "Private-Property Rights," 629, 643–44.
111. Peters, "Cuba's New Real Estate Market," 3.
112. Peters, "Cuba's New Real Estate Market," 4. A *notario*, translated as *notary* but performing a much more substantial role than a notary performs in the common law system, verifies the exchange and the title. Peters, "Cuba's New Real Estate Market," 6.
113. Peters, "Cuba's New Real Estate Market," 7.
114. The most well-known is www.revolico.com, which was launched by Cuban ex-pats living in Spain to help Cubans residing in-country to find a vast array of goods.
115. Peters, "Cuba's New Real Estate Market," 10.
116. Constitución de la República de Cuba, art. 29 (2019).
117. Peters, "Cuba's New Real Estate Market," 9.
118. Peters, "Cuba's New Real Estate Market," 15.
119. Peters, "Cuba's New Real Estate Market," 17.
120. This is happening in Puerto Rico and is gentrifying native Puerto Ricans out of some areas. See Coral Murphy Marcos and Patricia Mazzei, "The Rush for a Slice of Paradise in Puerto Rico," *The New York Times*, June 22, 2023, www.nytimes.com/2022/01/31/us/puerto-rico-gentrification.html.
121. The first post-Fidel constitution reconfigured Cuba's property regime, setting forth new categories of ownership, each with its own regulatory parameters in Art. 22. For explanation and elaboration on the Art. 22 schematic as well as a primer on socialist property theory, see Marta Fernández Martínez, "Comentario a las formas de propiedad como estatuto jurídico regulado en el artículo 22 constitucional," *Universidad de La Habana* 289 (2020). http://scielo.sld.cu/scielo.php?script=sci_arttex

t&pid=S0253-92762020000100071. See also Julio César Guanche, "The Constitutional Regulation of Private Property in Cuba: Legal Framework, Cultural Narratives, and Unwritten Rules," *Cuba Capacity Building Project at Columbia Law School*, January 28, 2022, https://horizontecubano.law.columbia.edu/news/constitutional-regulation-private-property. Property is now divided into seven categories, of which personal and private are two. While *personal* property remains that which is devoted solely "to satisfy material and spiritual necessities," *private* property is ownership "over the means of production." The other types include "socialist" property which belongs to the state, "cooperative" property which is owned by a workplace collective, two types of property belonging to certain permissible organizations, and "mixed" ownership which is a hybrid of two or more of the other types. Art. 22. See also Monzon, "Private-Property Rights," 650.

122. Adriel Reyes, "More Cubans Want the Deed to Their Homes," *Martí Noticias*, December 20, 2013, on file with author.
123. Asunto Circular No. 265 (2013), www.cubaencuentro.com/txt/cuba/articulos/al-cesar-lo-que-es-del-cesar-302033/tribunal-supremo-popular-circular-no-265; Peters, "Cuba's New Real Estate Market," 20–21.
124. Hynson, *Laboring for the State*, 143.
125. Asunto Circular No. 265 (2013), www.cubaencuentro.com/txt/cuba/articulos/al-cesar-lo-que-es-del-cesar-302033/tribunal-supremo-popular-circular-no-265; Peters, "Cuba's New Real Estate Market," 20–21.
126. David A. Grossman et al., "The Emergence of Entrepreneurship in Cuba: What We Can Learn," *KnE Social Sciences* 3, no. 10 (2018): 85, https://doi.org/10.18502/kss.v3i10.2886.
127. Grossman et al., "The Emergence of Entrepreneurship," 88–89.
128. Aldo Álvarez, "Foreign Investment in Cuba: New Opportunities for the Private and Non-State Sectors," *Cuba Capacity Building Project at Columbia Law School*, June 29, 2021, https://horizontecubano.law.columbia.edu/news/foreign-investment-cuba.
129. See Layz Reynet, "Inequality and the Informal Market in Cuba: Structural Barriers of Income Distribution in Light of Tourism and Economic Growth for Afro-Cubans" (unpublished master's thesis, Lund University, 2018), 24, 30, https://lup.lub.lu.se/student-papers/search/publication/8959045.

    Some Cubans have used internet sites such as Revolico.com to make a profit selling goods obtained from abroad. As Megan Janetsky reports, "President Miguel Díaz-Canel called for a crackdown on the practice, referring to the revendedores [resellers] as 'criminals, swindlers, riffraff, the lazy, and the corrupt.'" Megan Janetsky, "Cuba's Informal Market Finds New Space on Growing Internet," *The Associated Press*, November 27, 2022, https://apnews.com/article/technology-business-caribbean-havana-716544aa36e6f14a54293eb8411c8539.
130. Guanche, "Constitutional Regulation of Private Property."
131. Caroline Kuritzkes, "The End of Cuba's Entrepreneurship Boom," *Foreign Policy Magazine*, July 15, 2019, https://foreignpolicy.com/2019/07/15/the-end-of-cubas-entrepreneurship-boom/.
132. Kuritzkes, "Entrepreneurship Boom."
133. Guanche, "Constitutional Regulation of Private Property."
134. Riury Rodríguez Lorenzo, "Entrepreneurship in Cuba in 2021: A Race with Obstacles," *Cuba Study Group Blog*, January 28, 2021, http://cubastudygroup.org/blog_posts/entrepreneurship-in-cuba-in-2021-a-race-with-obstacles/.
135. Rodríguez Lorenzo, "Entrepreneurship in Cuba."

136. Cuba, Ministry of Justice, Gaceta Oficial no. 94, August 19, 2021, www.gacetaoficial.gob.cu/es/gaceta-oficial-no-94-ordinaria-de-2021.
137. Rodríguez Lorenzo, "Entrepreneurship in Cuba."
138. Rodríguez Lorenzo, "Entrepreneurship in Cuba."
139. Richard Feinberg, *Open for Business: Building the New Cuban Economy* (Brookings institution Press, 2016), 66–97.
140. Feinberg, *Open for Business*, 77.
141. Some non-state cooperatives have had access to foreign investment. Feinberg, *Open for Business*, 94.
142. Marc Frank, "Cuba Cracks Open Door to Foreign Investment in Domestic Trade," *Reuters*, August 16, 2022, www.reuters.com/world/americas/cuba-cracks-open-door-foreign-investment-domestic-trade-2022-08-16/. See also Álvarez, "Foreign Investment in Cuba," citing Law 118/2014 "Foreign Investment Law." Article 2, subsection m. www.gacetaoficial.gob.cu/sites/default/files/ley_de_inversion_extranjera.pdf.
143. Frank, "Cuba Cracks Open Door."
144. Feinberg, *Open for Business*, 69. It seems at least possible that access to foreign investment could free would-be entrepreneurs from reliance on family members living abroad, which has historically been a source of inequality among Cubans.
145. Feinberg, *Open for Business*, 166, 131–71. According to Feinberg, a Cuban middle class has emerged, defined by wages, education, or fertility. The only indicator of middle class status Cubans lack is access to consumer goods. Feinberg, *Open for Business*, 166–68.
146. Aníbal Rosario-Lebrón, "For Better and for Better: The Case for Abolishing Civil Marriage," *Washington University Jurisprudence Review* 5, no. 2 (2013): 189, https://openscholarship.wustl.edu/cgi/viewcontent.cgi?article=1047&context=law_jurisprudence.
147. Rosario-Lebrón, "For Better," 193. Kaiponanea Matsumura invokes Pierre Bourdieu's concept of *habitus* to similar effect - that is, as a critical aperture to the otherwise invisible, nonregulatory power of marriage to array conceptual possibilities for governing familial and intimate relationships. Kaiponanea Matsumura, "The Marital Habitus" *Washington University Law Review* 99 (2022): 2035.
148. On hegemony, see Antonio Gramsci, *Selections from the Prison Notebooks*, edited and translated by Quintin Hoare and Geoffrey Noewell Smith (International Publishers, 1971), 12.
149. Rosario-Lebrón, "For Better," 216.
150. This exemplifies an "inter-generational pattern," Hamilton observed, "of women attaining housing through formal or informal heterosexual relationships." Hamilton, *Sexual Revolutions in Cuba*, 162, 168.
151. Rosario-Lebrón, "For Better," 229.
152. "Where there is power, there is resistance," in Foucault's articulation. Foucault, *The History of Sexuality*, 95.
153. Rosario-Lebrón, "For Better," 229. Rosario-Lebrón turns here to George Lukács's concept of *reification* and the *dialectical* process by which an individual "returns to oneself as an active agent" capable of critical thought. Rosario-Lebrón, "For Better," 233–34. I hasten to note, per the tutelage of Karl Klare, that in my view, there is no "Archimedean point" positioned entirely outside of discourse. I lean toward Judith Butler's conception: "If conditions of power are to persist, they must be reiterated; the subject is precisely the site of such reiteration." Judith Butler, *The Psychic Life of Power* (Stanford University Press, 1997), 16. "It is precisely the possibility of a repetition which does not

consolidate … the subject, but which proliferates effects which undermine the force of normalization." Butler, *Psychic Life*, 93. See also Libby Adler, *Gay Priori*, 171.

154. Rosario-Lebrón, "For Better," 235.
155. Rosario-Lebrón, "For Better," 235 (citing Douglas Litowitz, "Reification in Law and Legal Theory," *Southern California Interdisciplinary Law Journal* 9, no. 2 (2000): 401, 414. Emphasis mine).
156. Judith Butler, *Gender Trouble: Feminism and the Subversion of Identity* (Routledge, 1990), 137–41.
157. Butler, *Gender Trouble*, 30.

4 QUEER ENCOUNTERS

1. Hollingsworth v. Perry, 570 U.S. 693 (2013), aff'g Perry v. Brown, 671 F.3d 1052 (9th Cir. 2012), aff'g Perry v. Schwarzenegger, 704 F. Supp. 2d 921 (N.D. Cal. 2010).
2. Transcript of Trial Proceedings, January 12, 2010, at 240, Perry v. Schwarzenegger, No. C 09-2292-VRW (N.D. Cal.), https://cases.justia.com/federal/district-courts/california/candce/3:2009cv02292/215270/453/0.pdf.
3. Perry v. Schwarzenegger, Trial Tr., January 12, 2010, 240.
4. Perry v. Schwarzenegger, Trial Tr., January 12, 2010, 241.
5. Perry v. Schwarzenegger, Trial Tr., January 12, 2010, 243–44.
6. Perry v. Schwarzenegger, Trial Tr., January 12, 2010, 244.
7. Perry v. Schwarzenegger, Trial Tr., January 12, 2010, 244–45. In his rich historical study of three 1970s litigations seeking legal approval for same-sex marriages, Michael Boucai observes that all three plaintiff couples were asked which of the intended spouses would perform the role of the husband and which would perform that of the wife:

> All three plaintiff couples resisted attempts by inquiring minds to assimilate their relationships to the traditional gendered model. When asked by reporters whether he or Barwick was the bride, Singer answered: "We don't believe in role playing. We're two people. We happen to be genital males …." Confronted with the same question on the steps of the Hennepin County Clerk's office, Baker said, "We don't play those kind of roles." In a televised interview he elaborated the point: "One problem we have in dealing with the public is that they go looking for role playing. Who's dominant and who's submissive? The nice thing about gay relationships is you both come into it as two equal human beings and then negotiate among yourselves as to how your relationship will be structured." In Louisville, when asked at trial whether she played one role and Jones another, Knight acknowledged being the "butch" in the couple, but she insisted, "there really are no roles. We're both women and we do not take a man's stand either in our social or sexual affairs …. The only real identity that a woman plays in a lesbian role is that of a woman who loves a woman …."
>
> A "companionate" as opposed to "conjugal" view of the marital relationship, arguably implicit in the very notion of gay marriage, was made explicit in the plaintiffs' legal arguments.

Boucai, "Glorious Precedents," 57 (citations omitted). It took another four decades for this line of inquiry to go out of date.

8. Hollingsworth, 570 U.S. 693.
9. *Oral Argument*, Hollingsworth v. Perry, No. 12-144, argued March 26, 2013, Supreme Court of the United States, audio recording, Oyez, www.oyez.org/cases/2012/12-144.

10. Some subcultural groups in the US reject gay identity for political or identitarian reasons, preferring terms such as "men who have sex with men," or MSM, and public health entities have accommodated men circulating in those subcultures by ratifying terminology that resists gay identity. See "CDC Sexually Transmitted Infections Treatment Guidelines 2021, Men Who Have Sex with Men (MSM)," www.cdc.gov/std/treatment-guidelines/msm.htm. A different lexicon also predominates in US prison culture, where penetrative versus receptive role is more likely to be definitional. (Terminology has varied over time and by region of the country, but some examples include wolf/punk, daddy/kid, pitcher/catcher, as well as butt-boy, fuck-boy, and prison-dime. See, e.g., "Prison Writers: Where Prisoners Have a Voice," https://prisonwriters.com/235-prison-slang-words/). Thanks to Adrienne Davis for pointing me in this direction. Moreover, leftist sex politics that exist to oppose gay normalization efforts as well as an increase in gender variance have together animated a preference for the term *queer*, the meaning of which is contested. *Queer* sometimes functions as a mere synonym for *gay*. Still, the sexual orientation conception of gay identity predominates in mainstream US discourse in psychology, NGO advocacy, mainstream media, diversity and inclusion efforts, and pop culture.
11. "Understanding Sexual Orientation and Homosexuality," American Psychological Association, www.apa.org/topics/lgbtq/orientation. But see Mairead Sullivan, *Lesbian Death* (University of Minnesota Press, 2022) 3–4, for a more "disruptive" idea of lesbian identity in its relationship to trans and queer.
12. For Cuban lesbians, it is not clear that the logic runs the same. White lesbians are reputed to valorize femininity and disdain butchness, which is associated with blackness. Saunders, "Grupo OREMI," 169.
13. Arenas, *Before Night Falls*, 106–7. Emilio Bejel, commenting on Arenas's memoir, observes that while "the narrator-protagonist dedicates his life to rebelling against the *machista* power structure" of Revolutionary Cuba, he nonetheless "declares his uncontrollable attraction toward, his tremendous desire to have sexual relations with, a 'real man' … the prototypical representative of the oppressive system …. In Cuban society, homoerotic relationships are often based on the masculine/feminine binary, and Arenas was unable to free himself from this mold." Bejel, *Gay Cuban Nation*, 149.
14. Gayle Rubin, "The Traffic in Women: Notes on the 'Political Economy' of Sex," in *Toward an Anthropology of Women*, ed. Rayna R. Reiter (Monthly Review Press, 1975).
15. Rubin, "The Traffic in Women," 165.
16. Rubin, "The Traffic in Women," 165.
17. Rubin, "The Traffic in Women," 203.
18. Rubin, "The Traffic in Women," 173.
19. In a subsequent blockbuster essay, Rubin checks the universalism of her claim. Gayle Rubin, "Thinking Sex: Notes for a Radical Theory of the Politics of Sexuality," in *Pleasure and Danger: Exploring Female Sexuality*, ed. Carole Vance, 307.
20. Rubin, "The Traffic in Women,"173.
21. Rubin, "The Traffic in Women," 175. In Rubin, "Thinking Sex," 308, she impugns a rival explanation for women's oppression offered by Catharine MacKinnon, that is, the expropriation of women's sexuality. MacKinnon, "Feminism, Marxism, Method and the State," 515–16. A key figure in "pro-sex feminism," Rubin strives to separate sex (as in eroticism) from sex-based oppression (as in male domination).
22. Rubin, "The Traffic in Women," 178. Rubin adds, "If biological and hormonal imperatives were as overwhelming as popular mythology would have them, it would hardly be necessary to insure heterosexual unions by means of economic interdependency." Rubin, "The Traffic in Women," 180.

23. This is not entirely different from Gary Becker's idea that the comparative advantage each sex category holds in a form of labor need only be slight to form the basis for a more pronounced division of labor. Gary S. Becker, *A Treatise on the Family* (Harvard University Press, 1981) 54–79.
24. Rubin, "The Traffic in Women," 188.
25. Rubin, "The Traffic in Women," 189.
26. Rubin, "The Traffic in Women," 189.
27. Rubin, "The Traffic in Women," 190–91.
28. Rubin, "The Traffic in Women," 192.
29. Rubin, "The Traffic in Women," 194.
30. Rubin, "The Traffic in Women," 195.
31. Rubin, "The Traffic in Women," 195.
32. Rubin, "The Traffic in Women," 196.
33. Rubin, "The Traffic in Women," 196.
34. Rubin, "The Traffic in Women," 196. As Rubin argues, feminists have long objected to this story, and "[t]o the extent that it is a rationalization of female subordination, this critique has been justified. To the extent," however, "that it is a description of a process which subordinates women, this critique is a mistake." Rubin, "The Traffic in Women," 197. Indeed, "since psychoanalysis is a theory of gender, dismissing it would be suicidal for a political movement dedicated to eradicating gender hierarchy." Rubin, "The Traffic in Women," 198.
35. Rubin, "The Traffic in Women," 198.
36. Rubin, "The Traffic in Women," 199. Here I acknowledge an observation of Kerry Rittich, who offers the corrective that the "functional load" has perhaps *eroded*, but not disappeared, that is, the sexual division of labor continues to serve *some* role in the contemporary economy. This sounds right. For my purposes, the exact extent of divergence is less important than the fact of it.
37. Rubin, "The Traffic in Women," 199.
38. Rubin, "The Traffic in Women," 199.
39. Rubin, "The Traffic in Women," 199.
40. Cuba, Council of Ministers, Family Code, Ley No. 1289, February 14, 1975, https://oig.cepal.org/sites/default/files/1975_ley1289_cub.pdf.
41. The original law prohibiting sex discrimination in the workplace was set forth in Código de Trabajo [Labor Code]. Law No. 49 of December 28, 1984. The current version is Código de Trabajo [Labor Code]. Law No. 116 of December 20, 2013. Earlier laws provided maternity leave. See, e.g., Ley de Maternidad. Law No. 1100 of 1963.
42. Sierra Madero, "Bodies for Sale," 6.
43. Gayle Rubin, "Sexual Traffic," interview by Judith Butler, *Feminism Meets Queer Theory*, ed. Elizabeth Weed and Naomi Schor (Indiana University Press, 1997).
44. Rubin, "Sexual Traffic," 74.
45. Rubin, "Sexual Traffic," 74.
46. Rubin, "Sexual Traffic," 75.
47. Rubin, "Sexual Traffic," 68, 74–75.
48. "[A]lthough the field of psychoanalysis always sought to distance the notion of sexual difference from an exclusively anatomical perspective, sexual difference nonetheless remained connected to 'the phallic value' as an example of potency, power and strength. However, this is a debate that has been carried out in dualistic terms while inverting the terms at play ...." Leticia Glocer Fiorini, "Polyphonies of Sexuality: Debates about Theories/Debates about Paradigms," *The International Journal of Psychoanalysis* 100, no. 6 (2019): 1261, https://doi.org/10.1080/00207578.2019.1674119.

"Importantly – and this is where Lacan's re-definition of the 'phallus' will be so crucial – these positions should not necessarily correspond to biological 'sex', that is, to having the biological body of a girl or a boy; these positions should instead correspond to maintaining a fundamental unconscious relationship to the phallus." Derek Hook, "Psychoanalysis, Sexual Difference and the Castration Problematic," in *The Gender of Psychology*, ed. Tamara Shefer, Floretta Boonzaier, and Peace Kiguwa (Juta Academic Publishing, 2006), 56.

49. Williams Institute. "More than 2.5 Million LGBTQ Adults Are Parenting Children under the Age of 18." *UCLA School of Law*, April 9, 2024; https://williamsinstitute.law.ucla.edu/press/lgbtq-parenting-2024-press-release/.
50. Law Professor Bernard Harcourt has argued that the "culture wars" in the US should be understood in a more fragmented fashion, rather than as two unified sides. See generally, Bernard Harcourt, "You Are Entering a Gay and Lesbian Free Zone': On the Radical Dissents of Justice Scalia and Other (Post-) Queers – [Raising Questions about Lawrence, Sex Wars, and the Criminal Law]," *Journal of Criminal Law & Criminology* 94 (2004). https://scholarship.law.columbia.edu/faculty_scholarship/646.
51. According to one poll, the majority of Cubans, including those who identify as gay or lesbian, favored legalization of same-sex marriage. "El 92.2 por ciento a favor del matrimonio LGBTIQ+: Estos fueron los resultados de una encuesta independiente realizada en Cuba," *Tremenda Nota*, October 8, 2021, https://s3.eu-central-1.amazonaws.com/qurium/tremendanota.com/el-92-2-por-ciento-a-favor-del-matrimonio-lgbtiq-estos-fueron-los-resultados-de-una-encuesta-independiente-realizada-en-cuba.html. On file with author.

    In addition, approximately two-thirds of voting Cubans supported the new Family Code knowing that it contained a provision legalizing same-sex marriage. Finally, media anecdotes suggest that at least some gay and lesbian Cubans want it. See, e.g., Victoria Bisset, "Cuba to Hold Referendum on Same-Sex Marriage," *The Washington Post*, July 23, 2022, www.washingtonpost.com/world/2022/07/23/cuba-same-sex-marriage-referendum-family/; Bodenheimer, "American Evangelicals," and Orlando Palma, "A New Campaign for Marriage Equality Announced,"*14 y Medio*, November 25, 2015, www.14ymedio.com/englishedition/Campaign-For-Marriage-Equality-Announced_0_1898210169.html.
52. Gayatri Chakravorty Spivak, *A Critique of Postcolonial Reason: Toward a History of the Vanishing Present* (Harvard University Press, 1999), 110 (reminding readers of her call for "a persistent critique of what we cannot not want").
53. Neville Hoad, "Arrested Development or the Queerness of Savages: Resisting Evolutionary Narratives of Difference," *Postcolonial Studies: Culture, Politics, Economy* 3, no. 2 (2000): 151, https://doi.org/10.1080/13688790050115277.
54. Hoad, "Arrested Development," 135. See also Dennis Altman, "Global Gaze/Global Gays" in *GLQ: A Journal of Lesbian and Gay Studies* 3, no. 4 (1997): 429, https://doi.org/10.1215/10642684-3-4-417.
55. Hoad, "Arrested Development," 147.
56. Butler, *The Psychic Life of Power*, 16.
57. Butler, *The Psychic Life of Power*, 16.
58. Annamarie Jagose, *Queer Theory: An Introduction* (Melbourne University Press, 1996), 132.
59. Jagose, *Queer Theory*, 3.
60. Ivana Isailovic, "Same Sex but Not the Same: Same-Sex Marriage in the United States and France and the Universalist Narrative," *The American Journal of Comparative Law* 66, no. 2 (2018): 271, https://doi.org/10.1093/ajcl/avy027.
61. Isailovic, "Same Sex," 270.
62. Isailovic, "Same Sex," 270.

63. See also Kim, "Historicizing Same-Sex Marriage Debate in the Legal Periphery," 213 on rejecting a "thin" approach to comparing national jurisdictions in the context of same-sex marriage.
64. Kees Waaldijk, "Small Change: How the Road to Same-Sex Marriage Got Paved in the Netherlands," in *Legal Recognition of Same-Sex Partnerships: A Study of National, European, and International Law*, ed. Robert Wintemute and Mads Andenæs (Hart Publishing, 2001), 437.
65. Waaldijk, "Small Change," 440.
66. Waaldijk, "Small Change," 440.
67. Waaldijk, "Small Change," 437.
68. Waaldijk, "Small Change," 439.
69. William N. Eskridge, Jr., "Comparative Law and the Same-Sex Marriage Debate: A Step-by-Step Approach toward State Recognition," *McGeorge Law Review* 31, no. 3 (2000): 641, https://openyls.law.yale.edu/entities/publication/30074b70-6cb0-4b5d-89d0-ca4ad190f909.
70. Eskridge, "Same-Sex Marriage Debate," 642.
71. Eskridge, "Same-Sex Marriage Debate," 647–48.
72. Dipesh Chakrabarty, *Provincializing Europe: Postcolonial Thought and Historical Difference* (Princeton University Press, 2000), 8.
73. Rahul Rao, *Out of Time: The Queer Politics of Postcoloniality* (Oxford University Press, 2020), 11 citing Anna Lowenhaupt Tsing, *Friction: An Ethnography of Global Connection* (Princeton University Press, 2005).
74. Hodge, "Colonization of The Cuban Body," 22.
75. Sierra Madero, "Bodies for Sale," 13.
76. Sierra Madero, "Bodies for Sale," 25.
77. Hodge, "Colonization of The Cuban Body," 22.
78. Hodge, "Colonization of The Cuban Body," 26–27.
79. G. Derrick Hodge, "Sex Workers of Havana: The Lure of Things," *NACLA*, September 25, 2007, https://nacla.org/article/sex-workers-havana-lure-things. Hodge has also reported hearing from pingueros that they physically "can't have sex without money" regardless of their partner's sex. Hodge, "Colonization of The Cuban Body," 26.
80. Stout, "When a *Yuma* Meets Mama," 671.
81. Hodge, "Colonization of The Cuban Body," 22.
82. Hodge, "Colonization of The Cuban Body," 27.
83. Hodge, "Colonization of The Cuban Body," 28.
84. Hodge, "Colonization of The Cuban Body," 23.
85. Sierra Madero, "Bodies for Sale," 11.
86. Leo Bersani, "Is the Rectum a Grave?" *AIDS: Cultural Analysis/Cultural Activism* 43 (1987): 197–222, https://doi.org/10.2307/3397574.
87. Bersani, "Is the Rectum a Grave?," 205.
88. Bersani, "Is the Rectum a Grave?," 206.
89. Bersani, "Is the Rectum a Grave?," 208.
90. Bersani, "Is the Rectum a Grave?," 213.
91. Andrea Dworkin, *Intercourse* (Free Press, 1987), 155.
92. Bersani, "Is the Rectum a Grave?," 212.
93. Bersani, "Is the Rectum a Grave?," 212.
94. Bersani, "Is the Rectum a Grave?," 217.
95. Bersani, "Is the Rectum a Grave?," 217. See also Janet Halley, *Split Decisions: How and Why to Take a Break from Feminism* (Princeton University Press, 2006), 160, 166.
96. Halley, *Split Decisions*, 160.

97. Bersani, "Is the Rectum a Grave?," 222.
98. Halley, *Split Decisions*, 161.
99. Bersani's essay did not take up precisely the problem of consent. He did acknowledge that "the idea of penis envy describes how men feel about having one, and, as long as there are sexual relations between men and women, this can't help but be an important fact *for women*." Bersani, "Is the Rectum a Grave?," 216.
100. Bersani, "Is the Rectum a Grave?," 215.
101. Associations among male anal receptivity, effeminacy, and decadent wealth can be traced back at least as far as the first century CE. An early example can be found in the Roman poet Juvenal's *Satire II, entitled Effeminate Rome*. Juvenal, "Satires" 2.1–35, 64–81, 149–70, trans. A. S. Kline, Poetry in Translation, 2001, www.poetryintranslation.com/PITBR/Latin/JuvenalSatires2.php.
102. Allen, *¡Venceremos?*, 160, 171–76. See also Sierra Madero, "Bodies for Sale," 13 (a "young man confessed [sic] me that the colour of his skin is a precious asset in the trade .... 'People come here [wanting] sex with blacks and mulattos because they say we are more handsome than whites...").
103. "[F]or the woman to get on top is just a way of letting her play the game of power for awhile." Bersani, "Is the Rectum a Grave?," 216. See also Halley, *Split Decisions*, 165, experimenting with female topping and whether "female masculinity [could be read as] drag or deadly serious."
104. Ruskola, "Raping Like a State," 1477.
105. MacKinnon, "Feminism, Marxism, Method, and the State," 532.
106. Queer theorist Tim Dean's book on barebacking (gay male intercourse without condoms) also introduces a neat analytical flip to Bersani's metaphor. According to Dean, masculine status is *enhanced* in barebacking subculture by a man's "voracious bottoming – by taking as many penises and as much semen inside him as he can .... The more men by whom one is penetrated, the more of a man he becomes." Tim Dean, *Unlimited Intimacy: Reflections on the Subculture of Barebacking* (University of Chicago Press, 2009), 3. In barebacking subculture, "being sexually penetrated is a matter of 'taking it like a man,' enduring without complaint any discomfort or temporary loss of status, in order to prove one's masculinity." Dean, *Unlimited Intimacy*, 4. Referring specifically to Bersani's metaphor, Dean adds,

> Bareback subculture's hypermasculinization of bottoming, its picturing erotic submission as a proof of manhood, could be seen as a compensatory response to modern society's feminization of male homosexuality – a response, that is, to the gender-inversion model of same-sex desire. But it also could be seen as a response to the feminizing potential of sex itself, namely, the way that intense pleasure overwhelms self-control, threatening the ego's coherence. Here I am thinking of Leo Bersani's contention that what people dislike about sex is its capacity to make them temporarily helpless: there comes a point in the pursuit of pleasure when even the most dominant partner must submit to something more powerful than himself....
>
> Through its commitment to no-excuses submission and no-limits endurance, however, bareback subculture conversely embraces masochism as proof positive of masculinity. That is to say, by remasculinizing masochism, barebackers have made self-loss into a confirmation rather than an effacement of manhood.

Dean, *Unlimited Intimacy*, 8–9. Thanks to Joe Fischel for pointing me to this.
107. Janet R. Jakobsen, "Queers Are Like Jews, Aren't They? Analogy and Alliance Politics," in *Queer Theory and the Jewish Question*, ed. Daniel Boyarin, Daniel Itzkovitz, and Ann Pellegrini (Columbia University Press, 2003), 64–89.

108. Jakobsen, "Queers Are Like Jews," 69, citations omitted.
109. Jakobsen, "Queers Are Like Jews," 70.
110. Sierra Madero, "Bodies for Sale," 18.
111. Sierra Madero, "Bodies for Sale," 18.
112. Sierra Madero, "Bodies for Sale," 24.
113. Rao, *Out of Time*, 11.
114. Nicola and Frankenberg, *Comparative Law*, 22.
115. Nicola and Frankenberg, *Comparative Law*, 22. Remember also that *law* refers not merely to codes and cases, but also to self-governance and the kind of shared cultural conceptions that Foucault would call "knowledge." Michel Foucault, "Two Lectures," 93–94.
116. The "rights" I refer to here include those abstract, typically constitutional rights associated with liberal legal systems, including rights related to expression, freedom of conscience, association, and privacy, as well as identity-based rights against discrimination. Cuba ostensibly offers some of these rights, but they are thoroughly subordinated to the interests of the state. Cuba does, on the other hand, guarantee health care and other rights that are better described as socio-economic and have historically been devalued in the US system.
117. Frances Robles, "Cubans Denounce 'Misery' in Biggest Protests in Decades" in *The New York Times*, July 11, 2021.

5 "DENTRO DE LA REVOLUCIÓN"

1. Staff Attorney at Greater Boston Legal Services, Immigration Unit; Northeastern University School of Law, JD 2022. The title "Research Assistant" undervalues Annery's contribution by a mile. Before the trip to Cuba, she had worked with me for a couple of years as both a TA and RA. She brought to her nascent legal career a background as a social worker. She came to the project with excellent interviewing skills, about ten years of professional maturity on her classmates, experience doing on-the-spot translation, powerful instincts for critical methodology, and a high level of perceptivity in connecting individual experience to social phenomena. Additionally, having been raised in a Dominican household (in the US), she is effectively a native Caribbean Spanish-speaker. The trip would not have succeeded without her.
2. Our interviews were few and modest, but for guidance on how we might conceptualize and approach them, I turned to the work of Margarete Sandelowski, including her article "The Problem of Rigor in Qualitative Research," *Advances in Nursing Science* 8, no. 3 (1986): 27–37, https://journals.lww.com/advancesinnursingscience/toc/1986/04000, which explains that "[t]he truth value of a qualitative investigation generally resides in the discovery of human phenomena or experiences as they are lived and perceived by the subjects, rather than in the verification of a priori conceptions of those experiences." Sandelowski, "The Problem of Rigor in Qualitative Research," 30. Thanks to Rodela Khan for directing me to this helpful resource.
3. Duncan Kennedy, "Legal History," July 30, 20215, https://duncankennedy.net/topics/legal-history/#legal-consciousness.
4. Ugo Mattei, "Comparative Law and Critical Legal Studies," 829. Some writers in the tradition of Law and Society study the evidence and impact of legal consciousness in "everyday life" – that is, as held by ordinary people (outside of the legal profession) as they work, navigate relationships, engage in commerce, and solve problems. See, e.g., Patricia Ewick and Susan S. Silbey, *The Common Place of Law: Stories from Everyday Life* (University of Chicago Press, 1998), xi. Legal consciousness as it is understood in this study, however, concerns itself with the consciousness of professionals working in the legal system.

5. Robert K. Yin, *Case Study Research: Design and Methods*, 5th ed. (Sage Publications, 2014), 110.
6. John W. Creswell and Cheryl N. Poth, *Qualitative Inquiry and Research Design: Choosing among Five Approaches*, 4th ed. (Sage Publications, 2018), 24.
7. Libby Adler, *Gay Priori*, 1–141.
8. Margarete Sandelowski, "Telling Stories: Narrative Approaches to Qualitative Research," *IMAGE: Journal of Nursing Scholarship* 23, no. 3 (1991): 161–66, https://doi.org/10.1111/j.1547-5069.1991.tb00662.x. "Narrative analyses … focus on discourse: on the tellings themselves and the devices individuals use to make meaning in stories." Sandelowski, "Telling Stories," 162.
9. *Cf.* Creswell and Poth, "Qualitative Inquiry and Research Design," 26, 246.
10. Yin, *Case Study Research*, 21, 40.
11. Yin, *Case Study Research*, 144.
12. Uwe Flick, *An Introduction to Qualitative Research*, 3rd ed. (Sage Publications, 2006), 136. Yin, *Case Study Research*, 21.
13. Margarete Sandelowski, "Theory Unmasked: The Uses and Guises of Theory in Qualitative Research," *Research in Nursing & Health* 16, no. 3 (1993): 214, 217, https://doi.org/10.1002/nur.4770160308.
14. "Cuba Prohibited Accommodations List Initial Publication," U.S. Department of State, September 20, 2020, www.state.gov/cuba-prohibited-accommodations-list-initial-publication/.
15. Dobbs v. Jackson, 597 U.S. 215 (2022).
16. See Zatz, *Producing Legality*, 60–65, discussing lawmaking as an educational process.
17. Zatz found in her research that legislation follows social change, rather than the other way around. Zatz, *Producing Legality*, 64.
18. "Positive law, which is the object of the pure theory of law, is an order by which human conduct is regulated in a specific way. The regulation is accomplished by such provisions which set forth how men ought to behave. Such provisions are called norms, and either arise through custom, as do the norms of the common law, or are enacted by conscious acts of certain organs aiming to create law, as a legislature acting in its law-making capacity …. If we say that a norm 'exists' we mean that a norm is valid …. Validity and efficacy are two completely distinct qualities …. Jurisprudence regards law as a system of valid norms …. It is [the] 'ought' which is expressed in the concept of validity as distinguished from efficacy." Hans Kelsen, "The Pure Theory of Law and Analytical Jurisprudence," *Harvard Law Review* 55, no. 1 (1941), 50–51, https://doi.org/10.2307/1334739.
19. Gustavo Silveira Siqueira, "Roscoe Pound and Hans Kelsen: The Friendship of Jurists in a World at War," *Law & History Review* 3, no. 3 (2020). https://lawandhistoryreview.org/article/roscoe-pound-and-hans-kelsen-the-friendship-of-jurists-in-a-world-at-war-1936-1945/.
20. Roscoe Pound, "Law in Books and Law in Action" (1910) in *American Legal Realism*, ed. William W. Fisher III, Morton J. Horwitz, and Thomas A. Reed (Oxford University Press, 1993).
21. See also Zatz, *Producing Legality*, 109, discussing Cuban legal education and the objective of getting beyond "rote" and to "creativity."
22. A classic instantiation of this argument is Paula Ettelbrick, "Since When Is Marriage a Path to Liberation?" in *Same-Sex Marriage: Pro and Con*, ed. Andrew Sullivan (Vintage Books, 1997), 118–24.
23. I could not ascertain who said this first, but there are plenty of citations for what has effectively become an aphorism. See, e.g., Brian Leiter, "Rethinking Legal Realism: Toward a Naturalized Jurisprudence," *Texas Law Review* 76, no. 2 (1997): 267–68; Joseph

William Singer, "Legal Realism Now," *California Law Review* 76, no. 2 (1988): 465, 467, 3480619.2307/3480619.

24. Thanks to Janet Halley for pushing me past my Anglo-American legal bias to this deeper interpretation.
25. Despite the work of Justice Oliver Wendell Holmes, Jr. and his American Legal Realist successors, judges still charge one another with infidelity to the text while claiming that their own methods most closely approximate the ideal of judicial neutrality. See, e.g., McDonald v. Chicago, 561 US 742 (2010), especially 791–805 (Scalia, J., concurring) and 858–912 (Stevens, J., dissenting).
26. John Adams, "Thoughts on Government," National Constitution Center, July 30, 2025, https://constitutioncenter.org/the-constitution/historic-document-library/detail/john-adams-thoughts-on-government-1776.
27. Duncan Kennedy, *A Critique of Adjudication: Fin de Siècle* (Harvard University Press, 1997), 305.
28. Kennedy, *A Critique of Adjudication*, 305.
29. William N. Eskridge, Jr., *The Case for Same-Sex Marriage: From Sexual Liberty to Civilized Commitment* (Free Press, 1996), 124.
30. Fidel famously declared, "Dentro de la Revolución, todo; contra de la Revolución, nada" (*Within the Revolution, everything; against the Revolution, nothing*). Allen, *¡Venceremos?*, 146.
31. "We emphasize the modest nature of the indeterminacy thesis. It is not a global claim about intrinsic properties of language, reason, texts, or interpretation." Dennis M. Davis and Karl Klare, "Critical Legal Realism in a Nutshell," in *Research Handbook on Critical Legal Theory*, ed. Emilios Christodoulidis, Ruth Dukes, and Marco Goldoni (Edward Elgar Publishing, 2019), 29.
32. Davis and Klare, "Critical Legal Realism," 30.
33. Davis and Klare, "Critical Legal Realism," 28–30.
34. Davis and Klare use the phrase "bend points." Davis and Klare, "Critical Legal Realism," 31.
35. David Kennedy, *A World of Struggle*, 7–10.
36. Deborah Stone, *Policy Paradox: The Art of Political Decision Making* (W. W. Norton & Company, 2002), 376.
37. Morton J. Horwitz, *The Transformation of American Law 1870–1960* (Oxford University Press, 1992), 176–78.
38. Lochner v. New York, 198 U.S. 45 (1905).
39. Lochner, 198 U.S. at 65 (Holmes, J., dissenting).
40. Horwitz, *The Transformation of American Law*, 169.
41. Horwitz, *The Transformation of American Law*, 181.
42. Kennedy, *A Critique of Adjudication*, 147–52.
43. "Cuba's Constitution of 2019," Constitute Project, November 25, 2019, https://faolex.fao.org/docs/pdf/cub184086E.pdf.
44. Miguel M. Díaz-Canel Bermúdez, "Our Horizon Continues to Be Socialist" (speech, Havana, Cuba, October 29, 2022), *Granma*, https://en.granma.cu/cuba/2022–11-11/our-horizon-continues-to-be-socialist.
45. Díaz-Canel, "Our Horizon Continues to Be Socialist."
46. Erik Olin Wright, *How to Be an Anti-Capitalist in the 21st Century* (Verso, 2019), 98.
47. Wright, *How to Be an Anti-Capitalist*, 59.
48. Wright, *How to Be an Anti-Capitalist*, 71.
49. Wright, *How to Be an Anti-Capitalist*, 4.
50. Wright, *How to Be an Anti-Capitalist*, 66.

51. Wright, *How to Be an Anti-Capitalist*, 66–67.
52. Wright, *How to Be an Anti-Capitalist*, 68.
53. Cuba. *Código de la Familia* [Family Code]. Law No. 1289, art. 29–42, February 14, 1975.
54. Cuba. *Ley General de la Vivienda* [General Housing Law]. Law No. 48/84, December 1984.

6 REFLECTIONS IN A CUBAN MIRROR

1. Matthew Dimick, "Is Capitalism 'a Thing'?," *The Law and Political Economy Project*, October 23, 2023, https://lpeproject.org/blog/is-capitalism-a-thing/.
2. Dimick, "Is Capitalism 'a Thing'?"
3. Dimick, "Is Capitalism 'a Thing'?"
4. Samuel Moyn, "Does LPE Need Theory?," *The Law and Political Economy Project*, September 4, 2023, https://lpeproject.org/blog/does-lpe-need-theory/. The longer version of Moyn's argument is at Samuel Moyn, "Reconstructing Critical Legal Studies," *Yale Law Journal* 134, no. 1 (2024): 77, https://papers.ssrn.com/sol3/papers.cfm?abstract_id=4531492.
5. Here is a very small sampling of first-rate CLS-influenced legal scholarship from the last twenty years originating outside the US: Helena Alviar Garcia and Laura Betancur-Restrepo, "Derecho Internacional y Justicia Transicional: Explorando Algunos Desafíos a Través del Caso Colombiano," *AJIL Unbound* 116 (2022): 297–301. ⟨10.1017/aju.2022.56⟩. ⟨hal-03845608⟩. Prabha Kotiswara, *Dangerous Sex, Invisible Labor: Sex Work and the Law in India* (Princeton University Press, 2011). Kerry Rittich and Joanne Conaghan, *Labour Law, Work and Family: Critical and Comparative Perspectives* (Oxford University Press, 2005). Inga K. Thiemann and Hila Shamir, "A Socio-Legal Analysis of Reforms in the Regulation of Sex Work: The Case Study of End Demand Legislation in Israel," *International Journal of Gender, Sexuality and the Law* 2 no. 1 (2022): 19.
6. Moyn, "Does LPE Need Theory?"
7. Moyn, "Does LPE Need Theory?"
8. Moyn, "Does LPE Need Theory?"
9. Moyn, "Does LPE Need Theory?"
10. Moyn, "Does LPE Need Theory?"
11. Moyn, "Does LPE Need Theory?"
12. Dimick, "Is Capitalism 'a Thing'?"
13. Dimick, "Is Capitalism 'a Thing'?"
14. Yochai Benkler, "The Role of Law in Capitalism," *The Law and Political Economy Project*, October 31, 2023, https://lpeproject.org/blog/the-role-of-law-in-capitalism/.
15. Benkler, "The Role of Law in Capitalism."
16. Benkler, "The Role of Law in Capitalism."
17. Max Weber, *The Protestant Ethic and the Spirit of Capitalism* (Dover Publications, 2012).
18. Charles de Montesquieu, *The Spirit of the Laws* (Cambridge University Press, 1989).
19. Benkler, "The Role of Law in Capitalism."
20. Benkler, "The Role of Law in Capitalism."
21. Benkler, "The Role of Law in Capitalism."
22. In a workshop, a graduate student asked me what government provisions (in the US) were inconsistent with capitalism, defined in such a unified manner. I started with public schools. He dismissed this on the grounds that schools were just preparing laborers for capitalist exploitation. I said, "ok, how about public parks?" He paused, uncertain. I urged him on: "You could respond that public parks exist merely to provide recreation to the laboring class to refresh them for further exploitation. You could say that public assistance

programs are just there to undermine revolt by the poor. But at this point, haven't you just created a tautology?" This is a classic structuralist fallacy.

23. The Moyn provocation resulted in a flurry of other interventions. Jedediah Britton-Purdy, a founding voice in the new LPE school, posted "In Defense of Theoretical Pluralism." He urged that "it is possible to be a democratic constructivist in the morning, a materialist skeptic of legal doctrine in the afternoon, and, perhaps, a more internal student of doctrine in the evening, without *becoming* any of these … or contradicting oneself." The "point" of LPE scholarship for Britton-Purdy "is to highlight the themes of power, distribution, and ideological colonization that a relatively hermetic economic or doctrinal discourse suppresses." This point, his post argues, does not require a consistent meta-theory. Jedediah Britton-Purdy, "In Defense of Theoretical Pluralism," *The Law and Political Economy Project*, September 12, 2023, https://lpeproject.org/blog/in-defense-of-theoretical-pluralism/."

A peaceable intervention by Sanjukta Paul argued for a "big step down from high-altitude social or legal theory" in favor of "mid-level legal and economic concepts that actually have the most effect in the world." Sanjukta Paul, "In Defense of Theoretical Quietism," *The Law and Political Economy Project*, October 3, 2023, https://lpeproject.org/blog/in-defense-of-theoretical-quietism/.

Bernard E. Harcourt's intervention left the internecine battles between leftist schools of legal thought to those with evident psychic investments, preferring instead to respond directly to Moyn by depicting a "dynamic relationship between critical legal theory and radical political practice." Bernard E. Harcourt, "Critical Legal Theory & Radical Political Praxis," *The Law and Political Economy Project*, October 19, 2023, https://lpeproject.org/blog/critical-legal-theory-radical-political-praxis/. Contrary to the "deference towards grassroots social movements" described by Moyn, Harcourt sees "a constant back-and-forth due to the inherent gap between the negativity of critique and the positivity of political praxis." Harcourt, "Critical Legal Theory & Radical Political Praxis." Harcourt urged "radical political experimentation in constant confrontation with critical theory," each crucial to the other. Harcourt, "Critical Legal Theory & Radical Political Praxis." He saw little purpose in "systematiz[ing] the critiques into a totalizing theory, or … impugn[ing] some critiques at the expense of others … as … Tzouvala seems to suggest," citing Adorno for the renunciation of "the question of totality." Harcourt, "Critical Legal Theory & Radical Political Praxis." Instead, Harcourt embraces the "combative … posture" between theory and praxis, where "new [critiques] emerge organically from the ruthless confrontation." Harcourt, "Critical Legal Theory & Radical Political Praxis."

24. Fred L. Block, *Capitalism: The Future of an Illusion* (University of California Press, 2018), 10. Block's full sentence reads "The core illusion is the idea that capitalism is a system that has its own logic and rules that must be obeyed or we risk losing the material well-being that has been achieved to date." Block, *Capitalism*, 10. I left out the end in the main text because I am only concerned here with the logical coherence of the system, not whether it is the best system for producing prosperity.
25. Block, *Capitalism*, 12.
26. Block, *Capitalism*, 12.
27. The classic illustration of background rules analysis is in Robert L. Hale, "Coercion and Distribution in a Supposedly Non-coercive State," *Political Science Quarterly* 38, no. 3 (1923): 470–94, https://doi.org/10.2307/2142367.
28. Thanks to Duncan Kennedy for proposing this apt description, drawn from Gilles Deleuze and Félix Guattari, *A Thousand Plateaus: Capitalism and Schizophrenia* (University of Minnesota Press, 1987).

29. I have illustrated this before, using the example of homeless lgbtq youth in the US and their means for self-support. Adler, *Gay Priori*, 183–206.
30. Davis and Klare, "Critical Legal Realism," 35–36.
31. Davis and Klare, "Critical Legal Realism," 35–36.
32. Davis and Klare, "Critical Legal Realism," 36–37.
33. Davis and Klare, "Critical Legal Realism," 36.
34. Amna A. Akbar, "Non-Reformist Reforms and Struggles over Life, Death, and Democracy," *Yale Law Journal* 132, no. 8 (2023): 2497, www.yalelawjournal.org/feature/non-reformist-reforms-and-struggles-over-life-death-and-democracy. Akbar explains, "The basic formulation of the non-reformist reform is twofold. First, a non-reformist reform aims to undermine the political, economic, and social system or set of relations as it gestures at a fundamentally distinct system or set of relations in relation or toward a particular ideological and material project of world-building. Second, a non-reformist reform draws from and builds the popular strength, consciousness, and organization of revolutionary or agential classes or coalitions .... It is part of a democratic project." Akbar, "Non-Reformist Reforms," 2527.
35. Akbar is multiply published on the LPE blog and her article in the Yale Law Journal was the subject of a separate LPE blog symposium. See https://lpeproject.org/symposia/non-reformist-reforms/.
36. Akbar, "Non-Reformist Reforms," 2519.
37. Block, *Capitalism*, 24.
38. Tzouvala, like Akbar, is multiply published in and closely associated with the LPE Project blog.
39. Ntina Tzouvala, "On Tariffs and the Ends of International Economic Law," *The Law and Political Economy Project*, April 29, 2025, https://lpeproject.org/blog/on-tariffs-and-the-ends-of-international-economic-law/.
40. Tzouvala, "On Tariffs and the Ends of International Economic Law."
41. Tzouvala, "On Tariffs and the Ends of International Economic Law."
42. Tzouvala, "On Tariffs and the Ends of International Economic Law." Emphasis added.
43. World Trade Organization, "Declaration on the TRIPS Agreement and Public Health," adopted November 14, 2001, WT/MIN(01)/DEC/2, www.wto.org/english/thewto_e/minist_e/min01_e/mindecl_trips_e.htm.
44. Tzouvala, "On Tariffs and the Ends of International Economic Law."
45. Tzouvala, "On Tariffs and the Ends of International Economic Law."
46. For example, Tzouvala contends in her first chapter that "contradictions of uneven and combined capitalist development … 'do not exist as a random flux but as a unity of difference.'" and Ntina Tzouvala, *Capitalism as Civilisation: A History of International Law* (Cambridge University Press, 2020), 3 (internal citation omitted).
47. Tzouvala, *Capitalism as Civilisation*, 6.
48. Akbar, "Non-Reformist Reforms," 2517.
49. Karl Klare, "What Non-Reformist Reforms Meant to Us," *The Law and Political Economy Project*, November 15, 2023, https://lpeproject.org/blog/what-non-reformist-reforms-meant-to-us/.
50. Kennedy, *A Critique of Adjudication*, 361.
51. Bianca D. M. Wilson et al., *LGBT Poverty in the United States: Trends at the Onset of COVID-19* (The Williams Institute, UCLA School of Law, February 2023), https://williamsinstitute.law.ucla.edu/wp-content/uploads/LGBT-Poverty-COVID-Feb-2023.pdf.
52. Adam P. Romero, Shoshana K. Goldberg, and Luis A. Vasquez, *LGBT People and Housing Affordability, Discrimination, and Homelessness* (The Williams Institute, UCLA

School of Law, April 2020), 14, https://williamsinstitute.law.ucla.edu/wp-content/uploads/LGBT-Housing-Apr-2020.pdf.

53. Brad Sears, Andrew R. Flores, and Jet Harbeck, *LGBT Adults, Food Insecurity, and Reliance on SNAP* (The Williams Institute, UCLA School of Law, June 2025), 7, https://williamsinstitute.law.ucla.edu/wp-content/uploads/SNAP-Reliance-Jul-2025.pdf.
54. Amira Hasenbush et al., *The LGBT Divide: A Data Portrait of LGBT People in the Midwestern, Mountain & Southern States.* (The Williams Institute, UCLA School of Law, December 2014) https://williamsinstitute.law.ucla.edu/wp-content/uploads/LGBT-Divide-Dec-2014.pdf.
55. Adler, *Gay Priori*, 19–141.
56. Bostock v. Clayton Cnty., Georgia, 590 U.S. 644 (2020).
57. *Civil Rights Act of 1964*, Pub. L. No. 88-352, Title VII, 78 Stat. 241, 253 (1964), codified at 42 U.S.C. § 2000e et seq.
58. Katie R. Eyer, "Statutory Originalism and LGBT Rights," *Wake Forest Law Review* 54 (2019): 63, https://papers.ssrn.com/sol3/papers.cfm?abstract_id=3244473#.
59. Brian J. Sutherland, *Petition for Writ of Certiorari, Bostock v. Clayton County*, No. 17-1618 (Supreme Court of the United States, May 25, 2018).
60. Bostock, 590 U.S. at 661–62.
61. Bostock, 590 U.S. at 662.
62. Bostock, 590 U.S. at 660.
63. Bostock, 590 U.S. at 660 (Alito, J., dissenting) (bold in original).
64. Brown v. Board of Education of Topeka, 387 U.S. 484 (1954).
65. Derrick Bell, *Silent Covenants*, 7.
66. Five years after *Bostock* and facing an even more daunting 6–3 conservative supermajority in the US Supreme Court, trans advocates together with the Biden administration challenged a Tennessee law that prohibited the use of certain medical interventions, including puberty blockers and hormones, by minors for the treatment of gender dysphoria. The question presented was whether intermediate scrutiny should be used to review the state law based on equal protection doctrine that would *require* that level of scrutiny for a sex-based classification or *could be found applicable* to the distinct class of transgender persons. Tennessee, which urged application of rational basis review, the most deferential level of review that the Supreme Court could apply, argued that the law did not classify persons based on sex or transgender identity, but rather on the basis of medical diagnosis. A minor, under the law, could be prescribed puberty blockers to treat precocious puberty but not to treat gender dysphoria. The Court accepted Tennessee's arguments, applied rational basis, and found that the standard was easily met by the state's interest in minors' well-being. U.S. v. Skrmetti, 605 U.S. __, 145 S. Ct. 1816 (2025).

    There is a lot to say about this case, but for purposes of further illustrating the problem of indeterminacy, it is perhaps most useful to point out that *a person who is transgender* and *a person with the medical condition gender dysphoria* are, to say the least, difficult to distinguish. Classifying the law as discriminatory against the former would have required the Court to engage in an analysis about what level of scrutiny appropriately applies (i.e., is the trait an immutable one that has no relevance to a bearer's ability to contribute to society; does the class defined by the trait have a history of state-sponsored discrimination; and is the class politically powerless?) Concurrences addressed these questions (and determined that rational basis should apply) (e.g., Skrmetti, 605 U.S. at __, 145 S. Ct. at 1855 (Barrett, J., concurring)) but the majority opinion did not reach them. Why? Because Chief Justice Roberts, author of the main opinion, did not see a class of transgender people, but rather a diagnosis of gender dysphoria. It is hard to imagine a more indeterminate decision-point (notwithstanding the Chief's characteristic tone of resolve). While the case exemplifies indeterminacy, in my view trans advocates had little choice but to petition for *certiorari* after the adverse decision out of the Court of Appeals for the Sixth Circuit, notwithstanding some commentary presenting the decision as a strategic error. (See Nicholas Confessore, "What to Know about the Transgender Rights Movement's Supreme Court Gamble," *New York Times*, June 19, 2025. www.nytimes.com/2025/06/19/magazine/transgender-supreme-court-skrmetti-takeaways.html.) The alternative was to capitulate to a cruel and harmful attack on trans health. Appreciating the problem of indeterminacy does not mean never bringing forth a legal question. Instead, the idea is to speculate thoughtfully about the (first, second, and third order) costs and benefits of succumbing *versus* those of *even a victory* and how the decision might legitimate bad outcomes.

67. In my prior work I set forth an elaborate alternative. Adler, *Gay Priori*, 175–211.
68. Ntina Tzouvala, "Legal Theory in the Lowercase," *The Law and Political Economy Project*, September 19, 2023, https://lpeproject.org/blog/legal-theory-in-the-lowercase/.
69. Tzouvala, "Legal Theory in the Lowercase."
70. Tzouvala, "Legal Theory in the Lowercase."
71. Talha Syed, "Did CLS Have (Much of) Any Theory?," *The Law and Political Economy Project*, October 16, 2023, https://lpeproject.org/blog/did-cls-have-much-of-any-theory/.
72. Syed, "Did CLS Have (Much of) Any Theory?"
73. Syed, "Did CLS Have (Much of) Any Theory?"
74. Syed, "Did CLS Have (Much of) Any Theory?"
75. Foucault, "Two Lectures," 92–108.
76. Foucault, "Two Lectures," 93.
77. Foucault, "Two Lectures," 95.
78. Duncan Kennedy, *A Critique of Adjudication*, 340.
79. Kennedy, *A World of Struggle*, 10.
80. Kennedy, *A World of Struggle*, 12.
81. Kennedy, *A Critique of Adjudication*, 342.
82. Kennedy, *A Critique of Adjudication*, 342.
83. Kennedy, *A Critique of Adjudication*, 342. Karl Klare, Kennedy's dear friend and former student, parts ways with him on this point.

> [M]y misgivings concern the unproductive way some leftists of all varieties discuss these issues. Unfortunately, Kennedy's polemic reflects the worst tendencies: exaggerated claims and mocking denigration of competing approaches. Kennedy thinks the left should encourage compulsive repetition of ritual fratricide. In my view, this is a tragic waste of the left's limited political and intellectual resources. We should give it a rest.

Karl Klare, "The Politics of Duncan Kennedy's *Critique*" *Cardozo Law Review* 22, no. 3–4 (2001): 1075–76, https://larc.cardozo.yu.edu/clr/vol22/iss3/21.

84. Kennedy, *A Critique of Adjudication*, 342.
85. On a zoom panel entitled *Key Words: CLS and LPE on 'Political Economy' and' Indeterminacy*,' sponsored by Yale LPE in 2022, law professor Amy Kapczynski proposed that the amount of trauma around us might call for a more reparative approach (following Eve Kosofsky Sedgwick) rather than one designed to jolt. You can watch the panel here: www.youtube.com/watch?v=7rpGK35S3ao. It covered much of the terrain in this section.
86. Klare, "What Non-Reformist Reforms Meant to Us."
87. Foucault, "Two Lectures," 99 (emphasis in original).
88. Kennedy, *A Critique of Adjudication*, 341.

89. Kennedy, *A Critique of Adjudication*, 341.
90. Syed, "Did CLS Have (Much of) Any Theory?"
91. Syed, "Did CLS Have (Much of) Any Theory?"
92. It seems to be the strand that Moyn values least. Moyn, "Reconstructing Critical Legal Studies," 91.
93. Kennedy, *A Critique of Adjudication*, 362.
94. Mario Mieli, *Towards a Gay Communism: Elements of a Homosexual Critique*, trans. David Fernbach and Evan Calder Williams (Pluto Press, 2018), 223.
95. Mieli, *Towards a Gay Communism*, 223.
96. Mieli, *Towards a Gay Communism*, 224 citing Herbert Marcuse, *Eros and Civilization* (Vintage Books, 1962), 46.
97. Mieli, *Towards a Gay Communism*, 224.
98. Mieli, *Towards a Gay Communism*, 224.
99. Mieli, *Towards a Gay Communism*, 225.
100. Mieli, *Towards a Gay Communism*, 226.
101. Mieli, *Towards a Gay Communism*, 228, italics in original.
102. Mieli is not the only homophilic writer to urge a structural correlation between political economy and sexuality. The playwright Tony Kushner proposes what he calls a "socialism of the skin": "If there is a relationship between socialism and homosexual liberation, perhaps this is it: an irritation of the skin." Tony Kushner, "Homosexual Liberation: A Socialism of the Skin," in *Homo Economics: Capitalism, Community, and Lesbian and Gay Life*, ed. Amy Gluckman and Betsy Reed (Routledge, 1997), 191. The irritation Kushner had in mind derives from Oscar Wilde's objection to capitalism as "the irritation of an extremely sensitive skin … combined with a pleasure-lover's annoyance at seeing other people so miserably wretched." Kushner, "Homosexual Liberation," 191, internal citations omitted. Kushner's excerpt from Wilde entails both compassion for the suffering of others and the carnal indulgence for which Wilde is known, but Kushner reconfigures two important aspects. First, he emphasizes the noble (as opposed to the profligate) "pleasure" and "annoyance" in Wilde, transforming them into "heart" and "soul": "Honoring the true desire of the skin, and the connection between the skin and heart and mind and soul, is what homosexual liberation is about." Kushner, "Homosexual Liberation," 191. Second, Kushner highlights sensation – sexuality and politics blend together as *feeling*. Kushner's essay offers more of an intuition than a fully elaborated political theory. He sounds a lot like Mieli, though, when he urges that socialism "must surely have as its ultimate objective the restitution of the joy of living we may have lost when we first picked up a tool," evoking our cave dwelling progenitors in a state of nature, unwittingly setting us on a course toward capitalism and homophobia for want of a hammer. Kushner, "Homosexual Liberation," 191.
103. Foucault, Two Lectures, 100.
104. Foucault, Two Lectures, 100.
105. Mieli, *Towards a Gay Communism*, 235. For a quite different and more literary interpretation of gay sameness and sexual positioning, see Leo Bersani, Homos (Harvard University Press, 1995), 170–71.
106. Michael Warner, *Fear of a Queer Planet*, xiii.
107. Cynthia Grant Bowman, "The Future of Socialist Feminism," *Journal of Law and Political Economy* 4, no. 1 (2023): 702, 704, https://doi.org/10.5070/LP64162694.
108. Bowman, "The Future of Socialist Feminism," 704, citing Zillah R. Eisenstein, "Constructing a Theory of Capitalist Patriarchy and Socialist Feminism," *Critical Sociology* 25, no. 2–3 (1999): 196. https://doi.org/10.1177/08969205990250020901.

109. Bowman, "The Future of Socialist Feminism," 704, citing Silvia Federici, *Revolution at Point Zero: Housework, Reproduction, and Feminist Struggle* (PM Press, 2012).
110. Judith Butler, "Merely Cultural," in *Adding Insult to Injury: Nancy Fraser Debates Her Critics*, ed. Kevin Olsen (Verso, 2008), 42–56.
111. Women's greater inclusion in the wage economy also set up a natural experiment to test the theory. Contemporary feminists focused on social reproduction have argued that capitalism adapted by shifting to a low-wage market in care employing immigrant labor. Deborah Dinner, "The Care Crisis: Covid-19, Labor Feminism, and Democracy," in *The Cambridge Handbook of Labor and Democracy*, ed. Mark Berenberg and Angela B. Cornell (Cambridge University Press, 2021), 217–34.
112. M. V. Lee Badgett, *The Economic Case for LGBT Equality: Why Fair and Equal Treatment Benefits Us All* (Beacon Press, 2020), 3.
113. Badgett, "LGBT Equality," 89–90, 91–95. See also Ball, *The Queering of Corporate America*, for a story about how employees pushed employers to adopt more lgbtq-friendly policies. But see Margot Canaday, *Queer Career: Sexuality and Work in Modern America* (Princeton University Press, 2023), 256–60, for the origins of "the business case" for lgbtq equality as well as an argument that "LGBT employees … fit the template of late capitalism," specifically how "in the 1970s, employers began to look for an escape from [Fordist] commitments to primary workers and their families …. [Gays and lesbians] worked hard for the company but also knew that being overly ambitious … exposed them to risk [and] they were simultaneously available to put in extra hours or work split shifts, travel for the company on a moment's notice, or be transferred to a different part of the country [because even those with partners] behaved as if they were single."
114. Badgett, "LGBT Equality," 88–89.
115. Badgett, "LGBT Equality," 88–89.
116. Badgett, "LGBT Equality," 97.
117. Badgett, "LGBT Equality," 97. Some wedding vendors have been less eager to enter the same-sex wedding market. See, e.g., 303 Creative LLC v. Elenis, 600 U.S. __; 143 S. Ct. 2298 (2023) regarding a website designer who successfully sued her state to avoid having to provide wedding websites for same-sex couples.
118. Altria Group, Inc., Brief of Amicus Curiae Supporting the Employees, Bostock v. Clayton County, Nos. 17-1618, 17-1623, and 18-107 (U.S. Sup. Ct. July 3, 2019), www.supremecourt.gov/DocketPDF/17/17-1618/106994/20190703124523964_17-1618.Amicus%20Altria.PDF. This is an astonishing turnaround for the corporation. The Philip Morris tobacco company was a major campaign contributor to the notoriously homophobic and racist US Senator Jesse Helms from North Carolina. Helms served from 1973 to 2003 and was a relentless foe of gay rights and funding for HIV/AIDS research.
119. Altria Group, *Amicus Brief*, 17.
120. Altria Group, *Amicus Brief*, 18–19. Badgett's argument is an old one in a longstanding debate comparing national economies regarded as market economies. See Peter A. Hall and David Soskice, eds., *Varieties of Capitalism* (Oxford Academic, 2003), https://doi.org/10.1093/0199247757.001.0001.
121. Tommy Tomlinson, "How the NFL Helped Kill Arizona's Anti-Gay Rights Bill," *Forbes*, February 27, 2014, www.forbes.com/sites/tommytomlinson/2014/02/27/arizona-gay-rights-and-the-super-bowl/.
122. Jana Kasperkevic, "PayPal Cancels North Carolina Center in Protest of Law That 'Denies Equal Rights,'" *The Guardian*, April 5, 2016, www.theguardian.com/technology/2016/apr/05/paypal-cancels-north-carolina-center-charlotte-law-lgbt-discrimination.
123. Badgett, "LGBT Equality," 107–33.

124. Rao, *Out of Time*, 11. Rao's *homocapitalism* picks up where Jasbir Puar left off when she coined her now widely cited concept of "homonationalism." Puar, Rethinking Homonationalism, 336. Homonationalism critiques the association of lgbtq progress with Western modernity. Rao advances the critique by adding an economic development dimension.
125. Rao, *Out of Time*, 12.
126. Cindy Patton, "Stealth Bombers of Desire: The Globalization of 'Alterity,'" in *Queer Globalizations: Citizenship and the Afterlife of Colonialism*, ed. Arnaldo Cruz-Malavé and Martin F. Manalanzan IV (New York University Press, 2002), 195, 200.
127. Rao, *Out of Time*, 138.
128. Rao, *Out of Time*, 139. Rao suggests that reference to self-interest rather than human rights is meant to "avoid the appearance of moralizing condescension." Rao, *Out of Time*, 139.
129. Rao, *Out of Time*, 146.
130. F. A. Hayek, *The Road to Serfdom: Text and Documents – The Definitive Edition*, ed. Bruce Caldwell (University of Chicago Press, 2007).
131. John Locke, *Two Treatises of Government* (Hafner Press, 1947), 133–46.
132. Alexandra Chasin, *Selling Out: The Gay and Lesbian Movement Goes to Market* (Palgrave Macmillan, 2000), Preface XVII.
133. Chasin, *Selling Out*, 3.
134. Chasin, *Selling Out*, 14.
135. Chasin, *Selling Out*, 14.
136. Chasin, *Selling Out*, 14.
137. Chasin, *Selling Out*, 15.
138. Chasin, *Selling Out*, 24.
139. Chasin, *Selling Out*, 24.
140. Chasin, *Selling Out*, 27.
141. Liz Montegary, *Familiar Perversions: The Racial, Sexual, and Economic Politics of LGBT Families* (Rutgers University Press, 2018), 5.
142. Montegary, *Familiar Perversions*, 6.
143. Montegary, *Familiar Perversions*, 24.
144. Montegary, *Familiar Perversions*, 25.
145. Montegary, *Familiar Perversions*, 26.
146. Ann Pellegrini, "Consuming Lifestyle: Commodity Capitalism and Transformations in Gay Identity," in *Queer Globalizations: Citizenship and the Afterlife of Colonialism*, ed. Arnaldo Cruz-Malavé and Martin F. Manalanzan IV (New York University Press, 2002), 134, 135, 141.
147. Pellegrini, "Consuming Lifestyle," 141.
148. Pellegrini, "Consuming Lifestyle," 141.
149. Michel Foucault, "Nietzsche, Genealogy, History," in *Language, Counter-Memory, Practice: Selected Essays and Interviews*, ed. D. F. Bouchard (Cornell University Press, 1977), 139–64.
150. Foucault, "Nietzsche, Genealogy, History," 142.
151. Foucault, "Nietzsche, Genealogy, History," 147.
152. Foucault, "Nietzsche, Genealogy, History," 152.
153. John D'Emilio, "Capitalism Made Gay Identity Possible. Now We Must Destroy Capitalism," interview by Meagan Day, *Jacobin*, August 15, 2020, https://jacobin.com/2020/08/gay-identity-capitalism-lgbt.
154. John D'Emilio, "Capitalism and Gay Identity," in *Making Trouble: Essays on Gay History, Politics, and the University* (Routledge, 1992), 3.

155. D'Emilio, "Capitalism and Gay Identity," 5.
156. D'Emilio, "Capitalism and Gay Identity," 7–8.
157. In a preface to the essay, D'Emilio explicitly disclaims that his argument is meant to establish causation. D'Emilio, "Capitalism and Gay Identity," 3.
158. D'Emilio, "Capitalism and Gay Identity," 8.
159. D'Emilio, "Capitalism and Gay Identity," 9.
160. D'Emilio, "Capitalism and Gay Identity," 5.
161. Jeffrey Escoffier, "The Political Economy of the Closet: Notes toward an Economic History of Gay and Lesbian Life before Stonewall," in *Homo Economics: Capitalism, Community, and Lesbian and Gay Life*, ed. Amy Gluckman and Betsy Reed (Routledge, 1997), 123–24.
162. Escoffier, "Political Economy," 126–27.
163. Foucault, "Nietzsche, Genealogy, History," 155.
164. Michael Warner, Fear of a Queer Planet, xvi–xvii.
165. "Silence itself – the things one declines to say, or is forbidden to name, the discretion that is required between different speakers – is less the absolute limit of discourse … than an element that functions alongside the things said …. There is no binary division to be made between what one says and what one does not say …. There is not one but many silences, and they are an integral part of the strategies that underlie and permeate discourses." Foucault, *The History of Sexuality*, 27.
166. Foucault, Two Lectures, 85.
167. Foucault, Two Lectures, 85.
168. Foucault, Two Lectures, 85.
169. Foucault, Two Lectures, 87.

CONCLUSION

1. "Yoan Capote: Immanence," Peabody Essex Museum. www.pem.org/exhibitions/yoan-capote-immanence.
2. "Yoan Capote: Immanence."
3. Andrew Buchwalter, "Hegel, Marx, and the Concept of Immanent Critique," *Journal of the History of Philosophy* 29, no. 2 (1991), https://dx.doi.org/10.1353/hph.1991.0037.
4. Yishai Blank and Issi Rosen-Zvi, "The Geography of Sexuality," *North Carolina Law Review* 90, no. 4 (2012): 958. https://scholarship.law.unc.edu/nclr/vol90/iss4/2958.
5. Elizabeth Grosz, "Bodies-Cities," in *Sexuality and Space*, edited by Beatriz Colomina (Princeton University Press, 1992), 250 (internal citations omitted).
6. *Looking for a Space: Lesbians and Gay Men in Cuba*, directed by Kelly Anderson, (Kelly Anderson, 1993), https://vimeo.com/411547632.
7. *Looking for a Space*, film's own translation.
8. BBC Learning English, "A Place for Love in Cuba," *BBC News Review*, aired July 4, 2017, on YouTube, www.youtube.com/watch?v=L_1VhmvJH1U.
9. Ernesto Perez Chang, "Rooms by the Hour in Old Havana," *Havana Times*, January 25, 2014, https://havanatimes.org/features/rooms-by-the-hour-in-old-havana/.
10. BBC Learning English, "A Place for Love in Cuba."
11. Chang, "Rooms by the Hour."
12. Coco Fusco, "Hustling for Dollars," 165. Guards can sometimes be bribed, but they then put themselves at risk of punishment. Fusco, "Hustling for Dollars," 165.
13. Cabezas, *Economies of Desire*, 98–99.

14. Cabezas, *Economies of Desire*, 76.
15. Fusco, "Hustling for Dollars," 165.
16. Stout, "When a *Yuma* Meets Mama," 679.
17. Judith Halberstam, "What's That Smell?: Queer Temporalities and Subcultural Lives," *The Scholar and Feminist Online* 2, no. 1 (2003). https://sfonline.barnard.edu/ps/printjha.htm.
18. J. Jack Halberstam, *In a Queer Time & Place: Transgender Bodies, Subcultural Lives* (New York University Press, 2005), 1.
19. Aaron Betsky, *Queer Space: Architecture and Same-Sex Desire* (William Morrow and Company, Inc., 1997), 8.
20. Betsky, *Queer Space*, 9.
21. Betsky, *Queer Space*, 9.
22. Amy J. Cohen and Stephen Healy, "Diverse Legalities: Towards a Legal Theory for a Postcapitalist Political Economy," *Law and Contemporary Problems* 88, no. 1 (2025) 91.
23. Cuban discourse contemplates an opposition between *la calle* (the street) and *la casa* (the home). Bayard de Volo, *Women and the Cuban Insurrection*, 89.
24. https://clandestina.co and https://clandestinaencasa.com.

Bibliography

Adams, John. "Thoughts on Government." National Constitution Center, July 8, 2025. https://constitutioncenter.org/the-constitution/historic-document-library/detail/john-adams-thoughts-on-government-1776.

Adler, Libby. *Gay Priori: A Queer Critical Legal Studies Approach to Law Reform*. Duke University Press, 2018.

Adler, Libby. "Life at the Corner of Poverty and Sexual Abjection: Lewdness, indecency, and LGBTQ Youth." In *Research Handbook on Gender, Sexuality and the Law*, edited by Chris Ashford and Alexander Maine. Edward Elgar Publishing, 2020.

Adler, Libby. "Distributive Justice for LGBTQ People." In *The Oxford Research Encyclopedia of Politics*, edited by Donald P. Haider-Markel. Oxford University Press, 2021. https://doi.org/10.1093/acrefore/9780190228637.013.1235.

Ahmed, Aziza. *Risk and Resistance: How Feminists Transformed the Law and Science of AIDS*. Cambridge University Press, 2025.

Akbar, Amna A. "Non-Reformist Reforms and Struggles over Life, Death, and Democracy." *Yale Law Journal* 132, no. 8 (2023): 2497–577. www.yalelawjournal.org/feature/non-reformist-reforms-and-struggles-over-life-death-and-democracy.

Allahar, Anton L. "Women and the Family in Cuba: A Study across Time." *Humboldt Journal of Social Relations* 20, no. 1 (1994): 87–120. www.jstor.org/stable/23262643.

Allen, Jafari S. *¡Venceremos?: The Erotics of Black Self-Making in Cuba*. Duke University Press, 2011.

Alpert, Jon, dir. *Mariela Castro's March: Cuba's LGBT Revolution*. HBO, 2016.

Altman, Dennis. "Global Gaze/Global Gays." *GLQ: A Journal of Lesbian and Gay Studies* 3, no. 4 (1997): 417–436. https://doi.org/10.1215/10642684-3-4-417.

Álvarez, Aldo. "Foreign Investment in Cuba: New Opportunities for the Private and Non-State Sectors." *Cuba Capacity Building Project at Columbia Law School*, June 29, 2021. https://horizontecubano.law.columbia.edu/news/foreign-investment-cuba.

Álvarez-Tabío Albo, Ana María. "General Overview of Cuban Family Law Legislation." *Florida Journal of International Law* 29, no. 1, art. 3 (2017): 19–33. https://scholarship.law.ufl.edu/fjil/vol29/iss1/3.

Alviar Garcia, Helena and Betancur-Restrepo, Laura. "Derecho Internacional y Justicia Transicional: Explorando Algunos Desafíos a Través del Caso Colombiano." *AJIL Unbound* 116 (2022): 297–301. ⟨10.1017/aju.2022.56⟩. ⟨hal-03845608⟩.

Amara, Emmanuel, Kai Christiansen, and Florian Dedio, dir. *The Cuba Libre Story*, episode 2, "War and Sugar." Netflix, December 11, 2015. www.netflix.com/watch/80117386?trackId=14277281.

Amara, Emmanuel, Kai Christiansen, and Florian Dedio, dir. *The Cuba Libre Story*, episode 4, "A Ragtag Revolution." Netflix, December 11, 2015. www.netflix.com/watch/80117388?trackId=200257859.

American Psychological Association. "Understanding Sexual Orientation and Homosexuality." www.apa.org/topics/lgbtq/orientation.

Anderson, Benedict. *Imagined Communities: Reflections on the Origin and Spread of Nationalism*. Verso, 1991.

Anderson, Kelly, dir. *Looking for a Space: Lesbians and Gay Men in Cuba*. Kelly Anderson, 1993. https://vimeo.com/411547632.

ARC International. "The Yogyakarta Principles." https://yogyakartaprinciples.org.

Arenas, Reinaldo. *Before Night Falls*. Translated by Dolores M. Koch. Penguin Books, 1993.

Arguelles, Lourdes and B. Ruby Rich. "Homosexuality, Homophobia, and Revolution: Notes toward an Understanding of the Cuban Lesbian and Gay Male Experience, Part I." *Signs* 9, no. 4 (1984): 683–99. www.jstor.org/stable/3173617.

Badgett, M. V. Lee. *The Economic Case for LGBT Equality: Why Fair and Equal Treatment Benefits Us All*. Beacon Press, 2020.

Ball, Carlos A. *The First Amendment and LGBT Equality: A Contentious History*. Harvard University Press, 2017.

Ball, Carlos A. *The Queering of Corporate America: How Big Business Went from LGBTQ Adversary to Ally*. Beacon Press, 2019.

Bayard de Volo, Lorraine. *Women and the Cuban Insurrection: How Gender Shaped Castro's Victory*. Cambridge University Press, 2018.

BBC Learning English. "A Place for Love in Cuba." *BBC News Review*. Aired July 4, 2017, on YouTube. www.youtube.com/watch?v=L_1VhmvJH1U.

Bejel, Emilio. *Gay Cuban Nation*. The University of Chicago Press, 2001.

Bell, Derrick. *Silent Covenants: Brown v. Board of Education and the Unfulfilled Hopes for Racial Reform*. Oxford University Press, 2004.

Benkler, Yochai. "The Role of Law in Capitalism." *The Law and Political Economy Project*. October 31, 2023. https://lpeproject.org/blog/the-role-of-law-in-capitalism/.

Berman, Nathaniel. "Aftershocks: Exoticization, Normalization, and the Hermeneutic Compulsion," *Utah Law Review* 1997, no. 2 (1997): 281–86. https://heinonline.org/HOL/LandingPage?handle=hein.journals/utahlr1997&div=22&id=&page=.

Bersani, Leo. "Is the Rectum a Grave?" *AIDS: Cultural Analysis/Cultural Activism* 43 (1987): 197–222. https://doi.org/10.2307/3397574.

Bersani, Leo. *Homos*. Harvard University Press, 1995.

Beschloss, Michael. *Presidents of War: The Epic Story, from 1807 to Modern Times*. Crown Publishing, 2019.

Betsky, Aaron. *Queer Space: Architecture and Same-Sex Desire*. William Morrow and Company, Inc., 1997.

Birnbaum, Pierre. "Political Antisemitism, 'State Jews' and Roosevelt's New Deal." In *Antisemitism before and since the Holocaust: Altered Contexts and Recent Perspectives*, edited by Anthony McElligott and Jeffrey Herf. Springer International Publishing, 2017.

Blank, Yishai and Issi Rosen-Zvi. "*The Geography of Sexuality*." *North Carolina Law Review* Vol. 90 (2012). https://scholarship.law.unc.edu/nclr/vol90/iss4/2958.

Blaustein, Albert P., and Gisbert H. Flanz, eds. *Constitutions of the Countries of the World*. Oceana Publications, 1996.

Block, Fred L. *Capitalism: The Future of an Illusion*. University of California Press, 2018.

Bodenheimer, Rebecca. "How American Evangelicals Helped Stop Same Sex Marriage in Cuba." Vice, August 20, 2019. www.vice.com/en/article/qvg8pw/how-american-evangelicals-helped-stop-same-sex-marriage-in-cuba.

Boucai, Michael. "Glorious Precedents: When Gay Marriage was Radical." *Yale Journal of Law & Humanities*, 27, no. 1 (2015). https://ssrn.com/abstract=2543686.
Bowman, Cynthia G. "The Future of Socialist Feminism." *Journal of Law and Political Economy* 4, no. 1 (2023). 702–25. https://doi.org/10.5070/LP64162694.
Britton-Purdy, Jedediah. "In Defense of Theoretical Pluralism." *The Law and Political Economy Project*, September 12, 2023. https://lpeproject.org/blog/in-defense-of-theoretical-pluralism/.
Bronski, Michael. *A Queer History of the United States*. Beacon Press, 2011.
Buchwalter, Andrew. "Hegel, Marx, and the Concept of Immanent Critique." *Journal of the History of Philosophy* 29, no. 2 (1991): 253–79. https://dx.doi.org/10.1353/hph.1991.0037.
Butler, Judith. *Gender Trouble: Feminism and the Subversion of Identity*. Routledge, 1990.
Butler, Judith. *The Psychic Life of Power*. Stanford University Press, 1997.
Butler, Judith. "Merely Cultural," In *Adding Insult to Injury: Nancy Fraser Debates Her Critics*, ed. Kevin Olsen. Verso, 2008.
Cabezas, Amalia L. *Economies of Desire: Sex and Tourism in Cuba and the Dominican Republic*. Temple University Press, 2009.
Canaday, Margot. *The Straight State: Sexuality and Citizenship in Twentieth-Century America*. Princeton University Press, 2009.
Canaday, Margot. *Queer Career: Sexuality and Work in Modern America*. Princeton University Press, 2023.
Carpenter, Dale. *Flagrant Conduct: The History of Lawrence v. Texas*. Norton, 2012.
Carpenter, Lenore. "Getting Queer Priorities Straight: How Direct Legal Services Can Democratize Issue Prioritization in the LGBT Rights Movement." *University of Pennsylvania Journal of Law and Social Change* 17 (2014): 107. https://papers.ssrn.com/sol3/papers.cfm?abstract_id=2424916#.
Castro, Fidel. "History Will Absolve Me." In *The Cuba Reader: History, Culture, Politics*, edited by Aviva Chomsky et al. Duke University Press, 2019.
Chakrabarty, Dipesh. *Provincializing Europe: Postcolonial Thought and Historical Difference*. Princeton University Press, 2000.
Chase, Michelle. *Revolution within the Revolution: Women and Gender Politics in Cuba, 1952–1962*. The University of North Carolina Press, 2015.
Chasin, Alexandra. *Selling Out: The Gay and Lesbian Movement Goes to Market*. Palgrave Macmillan, 2000.
Chauncey, George. *Gay New York: Gender, Urban Culture, and the Making of the Gay Male World 1890–1940*. Basic Books, 1994.
Clancy, Michael. "The Globalization of Sex Tourism and Cuba: A Commodity Chains Approach." *Studies in Comparative International Development* 36 (2002): 63–88. https://doi.org/10.1007/BF02686333.
Cohen, Amy J. and Stephen Healy. "Diverse Legalities: Towards a Legal Theory for a Postcapitalist Political Economy." *Law and Contemporary Problems* 88, no. 1 (2025): 79–115.
Cohen, Cathy J. "Punks, Bulldaggers, and Welfare Queens: The Radical Potential of Queer Politics?" In *Black Queer Studies: A Critical Anthology*, edited by E. Patrick Johnson and Mae G. Henderson. Duke University Press, 2005. https://doi.org/10.1515/9780822387220-004.
Coppola, Francis Ford, dir. *The Godfather Part II*. Paramount Pictures, 1974.
Cossman, Brenda. "Family Feuds: Neo-Liberal and Neo-Conservative Visions of the Reprivatization Project." In *Privatization, Law, and the Challenge to Feminism*, edited by Brenda Cossman and Judy Fudge. University of Toronto Press, 2002.
Creswell, John W. and Cheryl N. Poth. *Qualitative Inquiry and Research Design: Choosing among Five Approaches*. 4th ed. Sage Publications, 2018.

"Cuban Assets Control Regulations." *Code of Federal Regulations*, Title 31, Part 515 (2024). www.ecfr.gov/recent-changes?search%5Bhierarchy%5D%5Bpart%5D=515&search%5Bhierarchy%5D%5Btitle%5D=31&search%5Blast_modified_after%5D=2024-05-26.

"Cuba's Constitution of 2019." Constitute Project, November 25, 2019. https://faolex.fao.org/docs/pdf/cub184086E.pdf.

Daigle, Megan. *From Cuba with Love: Sex and Money in the Twenty-First Century*. University of California Press, 2015.

Davis, Dennis M. and Karl Klare. "Critical Legal Realism in a Nutshell." In *Research Handbook on Critical Legal Theory*, edited by Emilios Christodoulidis, Ruth Dukes, and Marco Goldoni. Edward Elgar Publishing, 2019.

Dean, Tim. *Unlimited Intimacy: Reflections on the Subculture of Barebacking*. University of Chicago Press, 2009.

D'Emilio, John, ed. "Capitalism and Gay Identity." In *Making Trouble: Essays on Gay History, Politics, and the University*, 3–16. Routledge, 1992.

D'Emilio, John, ed. "Dreams Deferred: The Birth and Betrayal of America's First Gay Liberation Movement." In *Making Trouble: Essays on Gay History, Politics, and the University*, 17–56. Routledge, 1992.

D'Emilio, John, ed. "The Homosexual Menace: The Politics of Sexuality in Cold War America." In *Making Trouble: Essays on Gay History, Politics, and the University*, 57–73. Routledge, 1992.

D'Emilio, John, ed. "A Meaning for All Those Words: Sex, Politics, History and Larry Kramer." In *The World Turned: Essays on Gay History, Politics, and Culture*, 63–77. Duke University Press, 2002.

D'Emilio, John. "Capitalism Made Gay Identity Possible: Now We Must Destroy Capitalism." Interview by Meagan Day. *Jacobin*, August 15, 2020. https://jacobin.com/2020/08/gay-identity-capitalism-lgbt.

De la Fuente, Alejandro. *A Nation for All: Race, Inequality, and Politics in Twentieth-Century Cuba*. The University of North Carolina Press, 2001.

De Montesquieu, *Charles: The Spirit of the Laws*. Cambridge University Press, 1989.

Dimick, Matthew. "Is Capitalism 'a Thing'?" *The Law and Political Economy Project*, October 23, 2023. https://lpeproject.org/blog/is-capitalism-a-thing/.

Dinner, Deborah. "The Care Crisis: Covid-19, Labor Feminism, and Democracy." In *The Cambridge Handbook of Labor and Democracy*, edited by Mark Berenberg and Angela B. Cornell. Cambridge University Press, 2021.

Dudziak, Mary L. *Cold War Civil Rights: Race and the Image of American Democracy*. Princeton University Press, 2002.

Dworkin, Andrea. *Intercourse*. Free Press, 1987.

Echols, Alice. *Daring to Be Bad: Radical Feminism in America 1967–1975*. University of Minnesota Press, 1989.

Eckstein, Susan. "The Rectification of Errors or the Errors of the Rectification Process in Cuba?" *Cuban Studies* 20 (1990): 67–85. www.jstor.org/stable/24486987.

Eckstein, Susan Eva. *Back from the Future: Cuba under Castro*. Princeton University Press, 1994.

Edelman, Lee. "Tearooms and Sympathy, or, The Epistemology of the Water Closet." In *Nationalisms and Sexualities*, edited by A. Parker, M. Russo, D. Sommer, and P. Yaeger, 263–83. Routledge (1992).

Eisenstein, Zillah R. "Constructing a Theory of Capitalist Patriarchy and Socialist Feminism." *Critical Sociology* 25, no. 2–3 (1999): 196–217. https://doi.org/10.1177/08969205990250020901.

English, T. J. *Havana Nocturne: How the Mob Owned Cuba … and Then Lost It to the Revolution*. HarperCollins, 2009.

Epps, Brad. "Proper Conduct: Reinaldo Arenas, Fidel Castro, and the Politics of Homosexuality." *Journal of the History of Sexuality* 6, no. 2 (1995): 231–83. www.jstor.org/stable/3704123.
Escoffier, Jeffrey. "The Political Economy of the Closet: Notes Toward an Economic History of Gay and Lesbian Life before Stonewall." In *Homo Economics: Capitalism, Community, and Lesbian and Gay Life*, edited by Amy Gluckman and Betsy Reed. Routledge, 1997.
Eskridge, William N., Jr. *The Case for Same-Sex Marriage: From Sexual Liberty to Civilized Commitment*. Free Press, 1996.
Eskridge, William N., Jr. "Comparative Law and the Same-Sex Marriage Debate: A Step-By-Step Approach toward State Recognition." *McGeorge Law Review* 31, no. 3 (2000): 641–72. https://core.ac.uk/download/pdf/303901707.pdf.
Eskridge, William N., Jr. *Dishonorable Passions: Sodomy Laws in America 1861–2003*. Viking 2008.
Esquirol, Jorge L. "The Fictions of Latin American Law (Part I)." *Utah Law Review* 425 (1997): 425–70. https://ecollections.law.fiu.edu/faculty_publications/330.
Ettelbrick, Paula. "Since When Is Marriage a Path to Liberation?" In *Same-Sex Marriage: Pro and Con*, edited by Andrew Sullivan, 118–24. Vintage Books, 1997.
Ewick, Patricia and Susan S. Silbey. *The Common Place of Law: Stories from Everyday Life*. University of Chicago Press, 1998.
Eyer, Katie R. "Statutory Originalism and LGBT Rights." *Wake Forest Law Review* 54 (2019): 63. https://papers.ssrn.com/sol3/papers.cfm?abstract_id=3244473#.
Faderman, Lillian. *Odd Girls and Twilight Lovers: A History of Lesbian Life in Twentieth-Century America*. Penguin Books, 1991.
Feinberg, Richard. *Open for Business: Building the New Cuban Economy*. Brookings institution Press, 2016.
Fernandez, Nadine. "Back to the Future: Women, Race, and Tourism in Cuba." In *Sun, Sex, and Gold: Tourism and Sex Work in the Caribbean*, edited by Kamala Kempadoo, 81–89. Rowman & Littlefield, 1999.
Fernández Martínez, Marta. "Comentario a las formas de propiedad como estatuto jurídico regulado en el artículo 22 constitucional." *Universidad de La Habana* 289 (2020): 71–86. http://scielo.sld.cu/scielo.php?script=sci_arttext&pid=S0253-92762020000100071.
Ferrer, Ada. *Cuba: An American History*. Scribner, 2021.
Flick, Uwe. *An Introduction to Qualitative Research*, 3rd ed. Sage Publications, 2006.
Foucault, Michel. "Nietzsche, Genealogy, History." In *Language, Counter-Memory, Practice: Selected Essays and Interviews*, edited by D. F. Bouchard. Cornell University Press, 1977.
Foucault, Michel. "Two Lectures" In *Power/Knowledge: Selected Interviews & Other Writings 1972–1977*. Edited and translated by Colin Gordon. Pantheon Books, 1980.
Foucault, Michel. *The History of Sexuality Volume 1: An Introduction*. Translated by Robert Hurley. Vintage Books, 1990.
Foucault, Michel. *The Birth of Biopolitics: Lectures at the Collège de France 1978–1979*. Translated by Graham Burchell. Palgrave Macmillan, 2008.
Frankenberg, Günter. *Comparative Law as Critique*. Edward Elgar Publishing, 2016.
Freyre, Gilberto. *The Masters and the Slaves: A Study in the Development of Brazilian Civilization*. University of California Press, 1986.
Fusco, Coco. "Hustling for Dollars: Jineterismo in Cuba." In *Global Sex Workers: Rights, Resistance, and Redefinition*, edited by Kamala Kempadoo and Jo Doezema, 151–66. Routledge, 1998.
Gabilondo, José. "Whither the Revolution? Framing Political Animosities between Sexual Minorities and Churches in Cuba's New Constitution." *Harvard Latin American Law Review* 23 (2020): 43–72. https://journals.law.harvard.edu/lalr/2021/09/

whither-the-revolution-framing-political-animosities-between-sexual-minorities-and-churches-in-cubas-new-constitution/.
Gelman, Andrew R., Todd J. Schneider, and David Shayne. "Perpetuities and Accumulations." In *Horner Probate Practice and Estates*, edited by Michael P. McElroy. Vol. 4, § 78:7. June 2025.
Ginsberg, Allen. *Deliberate Prose: Selected Essays 1952–1995*. HarperCollins, 2000.
Gjelten, Tom. *Bacardi and the Long Fight for Cuba: The Biography of a Cause*. Viking, 2008.
Glocer Fiorini, Leticia. "Polyphonies of Sexuality: Debates about Theories/Debates about Paradigms." *The International Journal of Psychoanalysis* 100, no. 6 (2019): 1256–69. https://doi.org/10.1080/00207578.2019.1674119.
González Pagés, Julio César. *Macho Varón Masculino: Estudios de Masculinidades en Cuba*. Editorial de la Mujer, 2010.
Gott, Richard. *Cuba: A New History*. Yale University Press, 2004.
Gramsci, Antonio. *Selections from the Prison Notebooks*. Edited and translated by Quintin Hoare and Geoffrey Noewell Smith. International Publishers, 1971.
Grossman, David A., Jeanie Murphy, and Paul Eberle. "The Emergence of Entrepreneurship in Cuba: What We Can Learn." *KnE Social Sciences* 3, no. 10 (2018): 85–92. https://doi.org/10.18502/kss.v3i10.2886.
Grosz, Elizabeth. "Bodies-Cities." In *Sexuality and Space*, edited by Beatriz Colomina. Princeton University Press, 1992.
Guanche, Julio César. "The Constitutional Regulation of Private Property in Cuba: Legal Framework, Cultural Narratives, and Unwritten Rules." *Cuba Capacity Building Project at Columbia Law School*, January 28, 2022. https://horizontecubano.law.columbia.edu/news/constitutional-regulation-private-property.
Guerra, Lillian. "Elián González and the 'Real Cuba' of Miami" In *The Cuba Reader: History, Culture, Politics*, edited by Aviva Chomsky et al. Duke University Press, 2019.
Guevara, Che. "Socialism and Man." In *The Cuba Reader: History, Culture, Politics*, edited by Aviva Chomsky, Barry Carr, Alfredo Prieto, and Pamela Maria Smorkaloff. Duke University Press, 2019.
Gutiérrez Alea, Tomás and Juan Carlos Tabío, dir. *Fresa y Chocolate*. Miramax Films, 1993.
Halberstam, J. "What's That Smell?: Queer Temporalities and Subcultural Lives." *The Scholar and Feminist Online* 2, no. 1 (2003). https://sfonline.barnard.edu/ps/printjha.htm.
Halberstam, J. Jack. *In a Queer Time & Place: Transgender Bodies, Subcultural Lives*. New York University Press, 2005.
Hale, Robert L. "Coercion and Distribution in a Supposedly Non-coercive State." *Political Science Quarterly* 38, no. 3 (1923): 470–94. https://doi.org/10.2307/2142367.
Hall, Peter A. and David Soskice, eds. *Varieties of Capitalism*. Oxford Academic, 2003. https://doi.org/10.1093/0199247757.001.0001.
Halley, Janet. *Split Decisions: How and Why to Take a Break from Feminism*. Princeton University Press, 2006.
Halley, Janet. "Introducing Governance Feminism." In *Governance Feminism: An Introduction*, edited by Janet Halley, Prabha Kotiswaran, Rachel Rebouché, and Hila Shamir. University of Minnesota Press, 2018.
Hamilton, Carrie. *Sexual Revolutions in Cuba: Passion, Politics, and Memory*. The University of North Carolina Press, 2012.
Harcourt, Bernard. "'You Are Entering a Gay and Lesbian Free Zone': On the Radical Dissents of Justice Scalia and Other (Post-) Queers – [Raising Questions about Lawrence, Sex Wars, and the Criminal Law]." *Journal of Criminal Law & Criminology* 94 (2004) 503–49. https://scholarship.law.columbia.edu/faculty_scholarship/646.

Harcourt, Bernard E. "Critical Legal Theory & Radical Political Praxis." *The Law and Political Economy Project*, October 19, 2023. https://lpeproject.org/blog/critical-legal-theory-radical-political-praxis/.

Härkönen, Heidi. *Kinship, Love, and Life Cycle in Contemporary Havana, Cuba: To Not Die Alone*. Palgrave Macmillan, 2016.

Hasenbush, Amira, Andrew R. Flores, Angeliki Kastanis, Brad Sears, and Gary J. Gates. *The LGBT Divide: A Data Portrait of LGBT People in the Midwestern, Mountain & Southern States*. The Williams Institute, UCLA School of Law, December 2014. https://williamsinstitute.law.ucla.edu/wp-content/uploads/LGBT-Divide-Dec-2014.pdf.

Hayek, F. A. *The Road to Serfdom: Text and Documents – The Definitive Edition*, edited by Bruce Caldwell. University of Chicago Press, 2007.

Hernández, Tanya K. *Racial Subordination in Latin America: The Role of the State, Customary Law, and the New Civil Rights Response*. Cambridge University Press, 2013.

Hirshman, Linda. *Victory: The Triumphant Gay Revolution*. HarperCollins, 2012.

Hoad, Neville. "Arrested Development or the Queerness of Savages: Resisting Evolutionary Narratives of Difference." *Postcolonial Studies: Culture, Politics, Economy* 3, no. 2 (2000): 133–58. https://doi.org/10.1080/13688790050115277.

Hodge, G. Derrick. "Colonization of the Cuban Body: The Growth of Male Sex Work in Havana." *NACLA Report on the Americas* 34, no. 5 (2001): 20–28. https://doi.org/10.1080/10714839.2001.11722597.

Hodge, G. Derrick. "Sex Workers of Havana: The Lure of Things." *NACLA*, September 25, 2007. https://nacla.org/article/sex-workers-havana-lure-things.

Hook, Derek. "Psychoanalysis, Sexual Difference and the Castration Problematic." In *The Gender of Psychology*, edited by Tamara Shefer, Floretta Boonzaier, and Peace Kiguwa. Juta Academic Publishing, 2006.

Hooker, Evelyn. "The Adjustment of the Male Overt Homosexual." *Journal of Projective Techniques* 21 (1957): 18–31. https://doi.org/10.1080/08853126.1957.10380742.

Horwitz, Morton J. *The Transformation of American Law 1870-1960*. Oxford University Press, 1992.

Hughes, Langston. *I Wonder as I Wander: An Autobiographical Journey*. Octagon Books, 1956, 1981.

Human Rights Campaign. "Marriage Equality around the World." Resources. www.equaldex.com/issue/marriage.

Hynson, Rachel. *Laboring for the State: Women, Family, and Work in Revolutionary Cuba, 1959–1971*. Cambridge University Press, 2019.

Isailovic, Ivana. "Same Sex but Not the Same: Same-Sex Marriage in the United States and France and the Universalist Narrative." *The American Journal of Comparative Law* 66, no. 2 (2018): 267–315. https://doi.org/10.1093/ajcl/avy027.

Jagose, Annamarie. *Queer Theory: An Introduction*. Melbourne University Press, 1996.

Jakobsen, Janet R. "Queers Are Like Jews, Aren't They? Analogy and Alliance Politics." In *Queer Theory and the Jewish Question*, edited by Daniel Boyarin, Daniel Itzkovitz, and Ann Pellegrini. Columbia University Press, 2003.

James, C. L. R. *The Black Jacobins: Toussaint L'Ouverture and the San Domingo Revolution*. Vintage Books, 1989.

Johnson, David K. *The Lavender Scare: The Cold War Persecution of Gays and Lesbians in the Federal Government*. The University of Chicago Press, 2004.

Juvenal. "Satires II": 1–35, 64–81, 149–70, translated by A. S. Kline. Poetry in Translation, 2001. www.poetryintranslation.com/PITBR/Latin/JuvenalSatires2.php.

Kasperkevic, Jana. "PayPal Cancels North Carolina Center in Protest of Law That 'Denies Equal Rights.'" The Guardian, April 5, 2016. www.theguardian.com/technology/2016/apr/05/paypal-cancels-north-carolina-center-charlotte-law-lgbt-discrimination.

Katyal, Sonia K. "Exporting Identity." *Yale Journal of Law & Feminism* 14, no. 1 (2019) 97–176. https://lawcat.berkeley.edu/record/1108613?v=pdf.

Kelsen, Hans. "The Pure Theory of Law and Analytical Jurisprudence." *Harvard Law Review* 55, no. 1 (1941): 44–70. https://doi.org/10.2307/1334739.

Kempadoo, Kamala. "Continuities and Change." In *Sun, Sex, and Gold: Tourism and Sex Work in the Caribbean*, edited by Kamala Kempadoo, 3–33. Rowman & Littlefield, 1999.

Kennedy, David. "Law and the Political Economy of the World." *Leiden Journal of International Law* 26, no. 1 (2013): 7–48. https://doi.org/10.1017/S0922156512000635.

Kennedy, David. *A World of Struggle: How Power, Law, and Expertise Shape Global Political Economy*. Princeton University Press, 2016.

Kennedy, Duncan, ed. "The Stakes of Law, or Hale and Foucault!" In *Sexy Dressing etc.: Essays on the Power and Politics of Cultural Identity*. Harvard University Press, 1993.

Kennedy, Duncan. *A Critique of Adjudication: Fin de Siècle*. Harvard University Press, 1997.

Kennedy, Duncan. "Legal History." Duncan Kennedy, July 8, 2025. https://duncankennedy.net/topics/legal-history/#legal-consciousness.

Khan, Ummni. *Vicarious Kinks: S/M in the Socio-Legal Imaginary*. University of Toronto Press, 2014.

Kim, Rama Hyeweon. "Historicizing Same-Sex Marriage Debate in the Legal Periphery: Savigny, Nakagawa, and the Korean Marriage." *Minnesota Journal of International Law* 33, no. 2 (2024): 155–214. https://scholarship.law.umn.edu/cgi/viewcontent.cgi?article=1003&context=minn-jrnl-intl-law.

Kirk, Emily J. "Setting the Agenda for Cuban Sexuality: The Role of Cuba's Cenesex." *Canadian Journal of Latin American and Caribbean Studies* 36, no. 72 (2011): 143–63. https://doi.org/10.1080/08263663.2011.10817018.

Kirk, Emily J. *Cuba's Gay Revolution: Normalizing Sexual Diversity Through a Health-Based Approach*. Lexington Books, 2017. EBSCOhost. www.google.com/books/edition/Cuba_s_Gay_Revolution/UwkvDwAAQBAJ?hl=en&gbpv=1.

Kirk, Emily J. and Robert Huish. "Transsexuals' Right to Health? A Cuban Case Study." *Health and Human Rights Journal* 20, no. 2 (2018): 215–22. https://pmc.ncbi.nlm.nih.gov/articles/PMC6293354/.https://pmc.ncbi.nlm.nih.gov/articles/PMC6293354/.

Klare, Karl. "The Politics of Duncan Kennedy's *Critique*." *Cardozo Law Review* 22, no. 3–4 (2001): 1073. https://larc.cardozo.yu.edu/clr/vol22/iss3/21.

Klare, Karl. "What Non-Reformist Reforms Meant to Us." *The Law and Political Economy Project*, November 15, 2023. https://lpeproject.org/blog/what-non-reformist-reforms-meant-to-us/.

Kotiswaran, Prabha. *Dangerous Sex, Invisible Labor: Sex Work and the Law in India*. Princeton University Press, 2011.

Kuritzkes, Caroline. "The End of Cuba's Entrepreneurship Boom." *Foreign Policy Magazine*, July 15, 2019. https://foreignpolicy.com/2019/07/15/the-end-of-cubas-entrepreneurship-boom/.

Kushner, Rachel. *Telex from Cuba*. Scribner, 2008.

Kushner, Tony. "Homosexual Liberation: A Socialism of the Skin." In *Homo Economics: Capitalism, Community, and Lesbian and Gay Life*, edited by Amy Gluckman and Betsy Reed. Routledge, 1997.

Labiosa, Wilfred W. *The LGBT Cuban Revolution*. Deletrea, 2023.

Lambe, Jennifer L. "Historicizing Sexuality in the Cuban Revolution: The Spectral 'Before.'" *Radical History Review* 2020 (2020): 217–32. http://dx.doi.org/10.1215/01636545-7857392.

Leiner, Marvin. *Sexual Politics in Cuba: Machismo, Homosexuality, and AIDS*. Westview Press, 1994.

Leiter, Brian. "Rethinking Legal Realism: Toward a Naturalized Jurisprudence." *Texas Law Review* 76, no. 2 (1997): 267–315. https://chicagounbound.uchicago.edu/cgi/viewcontent.cgi?article=2562&context=journal_articles.

Litowitz, Douglas. "Reification in Law and Legal Theory." *Southern California Interdisciplinary Law Journal* 9, no. 2 (2000): 401.

Locke, John. *Two Treatises of Government*. Hafner Press, 1947.

Lowinger, Rosa and Ofelia Fox. *Tropicana Nights: The Life and Times of the Legendary Cuban Nightclub*. Harcourt, 2005.

Luhur, Winston, Ilan H. Meyer, and Bianca D. M. Wilson. *Policing LGBQ People*. The Williams Institute, UCLA School of Law, May 2021. https://williamsinstitute.law.ucla.edu/wp-content/uploads/Policing-LGBQ-People-May-2021.pdf.

Lumsden, Ian. *Machos, Maricones, and Gays: Cuba and Homosexuality*. Temple University Press, 1996.

Lvovsky, Anna. *Vice Patrol: Cops, Courts, and the Struggle over Urban Gay Life before Stonewall*. University of Chicago Press, 2021.

MacKinnon, Catharine A. "Feminism, Marxism, Method, and the State: An Agenda for Theory." *Signs* 7, no. 3 (1982): 515–44. www.jstor.org/stable/3173853.

Marcuse, Herbert. *Eros and Civilization*. Vintage Books, 1962.

Matsumura, Kaiponanea. "The Marital Habitus." *Washington University law Review* 99, no. 6 (2022) 2033–61.

Mattei, Ugo. "Comparative Law and Critical Legal Studies." In *The Oxford Handbook of Comparative Law*, edited by Mathias Reimann and Reinhard Zimmermann, 805–36. Oxford University Press, 2006. https://doi.org/10.1093/oxfordhb/9780198810230.013.26.

Matthews, Herbert L. "The Cuban Story in the *New York Times*." In *The Cuba Reader: History, Culture, Politics*, edited by Aviva Chomsky et al. Duke University Press, 2019.

Merten, Paxtyn. "In Cuba, Santería Flourishes Two Decades after Ban Was Lifted." *The GroundTruth Project*, July 31, 2018. https://thegroundtruthproject.org/cuba-santeria-catholicism-religion-flourish-two-decades-freedom-granted/.

Mieli, Mario. *Towards a Gay Communism: Elements of a Homosexual Critique*. Translated by David Fernbach and Evan Calder Williams. Pluto Press, 2018.

Mill, John Stuart. "On Liberty." In *Three Essays*, edited by Jack Stillinger, 5–141. Oxford University Press, 1975.

Miller, Marilyn G. *Rise and Fall of the Cosmic Race: The Cult of Mestizaje in Latin America*. University of Texas Press, 2004.

Montano, Nicolas. *The Death, and Rebirth, of the Cuban Wedding Ceremony*. Brown University: Beyond the Sugar Curtain: Tracing Cuba-US Connections since 1959, December 2017. On file with author.

Montegary, Liz. *Familiar Perversions: The Racial, Sexual, and Economic Politics of LGBT Families*. Rutgers University Press, 2018.

Monzon, Renee. "Introducing Private-Property Rights to Cuba: How Cuba's New Constitution Paves the Way for Economic Growth." *Case Western Reserve Journal of International Law* 52, no. 1 (2020): 629–68. https://scholarlycommons.law.case.edu/jil/vol52/iss1/28.

Moyn, Samuel. "Does LPE Need Theory?" *The Law and Political Economy Project*, September 4, 2023. https://lpeproject.org/blog/does-lpe-need-theory/.

Moyn, Samuel. "Reconstructing Critical Legal Studies." *Yale Law Journal* 134, no. 1 (2024): 77–122. www.yalelawjournal.org/essay/reconstructing-critical-legal-studies.

NeJaime, Douglas. "Marriage Equality and the New Parenthood." *Harvard Law Review* 129, no. 5 (2016): 1185. https://harvardlawreview.org/print/vol-129/marriage-equality-and-the-new-parenthood/.

Nicola, Fernanda G. and Günter Frankenberg. *Comparative Law: Introduction to a Practice*. Edward Elgar Publishing, 2024.

Ojeda Bello, István. "Family Code a Year Later: People's History Is Not Only Written with DNA." *Periódico 26*, October 2, 2023. www.periodico26.cu/index.php/en/special-reports-2/15337-family-code-a-year-later-people-s-history-is-not-only-written-with-dna.

Ortiz, Jose A. "The Illegal Expropriation of Property in Cuba: A Historical and Legal Analysis of the Takings and a Survey of Restitution Schemes for a Post-Socialist Cuba." *Loyola of Los Angeles International and Comparative Law Review* 22, no. 3 (2000): 321–55. https://digitalcommons.lmu.edu/cgi/viewcontent.cgi?article=1497&context=ilr.

Padilla, Mark. *Caribbean Pleasure Industry: Tourism, Sexuality, and AIDS in the Dominican Republic*. University of Chicago Press, 2007.

Padura, Leonardo. *Havana Red*. Translated by Peter Bush. Bitter Lemon Press, 2005.

Parker, Andrew, Mary Russo, Doris Sommer, and Patricia Yaeger. "Introduction." In *Nationalisms and Sexualities*, edited by Andrew Parker, Mary Russo, Doris Sommer, and Patricia Yaeger, 1–18. Routledge, 1992.

Patton, Cindy. "Stealth Bombers of Desire: The Globalization of 'Alterity.'" In *Queer Globalizations: Citizenship and the Afterlife of Colonialism*, edited by Arnaldo Cruz-Malavé and Martin F. Manalanzan IV. New York University Press, 2002.

Paul, Sanjukta. "In Defense of Theoretical Quietism." *The Law and Political Economy Project*, October 3, 2023. https://lpeproject.org/blog/in-defense-of-theoretical-quietism/.

Peabody Essex Museum. "Yoan Capote: Immanence." www.pem.org/exhibitions/yoan-capote-immanence.

Pellegrini, Ann. "Consuming Lifestyle: Commodity Capitalism and Transformations in Gay Identity." In *Queer Globalizations: Citizenship and the Afterlife of Colonialism*, edited by Arnaldo Cruz-Malavé and Martin F. Manalanzan IV. New York University Press, 2002.

Peña, Susana. *¡Oye Loca!: From the Mariel Boatlift to Gay Cuban Miami*. University of Minnesota Press, 2013.

Peters, Philip. "Cuba's New Real Estate Market." Latin America Initiative Working Paper (Brookings, February 2014).

Pound, Roscoe. "Law in Books and Law in Action" (1910). In *American Legal Realism*, edited by William W. Fisher III, Morton J. Horwitz, and Thomas A. Reed, 39–44. Oxford: Oxford University Press, 1993.

Puar, Jasbir K. *Terrorist Assemblages: Homonationalism in Queer Times*. Duke University Press, 2007.

Puar, Jasbir. "Rethinking Homonationalism." *International Journal of Middle East Studies* 45, no. 2 (2013): 336–39. www.jstor.org/stable/43302999.

Rao, Rahul. *Out of Time: The Queer Politics of Postcoloniality*. Oxford University Press, 2020.

Reynet, Layz. "Inequality and the Informal Market in Cuba: Structural Barriers of Income Distribution in Light of Tourism and Economic Growth for Afro-Cubans." *Unpublished Master's Thesis*, Lund University, 2018. https://lup.lub.lu.se/student-papers/search/publication/8959045.

Rich, Ruby B. and Lourdes Arguelles. "Homosexuality, Homophobia, and Revolution: Notes toward an Understanding of the Cuban Lesbian and Gay Male Experience, Part II." *Signs* 11, no. 1 (1985). https://doi.org/10.1086/494203.

Rittich, Kerry and Joanne Conaghan. *Labour Law, Work and Family: Critical and Comparative Perspectives*. Oxford University Press, 2005.

Rivero, Yeidy M. *Tuning Out Blackness; Race and Nation in the History of Puerto Rican Television*. Duke University Press, 2005.

Roberts, Dorothy. *Shattered Bonds: The Color of Child Welfare*. Basic Civitas Books, 2002.

Rodríguez Lorenzo, Riury. "Entrepreneurship in Cuba in 2021: A Race with Obstacles." *Cuba Study Group Blog*, January 28, 2021. http://cubastudygroup.org/blog_posts/entrepreneurship-in-cuba-in-2021-a-race-with-obstacles/.

Rojas, Rafael. *Fighting over Fidel: The New York Intellectuals and the Cuban Revolution*. Princeton University Press, 2016.

Romero, Adam P., Shoshana K. Goldberg, and Luis A. Vasquez. *LGBT People and Housing Affordability, Discrimination, and Homelessness*. The Williams Institute, UCLA School of Law, April 2020. https://williamsinstitute.law.ucla.edu/wp-content/uploads/LGBT-Housing-Apr-2020.pdf.

Rosario-Lebrón, Aníbal. "For Better and For Better: The Case for Abolishing Civil Marriage." *Washington University Jurisprudence Review* 5, no. 2 (2013): 189–256. https://openscholarship.wustl.edu/cgi/viewcontent.cgi?article=1047&context=law_jurisprudence.

Roselle, Josephine, Brianna Navarre, and Megan Trimble. "Same-Sex Legalization by Country." U.S. News and World Report, February 15, 2024. www.usnews.com/news/best-countries/articles/countries-where-same-sex-marriage-is-legal.

Rubin, Gayle. "The Traffic in Women: Notes on the 'Political Economy' of Sex." In *Toward an Anthropology of Women*, edited by Rayna R. Reiter. Monthly Review Press, 1975.

Rubin, Gayle. "Sexual Traffic." *Interview by Judith Butler in Feminism Meets Queer Theory*, edited by Elizabeth Weed and Naomi Schor. Indiana University Press, 1997.

Rubin, Gayle. "Thinking Sex: Notes for a Radical Theory of the Politics of Sexuality." In *Culture, Society and Sexuality: A Reader, Second Edition*, edited by Richard Parker and Peter Aggleton. Routledge, 1999.

Ruskola, Teemu. "Raping Like a State." *UCLA Law Review* 57, no. 5 (2010): 1477–536. www.english.upenn.edu/sites/www.english.upenn.edu/files/Teemu-RapingLikeAState.pdf.

Sandelowski, Margarete. "The Problem of Rigor in Qualitative Research." *Advances in Nursing Science* 8, no. 3 (1986): 27–37. https://journals.lww.com/advancesinnursingscience/toc/1986/04000.

Sandelowski, Margarete. "Telling Stories: Narrative Approaches to Qualitative Research." *IMAGE: Journal of Nursing Scholarship* 23, no. 3 (1991): 161–66. https://doi.org/10.1111/j.1547-5069.1991.tb00662.x.

Sandelowski, Margarete. "Theory Unmasked: The Uses and Guises of Theory in Qualitative Research." *Research in Nursing & Health* 16, no. 3 (1993): 214, 217. https://doi.org/10.1002/nur.4770160308.

Saunders, Tanya L. "Grupo OREMI: Black Lesbians and the Struggle for Safe Social Space in Havana." *Souls* 11, no. 2 (2009): 167–85. https://doi.org/10.1080/10999940902910198.

Schnabel, Julian, dir. *Before Night Falls*. Grandview Pictures, 2000.

Sears, Brad, Andrew R. Flores, and Jet Harbeck. *LGBT Adults, Food Insecurity, and Reliance on SNAP*. The Williams Institute, UCLA School of Law, June 2025. https://williamsinstitute.law.ucla.edu/wp-content/uploads/SNAP-Reliance-Jul-2025.pdf.

Sedgwick, Eve K. *Between Men: English Literature and Male Homosocial Desire*. Columbia University Press, 2016.

Seidman, Sarah J. "Angela Davis in Cuba as Symbol and Subject." *Radical History Review* 136 (2020): 11–35. https://read.dukeupress.edu/radical-history-review/article-abstract/2020/136/11/148070/Angela-Davis-in-Cuba-as-Symbol-and-Subject?redirectedFrom=fulltext.

Serra, Ana. *The "New Man" in Cuba: Culture and Identity in the Revolution*. University of Florida Press, 2007.

Sierra Madero, Abel. "The Sex of Nations: An Interview with Abel Sierra Madero." Interview by Frances Negrón-Muntaner. *CSER Newsletter*, 1 (2011): 12–13.

Sierra Madero, Abel. "Bodies for Sale: Pinguerismo and Negotiated Masculinity in Contemporary Cuba." Translated by Lillian Guerra and Roberto Garcia, *Journal of the Association of Social Anthropologists* 10 (2015): 1–33. www.theasa.org/downloads/asaonline/PDF/asaonline0110.pdf.

Singer, Joseph William. "Legal Realism Now." *California Law Review* 76, no. 2 (1988): 465–544. 10.2307/3480619.

Siqueira, Gustavo Silveira. "Roscoe Pound and Hans Kelsen: The Friendship of Jurists in a World at War." *Law & History Review* 3, no. 3 (2020). https://lawandhistoryreview.org/article/roscoe-pound-and-hans-kelsen-the-friendship-of-jurists-in-a-world-at-war-1936-1945/.

Social Security, Office of Research, Evaluation, and Statistics. "Social Security Programs throughout the World: The Americas, 2019." December 19, 2024. www.ssa.gov/policy/docs/progdesc/ssptw/2018-2019/americas/cuba.html.

Spivak, Gayatri Chakravorty. *A Critique of Postcolonial Reason: Toward a History of the Vanishing Present*. Harvard University Press, 1999.

Stinchfield, Frederick H. *The American Constitution – Whose Heritage? The Self-Reliant or Those Who Would Be Wards of the Government?* American Liberty League, 1936.

Stone, Deborah. *Policy Paradox: The Art of Political Decision Making*. NY: W. W. Norton & Company, 2002.

Stout, Noelle M. "Feminists, Queers and Critics: Debating the Cuban Sex Trade." *Journal of Latin American Studies* 40 (2008): 721–42. doi:10.1017/S0022216X08004732.

Stout, Noelle M. *After Love: Queer Intimacy and Erotic Economies in Post-Soviet Cuba*. Duke University Press, 2014.

Stout, Noelle. "When a *Yuma* Meets Mama: Commodified Kin and the Affective Economies of Queer Tourism in Cuba." *Anthropological Quarterly* 88, no. 3 (2015): 665–91. https://dx.doi.org/10.1353/anq.2015.0040.

Suchlicki, Jaime. *Cuba: From Columbus to Castro and Beyond*. Brassey's Inc, 2002.

Sullivan, Mairead. *Lesbian Death*. University of Minnesota Press, 2022.

Syed, Talha. "Did CLS Have (Much of) Any Theory?" *The Law and Political Economy Project*, October 16, 2023. https://lpeproject.org/blog/did-cls-have-much-of-any-theory/.

Tabío, Juan Carlos, dir. *Se Permuta*. ICAIC, 1983.

Teichman, Judith. "Class and Race in Latin America's Left Populist Politics." *Race & Class* 64, no. 2 (2022): 55–74. https://doi.org/10.1177/03063968221103073.

Thiemann, Inga K. and Hila Shamir. "A Socio-Legal Analysis of Reforms in the Regulation of Sex Work: The Case Study of End Demand Legislation in Israel." *International Journal of Gender, Sexuality and the Law* 2, no. 1 (2022) 19. www.trafflab.org/_files/ugd/11e1f0_bee2fb38b0b74135b931603bda1c7c5b.pdf?index=true.

Tomlinson, Tommy. "How the NFL Helped Kill Arizona's Anti-Gay Rights Bill." *Forbes*, February 27, 2014. www.forbes.com/sites/tommytomlinson/2014/02/27/arizona-gay-rights-and-the-super-bowl/.

Tremenda Nota. "El 92.2 por ciento a favor del matrimonio LGBTIQ+: Estos fueron los resultados de una encuesta independiente realizada en Cuba." October 8, 2021. https://s3.eu-central-1.amazonaws.com/qurium/tremendanota.com/el-92-2-por-ciento-a-favor-del-matrimonio-lgbtiq-estos-fueron-los-resultados-de-una-encuesta-independiente-realizada-en-cuba.html. On file with author.

Tsing, Anna Lowenhaupt. *Friction: An Ethnography of Global Connection*. Princeton University Press, 2005.

Tzouvala, Ntina. *Capitalism as Civilisation: A History of International Law*. Cambridge University Press, 2020.

Tzouvala, Ntina. "Legal Theory in the Lowercase." *The Law and Political Economy Project*, September 19, 2023. https://lpeproject.org/blog/legal-theory-in-the-lowercase/.

Tzouvala, Ntina. "On Tariffs and the Ends of International Economic Law," *The Law and Political Economy Project*, April 29, 2025. https://lpeproject.org/blog/on-tariffs-and-the-ends-of-international-economic-law/.

United States General Accounting Office. Defense Force Management: DOD's Policy on Homosexuality. 1992. www.gao.gov/assets/nsiad-92-98.pdf.

U.S. Congress. Senate. *Employment of Homosexuals and Other Sex Perverts in Government*. 81st Cong., 2nd session, Sen. Doc. no. 241, 1950. https://web.archive.org/web/20120402035757/https://ecf.cand.uscourts.gov/cand/09cv2292/evidence/PX2337.pdf.

U.S. Department of State. "Cuba Prohibited Accommodations List Initial Publication." September 20, 2020. www.state.gov/cuba-prohibited-accommodations-list-initial-publication/.

Vaid, Urvashi. *Virtual Equality: The Mainstreaming of Gay and Lesbian Liberation*. Anchor Books, Doubleday, 1995.

Vance, Carole S. *Pleasure and Danger: Exploring Female Sexuality*. Routledge 1984.

Vasconcelos, José. *The Cosmic Race: A Bilingual Edition*. Johns Hopkins University Press, 1997.

Waaldijk, Kees. "Small Change: How the Road to Same-Sex Marriage Got Paved in the Netherlands." In *Legal Recognition of Same-Sex Partnerships: A Study of National, European, and International Law*, edited by Robert Wintemute and Mads Andenæs, 437–64. Hart Publishing, 2001.

Wade, Bex. "'Socialism Yes, Homophobia No!': A Day at Cuba's LGBTQ Rights March." Vice, June 6, 2016. www.vice.com/en_us/article/wnwwd4/socialism-yes-homophobia-no-a-day-at-cubas-lgbtq-rights-march.

Warner, Michael. "Introduction." In *Fear of a Queer Planet: Queer Politics and Social Theory*, edited by Michael Warner, vii–xxxi. University of Minnesota Press, 2000.

Weber, Max. *The Protestant Ethic and the Spirit of Capitalism*. Dover Publications, 2012.

West, D. J. "Parental Figures in the Genesis of Male Homosexuality." *International Journal of Social Psychiatry* 5, no. 2 (1959): 85–97. doi:10.1177/002076405900500201.

Williams Institute. "More than 2.5 Million LGBTQ Adults Are Parenting Children under the Age of 18." *UCLA School of Law*. April 9, 2024. https://williamsinstitute.law.ucla.edu/press/lgbtq-parenting-2024-press-release/.

Wilson, Bianca D. M., Soon Kyu Choi, Gary W. Harper, Marguerita Lightfoot, Stephen Russell, and Ilan H. Meyer. *Homelessness among LGBT Adults in the US*. The Williams Institute, UCLA School of Law, May 2020. https://williamsinstitute.law.ucla.edu/wp-content/uploads/LGBT-Homelessness-May-2020.pdf.

Wilson, Bianca D. M., Lauren J. A. Bouton, M. V. Lee Badgett, and Moriah L. Macklin. *LGBT Poverty in the United States: Trends at the Onset of COVID-19*. The Williams Institute, UCLA School of Law, February 2023. https://williamsinstitute.law.ucla.edu/wp-content/uploads/LGBT-Poverty-COVID-Feb-2023.pdf.

Wolfenden, John, et al. *Report of the Committee on Homosexual Offences and Prostitution*. London: Her Majesty's Stationery Office, 1957.

Wright, Erik Olin. *How to Be an Anti-Capitalist in the 21st Century*. Verso, 2019.

Yin, Robert K. *Case Study Research: Design and Methods*, 5th ed. Sage Publications, 2014.

Young, Allen. *Gays under the Cuban Revolution*. Grey Fox Press, 1981.

Young, Allen. "Cuba: Gay as the Sun." In *Out of the Closets: Voices in Gay Liberation*, edited by Karla Jay and Allen Young. New York University Press, 1992.

Zatz, Marjorie S. *Producing Legality: Law and Socialism in Cuba*. Routledge, 1994.

Index

For EU product safety concerns, contact us at Calle de José Abascal, 56–1°,
28003 Madrid, Spain or eugpsr@cambridge.org.

www.ingramcontent.com/pod-product-compliance
Ingram Content Group UK Ltd.
Pitfield, Milton Keynes, MK11 3LW, UK
UKHW020840290926
15470UKWH00004B/1459
9781009872324